Penguin Books

The Read-Aloud Handbook

JIM TRELEASE works full time addressing parents, teachers, and professional groups on the subjects of children, literature, and television. A graduate of the University of Massachusetts, he was an award-winning artist and writer for the *Springfield* (MA) *Daily News* from 1963 to 1983.

Initially self-published in 1979, *The Read-Aloud Handbook* has had six American editions as well as British, Australian, Japanese, Chinese, and Spanish editions. Mr. Trelease is also the editor of two popular read-aloud anthologies for Penguin: *Hey! Liste*~~[obscured]~~ or preteens and teens.

Since 1~~[obscured]~~ectures and seminars throughou~~[obscured]~~ *ithsonian* and *Reader's Digest*. Th~~[obscured]~~gfield, Massachusetts, with his wife, Susan, where they celebrate their four grandchildren's every escapade.

Although Mr. Trelease occasionally scolds American fathers for obsessing too much about sports, recent years have found him involved in one of professional sports' most famous moments when it was accidentally discovered that he had the only existing recording of the 1961 NBA basketball game in which Wilt Chamberlain scored one hundred points. A copy is now included in the archives of the Basketball Hall of Fame, just fifteen minutes from his home. (Visit his Web site, www.trelease-on-reading.com, for the story of how he came to make the recording.)

Jim Trelease's lectures are available on both video- and audiocassette. For information, write Reading Tree Productions, 51 Arvesta Street, Springfield, MA 01118, or visit his Web site.

The
Read-Aloud
Handbook

SIXTH EDITION

Jim Trelease

Penguin Books

PENGUIN BOOKS
Published by the Penguin Group
Penguin Group (USA) Inc., 375 Hudson Street, New York, New York 10014, U.S.A.
Penguin Group (Canada), 90 Eglinton Avenue East, Suite 700, Toronto,
Ontario, Canada M4P 2Y3 (a division of Pearson Penguin Canada Inc.)
Penguin Books Ltd, 80 Strand, London WC2R 0RL, England
Penguin Ireland, 25 St Stephen's Green, Dublin 2, Ireland (a division of Penguin Books Ltd)
Penguin Group (Australia), 250 Camberwell Road, Camberwell,
Victoria 3124, Australia (a division of Pearson Australia Group Pty Ltd)
Penguin Books India Pvt Ltd, 11 Community Centre,
Panchsheel Park, New Delhi - 110 017, India
Penguin Group (NZ), cnr Airborne and Rosedale Roads, Albany,
Auckland 1310, New Zealand (a division of Pearson New Zealand Ltd)
Penguin Books (South Africa) (Pty) Ltd, 24 Sturdee Avenue,
Rosebank, Johannesburg 2196, South Africa

Penguin Books Ltd, Registered Offices:
80 Strand, London WC2R 0RL, England

The Read-Aloud Handbook first published in the United States of America in Penguin Books 1982
First revised edition published 1985
Second revised edition (with title *The New Read-Aloud Handbook*) published 1989
Third revised edition published 1995
Fourth revised edition published 2001
This fifth revised edition published 2006

7   9   10   8

Copyright © Jim Trelease, 1979, 1982, 1985, 1989, 1995, 2001, 2006
All rights reserved

Portions of this book were originally published in pamphlet form.

Page 341 constitutes an extension of this copyright page.

LIBRARY OF CONGRESS CATALOGING IN PUBLICATION DATA
Trelease, Jim.
The read-aloud handbook / Jim Trelease.—6th ed.
p.   cm.
Includes bibliographical references and index.
ISBN 0 14 30.3739 0
1. Oral reading.   I. Title.
LB1573.5.T68 2006
372.45'2—dc22   2006041773

Printed in the United States of America
Set in Bembo

To my grandchildren, Connor, Tyler, Kiernan, and Tess—
the best audiences an old reader-aloud could hope to find.

And to Alvin R. Schmidt, a ninth-grade English teacher
in New Jersey who found the time a half-century ago
to write to the parents of one of his students to tell them
they had a talented child. Neither he nor the
vote of confidence has ever been forgotten.

Acknowledgments

This book could not have been written without the support and cooperation of many friends, associates, neighbors, children, teachers, and editors. I
especially wish to acknowledge my everlasting gratitude to the late Mary A.
Dryden, of Springfield, Massachusetts, who started it all by convincing me
to visit her class thirty-nine years ago in the school that is now named in her
honor.

I am also deeply indebted to my former editors at the *Springfield* (MA)
Daily News for their long-standing support of staff involvement with the
community's schoolchildren. It was this that provided the early impetus for
my experiences in the classroom. At the same time, I am particularly grateful to my dear friend Jane Maroney, whose guiding hand shaped the initial
concept of this book.

It is impossible to express adequately the gratitude I feel toward the hundreds of individuals who, over the last twenty-five years, have taken the
time to share with me their personal experiences with reading and children, only a fraction of which can I use in each edition. For this edition, I
am especially grateful to Melissa Olans Antinoff, Danny Brassell, Brenda
Chapman and her Ridgefield mothers and sons reading group, Bianca
Cotton and her family, Nancy Foote, Jed Gaines, Erin Hassett and her
family, Brigid Hubberman, Kathy Jackson, Larry LaPrise, Jade Malanson,

David Mazor, Susan Nelson, Don Nokes, Teresa Heitmiller Olea, Mike Oliver, Tom O'Neill Jr., Mark Ronnei, Schelly Solko, Amber Soucy, Jennifer Thomas and her family, Trudelle Thomas and her family, Karleen Waldman, and the Trelease-Keller-Reynolds clans of Massachusetts and New Jersey.

For the many clerical and manuscript needs that accompany a revision, I thank my long-suffering assistants, Linda Long and Helen Soucy, for their daily support.

In addition, I would like to thank my neighbor Shirley Uman, whose enthusiasm for my self-published edition back in 1979 was shared with a then-fledgling literary agent, Raphael Sagalyn, who carried it home to Penguin Books; Bee Cullinan for her early encouragement; my Penguin editors, Caroline White and Kathryn Court, for their faith and support through twenty-five years; and a lovely woman named "Florence of Arlington," who wrote the fateful letter to *Dear Abby* in 1983 that changed the Treleases' lives forever.

And, last but not least, I thank my wife, Susan, for her patience and sustenance during the long absences required for each revised edition.

Contents

Introduction

You may have tangible wealth untold:
Caskets of jewels and coffers of gold.
Richer than I you can never be—
I had a mother who read to me.
   —Strickland Gillilan,
    "The Reading Mother,"
    Best-Loved Poems
    of the American People

EVERY couple of years, someone writes a business book about what it is that great Fortune 500 CEOs do that makes them successful, and they're always written in such insider tones as "Psst! We ate breakfast with Bill Gates for a month and we found out that he . . ." Then tens of thousands of businesspeople rush out and buy the book.

Well, this book is like that. We know exactly how people raise readers, both in the home and in the classroom. We know what they do most often, what they seldom do, and what they demand of their children. Some of that research has been around for decades while some of it is new, and it's all wrapped up in the book you're holding.

My equivalent of a Fortune 500 CEO would be the Williams family. Of the four hundred thousand students taking the 2002 ACT exam with Christopher Williams, only fifty-seven had perfect scores—he was the fifty-eighth. When word got out that this kid from Russell, Kentucky (population 3,645), had scored a perfect 36, the family was besieged with questions, the most common being "What prep course did he take? Kaplan? Princeton Review?" It turned out to be a course his parents enrolled him as an infant, a free program, unlike some of the private plans that now cost up to $250 an hour.

In responding to inquiries about Christopher's prep courses, the Williamses simply told people—including the *New York Times*[1]—that he hadn't taken any, that he did no prep work. That, of course, wasn't *completely* true. His mother and father had been giving him and his younger brother free prep classes all through their childhoods, from infancy into adolescence: they read to them for thirty minutes a night, year after year, even well after they learned how to read for themselves.

Theirs is a house brimming with books but no *TV Guide,* GameCube, or Hooked on Phonics. Even though Susan Williams was a fourth-generation teacher, she offered no home instruction in reading before the boys reached school age. She and her husband, Tad, just read to them—sowed (and sewed) the sounds and syllables and endings and blendings of language into the love of books. Each boy easily learned to read, loved it, gobbled it up voraciously. Besides being a family bonding agent, reading aloud was used not as test prep as much as an "ensurance" policy—it *ensured* the boys would be ready for whatever came their way in school. That, combined with church and Scouting, would *ensure* they were ready for whatever life threw at them.

Christopher's situation didn't surprise me at all because I was already familiar with reading aloud as a prep course. Tom Parker recommends it all the time. He's the former admissions director for Williams College who is now at Amherst College, two of the most prestigious colleges in America. Parker tells anxious parents who ask about improving their child's SAT scores, "The best SAT preparation course in the world is to read to your children in bed when they're little. Eventually, if that's a wonderful experience for them, they'll start to read themselves."[2] Parker claims he's never met a student with high verbal SAT scores who wasn't a passionate reader. An ACT or SAT prep course can't package that passion, but parents like Susan and Tad Williams can and so can you.

Never before in American history has as much been written about the subject of reading as in the last five years. Never has so much money been spent to test children in any subject, and never have so many reading rules and regulations been imposed on schools. Strangely, the biggest impact seems to be on families that are the wealthiest and most educated. Where twenty years ago children were spending their after-school hours at dance classes and soccer practices, millennium moms and dads now have them enrolled in record numbers for after-school tutoring. The suburban paranoia over state tests has ballooned the tutoring business into a $4 billion industry, and not just for school-age children. In 2005, Sylvan Learning Centers announced it was opening its 1,200 centers to four-year-olds, while Kumon already was accepting two-year-olds. Where once these centers were mainly for remediation, half the enrollments now come from families looking to give their child an advantage—like the mother who told the *Wall Street Journal* she had enrolled her four-year-old because his scissor skills were not up to par. How about the parents (that's plural) who hire consultants to help their children make better "eye contact" and demonstrate "leadership qualities" with pre-school directors while they're being considered for preschool admission?[3]

Not that parents are alone in their extreme behavior. They have more than enough company among school boards and high-ranking politicians who think if you "fix the schools, they'll fix the kids." So, in Gadsden, Alabama, school officials eliminated kindergarten nap time in 2003 so the children would have more test-prep time.[4] Two hours away in Atlanta, school officials figured that if you eliminate recess, the kids will study more. And just in case those shifty teachers try to sneak it in, Atlanta started building schools without playgrounds. "We are intent on improving academic performance," said the superintendent. "You don't do that by having kids hanging on the monkey bars."[5] (See page 6 to find out how Finland uses its recess time while producing the highest reading scores in the world.) Meanwhile, Georgia's governor wanted the state to give Mozart CDs to newborns because research showed Mozart improved babies' IQs (which later proved to be mythical research).[6] Right behind him is Lincoln, Rhode Island, where they cancelled the district spelling bee because only one child would win, leaving all the others behind, thus violating the intent of No Child Left Behind—or, as they might say in Lincoln, *no child gets ahead*.[7]

In the current climate, everyone from superintendents, principals, and teachers to students, parents, and real estate agents waits with sweaty palms for the next wave of test results. That's at the elementary end of the learning spectrum. Up at the other end, however, there's another kind of restlessness. "We're training our children to be the most anxious, stressed-out, sleep-deprived, judged and tested, poorly nourished generation in history," exclaims Merilee Jones, who happens to be the dean of admissions at Massachusetts Institute of Technology (MIT).

At Harvard, the nation's oldest university and recipient of the largest number of advanced placement students, a thirty-year veteran of the admissions office said today's students "seemed like dazed survivors of some bewildering lifelong boot camp" and warned that "unless things change, we're going to lose a lot of them." In our pursuit of higher and higher scores, he said, "the fabric of family life has just been destroyed."[8]

If anything, the federal No Child Left Behind Act (NCLB) has exacerbated the paranoia, leaving me with two questions: (1) How do we raise smarter students for an increasingly complex work world *without* turning our schools into "boot camp" and our children into "dazed survivors"? and (2) What if NCLB doesn't work?

What about all the children who will have been left behind if NCLB's daily drilling and chanting, testing and penalizing don't work? What if all that drillwork just has them barking at type but when they have to put it all together in seventh grade and start reading *outside* school for the *inside* school tests, they won't read? What if we've been looking in the wrong place—and the weapon of mass instruction wasn't in school in the first place? Suppose the problem was someplace else? So just in case NCLB is wrong,[9] we'd best take out an *insurance* policy on our children like the one Christopher Williams was enrolled in, one that won't turn children into zombies.

Because I'm always being asked questions, I thought it might be helpful if I arranged this book under certain topic questions, such as:

Are You Suggesting This Reading Stuff Is the Job of the Parent? I Thought It Was the School's Job.

Let me introduce you to the sponge factor in education, the largest of all the missing ingredients in the NCLB legislation. We start with a young lady named Bianca Cotton, whom I met for the first time in 2002 on the morning my grandson Tyler began kindergarten. Families were invited in for the first hour to help break the ice, and I was snapping some pictures of Tyler and a new friend when I gradually became aware of an extended conversation going on behind me in the little housekeeping section of the kindergarten. Turning around, I found Bianca cooking up a make-believe meal on a make-believe stove while carrying on a make-believe conversation on a make-believe cordless phone. And, as you can see in the photo I snapped in the ensuing moments, she had all the body language down for talking on the phone and cooking at the same time.

Besides being our children, they're also our little sponges, soaking up everything we do and say.

While these are our children, they are also our little sponges. If Bianca had never seen an adult talking on the phone while cooking, she'd never think to grab a phone while "cooking" her first kindergarten meal. If Bianca isn't proof enough of the sponge-like quality of childhood, consider this one: Since 1956, no newspaper, network, or news agency has been able to correctly predict the outcome of all thirteen presidential elections— except for one group. Every four years for a half century, the quarter million children who vote in the *Weekly Reader* presidential poll have been right *every* time.

Like little sponges, they sit there in living rooms, kitchens, and cars, soaking up all the words and values of their parents, and then walk into a classroom and squeeze them onto a piece of paper. It's simple arithmetic: the child spends 900 hours a year in school and 7,800 hours outside school. Which teacher has the bigger influence? Where is more time available for change?

Jay Mathews, the *Washington Post*'s education writer, looked back on all the student achievement stories he'd done in twenty-two years and wrote: "I cannot think of a single instance in which the improvement in achievement was not tied, at least in part, to an increase in the amount of time students had to learn."[10] I've been saying the same thing for as many years. You either extend the school day (as have the successful KIPP Academies charters)[11] or you tap into the 7,800 hours at home. Since the dollar cost of lengthening the school day would be prohibitive in the neediest places, the most viable option is tapping the 7,800 hours at home, something government mistakenly sees as the equivalent of raising taxes.

Ronald F. Ferguson, a black scholar and Harvard lecturer, has long studied racial achievement gaps in public schools. Complicated as those issues are, Ferguson boils them down to one: "The real issue is historical differences in parenting. That is hard to talk about, but that is the root of the skill gap." According to Ferguson, black households traditionally see schooling as a job for teachers, while white families are more involved in schooling the child or paying for special services.[12]

Contrary to the doctrine that blames teachers for reading scores, research shows that the seeds of reading and school success are sown in the home, long before the child ever arrives at school. Twenty-one classes of kindergartners were examined for children who displayed either high or low interest in books. Those students' home environments were then examined in detail (see the table below).[13] The numbers reinforce the adage that "The apple doesn't fall far from the tree." Therefore, you change the tree if you want different apples.

Home Information	High Interest in Books (%)	Low Interest in Books (%)
Mother's leisure activities		
Watches TV	39.3	63.2
Reads	78.6	28.1
What mother reads		
Novels	95.2	10.5
Father's leisure activities		
Watches TV	35.1	48.2
Reads	60.7	15.8
What father reads		
Newspapers	91.1	84.2
Novels	62.5	8.8
Number of books in home	80.6 books	31.7 books
Child owns library card	37.5	3.4
Child is taken to library	98.1	7.1
Child is read to daily	76.8	1.8

Research like this helps crystallize education issues that politicians too often turn into fog. But research alone would bore the traditional parent and teacher, so I've also included the personal and anecdotal to bring the research alive.

By personal and anecdotal I mean people like Leonard Pitts Jr. and his mother. As he describes her, "She was not a learned woman, never finished high school. But then, it's hard to be learned when you grow up black in Depression-era Mississippi. Still, not being learned is not the same as not being smart." His mother "was a voracious consumer of books and newspapers, a woman filled with a thirst to know." With that in mind, picture this forty-six-year-old son sitting down at his computer in 2004, typing the following words:

> My first reader was a welfare mother with a heart condition. She lived in a housing project near downtown Los Angeles.
>
> This is circa 1962 or '63 and technically, she wasn't my reader back then but my listener. I would follow her around as she ironed clothes or prepared a meal, reading aloud from my latest epic, which, like all my epics, was about a boy who was secretly a superhero, with super strength and the ability to fly.
>
> Surely there came a point when the poor woman secretly regretted having taught the bespectacled child his ABCs, but she never let on. Just nodded and exclaimed in all the right places and when the story was done, sent me off to clean up my room or wash my hands for dinner.[14]

Leonard Pitts Jr. was writing a thank-you note to his mother. Even though she had died sixteen years earlier, he wanted her to know how grateful he was. After all, you don't win the Pulitzer Prize for commentary just any day of the week. His thank-you note became his syndicated *Miami Herald* column for that day. Mrs. Pitts couldn't afford to spend her son's 7,800 hours driving him around to tutoring classes. Instead, she tutored him herself by listening, enthusing, and reading. She couldn't afford high-priced "eye contact" tutors, but she skimped to buy him a toy typewriter when he was eight and a used one when he was fourteen. Loose change? Just enough so her son could buy the latest Spider-Man and Fantastic Four comic books. What Mrs. Pitts and the Williamses were doing is one of the great trade secrets in American education. Keeping that stuff a secret and focusing exclusively on testing is like telling people with cancer that they need to do something about their dandruff.

What the Williams and Pitts families did wasn't expensive, so income level need not be a blockade. It may not be easy for poor people, but it's not impossible. For example, the most comprehensive study of American schoolchildren (22,000 students)[15] showed us that while children in poverty made up 52 percent of the bottom quarter when they entered kindergarten, 6 percent scored in the highest quartile—right up there with the richest children in America. Furthermore, of all college graduates each year, 6 percent come from poverty.[16] They might be the same 6 percent—but collectively they demonstrate that it's not impossible to achieve at high levels *if* the parents do the right things.

Can We Really Change Families and Homes in America?

We did it once, why not again? Suppose we ran a national awareness campaign for what parents can, should, and must do in the home? And I don't mean a polite little campaign where the First Lady runs around and visits child-care centers, saying "Read to the kiddos!" I mean a real "in-your-face" crusade.

For the last forty years, an incessant antismoking campaign has been waged in this country, a three-pronged attack that could be adopted in the battle for family literacy. In the case of tobacco, we (1) informed, (2) frightened, and (3) shamed people into changing. Using all available media, we gave them statistics linking smoking to cancer and eventual death, we offered deathbed confessions from smokers who were speaking through artificial voice boxes, and we erected billboards that insulted and shamed smokers with statements like "Kissing a smoker is like licking an ashtray."

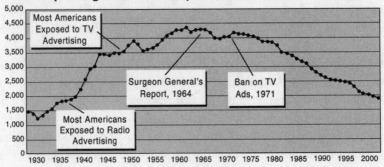

Per Capita Cigarette Consumption, United States 1930–2003

The amount of smoking was directly linked to the amount of positive or negative advertising. The same formula could be used in a national awareness campaign for family literacy.

Source: www.cdc.gov/tobacco/research_data?economics/consumpt./htm.

Gradually, public opinion swayed public practice, forcing legislation and litigation that would affect most homes and every public place in America. After forty years, fewer than 23 percent of Americans smoke, and hundreds of millions of lives and dollars have been saved.

Following that model, we could change parental practices in this country—not in one year or one presidential administration, but over several decades. It would work, however, only if we follow that three-pronged attack, because different people are motivated to change for different reasons. One size does not fit all families. We'd give parents the statistics on children's reading that you'll find in this book (to inform). There also would be information on the damage that is done to children's and grandchildren's futures if families fail to do the right things for literacy (to scare). And finally, we'd have to shame some families into doing the right thing, as we did with smokers.

I'm not talking about public shame, but rather the private kind that comes with feeling guilty about what you're doing to your child. Didn't we do that with people who smoked in front of their children? Didn't we do it with drunk drivers? Didn't we do it with parents who didn't know where their children were at 10 P.M.? Unfortunately, politicians have been reluctant to hold parents accountable because they're afraid of losing the parent vote, which is far larger than the teacher vote. It's time to change that kind of selfish thinking.

Will This Book Help Me Teach My Child to Read?

This is not a book about teaching a child *how* to read; it's about teaching a child to *want* to read. There's an education adage that goes, "What we teach children to love and desire will always outweigh what we make them learn." The fact is that some children learn to read sooner than others, while some learn better than others. There is a difference. For the parent who thinks that sooner is better, who has an eighteen-month-old child barking at flash cards, my response is: sooner is not better. Are the dinner guests who arrive an hour early better guests than those who arrive on time? Of course not.

However, I am concerned about the child who *needlessly* arrives late and then struggles through years of pain with books. Not only will he miss out on large portions of what he needs to know in school, he'll experience a pain in connection with print that may stay with him for a lifetime. There are things that families must do as "preventive maintenance" to ensure against those pains. You've already read some examples, and you'll find more in the chapters ahead.

Back in 1983, when the government issued the report *A Nation at Risk,* it sounded, in my opinion, a false alarm for schools to adopt a business approach to schooling. That report invited the private sector to come into schools and set up their cash registers; it forced schools to run like businesses, and the testing-accountability craze began. In the twenty-one years since that report, it's been disowned by its lead author, Terrell Bell (then the U.S. secretary of education), and most of its premises and promises have been exposed as false or fraudulent.[17]

One of the flaws in attempting to run a school like a business is that businesses depend on the efficiency of their employees and machinery, but children make awful machines. Businesspeople think in terms of packaging and on-time deliveries. While No Child Left Behind is in sync with the airline industry's "on-time departures and arrivals," children aren't planes or trains; they don't all depart or arrive on time, and some come with extra baggage.

There should be no rush to have your child reading before age six or seven. That's developmentally the natural time. Finland refuses to teach children to read until age seven and it boasts the world's highest reading scores (more on this in chapter 1). This book is not about raising precocious children. It's about raising children in love with print who want to keep on reading long after they graduate.

This is really two books in one. The first half comprises the evidence in support of reading aloud and the other practices that nurture lifetime readers; the second half is the "Treasury of Read-Alouds," a beginner's reference to recommended titles from picture books to novels. The Treasury is intended to take the guesswork out of reading aloud for busy parents and teachers (many of whom were never read to in their own childhoods) who want to begin reading aloud but don't have the time to take a course in children's literature.

Even I have to admit that the subject of children's reading is broader than simply reading aloud, passionate as I am about that subject. And that's why there's a chapter (5) devoted to sustained silent reading (SSR), reading aloud's silent partner, if you will. And just as the best baseball players come from countries and states where they can play baseball most often, research shows that children who have access to more print (magazines, newspapers, and books) have higher reading scores—because they end up reading more. That's explored in chapter 7.

There is also a section on television (9) that includes some new research correlating infants' daily TV exposure with attention deficit disorder by age seven. That chapter also includes information about a mechanical device for the TV that is the best electronic reading tutor in the world!

How Did a Parent Come to Write This Book?

Back in the 1960s, I was a young father of two children and working as an artist and writer for a daily newspaper in Massachusetts. Each night I read to my daughter and son, unaware of any cognitive or emotional benefits that would come of it. I had no idea what it would do for their vocabulary, attention span, or interest in books. I read for one reason: because my father had read to me and it made me feel so good I never forgot it and wanted my children to taste it too.

So there I was, reading to my young children each night, when one day I found myself doing some volunteer work in a classroom of sixth-graders in Springfield, Massachusetts (I'd been visiting classrooms on a weekly basis for several years, discussing my career as an artist and writer). After spending an hour with the class, I gathered my materials and prepared to leave when I noticed a little novel on the shelf near the door. It was *The Bears' House* by Marilyn Sachs, and it caught my eye because I'd just finished reading it to my daughter.

"Who's reading *The Bears' House*?" I asked the class. Several girls' hands went up. What followed was an unrehearsed lovefest about reading, talking with them about *The Bears' House* and other books I'd read to my children, and sharing secrets I knew about the authors: "Did you know that when Robert McCloskey was illustrating *Make Way for Ducklings,* he had a dreadful time drawing those ducks? He finally brought six ducklings up to his apartment to get a closer look. In the end, because they kept moving around so much, do you know what he did? You may find this hard to believe, but I promise you it's true: in order to get them to hold still, he slowed them down by getting them drunk on wine!")

It was forty-five minutes before I could say good-bye. The teacher subsequently wrote to say that the children had begged and begged to go to the library to get the books I'd talked about. At the time, I wondered what it was that I had said that was so unusual. All I'd done was talk about my family's favorite books. I'd been giving them *book reports* (just as Oprah would do twenty-five years later). As soon as I called it that, I realized what made it so special. It probably was the first time any of them had ever heard an adult give a book report—an unsolicited one, at that. I'd piqued the children's interest simply by giving them a book "commercial." From then on, whenever I visited a classroom, I'd save some time at the end to talk about reading. I'd begin by asking, "What have you read lately? Anybody read any good books lately?"

To my dismay, I discovered they weren't reading much at all. But I slowly began to notice one difference. There were isolated classrooms in which the kids *were* reading—reading a ton! How is it, I puzzled, that these kids are so turned on to reading while the class across the hall (where I had visited the previous month) wasn't reading anything? Same principal, same neighborhood, same textbooks. What's up?

When I pursued it further I discovered that the difference was standing in the front of the room: the teacher. In nearly every one of the turned-on classes, the teacher read to the class on a regular basis. Maybe there's something to this, I thought—more than just the feel-good stuff. In the libraries of the local teacher colleges I discovered research showing that reading aloud to children improves their reading, writing, speaking, listening—and, best of all, their attitudes about reading. There was one problem: the people who should have been reading the research weren't reading it. The teachers, supervisors, and principals didn't know it even existed. I also found that most parents and teachers were unaware of good children's books.

In the late 1970s, when I realized there was nothing generally available for parents on reading aloud, not even book lists (except those included in children's literature textbooks), I decided to compile my own—a modest self-published venture (costing me $650 for the first printing—the family vacation money for one summer). Some local bookstores took copies on consignment, and within three years the booklet had sold twenty thousand copies in thirty states and Canada. By 1982, Penguin Books had seen a copy and asked me to expand it into the first Penguin edition of the book you are reading now. There have also been British, Australian, Japanese, Chinese, and Spanish editions.

Even in this—the growth of this book—we can see the metaphor of "passing torches." A few months after the first Penguin edition of *The Read-Aloud Handbook* was published, someone gave a young graduate student a copy on the occasion of his becoming a new parent. He then gave a copy of it to an Arlington, Virginia, couple expecting a child and for whom he was doing part-time carpentry work. This Arlington mother, though, did more than just read it. She wrote and sent an unsolicited "book report" about it to a national syndicated advice columnist—a woman named Abigail Van Buren. And when her letter appeared in the *Dear Abby* column, with "Abby's" response, on February 23, 1983, Penguin received orders almost overnight for 120,000 copies of the book. February 23 is celebrated as Dear, Dear Abby Day in our house.

How Do I Convince My Husband He Should Be Doing This with Our Children?

As it happens, fathers are my pet project, even though there's always a shortage of dads at my seminars no matter where I travel. So here's the strategy to get your spouse involved with reading. First, get him to read this section, and then page 105 in chapter 6 (about a father and son in Cincinnati, Ohio).

The three things most dads think they understand best are business, sports, and boys. There have been some sea changes, however, involving those subjects since my first edition back in 1982. Back then, the world was round. Today it's flat. How's that for a sea change?

New York Times foreign affairs columnist Thomas L. Friedman, a three-time Pulitzer Prize winner, describes this in his book *The World Is Flat.* Twenty-five years ago, the power structure of the world consisted of highs and lows: the countries with the power and knowledge were at the top of the mountains and the rest were down in the valleys. A handful of countries ruled the world's economy because they monopolized the information, and information is power. The mountaintop countries were the United States, Britain, Germany, and Japan. Then came the Internet. Suddenly, those who were outside the information circuit, who were down in the valleys, were connected to the information network and linked to the knowledge base and thus to work flow.[18] These included India, Eastern Europe, South Korea, and now China. Don't believe it? Walk through Toys "R" Us and pick up any ten toys, checking each for where it was made. My last count: China, ten out of ten. The world's workforce has thus become "flattened."

In the old days, an educated English-speaking Indian from Bangalore had to emigrate to America or England to find professional work. That need ended with the Web. Friedman reports that in 2003, 25,000 U.S. tax returns were processed in India, outsourced by U.S. companies who wanted them done cheaply and correctly. Within two years, that number ballooned to 400,000. India now graduates 70,000 accountants a year. These are not necessarily smarter accountants than those in the United States, but they're not dumber and they sure are cheaper. Almost none of them is watching the clock. If you were playing a game and 3 *billion* new contestants entered the game, the game's flow would change, right? The Web opened the game of business to 3 billion new players.

America's best business students, who used to spend their summers laboring in Wall Street internships, increasingly are opting to do summer work in India. Talk about reverse migration! In the summer of 2005, one technology firm in Bangalore, India, had openings for forty interns; nine thousand applied.[19]

The only people who haven't heard about this sea change are the fathers and sons watching their third straight hour of ESPN, still clinging to the image of the swaggering male who doesn't need to play school. It's been twenty-five years since that idea had any wings, but too many dads are still trying to make it fly. Back in the mid-1970s, General Motors employed 86,000 hourly workers in the city of Flint, Michigan. By early 2006, that number stood for all the hourly workers GM had in the *entire* United States, and the Flint number was down to 17,000.[20] Where once the only thing that mattered for men was what they could do with their hands, it's now what they can do with their *heads* that counts. And without classroom success, today's male faces an impossible challenge from both intelligent women on the home front and foreigners willing to do the same job for less while sitting in an office not in Baltimore but in Bangalore.

So the first sea change has been the flattening of the world's workforce. The second change is a huge gender gap among American schoolchildren. Since 1970, there's been a steady gain in female achievement, accompanied by a steep drop in male performance. And this time, they're going to need more than pharmaceutical "performance enhancers" to cure the problem. In 1970, male enrollment in college was 59 percent, female 41 percent. Three decades later, it's almost completely reversed—57 percent female, 43 percent male.[21]

The top 10 percent of high school classes is 56 percent female, 44 percent male; among high school graduates who maintain an A average, 62 percent are female, 38 percent male.[22] Three out of five high school National Honor Society members are girls, and they outnumber boys 124 to 100 in Advanced Placement (AP) classes. As recently as 1987, boys had outnumbered girls in those classes.[23] If this were Major League Baseball, a lot of guys would be on the bus heading to the minor leagues.

We know what caused the rise in the girls' scores—their mothers' value systems about education changed thirty years ago. Mothers now expect more of their daughters intellectually. But how do we explain the nosedive on the part of the boys since 1970? Is it a coincidence that in that same year, 1970, we saw the birth of a national TV phenomenon called *Monday Night Football*? Prior to that, Madison Avenue pretty much thought it was a waste of time trying to advertise to men late at night—they were all asleep in their La-Z-Boys. Then along comes *MNF* and they've got millions of guys doing high fives on their chairs at 11 P.M. It didn't take long for the networks to catch on that sports at night could bring in a boatload of advertising dollars and thus was born ESPN, then ESPN2, followed by channels for golf, rodeo, NASCAR, wrestling, extreme sports—you name it, all sports, all the time, 24/7.

The impact on the young male of seeing his dad worshipping daily and nightly at the altar of ESPN, has to have played a damaging role in male attitudes about school. Girls read and write; guys hit, throw, catch, shoot, and fish. By 2000, moms were "taking their daughters to work," but dads were still taking their sons to the stadium.

The father who can find his way only to ball games with his kids is a "boy-man," whereas the father who can find his way to a ball game *and* to the library can be called a "grown man." Unfortunately, we have a growing shortage of grown men in America today. Once I asked members of an audience in Decatur, Georgia, if they thought they'd ever hear a president of the United States make a statement like that to the American people, and a woman replied, "Yes—as soon as she's elected!"[24]

The strange thing is that this "dumbing of Daddy" seems to affect families at all education levels. In a study comparing poverty-level families and university-educated families, fathers in both groups read to the children only 15 percent of the time, mothers 76 percent, and others 9 percent.[25] That could change if we publicized studies like one conducted in Modesto, California, which showed that (1) boys who were read to by their fathers scored significantly higher in reading achievement, and (2) when fathers read recreationally, their sons read more and scored higher than did boys whose fathers did little or no recreational reading. When the dads were surveyed, only 10 percent reported having fathers who read to them when they were children.[26] (See also page 17 in chapter 1.) But it's not just the dads who are to blame: the books we ask young males to digest may not exactly whet the appetite. That's explored on page 155 in chapter 8.

Is Reading Still Important in the Video Age?

The NCLB folks and I agree—reading is at the heart of education. Reading *is* first. The knowledge of almost every subject in school flows from reading. One must be able to read the word problem in math to understand it. If you cannot read the science or social studies chapter, you cannot answer the questions at the end of the chapter. A computer manual must be *read*, not *viewed*.

One can arguably state that reading is the single most important social factor in American life today. Here's a formula to support that. It sounds simplistic, but all its parts can be documented, and while not 100 percent universal, it holds true far more often than not.

1. The more you read, the more you know.[27]
2. The more you know, the smarter you grow.[28]
3. The smarter you are, the longer you stay in school.[29]
4. The longer you stay in school, the more diplomas you earn and the longer you are employed—thus the more money you earn in a lifetime.[30]
5. The more diplomas you earn, the higher your children's grades will be in school.[31]
6. The more diplomas you earn, the longer you live.[32]

The opposite would also be true:

1. The less you read, the less you know.
2. The less you know, the sooner you drop out of school.[33]
3. The sooner you drop out, the sooner and longer you are poor.[34]
4. The sooner you drop out, the greater your chances of going to jail.[35]

The basis for that formula is firmly established: poverty and illiteracy are related—they are the parents of desperation and imprisonment:

- Seventy to 82 percent of prison inmates are school dropouts.[36]
- Sixty percent of inmates are illiterate to semiliterate.[37]
- Sixty-three percent of inmates are repeat offenders.[38]

Why are such students failing and dropping out of school? Because they cannot read—which affects the entire report card. Change the graduation rate and you change the prison population—which changes the social climate of America.

Reading is the ultimate weapon, destroying ignorance, poverty, and despair before they can destroy us. A nation that doesn't read much doesn't know much. And a nation that doesn't know much is more likely to make poor choices in the home, the marketplace, the jury box, and the voting booth. And those decisions ultimately affect an entire nation—the literate and the illiterate.

Chapter 1

Why Read Aloud?

Education is not the filling of a bucket but the lighting of a fire.
—William Butler Yeats

ONE day I visited the same kindergarten room I had attended years earlier as a child at Connecticut Farms Elementary School in Union, New Jersey. Gazing up at me were the faces of about fifteen children, each of them seated expectantly on their story rug. "How many of you want to learn to read this year?" I asked. Without a second's hesitation, every hand shot into the air, many accompanied by boasts like "I already know how!" Their excitement matched what every kindergarten teacher has told me: every child begins school wanting to learn to read. In other words, we've got 100 percent enthusiasm and desire when they start school—that is, in chapter one of school life.

In five-year increments since then, the National Reading Report Card[1] has given the rest of the chapters:

♦ Among fourth-graders, only 54 percent read something for pleasure every day.
♦ Among eighth-graders, only 30 percent read for pleasure daily.
♦ By twelfth grade, only 19 percent read anything for pleasure daily.

We have 100 percent interest in kindergarten but lose 78 percent of our potential lifetime readers by senior year. Any business that kept losing that much of its customer base would be in bankruptcy.

A school's objective should be to create lifetime readers—graduates who continue to read and educate themselves throughout their adult lives. But the reality is that we create schooltime readers—graduates who know how to read well enough to graduate. At that point the majority take a silent vow: if I never read another book, it'll be too soon.

How are these childhood figures reflected in the adult population? The National Endowment for the Arts has been surveying adult reading habits for almost twenty-five years, and its most recent report coincided perfectly with the National Assessment of Educational Progress (NAEP) assessment of pleasure reading among thirteen- and seventeen-year-olds. Adult reading of literature (fiction, short stories, or poetry) was down 22 percent from its 1982 survey, and the decline was evidenced in every age, gender, ethnic, and educational category. By 2002, only 46.7 percent of 17,000 adults surveyed had read any fiction in the previous year.[2] When that was expanded in a different survey to include newspapers or any kind of book or magazine, the figure rose to only 50 percent of adults.[3] In short, half of America is aliterate.

In comparing 2004 NAEP scores with those of 1971, there is no change for seventeen-year-olds and an insignificant change for thirteen-year-olds.[4] That's thirty years—half of it devoted to national and state curriculum reform and higher standards—yet no improvement. Actually there *was* a change among the high school seniors in the last twenty years and it mirrored the change in adult reading habits. As I noted, adult recreational reading dropped 22 percent in the last twenty years. Among seventeen-year-olds (an age at which all the elementary instruction is supposed to take root and finally blossom), the percentage who never read anything for fun increased from 9 percent in 1984 to 19 percent in 2004. When you add those who read only once a month or a few times a year, the figure expands to 48 percent, pretty close to what you find among adults.

This trend was first noticed as far back as 1983, and a national committee was created to explore the causes and solutions. It was called the Commission on Reading, organized by the National Academy of Education and the National Institute of Education and funded through the U.S. Department of Education. It consisted of nationally recognized experts on how children develop, how they learn language, and how they learn to read. Since nearly everything in the school curriculum rested upon reading, the consensus was that reading was at the heart of either the problem or the solution. This commission was markedly different from the National Reading Panel (NRP) created in 2000, which established the Reading First reading curriculum under the No Child Left Behind Act. More on that later.

The 1983 commission took two years to pore through more than ten thousand research projects conducted in the previous quarter century to determine what works, what might work, and what doesn't work. In 1985, the commission issued its report, *Becoming a Nation of Readers.* Among its primary findings, two simple declarations rang loud and clear:

+ "The single most important activity for building the knowledge required for eventual success in reading is reading aloud to children."[5]
+ "It is a practice that should continue throughout the grades."[6] The commission found conclusive evidence to support reading aloud not only in the home but also in the classroom.

In their wording—"the single most important activity"—the experts were saying reading aloud was more important than work sheets, homework, assessments, book reports, and flash cards. One of the cheapest, simplest, and oldest tools of teaching was being promoted as a better teaching tool than anything else in the home or classroom. What exactly is so powerful about something so simple you don't even need a high school diploma in order to do it? And how exactly does a person get better at reading? It boils down to a simple, two-part formula:

+ The more you read, the better you get at it; the better you get at it, the more you like it; and the more you like it, the more you do it.
+ The more you read, the more you know; and the more you know, the smarter you grow.[7]

None of this is to be construed to mean we're a nation of illiterates. We are not. The average American student can read. And 95 percent of twenty-one- to twenty-five-year-olds, our alumni, can perform routine tasks using printed information (one paragraph of simple sentences).[8] Sixty-three percent attempt advanced education, compared to only 20 percent in 1940. The problem is not that they can't read; it's that they don't read very much as they mature and therefore aren't very good at it when they need to be. A major reason why only 27 percent of high school students advance beyond freshman year of college is that 78 percent spend less than three hours a week reading anything for school, including 68 percent of college-prep students.[9] The world is a lot more complex today than it was twenty-five years ago, so three hours or less doesn't cut it anymore.

Some in government propose that penalties, tests, and other measures will solve this problem, but that assumes it's a mechanical problem. When the "want-to" is missing, it's not a mechanical malfunction; it's an attitude problem. Instead of penalties, we should start with the advice of the man who founded compulsory education back in the 1830s, Horace Mann: "Men," he wrote in 1837, "are cast iron; but children are wax."

So we begin with the "wax"—children—and we use the findings of the Commission on Reading to shape them: We read aloud to them throughout the grades. Simple. Unlike most reforms, it will not increase the tax rate 1 percent, and, like Oprah's club, no one can fail it.

How Can Something as Simple as Reading to a Child Be So Effective?

We start with the brain. As lumber is the primary support for building a house, words are the primary structure for learning. There are really only two efficient ways to get words into a person's brain: either through the eye or through the ear. Since it is years before the eye in a young child is used for reading, the best source for ideas and brain building becomes the ear. What we send into that ear becomes the "sound" foundation for the rest of the child's "brain house." Those meaningful sounds in the ear now will help the child make sense of the words coming in through the eye later when learning to read.

We read to children for all the same reasons we talk with children: to reassure, to entertain, to bond, to inform or explain, to arouse curiosity, to inspire. But in reading aloud, we also:

+ condition the child's brain to associate reading with pleasure;
+ create background knowledge;
+ build vocabulary;
+ provide a reading role model.

One factor hidden in the decline of students' recreational reading is that it coincides with a decline in the amount of time adults read to them. By middle school, almost no one is reading aloud to students. If each read-aloud is a commercial for the pleasures of reading, then a decline in advertising would naturally be reflected in a decline in students' recreational reading.

There are two basic "reading facts of life" that are ignored in most education circles, yet without these two principles working in tandem, little else will work.

Reading Fact No. 1: Human beings are pleasure centered.
Reading Fact No. 2: Reading is an accrued skill.

Let's examine Fact No. 1. Human beings will voluntarily do over and over that which brings them pleasure. That is, we go to the restaurants we like, order the foods we like, listen to the radio stations that play the music we like, and visit the in-laws we like. Conversely, we avoid the foods, music, and in-laws we dislike. Far from being a theory, this is a physiological fact. We approach what causes pleasure, and we withdraw from what causes displeasure or pain.[10]

This fact applies to nearly everything we do willingly. Every time we read to a child, we're sending a "pleasure" message to the child's brain. You could even call it a commercial, conditioning the child to associate books and print with pleasure. There are, however, displeasures associated with reading and school. The learning experience can be tedious or boring, threatening, and often without meaning—endless hours of work sheets, intensive phonics instruction, and unconnected test questions. If a child seldom experiences the "pleasures" of reading but increasingly meets its "unpleasures," then the natural reaction will be withdrawal.

And that brings us to Reading Fact No. 2. Reading is like riding a bicycle, driving a car, or sewing: in order to get better at it you must do it. And the more you read, the better you get at it.

The last thirty years of reading research[11] confirms this simple formula—regardless of sex, race, nationality, or socioeconomic background. Students who read the most also read the best, achieve the most, and stay in school the longest. Conversely, those who don't read much cannot get better at it.

Why don't students read more? Because of Reading Fact No. 1. The large number of "unpleasure" messages they received throughout their school years, coupled with the lack of "pleasure" messages in the home, nullify any attraction books might have. They avoid books and print the same way a cat avoids a hot stovetop. There is ample proof for all these hypotheses in my answer to the next question.

Which Country Has the Best Readers and Why?

One of the most comprehensive international reading studies was conducted by Warwick Elley for the International Association for the Evaluation of Educational Achievement (IEA) in 1990 and 1991. Involving thirty-two countries, it assessed 210,000 nine- and fourteen-year-olds.[12] Of all those children, which ones read best?

For nine-year-olds, the four top nations were: Finland (569), United States (547), Sweden (539), and France (531). But the United States' position dropped to a tie for eighth when fourteen-year-olds were evaluated. This demonstrates that American children begin reading on a level that is among the best in the world, but since reading is an accrued skill and U.S. children appear to do less of it as they grow older, their scores decline when compared with countries where children read more as they mature. We also have a higher proportion of children in poverty, and their scores decline as they go through school (see page 88).

Can Finland's High Score Be Attributed to an Advanced Start?

Just the opposite. Finland's high scores should give pause to those who think an earlier reading start ("hothousing") will produce better results. They're really not into Baby Einstein toys over there. There was only three months' difference in age between the first-place Finnish children and second-place American students, yet the Finnish children—who are introduced to formal reading instruction only at age seven, two years later than American children—still managed to surpass them by age nine. Indeed, almost everything Finland does contradicts what some experts in America advocate: Most mothers work outside the home; most children are in child care by age one; school begins at age seven and then for half-days; the child remains in the same school from age seven to age sixteen; there are no gifted programs; class size often reaches thirty; there are fifteen minutes of recess for every forty-five-minute class; there is no national curriculum; all meals are free, as is university education; and there is a high family literacy rate, with reading to children emphasized heavily and supported by a powerful public library system.[13]

Finally, Finnish families are heavy users of a mechanical device that serves as a reading tutor for their children. More on that in chapter 9 (page 169). In the fifteen years since Elley's study, the Finns have remained atop the international scoreboard as measured by the Organization for Economic Cooperation and Development (OECD) every three years.

Do the Best Readers Share Any Common Denominators?

In Elley's study,[14] two of the factors that produced higher achievement (two others will be found later in chapter 7) are:

- The frequency of teachers reading aloud to students.
- The frequency of sustained silent reading (SSR), or pleasure reading in school. Children who had daily SSR scored much higher than those who had it only once a week.

Those two factors also represent the two Reading Facts we've just examined. Reading aloud is the catalyst for the child wanting to read on his own, but it also provides a foundation by nurturing the child's listening comprehension. In an international study of 150,000 fourth-graders, researchers found that students who were read to "often" at home scored thirty points higher than students who were read to "sometimes."[15] It stands to reason that the more often a child is read to, the more words are heard (bringing the child closer to comprehending more), and the more likely it is the child will associate reading with a daily pleasure experience.

Beyond the pleasure connection, reading aloud builds higher reading scores because listening comprehension comes before reading comprehension. If you've never heard a word, it's unlikely you'll ever say it. So how are you going to read it and write it? I'll explore this at greater length in chapter 2.

Where Does Phonics Fit into All This?

There's more than enough research to validate the importance of phonics in children's reading. Children who understand the mechanics of reading—who know that words are made up of sounds and can break the sound code—have a great advantage. But teaching a boy how to scrub his neck is no guarantee he'll have a clean neck, even if he knows how to use the washcloth and soap. The missing ingredient is motivation. If he knows how but doesn't want to wash his neck, it's going to stay dirty. But when that boy meets the right girl, he'll have a clean neck—thus you need the combination of know-how *and* motivation.

Phonics drills don't motivate—they can't, and no one knows that better than the folks who wrote the phonics chapter in the National Reading Panel (NRP) report,[16] the one that became the federal "rule book" for reading instruction in 2001. There were more than one hundred pages devoted to phonics, which is a story in itself. The NRP consisted of fourteen people, independent of each other and without support staff. It included eleven university professors (eight with reading background, two administrators, and one physician), along with a parent, a principal, and a middle school language arts teacher. Missing was anyone who might have actually taught a beginning reader. To create this kind of report without the input of reading teachers is, in my mind, the equivalent of NASA redesigning the shuttle program without seeking input from astronauts.

Although the NRP billed its report as completely "research-based" and "scientific," one of its members, Joanne Yatvin (the panel's principal and subsequently a district superintendent), wrote a withering rebuttal opinion of the report, finding it considerably less than "scientific." The most controversial and famous of the report's topics was phonics. With five months remaining before the report was to be turned over to Congress, the phonics topic was turned over to independent researchers outside the panel. The final phonics report was dropped in the lap of the NRP four days before press time. Yatvin wrote: "Thus the phonics report became part of the full report of the NRP uncorrected, undeliberated, and unapproved."[17] I offer that just in case you ever wondered about the NRP report and its "scientific" standards.

Nonetheless, the sounds of words are an important part of learning to read, but they're only a *part*. Equally important are motivation and background knowledge (often enlarged by reading more). If you ask doctors, coaches, even probation officers about the importance of motivation for the people they're dealing with, they all will tell you it's *crucial*. Good classroom teachers agree. Since there appeared to be a diminishing amount of motivation to read among secondary readers in the last thirty years, I was curious to see what the National Reading Panel's report would recommend to stanch the bleeding. Since the document is available as an Internet PDF file, it's entirely word-searchable by computer. I searched for the following words: "library," "phonics," "phonemic," derivatives of "motivate/motivation," and "book/literature."

Word Search of National Reading Panel Report

Word	No. of mentions
Phonemic	752
Phonics	178
Motivate (or motivation)	
to read more	19
Literature (children's)	7
Reading aloud (to child)	2
Library	1

There were an additional forty-six uses of "motivation" but all in conjunction with phonics usage in the classroom, not in association with children's desire to read more. Typical was: "Future research on phonics instruction should investigate how best to *motivate* children in classrooms to learn the letter-sound associations and to apply that knowledge to reading and writing."

Drill and skill don't motivate. What motivates fans to come back to baseball games are favorite players and favorite teams. Nobody has a favorite vowel or a favorite blend. What motivates children and adults to read more is that (1) they like the experience a lot, (2) they like the subject matter a lot, and (3) they like and follow the lead of people who read a lot (Oprah types). Writing a 449-page report on the teaching of reading and devoting seven sentences to literature and one sentence to libraries is like writing a 449-page book on the New York Yankees and devoting only one page to the players. Motivation is the kind of intangible that would be included in Einstein's observation: "Not everything that can be counted counts, and not everything that counts can be counted." Obviously the *desire* to read doesn't count with the bureaucrats.

The U.S. Department of Education's 1999 Early Childhood Longitudinal Study found that children who were read to at least three times a week had a significantly greater phonemic awareness when they entered kindergarten than did children who were read to less often, and that they were almost twice as likely to score in the top 25 percent in reading.[18] That being the case, wouldn't you figure the National Reading Panel would recommend that reading aloud continue in the classroom, especially for those children who never received the benefits at home (see the chart below)?[19] So, to even things up, I promise not to mention phonics again for the next four hundred pages.

So many read-aloud claims had accumulated in a thirty-year period that researchers subjected thirty-three of them to a meta-analysis to see if the

The higher the family's income (socioeconomic status, or SES), the more often the child was read to and the higher the child's literacy skills entering kindergarten.[20]

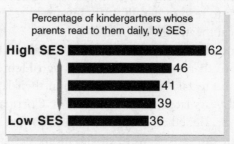

Percentage of kindergartners whose parents read to them daily, by SES

High SES ▮▮▮▮▮▮▮▮ 62
▮▮▮▮▮▮ 46
▮▮▮▮▮ 41
▮▮▮▮▮ 39
Low SES ▮▮▮▮▮ 36

Source: *An Uneven Start* by Richard J. Coley (Princeton, N.J.: Policy Information Center, ETS, 2002).

concept lived up to its claims. Looking at the impact of frequent household reading to preschoolers, the analysis showed clear, positive gains for phonemic awareness, language growth, and beginning reading skills. In addition, there was just as much of an impact for children of a lower socioeconomic status (SES) as there was for children with a higher SES, and the earlier or younger the reading began, the better the results.[21] Even when children reach primary grades, research has shown that repeated (at least three) picture book readings increases vocabulary acquisition by 15–40 percent, and the learning is relatively permanent.[22] The international assessment of

150,000 fourth-graders in 2001 showed an average thirty-five-point advantage for students who were read to more often by parents.[23]

As the child progresses through the grades, his or her reading can get bogged down in minutiae and fact-finding, and thus desire begins to flag. That's when an outside cheerleader helps with motivation. Hermitage, Missouri, recognized this in creating its Roving Reading Teacher position for Carolina George. Her job is to read aloud to students every day, from preschool through third grade. There are no tests or evaluations. Since the ultimate objective is to create lifetime readers, an immediate obstacle would occur if the child thought scorekeeping or testing was the purpose of reading. Ms. George is there to negate that impression.

Not everyone understands this. A few years after I'd lectured in a northern California community, one of its residents sent me a copy of a letter to the editor in the local paper. Prompting the letter was an article about a fifth-grade teacher who had been named teacher of the year, including a quote from another teacher who marveled at the honoree's ability with voices as he read to his students. That apparently outraged a father in the district, who wrote, "I also am disturbed by his apparent taking of class time to read aloud to his students, capturing 'the voices of the characters and the attention of the students.' When did our schools become baby-sitting centers with story time? By the time my daughter is in the fifth grade, I hope she is able to read to herself. If [he] wants to re-create characters, he should join a local theater group."

Far from being "babysitting," reading aloud has a rich intellectual history. More than two thousand years ago Hebrew fathers were urged by the Talmud to take their children upon their laps and read to them. One thousand years later, in that manual of Christian monastic life called the Rule of St. Benedict, chapter 38 specifies that meals be taken in silence, except for the spoken word of the monk designated to read aloud to the diners. Does anyone think this was "babysitting" the monks, the people who kept the lights on through the Dark Ages? I would also note that reading aloud "at table" is still practiced at least once a day among the Benedictines today—sometimes spiritual readings, other times secular—but they never read aloud textbooks. As of this writing, the monks at St. John's Abbey in Collegeville, Minnesota, are listening to Stephen Ambrose's *Custer and Crazy Horse: The Parallel Lives of Two American Warriors*.[24]

Then there is the history of the reader-aloud in the labor force. One could even argue that this foreshadowed audiobooks and subscription TV. I use the cigar industry as an example. When the cigar industry blossomed in the mid-1800s, the best tobacco came from Cuba (and the industry later moved to the Tampa area). These cigars were hand rolled by workers who became artisans in the delicate craft, producing hundreds of perfectly rolled specimens daily. Artistic as it might have been, it was still repetitious labor done in stifling factories. To break the monotony, workers hit upon the idea of having someone read aloud to them while they worked, known in the trade as *la lectura.*

From his elevated platform, the reader-aloud informed and entertained cigar makers in Cuba and the United States.

Source: Tampa-Hillsborough County Public Library System.

The reader (of which there were hundreds in the Tampa area alone) usually sat on an elevated platform or podium in the middle of the room and read aloud for four hours: hour 1—from local newspapers (often translating into Spanish); hour 2—from serialized novels (including classics by Cervantes, Hugo, and Dumas); hour 3—from political thinkers like Marx and Bakunin; and hour 4—Shakespeare or short stories. (Somehow none of this sounds like babysitting to me.)

As labor became more organized in the United States, the readings kept workers informed of progressive ideas throughout the world as well as entertained. (The Florida cigar makers were so taken with Alexandre Dumas' novel *The Count of Monte Cristo* that they named a premium cigar after it— the Montecristo.) When factory owners realized the enlightening impact of the readings, they tried to stop them but met stiff resistance from the workers, each of whom was paying the readers as much as twenty-five cents per week out of pocket.

The daily readings added to the workers' intellect and general awareness while civilizing the atmosphere of the workplace. By the 1930s, however, with cigar sales slumping due to the Great Depression and unions growing restive with mechanization on the horizon, the owners declared that the reader-aloud had to go.[25] Protest strikes followed but to no avail, and eventually readers were replaced by the radio, just as radio has been replaced by Walkmans and iPods in the listening population today.

Considering the stifling boredom in the American classroom and the fact that many high schools look like factories, schools seem to me to be the perfect setting for reading aloud. When you couple the history of reading aloud with the academic benefits noted in this chapter, how can the 2000 commission not have seen what the 1983 commission saw so clearly? As for babysitting, any babysitter who could accomplish all of that would be a bargain.

You Mentioned "Background Knowledge"—What Is It?

The easiest way to understand "background knowledge" is to read the following two paragraphs and see if there is a difference in your understanding of each. (I'm assuming you're a good enough reader to be able to "sound out" all the words.)

1. Mike Piazza and Robin Ventura singled to start the eighth inning. After a Braves pitching change to bring in Mike Remlinger, Melvin Mora—the first of a series of pinch-hitters—came to the plate for Benny Agbayani. Mora bunted, moving Piazza and Ventura over.
2. Kallis and Rhodes put on 84 but, with the ball turning, Mark Waugh could not hit with impunity and his eight overs cost only 37. The runs still had to be scored at more than seven an over, with McGrath still to return and Warne having two overs left, when Rhodes pulled Reiffel to Beven at deep square leg.

You probably had an easier time with the first paragraph, a newspaper account of a baseball game in 1999. The second paragraph came from a newspaper story on the World Cricket Championship in the same year. Any confusion was because the less you know about a subject or the vocabulary associated with that subject, the slower you must read, the more difficult comprehension becomes, and the less you understand.[26] Sounding out the cricket paragraph wouldn't have helped much, would it?

Background knowledge is one reason children who read the most bring the largest amount of information to the table and thus understand more of what the teacher or the textbook is teaching. Children whose families take them to museums and zoos, who visit historic sites, who travel abroad, or who camp in remote areas accumulate huge chunks of background knowledge without even studying. For the impoverished child lacking the travel portfolio of affluence, the best way to accumulate background knowledge is by either reading or being read to. (Yes, educational film and TV can help, but most such children are not exposed to it often enough.)

The lack of background knowledge surfaces very early in a child's school life. In the longitudinal kindergarten study, researchers found that more than

50 percent of children coming from the lowest education and income levels finished in the bottom quartile in background knowledge.[27]

What Are the Skills a Child Needs for Kindergarten?

Each time you read aloud to a child or class, you offer yourself as a role model. One of the early and primary abilities of children is imitation.[28] They imitate much of what they see and hear, and it is this ability that allows a fifteen-month-old child to say his first words. By age two, the average child expands his vocabulary to include nearly three hundred words, and it triples again in the next year. These aren't words the child is *saying* but the ones he or she *understands.* By age four, the child already understands two-thirds to three-quarters of the words he will use in future daily life.[29] Once he learns to talk, he'll average as many as ten new words a day, not one of which is on a flash card.[30] Much of that pace is determined by the amount and richness of the language he hears from you and others around him.

As you read to a child, you're pouring into the child's ears (and brain) all the sounds, syllables, endings, and blendings that will make up the words he or she will someday be asked to read and understand. And through stories you are filling in the background knowledge necessary to understand things that aren't in his neighborhood—like war or whales or locomotives.

There is one prekindergarten skill that matters above all others, because it is the prime predictor of school success or failure: the child's vocabulary upon entering school. Yes, the child goes to school to learn new words, but the words he or she already knows determine how much of what the teacher says will be understood. And since most instruction for the first four years of school is oral, the child who has the largest vocabulary will understand the most, while the child with the smallest vocabulary will grasp the least.

Once reading begins, personal vocabulary feeds (or frustrates) comprehension, since school grows increasingly complicated with each grade. That's why school-entry vocabulary tests predict so accurately.

How Is It That Some Kids Get a Head Start on Vocabulary?

Conversation is the prime garden in which vocabulary grows, but conversations vary greatly from home to home. The eye-opening findings of Drs. Betty Hart and Todd Risley at the University of Kansas, from their research on children's early lives, demonstrate the impact of this fact. But before I get into the details of their research, let me tell you how I share this information with parents, because I'm often asked by educators how I manage to convey it without insulting someone. Here's how I introduced it to 150 Title 1 (poverty level) parents in Tennessee one morning:

> I'm going to tell you a secret now—a *government* secret. It's the equivalent of all that smoking and cancer research—except this tells us why certain kids' brains live long and why other children's brains die young. The government has known this since 1996, yet no president has talked about it publicly; Democrat or Republican, no governor will talk about it. They're all afraid that if they shared this research, some of you might be insulted and then they'd lose votes. Instead, they told you a lie, that it was all the fault of schools and the awful *teachers.* That gets them some votes—but it's a lie. I'm not running for office, so I don't have to lie. I hope you're not insulted by what I'm going to tell you, but honestly, I'm more interested in helping your child than saving your feelings. So here's the secret. Here's what *helps* your children the most and here's what *hurts* them the most.

And then I told them about the research that follows. Afterward, they gave me a standing ovation, so I guess they felt more informed than insulted.

Published as *Meaningful Differences in the Everyday Experience of Young American Children,*[31] the research began in response to what Hart and Risley saw among the four-year-olds in the university lab school. With many children, the lines were already drawn: some were far advanced and some far behind. When these same children were tested at age three and then again at nine, the differences held. What caused the differences so early?

The researchers began by identifying forty-two normal families representing three socioeconomic groups: welfare, working class, and professional. Beginning when the children were seven months old, researchers visited the homes for one hour a month and continued their visits for two and a half years. During each visit, the researcher tape-recorded and transcribed by hand any conversations and actions taking place in front of the child.

Through 1,300 hours of visits, they accumulated 23 million bytes of information for the project database, categorizing every word (noun, verb, adjective, etc.) said in front of the child. They also defined the kinds of sentences used with the child, breaking them down into three distinct types:

♦ Question ("Can you find the ball?")
♦ Affirmation ("You're so smart!")
♦ Prohibition ("Stop that! Bad boy!")

The project held some surprises: Regardless of socioeconomic level, all forty-two families said and did the same things with their children. In other words, the basic instincts of good parenting are there for most people, rich or poor.

Then the researchers received the data printout and saw the "meaning-ful differences" among the forty-two families. When the daily number of words for each group of children is projected across four years, the four-year-old child from the professional family will have heard 45 million words, the working-class child 26 million, and the welfare child only 13 million. All three children will show up for kindergarten on the same day, but one will have heard 32 million fewer words. If No Child Left Behind expects the teacher to get this child caught up, she'll have to speak 10 words *a second* for nine hundred hours to reach the 32-million mark by year's end. I hope they have life support ready for her.

Total words (in millions) heard by child by age 4

45
26
13

■ professional
▨ working class
☐ poverty

The word gap among those children has nothing to do with how much their parents love them. They all love their children and want the best for them, but some parents have a better idea of what needs to be said and done to reach that "best." They know the child needs to hear words repeatedly in meaningful sentences and questions, and they know that plunking a two-year-old down in front of a television set for three hours at a time is more harmful than meaningful. Soci-ologists George Farkas and Kurt Beron stud-ied the research on 6,800 children from ages three to twelve, and found that children from the lower SES were far more likely to arrive at school with smaller vocab-ularies (twelve to fourteen months behind) and they seldom made up the loss as they grew older.[32] (See the summer-loss chart on page 88.)

The message in this kind of research is unambiguous: It's not the toys in the house that make the difference in children's lives; it's the words in their heads. The least expensive thing we can give a child outside of a hug turns out to be the most valuable: words. You don't need a job, a checking ac-count, or even a high school diploma to talk with a child. If I could select any piece of research that all parents would be exposed to, *Meaningful Dif-ferences* would be the one. And that's feasible. The authors took their 268-page book and condensed it into a six-page article for *American Educator,* the journal of the American Federation of Teachers, which may be freely reproduced by schools.[33]

If schools are to enlist the help of the 7,800-hour curriculum, then we must stop telling parents lies about schools, and tell them the truth about what helps and hurts children the most.

Where Is the Better Vocabulary: Conversation or Reading?

Most conversation is plain and simple, whether it's between two adults or with children. It consists of the five thousand words we use all the time, called the Basic Lexicon. (Indeed, 83 percent of the words in normal conversation with a child come from the most commonly used thousand words, and it doesn't change much as the child ages.)[34] Then there are another five thousand words we use in conversation less often. Together, these ten thousand words are called the Common Lexicon. Beyond that ten thousand mark are the "rare words," and these play a critical role in reading. The eventual strength of our vocabulary is determined not by the ten thousand common words but by how many "rare words" we understand.

If we don't use these rare words very often in conversation, where do we find them? The chart below shows that printed text contains the most rare words. Whereas an adult uses only nine rare words (per thousand) when talking with a three-year-old, there are three times as many in a children's book and more than seven times as many in a newspaper. As you can see from the chart, oral communication (including a TV script) is decidedly inferior to print when building vocabulary. As shown by the data for printed material (children's book), the number of rare words increases sig-

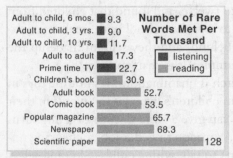

	Number of Rare Words Met Per Thousand
Adult to child, 6 mos.	9.3
Adult to child, 3 yrs.	9.0
Adult to child, 10 yrs.	11.7
Adult to adult	17.3
Prime time TV	22.7
Children's book	30.9
Adult book	52.7
Comic book	53.5
Popular magazine	65.7
Newspaper	68.3
Scientific paper	128

■ listening   ■ reading

Regular family conversations will take care of the basic vocabulary, but when you read to the child, you leap into the rare words that help most when it's time for school and formal learning. Simultaneously, you're familiarizing the child with books and print in a manner that brings him or her pleasure.

Source: Hayes and Ahrens, *Journal of Child Language.*[35]

nificantly. This poses serious problems for at-risk children who watch large amounts of TV, hear fewer words, and encounter print less often at home. Such children face a gigantic word gap that impedes reading progress throughout school. And that gap can't possibly be breached in 120 hours of summer school[36] or through more phonics instruction.

How Can I Give My Kid Words If I Don't Have Them?

This is a question I've heard from parents who have learning disabilities or for whom English is a second language. While there are few easy answers in parenting, this one is easier than most. There is a public agency that comes to the rescue in such instances; in fact, it's been doing this job for more than a century. What the agency does is take all the nouns, verbs, and adjectives a person would ever need, and bundles them into little packages for anyone to borrow—free. It asks only that you bring the "packages" back in a few weeks. I'm referring to the American free public library—the "people's university." And for those who can't read the words, they are now available on audiocassette or CD. Forty years ago you had to be blind to get a recorded book in America; now anyone can. More on this subject in chapter 9.

How Important Is It That the Parent Be a Reader?

My wife, Susan, is a great pie maker. Do you think it's coincidental that her mother was too? The apple (pie maker) doesn't fall far from the tree. My favorite example in research is the study of thirty men who were identified as growing up in working-class, blue-collar families.[37] Fifteen of the thirty men eventually became college professors and fifteen remained in blue-collar careers. In handpicking the thirty, the researchers made sure all came from similar socioeconomic backgrounds with similar family traumas (family alcoholism, parent death, divorce, etc.).

If the thirty men began life in similar circumstances, how can we explain the fifteen who rose so far above their beginning stations? In extensive interviews with the thirty, significant differences appeared regarding books and reading as children.

- Twelve of the fifteen professors were read to or told stories by their parents, compared to only four of the blue-collar workers.
- Fourteen out of fifteen professors came from homes where books and print were plentiful; among blue-collar workers, only four had books.
- Thirteen of the professors' mothers and twelve of the fathers were

identified as frequent readers of newspapers, magazines, or books; blue-collar workers identified six mothers and four fathers.
* All of the fifteen professors were encouraged to read as children, compared with only three of the blue-collar workers.

A significant part of the study was what the fifteen professors found motivating or interesting in their childhood reading. They identified reading that provided answers or information relating to problems in their lives. The book, in a manner of speaking, became food for the starving child. Typical in this respect was Professor Respondent No. 2, "a sociologist whose mother died when he was seven years old, with the result that the respondent was put into an orphanage, where he stayed until he was 'on my own' at about age seventeen. This respondent experienced great anxiety at being put into an orphanage and he identified the chief problem as being the 'uncertainty of what happens to orphans.'"

He explained: "'All of a sudden my mother was dead and I was in this place. I felt I didn't know what would happen to me. I was scared and had continually in my mind the question of what would happen to me and to others in that place. What happened to kids in orphanages?'"

The report continues: "In the orphanage library, at about age eight, this respondent discovered the Horatio Alger books. The discovery had a profound impact on him because all of a sudden he 'realized that I could create my own life' even if he was in an orphanage. He had been looking for an answer to the question of what would become of him and now he realized that what would become of him was up to him. Horatio Alger books provided him with the model of a boy whose life was his own and who could create it as he chose."

Ultimately, the purpose of literature, especially fiction, is to provide meaning in our lives—which is really the purpose of all education. Child psychologist Bruno Bettelheim wrote that finding this meaning is the greatest need and most difficult achievement for any human being at any age. Who am I? Why am I here? What can I be?[38] In *The Uses of Enchantment*, Bettelheim writes that the two factors most responsible for giving the child this belief that he can make a significant contribution to life are parents or teachers and literature—that is, life experience and stories about life experience.

Literature is considered such an important medium—more than television, more than films, more than art or overhead projectors—because literature brings us closest to the human heart. And of the two forms of literature (fiction and nonfiction), the one that brings us closest and presents the meaning of life most clearly to the child is fiction. That is one reason most of the recommendations for read-alouds at the back of this book are fiction. It's also worth noting that in the OECD study of 250,000 teens in thirty-two nations, those who read the widest variety of material, but the most fiction, had the highest literacy scores.[39] The suggestion here is that all reading helps us get better at reading, but fiction forces us to concentrate the most in order to find meaning, and therefore deepens our "engagement" and helps comprehension. One other finding in that study is worth noting: in all thirty-two nations, the male fifteen-year-olds scored lower than females. They also read less fiction. Perhaps it's a coincidence, but if you walk into one of those mega-bookstores, where do you find the fewest males? The fiction section.

Has Anyone Ever Applied Reading Aloud and SSR to an At-Risk School?

Just as parents in low-income situations need to be reminded that their task is not insurmountable, so too do educators who work with children coming from those homes. Reading achievement and "pleasure" do not have to be mutually exclusive. During his ten years as principal of Boston's Solomon Lewenberg Middle School, Thomas P. O'Neill Jr. and his faculty proved it. The pride of Boston's junior high schools during the 1950s and early 1960s, Lewenberg subsequently suffered the ravages of urban decay, and, by 1984, with the lowest academic record and Boston teachers calling it the "loony bin" instead of Lewenberg, the school was earmarked for closing. But first, Boston officials would give it one last chance.

The reins were handed to O'Neill (no relation to the former Speaker of the House), an upbeat, first-year principal and former high school English teacher whose experience there had taught him to "sell" the pleasures and importance of reading.

The first thing he did was abolish the school's intercom system. ("As a teacher I'd always sworn someday I'd rip the thing off the wall. Now I could do it legally.") He then set about establishing structure, routine, and discipline. "That's the easy part. What happens after is the important part—reading. It's the key element in the curriculum. IBM can teach our graduates to work the machine, but we have to teach them to read the manual." In O'Neill's first year, sustained silent reading (see chapter 5) was instituted for the nearly four hundred pupils and faculty for the last ten minutes of the day—during which everyone in the school read for pleasure. Each teacher was assigned a room—much to the consternation of some who felt those last ten minutes could be better used to clean up the shop or gym.

"Prove to me on paper," O'Neill challenged them, "that you are busier than I am, and I'll give you the ten minutes to clean." He had no takers.

Within a year, critics became supporters and the school was relishing the quiet time that ended the day. The books that had been started during SSR were often still being read by students filing out to buses—in stark contrast to former dismissal scenes that bordered on chaos.

The next challenge was to insure that each sixth-, seventh-, and eighth-grade student not only saw an adult reading each day, but also heard one. Faculty members were assigned a classroom and the school day began with ten minutes of reading aloud—to complement the silent ending. Soon reading aloud began to inspire awareness, and new titles sprouted during SSR. In effect, the faculty was doing what the great art schools have always done: providing "life" models from which to draw.

In the first year, Lewenberg's scores were up; in the second year, not only did the scores climb but so too did student enrollment in response to the school's new reputation.

Three years later, in 1988, Lewenberg's 570 students had the highest reading scores in the city of Boston; there was a fifteen-page waiting list of children who wanted to attend, and O'Neill was portrayed by *Time* as a viable alternative to physical force in its cover story on Joe Clark, the bullhorn- and bat-toting principal from Paterson, New Jersey.[40]

Today, Tom O'Neill is retired, but the ripple effect of his work has reached shores that not even his great optimism would have anticipated. In the early 1990s, a junior high school civics teacher in Japan, Hiroshi Hayashi, read the Japanese edition of *The Read-Aloud Handbook*. Intrigued by the concept of SSR and Tom O'Neill's example, he immediately decided to apply it in his own school. (Contrary to what most Americans believe, not all Japanese public school students are single-minded overachievers, and many are rebellious or reluctant readers—if they are readers at all.)[41]

Although SSR was a foreign concept to Japanese secondary education, Hayashi saw quick results in his junior high school with just ten minutes at the start of the morning. Unwilling to keep his enthusiasm to himself, he spent the next two years sending forty thousand handwritten postcards to administrators in Japanese public schools, urging them to visit his school and adopt the concept. His personal crusade has won accolades from even the faculty skeptics: to date, more than 3,500 Japanese schools use SSR to begin their school day, and their ranks are increasing each year.

Of all the endorsements for reading aloud, the following is the most unusual. Back in the mid-1990s, two men and a woman sat talking in an office of the University of Kentucky Medical Center. One man was an epidemiologist, the other man was a neurologist, and the woman was a psycholinguist. All were involved in what would become one of the most celebrated Alzheimer's studies to date. Two of them had been researching an order of nuns who had consented to regular mental examinations and brain autopsies upon death, and had turned all their personal records over to the researchers. The brain autopsies, when coupled with autobiographical essays written by the nuns when they were about twenty-two years old, showed a clear connection: those with the densest sentences (the most ideas jam-packed into a sentence without breaking them into separate clauses) were far less likely either to develop the disease or to show its ravages. Simply put, the larger the vocabularies and the more complex the thinking processes in youth, the less chance of Alzheimer's damage. Sample sentences from two nuns' essays:

> I was born in Eau Claire, Wis., on May 24, 1913, and was baptized in St. James Church. —Sister Helen

> It was about a half-hour before midnight between February twenty-eighth and twenty-ninth of the leap year nineteen-hundred-twelve when I began to live and die as the third child of a mother, whose maiden name was Hilda Hoffman, and my father, Otto Schmitt." —Sister Emma

Could the rich vocabulary and crammed thinking process in one's youth be an early insurance policy against Alzheimer's? As the three discussed these issues, the neurologist, Bill Markesbery, father of two, asked Susan Kemper, the psycholinguist, "What does this mean for our children?"

In his absorbing book about the study, *Aging with Grace,* David Snowden, the epidemiologist, describes what followed:[42]

> The question caught me off guard. But when I saw the look on his face, I realized that he was speaking as a father, not as a scientist. Bill has three grown daughters, and it was clear he wanted to know whether he and his wife, Barbara, had done the right things as parents.
>
> "Read to them," Susan answered. "It's that simple. It's the most important thing a parent can do with their children."
>
> Susan explained that idea density depends on at least two important learned skills: vocabulary and reading comprehension. "And the best way to increase vocabulary and reading comprehension is by starting early in life, by reading to your children," Susan declared.
>
> I could see the relief spread over Bill's face. "Barbara and I read to our kids every night," he said proudly.

. . . In the years since our study came out, I have been asked Markesbery's question many times. Parents ask me if they should play Mozart to their babies, or buy them expensive teaching toys, or prohibit television, or get them started early on the computer. I give them the same simple answer Susan Kemper gave to Markesbery: "Read to your children."

Chapter 2

When to Begin (and End)
Read-Aloud

What we learn in childhood is carved in stone.
What we learn as adults is carved in ice.
—David Kherdian, poet

How old must a child be before you start reading to him?" That is the question I am most often asked by parents. The next is: "When is the child *too* old to be read to?"

In answer to the first question, I ask one of my own: "When did you start *talking* to the child? Did you wait until he was six months old?"

"We started talking to him the day he was born," parents respond.

"And what language did your child speak the day he was born? English? Japanese? Italian?" They're about to say English when it dawns on them the child didn't speak *any* language yet.

"Wonderful!" I say. "There you were, holding that newborn infant in your arms, whispering, 'We love you, Tess. Daddy and I think you are the most beautiful baby in the world.' You were speaking multisyllable words and complex sentences in a foreign language to a child who didn't understand one word you were saying! And you never thought twice about doing it. But most people can't imagine *reading* to that same child. And that's sad. If a child is old enough to talk to, she's old enough to read to. It's the same language."

Obviously, from birth to six months of age we are concerned less with "understanding" than with "conditioning" the child to your voice and the sight of books. Dr. T. Berry Brazelton, when he was chief of the child development unit of Boston Children's Hospital Medical Center, observed that new parents' most critical task during these early stages is learning how to calm the child, how to bring it under control, so he or she can begin to look around and listen when you pass on information.[1] Much the same task confronts the classroom teacher facing a new class each September.

Is "In Utero Learning" a Myth?

We've long known the human voice is one of the most powerful tools a parent has for calming a child. And what many previously suspected is now firmly established in research indicating that the voice's influence starts *even earlier than birth*. University of North Carolina psychologist Anthony De-Casper and colleagues explored the effects of reading to children in utero, thinking that infants might be able to recognize something they had heard prenatally.

DeCasper asked thirty-three pregnant women to recite a specific paragraph of a children's story three times a day for the last six weeks of pregnancy. Three different paragraphs were used among the thirty-three women, but each woman used just one passage for the entire recitation period. Fifty-two hours after birth, the newborns were given a special nipple and earphones through which they could hear a woman (not the mother) reciting all three paragraphs. By measuring each child's sucking rate, researchers concluded the infants preferred the passages their mothers had recited during the third trimester.[2]

"The babies' reactions to the stories had been influenced by earlier exposure," DeCasper concluded. "That constitutes learning in a very general way." In a similar experiment involving reading to fetuses during the two and one-half months before birth, DeCasper found the child's heartbeat increased with the new story and decreased with the familiar one.[3] Both of these experiments clearly establish that a child becomes familiar with certain sounds while in utero and begins associating those tones with comfort and security. The baby is being conditioned—his first class in learning. Imagine how much can be accomplished when a child can see and touch the book, understand the words, and feel the reader.

What About Reading Aloud to Children with "Special Needs"?

In *Cushla and Her Books,* author Dorothy Butler described how Cushla Yeoman's parents began reading aloud to her when she was four months of age.[4] By nine months the child was able to respond to the sight of certain books and convey to her parents that these were her favorites. By age five she had taught herself to read.[4]

What makes Cushla's story so dramatic is that she was born with chromosome damage that caused deformities of the spleen, kidney, and mouth cavity. It also produced muscle spasms—which prevented her from sleeping for more than two hours a night or holding anything in her hand until she was three years old—and hazy vision beyond her fingertips.

Until she was three, the doctors diagnosed Cushla as "mentally and physically retarded" and recommended that she be institutionalized. Her parents, after seeing her early responses to books, refused; instead, they put her on a dose of fourteen read-aloud books a day. By age five, Cushla was found by psychologists to be well above average in intelligence and a socially well-adjusted child.

The story of Cushla and her family has appeared in each edition of *The Read-Aloud Handbook,* and each time it has been my hope that it would inspire an unknown reader someplace. One day I received a letter from Marcia Thomas, then of Memphis, Tennessee:

> Our daughter Jennifer was born in September 1984. One of the first gifts we received was a copy of *The Read-Aloud Handbook.* We read the introductory chapters and were very impressed by the story of Cushla and her family. We decided to put our daughter on a "diet" of at least ten books a day. She had to stay in the hospital for seven weeks as a result of a heart defect and corrective surgery. However, we began reading to her while she was still in intensive care; and when we couldn't be there, we left story tapes and asked the nurses to play them for her.
>
> For the past seven years we have read to Jennifer at every opportunity. She is now in the first grade and is one of the best readers in her class. She consistently makes 100 on reading tests and has a very impressive vocabulary. She can usually be found in the reading loft at school during free time, and at home she loves to sit with my husband or me and read a book.
>
> What makes our story so remarkable is that Jennifer was born with Down syndrome. At two months of age, we were told Jennifer most likely was blind, deaf, and severely retarded. When she was tested at age four, her IQ was 111.

Jennifer Thomas graduated from her Concord, Massachusetts, high school, passing her MCAS test, and was a member of the National Honor Society. I was honored to have been an invited guest at her graduation party. A talented artist, Jennifer competed in the juried VSA competition in 2003 for artists between the ages of sixteen and twenty-five who live in the United States and have a disability. Her piece was one of the fifteen chosen to tour the United States. In September 2005, Jennifer began undergraduate classes at Lesley University in Cambridge, Massachusetts.

If the Yeomans and the Thomases can accomplish all they did with their children, imagine how much can be realized by average families if they begin reading to their children early and in earnest.

What Could You Expect If You Started Reading to a Child on Day One?

Erin had no idea what a lucky girl she was when Linda Kelly-Hassett and her husband, Jim, brought her home from the hospital that Thanksgiving Day in 1988—but she soon found out. A few years later, I found out, too, when Erin's mom shared with me her journal of reading experiences. Since I didn't keep such a document with my own children, and since Linda began even earlier than I did (ignorant parent that I was back in those days), I think her words speak louder than anything I might write in this space.

Linda had been an elementary-grade teacher for twenty-two years when Erin was born and a devoted reader-aloud to her students. Everything she did in class, and recommended to the parents of her students, she applied to Erin. Not every parent has the time to do all that Linda did, but if they did even half as much, all children's futures would be brighter. In the following essay by Linda, note the unforced and gradual manner in which books were introduced to Erin and the way in which they were tied to everyday events.

> Erin's first book, on her first day of life, was *Love You Forever* by Robert Munsch. My husband videotaped me reading it. He was unfamiliar with the story and was moved to tears as we rocked "back and forth, back and forth." That video went to relatives and friends, helping to bring Erin into their lives in a special way, and it also went to my former class of third-graders—planting a seed for the next generation.
>
> Erin's first four months saw mostly soft chunky books, board books, and firmer-paged, lift-the-flap books. These were not only read but tasted and enjoyed. When she was four months old she began to enjoy time in her Johnny Jump Up, often spending forty-five minutes at a time, two or three times a day, jumping happily to

poems, songs, and pop-up books. Over and over we read poems from *Read-Aloud Rhymes for the Very Young* by Jack Prelutsky and sang along with the *Wee Sing* tapes.

The enjoyment of Johnny Jump Up diminished around eight months when crawling and seeking her own entertainment took over. She loved tearing paper at this time, so we put out lots of magazines, but only very durable books. At reading time we stayed with the same kind of book until she was around ten months. At this stage, I became so eager to read storybooks to her that I decided to read these to her while she was in her highchair (so she couldn't tear the pages). It worked beautifully and provided some surprises.

For starters, we never had any food battles because I was too busy reading to let myself become overly concerned with her food intake. As I read, she ate her finger foods while I spooned in some baby fruit and veggies. Mealtime was fun, positive, and usually ended with her pointing to the bookshelf and requesting another "Boo(k)." This practice set a precedent that followed through the years. I continued to read to her at breakfast and lunchtime. When she had friends over, we always had a story or two at snack time. Using big books from my teaching days was a special treat.

Several memorable events happened during this period of early reading. My husband was transferred to the East Coast and got home every other weekend. Between Erin's tenth and fifteenth months, we were pretty much by ourselves when eating, so mealtime reading grew in length. It was nothing for her to actively listen to stories from twenty to forty minutes after a meal. A note in my journal for February 4, 1990, reads: "9 books after breakfast; 10 books and 4 poems after lunch; 7 books after dinner." This was not an unusual day's reading.

Ten days later, February 14, 1990, I wrote this entry: "After breakfast, Erin asked for a book. Since we were moving at the end of the month, I read her *Good-Bye House* by Frank Asch. She kept asking for another book as soon as I finished one. I ended up reading seventy-five minutes, covering twenty-five books. At fourteen months of age, she had sustained interest in the stories—actively listening, pointing, saying words, and making sounds."

I want to note that all these books were familiar to Erin. She did not immediately take to a new book. I would introduce it to her over a period of days. The first day we would look at the cover and "talk" about it. On the second day, I would then proceed to read the first page or so. I would read a few more pages each additional day until about the fifth or sixth day, when the book would be familiar enough for me to read it in its entirety.

Shortly after our move to Pennsylvania, I was reading her *The Very Hungry Caterpillar* by Eric Carle—as I had been doing for the last six months. This time, during the reading of the second sentence ("One Sunday morning the warm sun came up and—pop!—out of the egg came a tiny and very hungry caterpillar"), while I was still forming my mouth to say "pop," Erin said the word "pop!" and with perfect inflection. She was seventeen months that day and it was the start of her inserting words into familiar stories. What an addition to an already pleasant experience.

Beyond the love of reading nurtured by these parent-child experiences, Erin's verbal skills were growing. She spoke in complete sentences at twenty-one months and had a vocabulary of a thousand words by twenty-four months—all achieved without flash cards or "drill and skill." Erin's father wasn't excluded from the readings, and the two had a collection of books she labeled "Daddy Books" that became a personal cache.

With all of this reading, Erin's attention span and interests grew by leaps and bounds. By four years of age, she was listening to hundred-page novels along with her picture books. When it came time to attend school, Erin's mom decided to use her own years of professional teaching experience and homeschool Erin. Homeschooling wasn't a political or religious issue with the Hassetts; they felt that their only child should receive the best they could possibly give her—a veteran twenty-two-year teacher called Mom. Furthermore, with the head start she received at home, much of her first years in formal school would have been redundant and probably would have bored her to tears. In the ensuing years, Linda and Erin would be involved in weekly cooperative ventures with other community homeschoolers, and by age twelve, Erin began taking band and physical education at the local middle school for five hours a week.

Aware of the bonding that occurs during read-aloud as well as the difference between a child's listening level and reading level (more on that later), the Hassetts continued to read to Erin. For a list of all the novels heard by Erin from ages four to twelve, see my Web site (www.trelease-on-reading.com/erinlist.html).

Erin's progress in learning to read is a story in itself. After expressing a desire at age five to know her letters and sounds, she quickly mastered them but balked at formal reading. Listening to Mom and Dad reading novels was still a daily experience, but when her mother began to press her about reading herself in first grade, Erin declared, "I don't want to read those dumb books, those baby books (primers and easy-readers). I'm not going to read until I can do chapter books."

Her mother backed off—to a degree. There was a local Head Start program of four- and five-year-olds that Linda and Erin had begun visiting as volunteers once a week, and one of the activities was reading to the children. Since the children quickly began to look up to Erin, she hedged on her determination and agreed to read some "big books" like Eric Carle's *The Very Hungry Caterpillar* to these classes. Obviously, Erin had learned *how* to read.

Erin Hassett today.

In the summer between first and second grade, the Hassetts were visiting friends who had a daughter three years older than Erin. Though the two girls went to bed at the same time, Erin was a night owl and not at all tired. When she was told she could read in bed, the older girl gave her some chapter books she had outgrown. The next morning, Erin came down to breakfast, handed her mother a novel, and said, "I read that last night." Thinking she meant she had glanced through it, Linda said that was nice and didn't think more about it. When it happened with a second novel the following morning, Linda asked her to read aloud a chapter. Erin did, with perfect inflection, and didn't miss a word.

By the end of third grade, Erin was scoring in the ninety-ninth percentile in reading and listening comprehension as well as vocabulary—and she had never done a workbook page in her life. Nearing age twelve, she read the 732-page *Harry Potter and the Goblet of Fire* in a weekend.

Through the years, thanks to that initial letter from her mom, I've lunched and dined with Erin, even interviewed her in front of seminar audiences in Pennsylvania and Colorado. She is poised, enthusiastic, articulate, talented, and one of the most extraordinary young ladies I've ever known. Despite her abilities and accomplishments, Jim and Linda continue to read to her. By age sixteen they'd done 652 novels together. And far from being a bookworm, she loves swimming, softball, and singing. In fact, in 2005 she was accepted to Michigan's Interlochen Arts Camp vocal program, and was grand prize winner of the Rocky Mountain District "Stars of Tomorrow" competition (won by Judy Collins back in 1958). Add to that several years competing in "Odyssey of the Mind" competitions and you've got an all-American kid.

Can You Recommend Something That Will Teach My Child to Read Before Kindergarten?

We can have instant pudding, instant photos, instant coffee—but there are no instant adults. Yet some parents are in a hurry to make their children old before their time. However, Finland has higher reading scores than the United States and everyone else despite the fact that its laws forbid the formal teaching of reading until the child is seven years of age.[5] In fact, in Warwick Elley's thirty-two-country study of more than two hundred thousand readers, four of the top ten countries don't begin formal reading instruction until age seven.[6]

Dr. T. Berry Brazelton is on record as noting that an interest in your child's intellectual growth is important, but you can expect negative consequences if this interest takes the form of an obsession with teaching your child to read.

"I've had children in my practice," Brazelton explained to National Public Radio's John Merrow (*Options in Education,* September 3, 1979), "who were reading from a dictionary at the age of three and one-half or four, and had learned to read and type successfully by age four. But those kids went through a very tough time later on. They went through first grade successfully, but second grade they really bombed out on. And I have a feeling that they've been pushed so hard from outside to learn to read early, that the cost of it didn't show up until later."

Experts like Brazelton and David Elkind[7] aren't saying that "early reading" is intrinsically bad; rather, they feel the early reader should arrive at the skill naturally, on his own, without a structured time each day when the mother or father sits down with him and teaches him letters, sounds, and syllables. The "natural way" is the way Scout learned in Harper Lee's *To Kill a Mockingbird*—by sitting on the lap of a parent and listening, listening as the parent's finger moves over the pages, until gradually, in the child's own good time, a connection is made between the sound of a certain word and the appearance of certain letters on the page.

There are, however, children who come to reading prematurely, who arrive at the kindergarten door already knowing how to read without having been formally taught. These children are called *early fluent readers* and they're more than worth our attention. During the last forty years, intensive studies have been done of such children.[8] The majority of them were never formally taught to read at home, nor did they use any commercial reading programs.

The research, as well as studies done of pupils who respond to initial classroom instruction without difficulty, indicates four factors are present in the home environment of nearly every early reader:

1. The child is read to on a regular basis. This is the factor most often cited among early readers. In Dolores Durkin's 1966 study, *all* of the early readers had been read to regularly. In addition, the parents were avid readers and led by example. The reading included not only books but package labels, street and truck signs, billboards, and so on. International research forty years later with fourth-graders and their families in thirty-five countries mirrored this with the highest scoring students.[9]

2. A wide variety of printed material—books, magazines, newspapers, comics—is available in the home. Nearly thirty years after Durkin's study, NAEP studies reported that the more printed materials found in a child's home, the higher the student's writing, reading, and math skills,[10] and chapter 7 here is devoted largely to the influence of the print climate, both at home and in school.

3. Paper and pencil are readily available for the child. Durkin explained: "Almost without exception, the starting point of curiosity about written language was an interest in scribbling and drawing. From this developed an interest in copying objects and letters of the alphabet."

4. The people in the child's home stimulate the child's interest in reading and writing by answering endless questions, praising the child's efforts at reading and writing, taking the child to the library frequently, buying books, writing stories that the child dictates, and displaying his paperwork in a prominent place in the home. This also is supported by the aforementioned study of 150,000 fourth-graders and their families in thirty-five countries,[11] as well as by the anecdote about the role of Leonard Pitts's mother in his winning a Pulitzer Prize (introduction, page xvi).

I want to emphasize that these four factors were present in the home of nearly every child who was an early reader. None of these factors involved much more than interest on the part of the parent.

How Is My Child's Reading Going to Get Better If *I'm* Doing the Reading?

Listening comprehension feeds reading comprehension. Sounds complicated, right? So let's make it simple. We'll use the most frequently used word in the English language: *the.* I always ask my lecture audiences if there is anyone present who thinks this little three-letter word is a difficult word to understand, and out of three hundred people I'll get about five who raise their hands—amid snickers from the rest.

I then ask those who *didn't* raise their hands "to pretend I am a Russian exchange student living in your home. It's also important to know there is no equivalent word in Russian for 'the,' as we use it." Indeed, many languages don't have such articles—Chinese, Japanese, Korean, Persian, Polish, Punjabi, Croatian, and Vietnamese.

"Now, as the Russian exchange student, I've been living in your home and listening to you and your family for three weeks when one day I come to you and say, 'Don't understand word you use over and over. What means word "the"?'"

How would you begin to explain the meaning of the word to this person? No one ever volunteers to explain it, and everyone laughs in embarrassment. Explaining this simple word turns out to be pretty difficult. Nevertheless, we do know how to *use* it. And you knew it when you showed up for kindergarten.

How did you learn it? One morning when you were three years old, did your mother take you into the kitchen, sit you down at the table with a little workbook, and say, "'The' is a definite article. It comes before nouns. Now take your green crayon and underline all the definite articles on the page"? Of course not.

We learned the meaning of this tiny but complex word by *hearing* it. In fact, we heard it three ways:

1. Over and over and over (immersion);
2. From superheroes—Mom, Dad, brother, and sister (role models);
3. In a meaningful context—the cookie, the nap, the crayons, and the potty.

Whenever an adult reads to a child, three important things are happening simultaneously and painlessly: (1) a pleasure connection is being made between child and book, (2) both parent and child are learning something from the book they're sharing (double learning), and (3) the adult is pouring sounds and syllables called words into the child's ear.

Inside the ear these words collect in a reservoir called the listening vocabulary. Eventually, if you pour enough words into it, the reservoir starts to overflow—pouring words into the speaking vocabulary, reading vocabulary, and writing vocabulary. All have their origin in the listening vocabulary.

One-on-one time is a key factor in how soon a child learns the purpose of books.

The research on oral versus reading comprehension certifies this concept and offers a sobering note about those children who enter school with small vocabularies. Where you might expect school to narrow the gap between children with small oral vocabularies and those with larger ones, the reverse is true: the gap widens instead of narrows.[12]

The reason for this is twofold: (1) Since children in the early grades are reading only words most of them already know (the "decodable text" decreed by Reading First), neither the slow nor the advanced child is meeting many new words in class; and (2) The students' only exposure to new or advanced language, therefore, would have to be via parents, peers, teachers, and television. While there's a shortage of new words in school, at home the advantaged child is more likely to be read to from advanced books, to be exposed to educational television, and to be engaged in meaningful conversation for longer periods of time. The child with the smaller vocabulary ends up hearing the same routine words at home.

To make matters worse, the advantaged child is more apt to be in a school that recognizes the advantages of reading aloud and will hear even more new words. In Nell Duke's study of twenty first-grade classes (ten urban, ten suburban), seven out of the ten suburban classes were read chapter books while only two of the ten urban classes experienced chapter books.[13] The children with the smallest vocabularies were exposed to the fewest words and the least complex sentences; thus the gap widens. Another factor is "summer slump," explained on page 87.

Narrowing the *achievement* gap, a noble objective in No Child Left Behind and Reading First, depends entirely on bridging the *vocabulary* gap. The most efficient way to do that is to tap into the 7,800 hours the child spends at home. Imagine the impact if even half the parents of at-risk children were reading to them from library books beginning at infancy (or listening to books on tape if family literacy is a problem). A second way, though not as efficient, would be for the classroom teacher to read aloud from richer literature—at least richer than the "decodable text"—in class. Children's books, even good picture books, are much richer than ordinary home or classroom conversation, as the chart indicates on page 16.

How Can I Expand My Child's Attention Span?

The best tool for expanding attention span is one-on-one time with the child; it is by far the most effective teaching/bonding arrangement ever invented. In studying methods to reverse language problems among disadvantaged children, Harvard psychologist Jerome Kagan found intensified one-on-one attention to be especially effective.[14] His studies indicate the advantages of reading to children and of listening attentively to their responses to the reading, but they also point to the desirability of reading to your children separately, if possible.

I recognize this approach poses an extra problem for working mothers and fathers with more than one child. But somewhere in that seven-day week there must be time for your child to discover the specialness of you, one-on-one, even if it's only once or twice a week.

One-on-one time between adult and child—be it reading or talking or playing—is essential to teaching the *concept* of books or puppies or flowers or water. Once the concept of something has been learned, the foundation has been laid for the next accomplishment: attention span. Without a concept of what is happening and why, a child cannot pay attention to it for any appreciable amount of time.

Here, for example, are two concepts entirely within the grasp of a three-year-old:

♦ The telephone can be used to make and receive calls.
♦ Books contain stories that give me pleasure if I listen and watch.

Nearly twenty-five years ago, my friend and neighbor Ellie Fernands, now a retired elementary school principal, returned to teaching after a ten-year hiatus. Since her former experience was in junior high, this new job—preschool—was almost extraterrestrial. I vividly recall Ellie telling me of her experiences on the first day of school with those two concepts: telephone and books. She said, "All morning the three-year-olds used the toy telephone in class to make pretend calls to their mothers for reassurances that they'd be picked up and brought home. They dialed make-believe numbers, talked for long periods of time, and even used telephone etiquette." Understanding the concept of the telephone, these children were able to use and enjoy it for a considerable length of time. Their telephone attention span was excellent.

Let's compare that with story time in the same class. "Thirty seconds after the story began, two of the children stood up and moved away from the circle, obviously bored. More children quickly joined them. Within two minutes, half the children had abandoned the story." (Ellie later learned that one of the two children who listened through the entire story was a child who had been read to from day one.)

The difference between the attention spans for each of these two activities is based on the concept that each child brought to the activity. When a child has little or no experience with books, it is impossible for him to have a concept of them and the pleasure they afford. No experience means no attention span.[15]

Is There Something I Could Buy That Would Help My Child Read Better?

Since parents often think there are quick fixes they can buy, some kind of kit or phonics game to help a child do better at school, I began asking my associates years ago, "What did you have in your home as a child that helped you become a reader? Things your folks had to buy." Besides the library card they all named, which is free, their responses form what I call the Three Bs, an inexpensive "reading kit" that nearly all parents can afford:

The first B is books: Ownership of a book is important, with the child's name inscribed inside, a book that doesn't have to be returned to the library or even shared with siblings. Chapter 7 here shows the clear connection between book ownership or access and reading achievement.

The second B is book basket (or magazine rack), placed where it can be used most often: There is probably more reading done in the bathrooms of

America than all the libraries and classrooms combined. Put a book basket in there, stocked with books, magazines, and newspapers.

Put another book basket on or near the kitchen table. Take a hint from all those newspaper coin boxes standing in front of fast-food restaurants; they're not for decoration. If you sit in your car in the parking lot and watch who uses those coin boxes, invariably it's the person who's eating alone. I'm convinced most human beings want or need to read when they're eating alone. And with more and more children eating at least one daily meal alone, the kitchen is a prime spot for recreational reading. If there's a book on the table, they'll read it—unless, of course, you're foolish enough to have a television in your kitchen, as do 58 percent of parents in America.[16] Morrow's study of twenty-one classes of kindergartners showed that children with the most interest in reading came from homes where books and print were spread throughout the house, not just in one or two places.[17]

A book basket offers easy, immediate access to print during "captive moments."

The third B is bed lamp: Does your child have a bed lamp or reading light? If not, and you wish to raise a reader, the first order of business is to go out and buy one. Install it, and say to your child: "Elizabeth, we think you're old enough now to stay up later at night and read in bed like Mom and Dad. So we bought this little lamp and we're going to leave it on an extra fifteen minutes [or longer, depending on the age of the child] *if* you want to read in bed. On the other hand, if you don't want to read—that's okay, too. We'll just turn off the light at *the same old time.*" Most children will do anything in order to stay up later—even read.

At What Age Should I Stop Reading to My Child?

Almost as big a mistake as not reading to children at all is stopping too soon. The 1983 Commission on Reading stated that reading aloud is "a practice that should continue throughout the grades."[18] In this recommendation the commission was really asking us to model the extremely successful marketing strategy of McDonald's. The fast-food chain has been in business for a half century and has never cut its advertising budget. Every year McDonald's spends more money on advertising than it did the previous year, which comes to more than $1 million *per day.* Its marketing people never think, "Everyone has heard our message. They should be coming to us on their own, instead of our spending all this money on advertising."

Every time we read aloud to a child or class, we're giving a commercial for the pleasures of reading. But, unlike McDonald's, we often cut our advertising each year instead of increasing it. The older the child, the less he is read to—in the home and in the classroom. A thirty-year survey of graduate students confirms how seldom they were read to in middle and upper grades.[19]

Parents (and sometimes teachers) say, "He's in the top fourth-grade reading group—why should I read to him? Isn't that why we're sending him to school, so he'll learn how to read by himself?" There are many mistaken assumptions in that question.

Let's say the student is reading on a fourth-grade level. Wonderful. But what level is the child *listening* on? Most people have no idea that one is higher than the other—until they stop and think about it. Here's an easy way to visualize it: For seven years, the most popular show on American television was *The Cosby Show,* enjoyed by tens of millions each week—including first-graders. Even in reruns it's still one of the most-watched shows all over the world. On what reading level would you estimate the script to have been written? When a *Cosby* script[20] was subjected to the Harris-Jacobson Wide Range Readability Formula, it came out to approximately a fourth-grade level (3.7).[21]

Few, if any, of the first-graders watching the show would be able to read the script of the show. But most could understand it if it was *read to them*— that is, recited by the actors. According to experts, it is a reasonable assertion that reading and listening skills begin to converge at about eighth grade.[22] Until then, kids usually listen on a higher level than that on which they read. Therefore, children can *hear* and *understand* stories that are more complicated and more interesting than anything they could read on their own—which has to be one of God's greatest blessings for first-graders. The last thing you want first-graders thinking is that what they're reading in first grade is as good as books are going to get! First-graders can enjoy books written on a fourth-grade level, and fifth-graders can enjoy books written on a seventh-grade reading level. (This is, of course, contingent upon the social level of the books' subject matter; some seventh-grade material is above the fifth-grader's social experience and might be off-putting.)

Now that I've established the idea in your mind that there is a significant difference between listening level and reading level, you can better understand why one should continue to read aloud to children as they grow older, as the Hassetts did with Erin. Beyond the emotional bond that is established between parent and child (or teacher and class), you're feeding those higher vocabulary words through the ear; eventually they'll reach the brain and register in the child-reader's eyes.

That's the argument for continuing the reading to a higher level. Now let's divert to a lower level. If you've got a beginning reader in your home or classroom—five-, six-, and seven-year-olds—and you're still reading to the child, wonderful! Keep it up. But, if you're still reading those Dr. Seuss controlled-vocabulary books to the child—like *The Cat in the Hat* or *Hop on Pop*—you're insulting the six-year-old's brain cells nightly!

With either book, you have a volume of 225 words and a six-year-old with a 6,000-word vocabulary. The child has understood and been using all 225 of those words since he was four years old. If this is what you're still reading to the child every night, there's something wrong with the child if he's not lying in bed at night thinking, "One of us here is brain dead!"

At age six, you're a beginning reader. As such, you've got a limited number of words you can decode by sight or sound. But you're not a beginning *listener*. You've been listening for six years; you're a veteran listener! Dr. Seuss deliberately wrote the controlled-vocabulary books to be read *by* children to themselves. And just to make sure people understood this was a book to be read *by* the child and not *to* the child, the covers of the controlled-vocabulary books like *The Cat in the Hat* and *Hop on Pop* contain a logo with the words "I Can Read It All by Myself."[23] The "myself" refers to the *child*, not the *parent*!

In chapter 3, I explore what you could be reading instead of controlled-vocabulary books, including some chapter books that kindergarten and preschool teachers have used successfully in their classes.

Aren't We Wasting Time Reading to Preteens and Teens?

Here are two arguments in favor of reading to older children: First, do you know anyone who thinks today's teenagers read too much or even enough? Second, do you think adults in America read enough? If you answer no on both counts, then I suggest the old formula—that is, not reading to children as they grow older, and increasing the amount of work associated with books—hasn't worked all that well. It's resulted in huge numbers of schooltime readers who have developed a sweat mentality about books and choose to avoid them in adulthood.

While I'm not suggesting school become a vacation, we should accept the fact that when we try to interest children in reading, we're in the sales business. From that perspective, consider the words of David Ogilvy, whose writings were the bible of the advertising industry during the last half of the twentieth century. Ogilvy gave this advice to new copywriters who would be writing ads for the likes of Rolls-Royce, Hathaway, Procter & Gamble, Guinness, and Sears: "You cannot *bore* people into buying your product. You can only *interest* them in buying it."[24] Reading is the product being sold here. Every read-aloud is an advertisement for pleasure, every work sheet is an ad for pain. If the pain outweighs the pleasure, the customers go elsewhere.

In multiple studies of children's reading habits in SSR, or independent reading, their first choice is for books that have been previously read aloud to the class or are associated with movies they have seen.[25] Awareness comes before desire. Read-aloud is the single best advertisement for reading and this is demonstrated perfectly on page 62 with the example of a teacher's daily read-alouds and subsequent impact on a very reluctant fourth-grade student.

Is There One Book I Can Read to Both My Four-Year-Old and My Nine-Year-Old?

Here's a little rule of thumb for parents: If you can't squeeze your kids into the same size underwear, don't try to squeeze them into the same size book! In doing that, you end up watering down the reading material to accommodate the lowest common denominator—the four-year-old—and boring the nine-year-old. The solution is to read to them individually, especially if there is more than three years' difference in their ages.

When my children were young, we all read the picture books together. But once Elizabeth was ready for novels, I read nearly all of our novels individually—one-on-one. Today my children are forty-one and thirty-seven, and there's no social or emotional gap between them, but when the same two children were eleven and seven, the gap was sizable. The book that Elizabeth could handle at eleven, Jamie either wasn't ready for or interested in at seven.

A father in New Jersey, after hearing me suggest reading to children separately, interjected, "Excuse me, but doesn't that take longer?" Yes, it does, sir. Parenting is not supposed to be a time-saving experience. Parenting is time-*consuming,* time-*investing*—but not time-*saving.*

Is Reading Aloud Only About Vocabulary and Learning?

Beyond the building of attention span and vocabulary, something else is built during these one-on-one hours with a child. When you get to the "heavy stuff" in books, it usually brings to the surface some of the child's own "heavy stuff"—his or her deepest hopes and fears. And when that happens, if there is not an obnoxious older sister or younger brother present, children will tell you their secrets. And when they share their secrets, the chemistry that occurs is called "bonding"—and that's what *really* holds families together.

Relatively little of what most people do collectively or communally nurtures bonding. Don't tell me the family trip to Disney World is a bonding time. I've been in the lobby of Disney hotels at 9:30 at night and seen the families come back from a day of "bonding." It's not a pretty sight.

When do we bond best with the young? Whenever it's one-on-one: one-on-one walk, one-on-one talk, or one-on-one read. You will discover you have far fewer arguments or problems with a child when you're in a one-on-one situation.

It is far easier to convince a parent to begin reading to an infant than it is to convince people to begin (or continue) reading to older children, yet the older the child, the more complicated the books become, and the more enjoyable or meaningful they are for the adult reader as well. Some of the novels I read to Jamie and Elizabeth in their middle-grade years were as good as anything I was reading on my own: *A Day No Pigs Would Die* by Robert Newton Peck, *Slake's Limbo* by Felice Holman, *Roll of Thunder, Hear My Cry* by Mildred Taylor, *North to Freedom* by Ann Holm, *The Foxman* by Gary Paulsen, and Willie Morris's *Good Old Boy.* Worth noting: they're all still in print today.

Would Reading Aloud to Them Help Children with Grammar?

Grammar is more caught than taught, and the way you catch it is the same way you catch the flu: you're exposed to it. By hearing the language spoken correctly, you begin to imitate the pattern—both in what you say and in what you write. The easiest test of whether something is grammatically correct or not is to say it out loud. If, in response, you find yourself saying "That doesn't sound right," there's a good chance it's not correct. The only way of telling if it sounds "right" or "wrong" is if you've read it or heard it said correctly. Therefore, those who seldom read and/or live with people who speak incorrect English have little chance of ever mastering grammar.

This predicament about grammar is not restricted to ESL (English as a second language) students. Those of us exposed to annoying public cell phone conversations now know that many native-born people bring new meaning to the term "English as a second language."

In a nation that is becoming a more and more service-oriented economy, oral communication is an essential skill in the workplace. The richer the words you hear, the richer will be the words you give back—in speech or writing. Reading aloud to all students—ESL or native born—beginning as early in their lives as possible and continuing through the grades will expose them to a rich, organized, and interesting language model as an alternative to the tongue-tied language of their peers.

Discounting sign language and body language, there are two main forms of language: spoken and written. While they are intimately related to each other, they are not twins. As I showed in the chart on page 16, written words are far more structured and complicated than spoken words. Conversation is imprecise, rambling, often ungrammatical, and less organized than print. Therefore, children who enjoy conversations with adults *and* hear stories are exposed to richer language than is the child who experiences only conversation.

In listening to stories being read aloud, you're learning a second language—the standard English of books, the classroom, and most of the workplace. Most of us process at least two spoken languages—*home* language and *standard* language.

This gift of *standard* English cannot be overemphasized. I say that not because I am a native speaker of English, but for purely practical reasons. Standard English is the primary tongue of the classroom and the business world, yet children who spend twenty-eight hours a week watching television learn little of it. In *The Story of English,*[26] we find what amounts to a "state of the language" report on English:

Of all the world's languages (which now number some 2,700), [English] is arguably the richest in vocabulary. The compendious *Oxford English Dictionary* lists some 500,000 words; and a further half million technical and scientific terms remain uncatalogued. According to traditional estimates, neighboring German has a vocabulary of about 185,000 words and French fewer than 100,000. . . . Three-quarters of the world's mail, and its telexes and cables, are in English. So are more than half the world's technical and scientific periodicals. It is the language of technology from Silicon Valley to Singapore. English is the medium for 80 percent of the information stored in the world's computers. Nearly half of all business deals in Europe are conducted in English. . . . American technology and finance has introduced 20,000 English words into regular use in Japan.

And since 1944, it is the official language governing conversations between pilots and control towers across the world.[27]

Today's student needs home English for the neighborhood and standard English in the marketplace, and hearing it aloud is an easy and contagious manner in which to meet it in large doses.

How Do I Handle the Words I Don't Know How to Pronounce?

If it's the odd word that's not integral to the story, admit you're not certain about it, give it a try, and move on. On the other hand, if it's an important word or if you and the listeners are sincerely interested in the correct pronunciation, then you do a maximum of two minutes' worth of homework.

Professional readers-aloud—the ones who read for commercial audio-book companies—often encounter pronunciation problems. Until recently, professional readers had a great advantage over the rest of us: paid linguists sat in the studio with them to assist with pronunciations.[28] Now, thanks to the Internet, the rest of us have the same advantage, except ours is free. When you encounter a confusing word, turn your Web browser to a dictionary site such as Merriam-Webster Online (http:www.m-w.com), enter the word you're looking for, and, along with the definition, you'll find an icon that enables you to hear it pronounced.

How Do We Improve the Basics Like Writing and Spelling?

By reading, reading, reading. Vocabulary and spelling are not learned best by looking up words in the dictionary. You learn the meanings and spellings in the same way teachers learn the names of students and parents learn the names of neighbors: by seeing them again and again, and making the connection between the face and the name.

Nearly everyone spells by visual memory, not by rules. (There is ample research to indicate that people who have the best recall of graphic or geometric symbols are also the best spellers. This, say the scientists, may have more to do with your memory genetics than with anything else.)[29] Most people, when they doubt the correctness of what they have just spelled, write the word out several different ways and choose the one that *looks* correct. The more a child looks at words in sentences and paragraphs, the greater the chances he will recognize when the word is spelled correctly or incorrectly. Conversely, the less you read, the fewer words you meet and the less certain you are of both meaning and spelling.[30]

As for writing, there is the traditional approach, what you might call the "Vince Lombardi school of writing." That is, you write, write, write until you bleed it across the paper and the curriculum. You get better at writing the way you get better at tackling! Do it over and over. The trouble with this approach is that it is not supported by research. Students who write the most are not the best writers.[31] Indeed, for all the testing and portfolio collections and the raising of writing standards over the last fifteen years, the NAEP assessments show no significant change in national writing scores.

Now, before someone suffers apoplexy, I'm *not* suggesting we do away with writing in school. I'm just suggesting—strongly—that we back off a bit, that we might be doing too much writing in some places. Good writers are like baseball players. Baseball players have to play regularly, but they spend most of their time either in the field or in the dugout, watching *others* run, hit, catch, and throw. Good writers do the same—they write, but they *read* even more, and they watch how *other* people throw words around to catch meaning. The more you read, the better you write—and the NAEP Writing Report Card proves it.[32] The highest-scoring student writers were not those who wrote the most each day, but rather the students who *read* the most recreationally, had the most printed materials in their homes, and did regular essay writing in class.

What is flawed in our current writing curriculum is our failure to grasp the simple observation that Jacques Barzun once made—that writing and speaking are "copycat" experiences: "Words get in through the ear or eye and come out at the tongue or the end of a pencil."[33]

We say what we hear and we write what we see. When I ask relatives in Georgia, "What do you call these things on either side of my nose?" they often respond with something that sounds like, "Those are yer ahzzs [eyes]." On the other hand, ask my cousins in New Jersey the same question, and the answer often sounds like "Those're yer oiys." Depending on where you live, you can say the word "eyes" one way or another. But in the end, we usually say what we hear most often. That's why my niece and nephew in Georgia don't sound like my cousins in New Jersey but still speak the same language. What goes in the ear comes out the mouth.

To a degree, it's even true with drawing. Ask children in Alaska and Wisconsin to draw pictures of cows and you end up with very different looking cows. All the Alaskan cows look like husky dogs with udders, but those Wisconsin kids draw cows so lifelike you can almost smell them. Why the difference? Cows are tough to draw if you haven't seen them.

The same principle holds for writing. It's tough to write compound, complex, or good old simple sentences if you haven't seen them that often. And when do you see them most often? When you read—over and over and over. Reading only your own written sentences is about as helpful as speaking Spanish to yourself.

Yes, practice is important, but when I encounter school after school in which children spend more time writing than reading, where they complain there's no time for SSR, I'm convinced they've got the cart in front of the horse. In 2005, most of the major testing agencies added essays to their exams (on the SAT, this now accounts for one-third of the score). Although some educators had been complaining about writing scores for decades, it was the mushroom cloud of business e-mail at the end of the 1990s that sparked the greatest change. Almost overnight, corporate America switched from telecommunication to written communication and, in the process, discovered how many CEOs, CFOs, and mid-level executives couldn't string ten words together in a coherent sentence. Corporations were suddenly spending almost $3 billion a year to teach college-educated employees how to write, but the crisis was so deep it was often a case of "the blind leading the blind," like this request to an online writing consultant: "i need help i am writing a essay on writing i work for this company and my boss want me to help improve the workers writing skills can yall help me with some information thank you."[34]

Given that these executives grew up spending more time watching TV than reading, this means they saw fewer printed words and sentences than any previous generation. True, television is composed of words and e-mail is composed of words, but there are major differences. Nearly all the words on TV are dialogue, or characters talking to each other, and much conversation is composed of verbal shorthand, often missing subjects or verbs. But subjects or verbs that can be safely dropped from conversation *have* to be included in an e-mail or letter if they are to be understood (or become a matter of the corporate record).

But here is the most glaring fact to consider about the reading and writing connection: visual receptors in the brain outnumber the auditory receptors, 30 to 1.[35] In other words, the chances of a word (or sentence) being retained in our memory bank are thirty times greater if we see it instead of just hear it. Business executives whose experience with language consists largely of television dialogue and conversation will never be able to write coherent sentences until they see a lot more coherent sentences, and it might even be too late for many of them. Learning to write well at age thirty-five is a lot like learning to Rollerblade or speak a foreign language at age thirty-five: it's not as easy as it would be at age seven. Vocabulary and coherent sentences can't be downloaded onto paper unless they've first been uploaded to the head—by reading.

As for the new examination standards improving students' writing, surely you jest. The millions of essays are being graded by part-time high school teachers spending an average of one to two minutes per essay. As someone noted, "The chances of such tests identifying good writers and writing are less than those of your local weather forecaster's being accurate." When three executives from the nation's premier test-prep company, the Princeton Review, applied the SAT writing standards to the writings of Shakespeare, Hemingway, Gertrude Stein, and Theodore Kaczynski (the Unabomber), the highest score went to—Kaczynski.[36] Not a good sign there.

Is It Ever Too Late to Start Reading to a Child?

They're never too old—but it's not as easy with older children as it is when they're two or six years old.

Because she has a captive audience, the classroom teacher holds a distinct advantage over the parent who suddenly wants to begin reading to a thirteen-year-old. Regardless of how well-intentioned the parent may be, reading aloud to an adolescent at home can be difficult. During this period of social and emotional development, teenagers' out-of-school time is largely spent coping with body changes, sex drives, vocational anxieties, and the need to form an identity apart from that of their families. These kinds of concerns and their attendant schedules don't leave much time for Mom's and Dad's reading aloud. (See also page 72.)

But the situation is not hopeless *if you pick your spots*. Don't suggest that your daughter listen to a story when she's sitting down to watch her favorite television show or fuming after a fight with her boyfriend. Along with timing, consider the length of what you read. Keep it short—unless you see an interest in more.

When the child is in early adolescence, from age twelve to fourteen, try sharing a small part of a book, a page or two, when you see he is at loose ends—and downplay any motivational or educational aspects connected with the reading. When Jamie and Elizabeth were teens, I was always reading excerpts to them from whatever I was reading myself—be it fiction or nonfiction. Late one evening I was reading Ferrol Sams's *Run with the Horseman,* a wonderful Southern novel by a Georgia physician. When I came to a scene in which a boy has two outrageously funny incidents with a mule in a field and a rooster in an outhouse, I thought, "Oh, Jamie will love these!"

So in the morning, I caught up with him. "Hey, Jamie—listen to this!"

Edging to the door, he said, "Sorry, Dad, but I gotta run. I'm supposed to meet the guys."

"I know, but it'll just take a minute—I promise." Rolling his eyes, he reluctantly sat and I began to read it aloud. And, as I expected, he loved it. And several hours later he was back with his buddies in tow, asking me to read it to them too.

Because so many parents and teachers seem at loose ends over what to read to this age group, I created an anthology of fifty read-aloud selections for preteens and teens called *Read All About It!* It contains a broad cross section of fiction and nonfiction, short stories and chapters from novels (which will whet the child's appetite for the rest of the book), newspaper columns, and biographical sketches of each author. I'll bet you think all those yellow-ribbon bumper stickers ("Support our troops") began with Tony Orlando and Dawn's rendition of "Tie a Yellow Ribbon." Wrong. Check out Pete Hamill's "The Yellow Handkerchief" column in *Read All About It!*

How Does This Fit with the Calls for Higher National Standards?

As a nation, we want to be sure to raise *all* the standards. Since 1983's *A Nation at Risk* report, CEOs and politicians have emphasized only one standard: IQ. And as the demands for higher scores are pressed on superintendent, principal, and teacher, the curriculum narrows to only what will be on the standardized test. Since the tests include only IQ subjects, there remains little or no time for HQ subjects—the "heart quotient." Who has time for the teachable moment when the class hamster dies but you've got test-prep to cover? Who bothers to discuss the ethical thing to do if there are no ethics questions on the state standards exam?

As the late Clifton Fadiman once said, "There is no shortage of smart people. We've got lots of those. The real shortage is in *better* people." And you make better people by educating children's brains *and* hearts. Daniel Goleman's *Emotional Intelligence* is perhaps the most eloquent argument in support of that.

Consider the following headlines (my short list), all of them involving people of high IQ, graduates of our finest colleges and universities, many with advanced degrees; but one must wonder at their HQ scores:

- HealthSouth to Settle Fraud Charges for $100 Million
- Bristol-Myers Pays $300 Million in Fraud Penalties
- Time Warner and S.E.C. Settle for $300 Million
- Wal-Mart to Pay $11M for Illegal Immigrants
- Insurers Say Doctors Filed $1 Billion in False Fees
- Deloitte & Touche Pay Largest Accounting Fine Ever
- Top Execs at 6th-Largest Cable Firm Guilty of Looting Millions
- 3 Major Newspapers Admit to Years of False Circulation Figures
- World's Biggest Insurance Broker to Pay $850M for Fraud
- Drug Giant Agrees to Pay $350 Million for Cheating Medicaid
- NEC Unit Fined $20.7 Million for Defrauding Schools
- Catholic Church's Costs Pass $1 Billion in Abuse Cases
- Enron Agrees to Pay $1.52 Billion for Manipulating Energy Crisis
- Microsoft to Pay $1.1B for Overcharging Customers
- 2 Drug Makers to Pay $875 Million to Settle Fraud Case

Those headlines weren't caused by a lack of algebraic skills, nor were they the result of former remedial students being in charge. The people behind those scandals were the gifted and talented guys, the ones from the head of the class.[37] To ignore students' emotional and social education (as the standards exams do) is to invite a plethora of such headlines and behaviors.

If all we're doing in school is teaching students how to answer the calls they'll someday get on their pagers or cell phones, then the curriculum is worthless. The most important calls won't come on pagers; instead they'll be the daily calls for love, justice, courage, and compassion. The most important calls at Enron and WorldCom were the ones that weren't returned: "Hey, ——, I've been looking at this quarter's numbers and—well—something doesn't add up."

Yes, student exam scores are important, but both scores must be addressed—the IQ and the HQ. When we focus exclusively on paper scores, we need to remember that the most educated nation in nearly two thousand years led the world in math and science in 1930. It also became the Third Reich. The Holocaust could never have happened if the German *heart* had been as well educated as the German *mind*.

So how do we educate the heart? There are really only two ways: life experience and stories about life experience, which is called literature. All the great preachers and all the great teachers of the heart have used stories to get their lesson plans across—Aesop, Socrates, Confucius, Moses, and Jesus—stories about mustard seeds and shepherds and vineyards and prostitutes and fishermen and travelers. It is the power of story to educate upstairs as well as downstairs.

Chapter 3

The Stages of Read-Aloud

Few children learn to love books by themselves. Someone has
to lure them into the wonderful world of the written word;
someone has to show them the way.

—Orville Prescott,
A Father Reads to His Children

Until a child is four months old, it doesn't matter a great deal *what*
you read, as long as you are reading. Doing so lets the child become accustomed to the rhythmic sound of your reading voice and to associate it with
a peaceful, secure time of day. Mother Goose, of course, is always appropriate, but my neighbor read aloud Kipling when she was nursing her
daughter, who eventually went on to both Princeton and Harvard. Did Kipling have anything to do with that? Not much, compared to her mother's
reading to her day in and day out.

Over the last decade or so, known in some circles as the Decade of the
Brain, a heated debate has raged over the importance of the infant years in
a person's brain development. Although psychologists and neuroscientists
have argued in public conferences, news magazines, and professional journals, the jury remains out on exactly how critical the first three years of life
really are. Do the doors of opportunity really slam shut after age three, or
are there second, third, or fourth chances later on?

I personally tend to compromise between the two extremes: Learning
(and life) is easier if the first three years are enriched, but later opportunities
can be rewarding if there is an ideal learning environment. Still, later learning will be more arduous. Anyone wishing to pursue the debate will find
it fully explored in *The Scientist in the Crib: Minds, Brains, and How Children*

Learn by Gopnick, Melzoff, and Kuhl and *The Myth of the First Three Years* by John T. Bruer. You can also listen via the Internet to a presentation by Dr. Jack Shonkoff, pediatrician, dean of the Heller Graduate School at Brandeis University, and chairman of the Committee on Integrating the Science of Early Childhood Development, as he cautions against some of the learning mandates imposed today by federal education authorities in the name of science and brain research.[1]

What is firmly established by the research is that measurable long-term storage of sound and word patterns begins as early as eight months of age. Children hearing the most language will have the best chance of having the best language skills.[2] There are only two ways for words to enter a child's brain: through the eyes or through the ears. Since the child isn't reading yet, that leaves just the ears.

Let me reiterate an earlier statement: None of this is intended to create a super-baby. The focus should be on nurturing whatever abilities are already there, building an intimate bond between parent and child, and constructing a natural bridge between child and books that can be crossed whenever the child is developmentally ready as a reader to cross it.

Which Books Are Best for Infants?

Your book selections for the first year should be ones that stimulate your child's sight and hearing—colorful pictures and exciting sounds upon which the child can focus easily. One of the reasons for Mother Goose's success is that she echoes the first sound a child falls in love with—the rhythmic, rhyming *beat-beat-beat* of a mother's heart.

Mother Goose and Dr. Seuss not only rhyme in name and text, they also must have sensed what researchers would later prove. According to learning specialists at the National Institute of Child Health and Human Development in Bethesda, Maryland, the ability to find words that rhyme appears to be an important ability in children. Indeed, kindergartners who struggle to find words that rhyme with "cat" are prime candidates for later reading problems. Moreover, considering the many rhyming chants found in children's games (such as jump-rope rhymes) and popular children's books like Seuss's *The Sleep Book* and *The Foot Book,* it's obvious that children find pleasure in words that rhyme. But why? Researchers say it is for the same reason humans subconsciously enjoy looking at stripes and plaids or listening to musical harmony—they help to arrange a chaotic world.

With that in mind, a prime recommendation is that parents frequently read aloud books and stories that rhyme. You can find a list of such titles on pages 282–83.

The impact of rhyme can be traced as early as the womb. For one study, women in the last trimester of pregnancy repeatedly read aloud Dr. Seuss's *The Cat in the Hat*; then, fifty-two hours after birth, monitored infants were able to distinguish Seuss's rhyming verse from a book without rhymes.[3]

We don't turn to Mother Goose for the plot. We turn to her because she takes all those sounds, syllables, endings, and blendings and mixes them in with the rhythm and rhyme of language for us to feed to a child who already takes delight in rocking back and forth in his crib, repeating a single syllable over and over: "Ba, ba, ba, ba, ba . . ." There are many collections of Mother Goose, but my two present favorites are *The Lucy Cousins Book of Nursery Rhymes* and *The Neighborhood Mother Goose* by Nina Crews.

Many parents find that singing or reciting these rhymes during the appropriate activity further reinforces the relationship between rhyme and activity in the child's mind. Compact disks, long-playing records, and tapes of these rhymes are available at your library and local bookstore.

Also keep in mind the physical bonding that occurs during the time you are holding the child and reading. To make sure you never convey the message that the book is more important than the child, maintain skin-to-skin contact as often as possible, patting, touching, and hugging the child while you read.[4] Linked with the normal parent-infant dialogue, this reinforces a feeling of being well-loved.

What Is Normal Behavior by the Infant or Toddler During Readings?

Recent interest in early learning has spurred investigations into how infants and their parents react in read-aloud situations, though any reading parent can tell you a child's interest in and response to books varies a great deal. But if you are a *new* parent, any seeming lack of interest can be discouraging. Here is a forecast so you'll not be discouraged or think your child is hopeless.

- At four months of age, since he has limited mobility, a child has little or no choice but to listen and observe, thus making a passive and noncombative audience for the parent, who is probably thinking, "This is easy!"
- Your arms should encircle the child in such a way as to suggest support and bonding, but not imprisonment, allowing the child to view the pages if you're reading a picture book.
- By six months, however, the child is more interested in grabbing the book to suck on it than listening (which he's also doing). Bypass the problem by giving him a teething toy or other distraction.

- At eight months, he may prefer turning pages to steady listening. Allow him ample opportunity to explore this activity, but don't give up the book entirely.
- At twelve months, the child's involvement grows to turning pages for you, pointing to objects you name on the page, even making noises for animals on cue.
- By fifteen months and the onset of walking, his restlessness blossoms fully, and your reading times must be chosen so as not to frustrate his immediate interests.

In nearly all these studies,[5] attention spans during infant reading time averaged only three minutes in length, though several daily readings often brought the total as high as thirty minutes a day. There are some one-year-olds who will listen to stories for that long in one sitting, but they are more the exception than the rule.

As babies mature, good parent-readers profit from earlier experiences. They don't force the reading times; they direct attention by pointing to something on the page, and they learn to vary their voices between whispers and excited tones. They also learn that attention spans are not built overnight—they are built minute by minute, page by page, day by day.

Once the child starts to respond to the sight of books and your voice, begin a book dialogue, *talking* the book instead of just *reading* it. Reading aloud with a young child shouldn't be a solitary, passive experience. As much as possible you want the child to interact with you and the book. You elicit the interaction by the questions or comments you interject in the reading, as you'll see in a moment. What you want in the reading is the same thing you want when you talk with a child—give and take, or, as one educator put it, "Play Ping-Pong, not darts." When you simply throw words or orders at a child, you're playing verbal darts. Here is a sample dialogue between a mother and her twenty-month-old during a reading of *Blueberries for Sal* by Robert McCloskey. Note that the parent doesn't stay tied to the exact text, which is underlined here.

> **Parent:** <u>Little Bear's mother turned around to see what on earth could make a noise like *kuplunk*!</u> And there, right in front of her, was—Sal!
> **Child:** Saa.
> **Parent:** Right, Sal. And <u>mother bear</u> was *very* surprised to see Sal and not <u>Little Bear</u> behind her. Look at the surprised look on her face. Sal looks a little surprised, too, don't you think?

Child: Yeh.
Parent: Yes. *"Garumpf!"* she cried. This is not my child! Where is Little Bear? And mother bear ran off to find him. Where do you think Little Bear is?
Child: D-no.
Parent: You don't know? Well, let's turn the page—you can turn it—and maybe we'll find him *there*.

In this simple exchange, a number of important things are being accomplished with language.

1. Parent and child are sharing the pleasures of a book together, a story that unfolds gradually at their pace (not a video's pace) on pages that have illustrations that are stationary enough for the child to study or scrutinize closely.
2. The mother uses both her own words and the words in the book. How closely you follow the exact text is determined by the age of the child and the attention span.
3. The dialogue is interactive—that is, the parent interjects simple questions that elicit responses.
4. When the child answers, the parent affirms the response ("Right") and/or corrects it (pronouncing "Sal," "yes," and "don't know" correctly).

When a middle-class mother and her child were monitored for ten months, researchers found that 75 percent of the labeling of objects done by the mother was done in the context of a book, and the child's responses were corrected or reinforced 81 percent of the time.[6] A similar study of lower-income mothers found this behavior was much less likely to occur.[7]

What Comes After Mother Goose?

During the toddler stage, an important parental role is to serve as a welcoming committee—welcoming the child to your world. Think of yourself as the host of a huge party, with your child as the guest of honor. Naturally, you want to introduce him to all the invited guests to make him feel at home. As the child grows older a huge number of "things" become objects of fascination: holes, cars, snow, birds, bugs, stars, trucks, dogs, rain, planes, cats, storms, babies, mommies, and daddies. This stage is called "labeling the environment."

Picture books are perfect teaching vehicles at this stage. Point to the various items illustrated in the book, call them by name, ask the child to say the name with you, and praise any responses. Two books are excellent for this purpose: *The Everything Book* by Denise Fleming (Holt), and *My First Word Book* by Jane Yorke (DK). The latter is a collection of photographs of one thousand common items and is aimed at children eighteen to thirty-six months, while *The Everything Book* focuses on infants up to eighteen months and contains a smaller number of images, including animals, shapes, colors, rhymes, finger games, food, faces, letters, traffic, and toys.

The very best picture book at this stage may be the one you make, using photographs taken in your home and of your family. Desktop printing has made this kind of publishing easy for families. Take photos of your child's day and environment, add some captions, print them out on your home printer, laminate the pages, punch a couple of holes and you've got a homemade family book. Of course, if you have access to Apple iPhoto capabilities, you can have the book printed and bound by professionals, all via the Internet.

Why Do They Want the Same Book Read Over and Over?

Just as you didn't learn the names of everyone in your neighborhood or parish overnight, children also need repeated readings in order to learn. Thus, although reading a different book every day may keep the adult from being bored, it prevents the child from getting the reinforcement he needs for learning. Prior to age two, repeated readings of fewer books is better than a huge collection read infrequently.

Those of us who have seen a movie more than once fully realize how many subtleties escaped us the first time. This is even more the case with children and books. Because they're learning a complex language at the adult's speaking pace, there often are misunderstandings that can be sorted out only through repeated readings.

Parents sometimes are irritated by a child's incessant questions: "My child interrupts the book so often for questions, it ruins the story." First, you need to define the kinds of questions. Are they silly? Are they the result of curiosity or extraneous to the story? Is the child sincerely trying to learn something or just postponing bedtime? You can solve the latter problem if you make a regular habit of talking about the story when you finish instead of simply closing the book, kissing the child good night, and turning off the light.

In the case of intelligent questions, try to respond immediately if the child's question involves background knowledge ("Why did Mr. MacGregor put Peter's father in a pie, Mom? Why couldn't he just hop out?"), and thus help the child better understand the story. Extraneous questions can be handled by saying, "Good question! Let's come back to that when we're done." And be sure to live up to that promise. Ultimately, one must acknowledge that questions are a child's primary learning tool. Don't destroy natural curiosity by ignoring it.

As boring as repeated readings may be for the adult, they can accomplish very important things within a child. To begin with, he will learn language by hearing it over and over—this is called immersion. Hearing the same story over and over is definitely a part of that immersion process.

For as long as possible, your read-aloud efforts should be balanced by the outside experiences you bring to the child. Barring cases of bedridden children, it is not enough simply to read to the child. The background knowledge I noted earlier applies to life experience as well. The words in the book are just the beginning. What you as a parent or teacher do *after* the reading can turn a mini-lesson into a sizable learning experience. For example, *Corduroy* by Don Freeman is a much-loved children's book about a little girl and a department store teddy bear. The story alone is heartwarming, but the name Corduroy could also be used as a springboard to a discussion and comparison of other common fabrics like denim, wool, cotton, canvas, and felt. And it works in reverse as well: when you find a caterpillar outside, read Eric Carle's *The Very Hungry Caterpillar* inside the house or classroom.

What About Vocabulary Words the Child or Class Might Not Know?

While it's not necessary to turn every book into a lesson, there are some reading styles that are shown to be more effective than others. For example, Warwick Elley had teachers of six classes of eight-year-olds read picture books to the students using different styles. Certain target words were identified to teachers beforehand, and students were given a pretest into which those words were subtly inserted.[8]

Group A classes heard the book with the teacher giving brief explanations of unknown words, either using synonyms for the word or pointing to a picture on the page of, for example, a "roadster." This was the "reading with explanation" style. In a period of seven days, the class heard the story three times.

Group B classes heard the same book three times in the same period but without explanations of the target words ("no explanation" style). Additionally, there was a control group of children who did not hear the story at all.

Using pretests, posttests, and three-month delayed posttests, Elley found the "with explanation" classes had a 39.9 percent vocabulary gain while the "no explanation" classes gained 14.8 percent, and the control group (hearing none of the books) gained less than 2 percent. Students scoring low on the pretest showed posttest gains as large as their classmates'.[9]

In looking at readings of various books and the difference in results (some more modest than others), researchers noted that books which hold children's attention will garner larger learning benefits, especially books that include "novelty, humor, conflict, and suspense." In other words, the more interesting the book, the keener the child's attention and the more learning results.

Won't a Video Do My Child as Much Good as a Picture Book?

Film and print are separate art forms that often have a common audience—in this case, the child. On page 16, I showed the difference in vocabulary level between a children's book and TV. But there is another issue to consider, especially for preschoolers or younger: the image on the film moves, but the one on the page is static. Let's see how important that might be.

In a typical film, the image of an insect speeds across the screen at a pace of 24 frames per second. In a two-hour film, that would be more than 170,000 frames—few of which could be studied for details. As soon as you stop the film, the image blurs.

On a page, the insect's image remains in focus and in one place, allowing the child to scrutinize it for details. Because visual literacy comes before print literacy, two-thirds of the questions and comments from young children are about the illustrations.[10] In a study of nine children, ages three to five, 150 hours of parent story-readings were audiotaped and analyzed for the kinds of questions asked by the children.[11] They asked a total of 2,725 questions, the vast majority of which focused on the illustrations. On average, the children asked 7 questions per book, and picture queries outnumbered story questions by a two-to-one ratio. Surprisingly, less than 10 percent of the questions concerned letters or sentences (text), and 5 percent were about word meanings.

How Can Illiterate or Semiliterate Parents Read to Children?

Forty years ago, this would have been an insurmountable problem, but not now. One kind of book and a piece of technology help to save the day. The books are wordless and predictable books (or easy readers) and the technology is the tape deck or CD player.

Thirty thousand years ago, in a step toward writing, our ancestors used cave drawings to tell stories without words. Wordless books follow that tradition. These books convey a story without using words; pictures (interpreted orally by the reader) tell the whole story—as books in pantomime, if you will. The parent who can't read (or can't read English) has little difficulty in looking at the pictures and talking the book to the child.[12] The popularity of this genre has increased in recent years, and there are now dozens of wordless books in print, from the simple (like *Deep in the Forest* by Brinton Turkle) to the complex (*The Silver Pony* by Lynd Ward, or *Tuesday* by David Wiesner). Ask your librarian for the wordless books in the library's collection, or consider the beginner's list on page 179.

Forty years ago, a person had to be blind to obtain a book on tape in America. Now thousands of titles are available for parents or anyone wishing to listen, learn, and enjoy a good book, all for free at the public library. Illiterate or semiliterate parents can listen to these recorded books along with the child, and, hearing them often enough, will begin to memorize them. The illiterate parent and child can sit together and listen to a book, even follow along on the page. They're sharing time and a common story. Is someone else's voice better than the parent's? No, but it's a whole lot better than no story at all. Taking the time to listen beside the child—instead of watching TV or talking on the phone—sends a message to the child about the importance the parent places on books. For parents or teachers of older children, see page 171 in chapter 9 for a discussion of children's books on audiocassette.

What Is the Purpose of Fairy Tales?

Before most parents realize it, a growing child is ready, in his own mind at least, to go out and challenge the world. In the last two thousand years, nothing has helped this exploratory need as much as the fairy tale.

I know what you may be thinking. "Fairy tales? Is he kidding? Why, those things are positively frightening. Children see enough violence on television—they don't need kids pushing witches into ovens and evil spells and poisoned apples."

Stop for a minute and remind yourself how long the fairy tale has been with us—in every nation and in every civilization. Surely there must be something significant here, an insight so important as to transcend time and mountains and cultures to arrive in the twenty-first century still intact. There are, for example, more than seven hundred different versions of *Cinderella* from hundreds of cultures. Nevertheless, they all tell the same story—a truly universal story. (See *Ella's Big Chance* by Shirley Hughes in the Treasury.)

What distinguishes the fairy tale is that it speaks to the very heart and soul of the child. It admits to the child what so many parents and teachers spend hours trying to cover up or avoid. The fairy tale confirms what the child has been thinking all along—that it is a cold, cruel world out there and it's waiting to eat him alive.

Now, if that were *all* the fairy tale said, it would have died out long ago. But it goes one step further. It addresses itself to the child's sense of courage and adventure. The tale advises the child: Take your courage in hand and go out to meet the world head on. According to Bruno Bettelheim, the fairy tale offers this promise: If you have courage and if you persist, you can overcome any obstacle, conquer any foe.

By recognizing a child's daily fears, appealing to his courage and confidence, and by offering hope, the fairy tale presents the child with a means by which he can understand the world and himself. And those who would deodorize the tales impose a fearsome lie upon the child. J. R. R. Tolkien cautioned, "It does not pay to leave a dragon out of your calculations if you live near him." Judging from the daily averages, our land is filled with dragons:

+ Advocacy groups receive three million child-abuse calls each year, with at least 40 percent substantiated.[13]
+ Over 1,200 children are abused to death each year, and one-half of all abuse victims are under one year of age.[14]
+ Every twelve seconds a man batters his wife or ex-wife or girlfriend.[15]

To send a child into that world unprepared is a crime.

Similar to the temptation to avoid fairy tales is the tendency of some adults to choose books that will keep the child forever young, books without problems, conflict, or drama. And then all too soon these same parents are asking why their children have lost interest in books. Of all the things we ask our books to be, few are as important as "believable." Fiction, nonfiction, biographies, fantasies—the good ones work because they are believable. A world that is "forever pink," as author Natalie Babbitt once put it, doesn't work because children eventually realize its fakery.

Isn't the Fairy Tale's "Prince Charming" a Bit Dated?

If there is one flaw in the fairy tale, it's that many of the more famous tales are top-heavy with heroes and short on heroines. For balance, readers-aloud will want to try these collections of fairy and folk tales focusing on heroines: Ethel Johnston Phelps's *Tatterhood and Other Tales*; *Not One Damsel in Distress: World Folktales for Strong Girls* collected by Jane Yolen; and *Fearless Girls, Wise Women, and Beloved Sisters: Heroines in Folktales from Around the World* by Kathleen Ragan. For nonfiction—*Girls Think of Everything: Stories of Ingenious Inventions by Women* by Catherine Thimmesh; *How High Can We Climb? The Story of Women Explorers* by Jeannine Atkins; and *Mighty Jackie* by Marissa Moss.

Ella Enchanted by Gail Carson Levine gives us a novelized and more believable Cinderella than the ones offered by Perrault and Disney, and Shirley Hughes's picture book account of Cinderella in the Jazz Age, *Ella's Big Chance,* is in the same vein. To see how far we've come with our heroines, check out these three picture books by Emily Arnold McCully about a young French girl: *Mirette on the High Wire, Starring Mirette & Bellini,* and *Mirette & Bellini Cross Niagara Falls.* On page 290, you'll also find a list of picture book parodies of traditional fairy tales in the vein of *The True Story of the Three Little Pigs* by Jon Sczieska.

If We Only Have a Small Amount of Time for Read-Aloud, How Do We Incorporate Discussion?

Steal more time! If that sounds daring, consider the words of education writer Alfie Kohn: "Before a teacher, especially a middle school, high school or college instructor sits down to plan a course, even a unit, or thinks about evaluation, he or she should ask the question 'What can I reasonably expect that students will retain from this course after a decade?' I know that if I'd been asked that question when I was teaching in high school and college, I would have found it profoundly unsettling, because I knew well, or would have known if I had been brave enough to face the question head-on, that all they would have left was a fact here, a stray theory there, a disconnected assumption or passage from a book. That should lead us to ask what it is we're doing. We sometimes end up making elaborate snow sculptures on the last day of winter."[16]

Discussion after the story is of critical importance. Students from classrooms where there were more book discussions tend to score higher in national reading assessments[17] and read more outside school.[18] In chapter 8, I explain the role that discussion plays in the success of Oprah's Book Club, which has helped put more than fifty books on the *New York Times* bestseller list, and not one was required reading for anyone. How many books do you think the state tests will put there?

Is There a Natural Transition from Picture Book to Novel?

Thanks to our primal need to find out what happens next, read-aloud is a particularly effective tool in stretching children's attention spans. Just keep in mind that endurance in readers, like runners, is not built overnight; start slowly and build gradually. Start with short picture books, then move to longer ones that can be spread over several days, then to short novels (already broken into convenient chapters), and finally to full-length novels (longer than one hundred pages).

The amount of text on a page is a good way to gauge how much the child's attention span is being stretched. When my grandson Tyler was two years old, he regularly heard books with just a few sentences on a page, but by three and a half he was listening to books that had three times as much text (see illustration below). The transition from short to longer should be done gradually over many different books. While you don't want to drown the child in words, you do want to entice him away from a complete dependence on illustrations for comprehension and into more words.

If I had a primary class (or child) that had never been read to (like the ones who spent all of kindergarten filling in blanks and circling letters), I'd

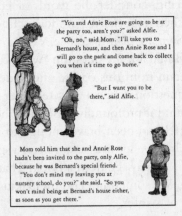

From All About Alfie *by Shirley Hughes. The amount of text on the page should grow with the child's attention span.*

start the year with: the repetition of *Tikki Tikki Tembo* by Arlene Mosel, the poignancy of *The Biggest Bear* by Lynd Ward, the mystery of *The Island of the Skog* by Steven Kellogg, the humor of *Here Come the Aliens!* by Colin McNaughton, and the suspense of Paul Zelinsky's retelling of *Rumpelstiltskin*.

Then I'd do a week of new picture books from the Treasury at the back of this book, including *Are You Going to Be Good?* by Cari Best (humor), *Nora's Ark* by Natalie Kinsey-Warnock (nonfiction), *Bridget and the Gray Wolves* by Pija Lindenbaum (bossy classmate), *The Great Fuzz Frenzy* by Janet Stevens and Susan Stevens Crummel (copycatting), and *Micawber* by John Lithgow (art).

Next would be "Red Riding Hood Week," focusing on different versions of that famous red-hooded pilgrim—starting with Trina Schart Hyman's *Little Red Riding Hood* and followed by books chosen from the titles listed with it in the Treasury.

Then I'd schedule several "author weeks," each focusing exclusively on one author's books. I'd start with Kevin Henkes, who uses his mouse tales to read the pulse of childhood so touchingly (see the list of his books accompanying *Lilly's Purple Plastic Purse* in the Treasury). As their attention grew, I'd have a "Bill Peet Week," choosing a week's worth of reading listed with *The Whingdingdilly* in the Treasury. On the day I read *Kermit the Hermit* (about a stingy hermit crab), I'd introduce it with "Hector the Collector" from Shel Silverstein's poetry collection *Where the Sidewalk Ends.* From then on I would sprinkle poetry throughout the day: waiting for the bell in the morning, between classes, et cetera.

Then I'd move on to a picture book *series,* with each volume treated as a chapter in an ongoing book—like Bernard Waber's seven-book Lyle the Crocodile series that begins with *The House on East 88th Street.* (See its Treasury listing for titles in the series.)

Once you've built a child's or class's attention span, it's an easy jump to "chapter books"—either long picture books or short novels of sixty to one hundred pages. These are books that don't have to end with Monday but can be stretched into Tuesday and Wednesday. Preschoolers can enjoy picture books that are divided into chapters, like Barbara Brenner's *Wagon Wheels* and *The Josefina Story Quilt* by Eleanor Coerr. Then I'd do a collection of stories in one volume about one family. One of the best is *All About Alfie* by Shirley Hughes, a collection of four stories about a spirited preschooler and his family. These can be expanded to the other collections about Alfie: *The Big Alfie and Annie Rose Storybook* and *Annie Rose Is My Little Sister.*

Sometimes you'll encounter a picture book that may be too long for one sitting. Simply divide it into chapters yourself.

As for actual short novels, my immediate nominees would be *My Father's Dragon* by Ruth Stiles Gannett, William McCleery's *Wolf Story,* Johanna Hurwitz's *Rip-Roaring Russell* (see the Treasury's short novel listings for the other books in the Russell series), and Dick King-Smith's *The Water Horse.*

At What Age Can You Begin Chapter Books?

Let me give you an idea of how widespread the misunderstanding of listening and reading levels is, as well as the magic that can occur when they are understood. About ten years ago I was doing an all-day seminar in a blue-collar community on the Jersey Shore. At lunch, a young teacher named Melissa Olans Antinoff introduced herself and said, "You'd *love* my kindergarten class!" She explained that she read one hundred picture books a year to the class, but also read ten to twelve chapter books. The socio-economic level of the class had 60 percent of the children on free lunch, and Antinoff was in only her fourth year of teaching.

When the seminar resumed after lunch, I asked how many kindergarten teachers were in the room and learned there were eight. Further investigation showed that Antinoff was the only one who read chapter books to her class. Which of those eight classes will be better prepared for first grade: the ones that heard 150 four-minute picture books, or the one that heard 100 picture books along with a dozen novels? Which class will have the longer attention spans at the end of the year, and the larger vocabularies? Which class will have exercised more complex thinking, having to recall what happened in Thursday's and Wednesday's chapter in order to understand Friday's chapter?

Today Melissa Antinoff teaches fourth grade in a different town but is still reading aloud to her students. She shared this anecdote with me recently:

> "Bobby" hated to read when fourth grade started. In fact, in the beginning he didn't want to sit still when I read aloud. He'd wiggle, poke people, want to sit at his desk, etc.
>
> I began the year with Louis Sachar's *There's a Boy in the Girls' Bathroom.* Eventually, by the end of September, he not only sat still, he moved so that he was sitting in front of me when I was reading, and then, around the beginning of November, he began asking to read ahead in the novel when there was free time.
>
> I was amazed. This is a boy who, at the beginning of the year, was in the lowest reading group (I hate that term, but I'm not sure what else to use) and had great difficulty answering any questions about what he had read. I rarely used the basal readers this year and we

read a ton of novels. By October, Bobby was the first one in his reading group to raise his hand to answer a question. In fact, I moved him up to one of my middle groups at the start of the second marking period. What excited me the most was that Bobby began reading on his own—every chance he could. (My general rule is that, if a student finishes any work in any subject early, he or she should read.)

By the time parent conferences came around, Bobby was reading three books—three! When I asked him why he didn't just read one book at a time, he told me he liked them all and couldn't decide which one to start, so he was reading all three. It got so that I had to specifically walk up to him and get his attention back to what we were doing, he was so engrossed in the books.

All of this came up at his conference. Bobby had come with his mother and was participating in the discussions concerning his progress for the first marking period. He was describing one of the books he was reading, and his mother was marveling at her son. I asked Bobby why he seemed to dislike anything to do with reading in September and three months later couldn't get enough of books.

He replied, "Well, at first I was really bored, especially when you read aloud, because I had to pretend to pay attention. But when you read, you made it sound so interesting, and I liked Bradley (the main character in *There's a Boy in the Girls' Bathroom*), and I wanted to see if it was as good if I read it myself, so I started reading about Bradley. It was. So I tried a book you weren't reading and liked it."

Could You Read Chapter Books at Preschool Level?

In 1999, my daughter came home for Thanksgiving with a letter she had received from my grandson Connor's preschool teacher at Battery Park City Day Nursery in New York City. "You're going to love this!" she exclaimed as she handed it to me. I've shared it with almost every teacher and parent audience I've had since then. The teacher was a talented young woman with fourteen years' experience working with four- and five-year-olds, and here's what she wrote:

Dear Parents:

Ordinarily, I do not go out of my way to recommend movies to my students' parents; however, there is a movie coming out which could help to extend your child's learning. On December 19th, the movie *Stuart Little* will be opening. It just so happens that we have just finished reading the book by E. B. White, which the movie is based on.

Throughout the year we will be selecting a few chapter books to read to the children who stay for nap time. Year after year, *Stuart Little* is always my first selection because each chapter of the book is short enough to be read in one sitting, and, most especially, I choose it because Stuart is a character that can easily capture the imagination of a young child. You see, Stuart is a young boy who just happens to look like a mouse! Because of his diminutive stature Stuart gets into all kinds of wild and crazy adventures.

Reading chapter books such as *Stuart Little* helps to build a child's visualization skills and helps them to appreciate stories that are told over more than one sitting. By taking your child to the movie, you may be able to initiate a conversation about the similarities and differences between the chapter book and the movie version, as well as the similarities and differences between watching a movie and reading a story. Your child might also enjoy rereading the book with you at home. If you haven't ever read a chapter book to your child, *Stuart Little* might be just the right book for you to get started with.

Happy Reading (& movie-viewing),

Karleen Waldman

For anyone unfamiliar with *Stuart Little,* it's a charming 130-page novel by the same person who wrote the classic *Charlotte's Web.* Karleen Waldman understood that children are ready for chapter books long before most people think they are. Our continued exclusive reliance on four-minute picture books is an insult to their growing minds and attention spans. No, Ms. Waldman didn't begin the year with a novel, nor did she abandon picture books for chapters. She began with picture books and built the children's attention spans. By the end of the year, these same children had also heard *A Cricket in Times Square* by George Selden and *Mr. Popper's Penguins* by Florence and Richard Atwater. I'm not suggesting we abandon picture books. Instead, add a few novel pages and then a daily chapter to the picture books you read to preschoolers.

At What Age Do You Stop the Picture Books?

Although I understand the impatience to get on with the business of growing up, I wince whenever I hear that question. A good story is a good story, whether it has pictures or not. All those pictures in museums don't have a lot of words under them but they still move us, right?

I know nursery school teachers who read Judith Viorst's *Alexander and the Terrible, Horrible, No Good, Very Bad Day* to their classes, and I know a high school English teacher who reads it to his sophomores twice a year—first in September and again, by popular demand, in June. A picture book should be someplace on the reading list of every class at every grade level.

Many U.S. high school students were not read to regularly in middle grades and do little or no recreational reading on their own. I remember talking with a remedial class of ninth-graders in California one day. Of the twenty-one students, not one had ever heard of the Pied Piper, none had heard of the Wright brothers, and only two had heard of David and Goliath. Their mainstream cultural references were a bit shallow and ripe for planting.

Some recommendations to win over those who think older students won't respond to picture books include:

+ *Johnny on the Spot* by Edward Sorel. (Johnny and his adult neighbor accidentally invent a radio that broadcasts events one day in advance; the conflict arises when Johnny is sworn to secrecy and forbidden to interfere with the future—even if he knows a calamity is about to occur.)
+ *The Man Who Walked Between the Towers* by Mordicai Gerstein. (Winner of the 2003 Caldecott Award, this is the true story of the young Frenchman who strung a tightrope between the two unfinished towers of the World Trade Center in 1974 and walked between them for two hours during morning rush hour. The story focuses on that event and not on the 9/11 tragedy twenty-seven years later, although there is a fleeting reference to the fact that the towers are no more.)
+ *An Orange for Frankie* by Patricia Polacco. (A great story that happens to have pictures to go with it. In this tale from the author's family history, we have a family of nine on Christmas Eve, a father missing in a snowstorm, a boxcar of hungry and freezing hobos, one missing sweater, and a lost Christmas orange—all of it neatly tied into a happy holiday ending. This is as good as holiday stories get!)

Are There Pitfalls to Avoid in Choosing Long Novels?

The difference between short novels and full-length novels (I use approximately one hundred pages as a demarcation point) is sometimes found in the amount of description, the shorter ones having less detail, the longer ones requiring more imagination on the part of the listener-reader. Children whose imaginations have been atrophying in front of a television for years are not comfortable with long descriptive passages. But the more you read to them, the less trouble they have in constructing mental images. Indeed, research shows us that listening to stories stimulates the imagination significantly more than television or film.[19]

In approaching longer books, remember that all books are not meant to be read aloud; indeed, some books aren't even worth reading to yourself, never mind boring a family or class with them. Some books are written in a convoluted or elliptical style that can be read silently but not aloud.

One of the best rules on the difference between *listening* to text and *reading* text was defined by the great Canadian adult novelist Robertson Davies in the preface to a volume of his speeches. He asked readers to remember they were reading *speeches,* not essays: "What is meant to be heard is necessarily more direct in expression, and perhaps more boldly coloured, than what is meant for the reader."[20] This is a fact missed by many speakers, preachers, and professors who write their speeches as if the audience were going to read them instead of listen to them. Be sure to take Davies' advice into consideration when choosing your longer read-alouds.

Also be alert to the subject matter of the novels. With longer books, it is imperative for the adult to preview the text before reading it aloud. The length of such books allows them to treat subject matter that can be very sensitive, far more so than a picture book could. As the reader, you should first familiarize yourself with the subject and the author's approach. Ask yourself as you read it through: "Can my child or class handle not only the vocabulary and the complexity of this story, but its emotions as well? Is there anything here that will do more harm than good to my child or class? Anything that might embarrass someone?"

Along with enabling you to avoid that kind of damaging situation, reading the book ahead of time will enable you to read it the second time to the class or child with more confidence, accenting important passages, leaving out dull ones (I mark these lightly in pencil in the margins), and providing sound effects to dramatize the story line (I'm always ready to knock on a table or wall where the story calls for a "knock at the door").

What Makes a Good Read-Aloud?

For infants and young toddlers, the ideal read-aloud floats on its sounds— good rhythm and rhyme, lots of repetition, sounds that are silly or dramatic or exciting, and lots of splashy color, along with plenty of the familiar.

For a child aged two and a half to three, the idea of plot begins to creep in, but nothing too complicated: the lost puppy, the lost mitten. Good examples are *You Can Do It, Sam* by Amy Hest or Martin Waddell's bear cub series that includes *You and Me, Little Bear.* Language is still exciting and repetitious, if possible, but with a little more narrative. *Whistle for Willie* by Ezra Jack Keats is one example, because it has enough of a story to keep the very young interested and pleased when, in the end, the boy is able to master the art of whistling, something that can be demonstrated to the child listener.

Beginning at around age three, plot plays an increasingly important role in holding the child's or class's attention. What does the story add up to? What happens next? While we want to be involved with the characters, we still need to be pulled through the pages by this abstract thing called a plot—the wind beneath the story's wings.

The challenge arrives as the child approaches eight or nine years of age, and the literature takes on a more realistic tone. The plots begin to center on social and emotional issues, many of them growing more severe as the books creep into what is called "young adult" literature: divorce, incest, child abuse, death, substance abuse, and violence. None of those are new issues to literature—Dickens handled them all.

In choosing books that explore such issues, however, we must ensure they do so at an appropriate developmental level. What a thirteen-year-old can handle in a story may not be appropriate for a nine-year-old. There is a great advantage to having certain serious issues shared between an adult and a child or teachers and students because the adult can then serve as a guide through the pain of the book's events.

But we must also make the distinction, as children grow older, between books that are emotionally appropriate for *hearing* and those for *reading*. The subject matter of some books may be too personal to be shared out loud, especially in a classroom. It would have to be a highly unusual circumstance for me to read aloud to a class of teenagers a book that had incest as its central focus. What you might read one-on-one with a daughter or son could come across very differently in a public classroom.

A book that was the Newbery runner-up in 2003 and ranks as one of the best children's novels I've read in a long time would be a difficult one to use in some classrooms because of certain subject matter. It's *A Corner of the Universe* by Ann Martin (Scholastic)—yes, the same Ann Martin of *Babysitters Club* fame. The really good books are the ones that stay with you long after the cover has been closed, enveloping the reader in a cocoon of sounds, smells, and images. This is that kind of book. When Hattie turns twelve, she discovers she has an uncle she never knew she had. Uncle Adam, twenty-three, is mentally disabled and his special school is closing, so he's returning home to his parents (Hattie's grandparents) until a new location is found for him. Adam is an idiot-savant, able to recite every *I Love Lucy* script he's ever heard. His mind never stops, wandering impulsively from one subject to the next, very much like a little boy's. Hattie readily adopts him as her personal project, which provides some funny and some frightening moments. As she puts it, "I feel a little like his baby-sitter, a little like his mother, not at all like his niece, and quite a bit like his friend." Hattie's parents run a boarding house and Adam becomes innocently infatuated with a young female bank clerk residing there. When he accidentally barges in on a heavy petting scene between the girl and her "illegal" guest, the trauma, coupled with his frustration with his overbearing parents, causes him to commit suicide.

Far from being a depressing experience, this book is a celebration of one girl's life and family, a serious (though sometimes humorous) exploration of mental illness and one child's determination to make a difference in her corner of the universe—and she does. I miss having a daughter to share this book with—my daughter is forty-one now. We would have cried and laughed over this one and remembered it always, just as we have never forgotten *Caddie Woodlawn*.

Nonfiction will often read like a boring textbook unless there's a strong narrative to it. One of the publishing highlights of the last two decades has been the proliferation of outstanding picture books devoted to American history and containing a strong story line. Here are some that make excellent read-alouds:

Saving the Liberty Bell
   by Megan McDonald
The Flag Maker
   by Susan Campbell Bartoletti
Mary Anning and the Sea Dragon
   by Jeannine Atkins
The Dinosaurs of Waterhouse Hawkins
   by Barbara Kerley
The Boy Who Drew Birds: The Story of John James Audubon
   by Jacqueline Davies
The Bobbin Girl
   by Emily Arnold McCully
Thank You, Sarah
   by Laurie Halse Anderson

The Last Princess: The Story of Princess Ka'iulani of Hawai'i
   by Fay Stanley
Alice Ramsey's Grand Adventure
   by Don Brown
When Esther Morris Headed West: Women, Wyoming, and the Right to Vote
   by Connie Nordhielm
Liberty Rising: The Story of the Statue of Liberty
   by Pegi Deitz Shea
You're on Your Way, Teddy Roosevelt
   by Judith St. George
Odd Boy Out: Young Albert Einstein
   by Don Brown

Eleanor
  by Barbara Cooney
Baseball Saved Us
  by Ken Mochizuk
My Brother Martin
  by Christine King Farris

The Story of Ruby Bridges
  by Robert Coles
Harvesting Hope: The Story of
  Cesar Chavez
  by Kathleen Krull

When It's Obvious You've Made a Poor Choice of a Book, Is It Okay to Abandon It, or Parts of It, and Move On?

I know very learned people who are adamant that if you start a book, you finish it. In my mind, these are people who need either a second job or larger families. Instead, I side with those who will give a book several chapters before setting it aside. (And rather than drag the child through the boredom, read the first couple of chapters yourself before choosing it as a read-aloud.)

My support in this approach comes from Nancy Pearl, former executive director of the Washington Center for the Book, who conceived the "One Book, One City" movement that has swept many American cities and towns. In *Book Lust,* Pearl offers advice to adults that can apply to both reading to children and to children's own reading. She calls it the "Rule of 50": If you're fifty or younger, give every book about fifty pages. If you're over fifty, then subtract your age from one hundred and give it that many pages.[21]

Simply put, there's a limit to how much mental punishment anyone should have to endure from an author. If the book becomes an endurance test, it belongs in the Olympics, not on your bookshelf.

As for the long descriptive passages, I follow the Charles Dickens policy: When reading aloud, bowdlerize the text where needed. When the great author was reading aloud his texts to audiences, he used abbreviated versions, excising his own long descriptive passages. I always read ahead, and when I find long passages that slow things down, I put a small check mark out in the margin and skip that section when I read aloud.

Do Children Have to Follow Along in a Book as You Read Aloud?

No, not at all, and usually there aren't enough copies for everyone in the class. But following along in the text has proven to be very effective with remedial students. These students often need repeated readings, which wearies a parent or teacher but coincides perfectly with the recorder's purpose.

Back in the 1970s, a young graduate student named Marie Carbo[22] began recording stories and books for her students who were labeled learning disabled. Eventually she hit upon the idea of recording the stories at different paces—slower for the initial hearings and faster for subsequent hearings. Students followed along in their own books and as they became more confident selected the faster versions.

Describing a particular case, Dr. Carbo wrote:

> The greatest gain in word recognition was made by Tommy, a sixth-grade boy reading on a 2.2 level. Prior to working with the tapes he had faltered and stumbled over second-grade words while his body actually shook with fear and discomfort. Understandably, he hated to read. Because a beloved teacher had once read *Charlotte's Web* to him, he asked me to record his favorite chapter from the book. I recorded one paragraph on each cassette side so that Tommy could choose to read either one or two paragraphs daily. The first time that he listened to a recording (five times) and then read the passage silently to himself (twice), he was able to read the passage to me perfectly with excellent expression and without fear. After this momentous event, Tommy worked hard. At last he knew he was capable of learning to read and was willing to give it all he could. The result was a fifteen-month gain in word recognition at the end of only three months. Every learning-disabled child in the program experienced immediate success with her or his individually recorded books.[23]

Ellen Beck of Crosby, Texas, read about Marie Carbo's methods in an earlier edition of *The Read-Aloud Handbook* and thought it might be worth a try. Her librarian at Newport Elementary located a set of the Carbo tapes, and she set up shop with her students. Beck wrote to me:

> I had one student—let's call her Mary—who was officially removed from special education classes by parent request because her mother felt it wasn't benefitting her. She began the new year with me—and struggled. On her initial reading test, she scored only 25 percent. I was mortified and wondered how to help her. Her mother requested that we put her in the third-grade reader so she would be reading the same material as other children in her grade, and I'm forever grateful for that suggestion.

When I told my principal that I wanted to get cassettes and record stories, he suggested I target certain students and do a test run. I selected ten, including Mary. Using the tape approach, Mary scored 60 percent at the end of six weeks; in fact, the scores improved for all the students listening to the tapes. The principal approved buying two cassette players and five headsets (I'd been borrowing the library's), along with two hundred cassettes.

Mary's scores continued to climb. She was up to 70, 75, back to 70, then up to 89. She proudly read to the principal, who was a big encouragement to her, and continued to astound us all. Though other students' scores were improving as well, every child is different, and therefore their needs were different. Mary's needs were sight words. She was highly trained in phonics, but obviously it doesn't always help when you have a strange sight word. The recorded repetition of third-grade vocabulary was the perfect antidote for her problems. On the year-end Texas Assessment of Academic Skills (TAAS) test, she scored 97 percent, missing only one of thirty-six questions, and she did as well the following year.

Needless to say, I'm sold on taped stories, but ten minutes of SSR (with free choice of books) is basic to my classroom, and I read aloud to them daily.[24]

For more on audio books, see chapter 9.

Where Can I Find More Information About Authors?

I don't know of a single lifetime reader who doesn't have a favorite author or two or three. We seek them out in books, magazines, and newspapers. For years I bought certain New York newspapers just on the days when my favorite columnists were appearing. While too often in the past schools focused on dead authors, Oprah Winfrey's influence has been felt in recent years and more is being done with living authors.

The best resources for extensive author information are Something About the Author and its smaller partner, the Author Autobiography series (both from Gale and found in most large public libraries). The former is a series of more than one hundred volumes containing photos and documentation about almost anyone who has written or illustrated for children in the twentieth century. Other excellent resources: *Fifth Book of Junior Authors and Illustrators* (Wilson) and Anita Silvey's *Children's Books and Their Creators* (Houghton).

Of course these days there are very few authors who don't have their own Web sites, some personal, some hosted by their publishers, and some hosted by fans, as in the case of deceased authors such as C. S. Lewis. To find the author's Web site or biographical information, simply "Google" the name. Be aware, however, that not everything on the Internet is verified or true.

How Do I Get My Twelve-Year-Old to Sit Still Long Enough for a Story?

Try reading aloud while your child is eating breakfast or dessert. When Jamie and Elizabeth were teenagers, their household responsibilities alternated between setting the table and doing the dishes. And while they did the dishes, I read to them, usually from magazines, newspapers, or anthologies. If I came across an interesting article—maybe an obituary for a rock star or a *Time* magazine essay on hairstyles—that would be the night's reading; *Paul Harvey's The Rest of the Story* collections were also popular.

Whenever I show parent audiences this photograph of Jamie doing the dishes when he was in seventh grade, I get some strange looks, to which I respond: "Now, if you have a preteen or teen who *doesn't* do the dishes in your home, then the child's IQ is higher than yours. Not a good thing, folks."

Read-aloud selections don't even have to be books; short pieces work

The perfect time for a teenager to hear a read-aloud? While doing the dishes.

too. The ultimate objective is to make positive connections between the child and the reading experience to the point where he or she will ask, "Do you have any more books like that one?" Never mind any misgivings you might have about the title; check out *Uncle John's Great Big Bathroom Reader.* Everyone has a hard time resisting the short but true anecdotes included: thousands of articles covering history, politics, family, death, movies, science, law and order, and myths. They've just published a special edition called *Uncle John's Bathroom Reader for Kids Only!* See page 289 in the Treasury for details or look online at www.bathroomreader.com. For high school students, consider the Best American series that has been a showcase for America's best short fiction and nonfiction since 1915 when the series began. *Best American Nonrequired Reading* features current fiction, nonfiction, satire, investigative reporting, alternative comics, and more from a variety of publishing venues. If you want a sample of how good the writing can be, go online to read or print LA sportswriter Bill Plaschke's now famous essay on Sarah Morris, a cerebral palsy sufferer who is a baseball fan unlike any you may ever know (http:www.thestlcardinals.homestead.com/SarahMorris.html). Plaschke's story originally appeared in the *Los Angeles Times* and then was selected for *Best American Sports Stories 2002*.

And if you're looking for a fast-moving novel that will grab even the most reluctant teen audience, try Avi's *Wolf Rider* (see page 280 for a description).

What Should Be Our Goals in Reading to Teenagers?

Beyond eighth grade, the prime objective will usually be motivational. In some cases, you're planting seeds that will bear fruit with the students' future children. It might even be motivating enough to get students to class on time or more regularly. Consider the experience of Nancy Foote of Higley, Arizona, former recipient of the Presidential Award for Excellence in mathematics and science teaching, but a devotee of reading aloud and its impact on reluctant teens. As she explains it:

> I was a teacher for almost 20 years in traditional schools. For several years, I taught at an alternative high school. Many of my students were convicted felons who were on probation. Some of my students were on house arrest, allowed to leave home only to go to school. Many had drug addictions that they were fighting. They were wonderful kids who had bigger problems than I could ever imagine.
>
> We had a relatively long passing between classes, amounting to five minutes. Our campus was rather small, so there was no reason for kids to come late to class. Yet day after day they arrived late—sometimes just a minute or two, other times much longer. I wanted to find a way to motivate them to get to class on time. I thought about the book *Frindle* by Andrew Clements, a book I had heard

you talk about in your workshops. I wasn't sure if these kids would like the book—they were tough kids—but decided to give it a try.

Exactly three minutes before the tardy bell rang, I would begin reading aloud from the book. Once the tardy bell rang, I continued reading until I finished the chapter. At first, I felt sort of foolish. I was reading to a totally empty classroom! That was OK because I loved the story and Nick is one of my favorite characters. Within a few days, the kids started getting to class early so that they could hear about Nick. Within one week, I no longer had problems with tardy students. Once we finished *Frindle,* we moved on to *Loser* by Jerry Spinelli and then Clements's *Things Not Seen.*

Not only did reading aloud get my students to class on time, attendance improved. Whenever someone came back to school after being absent, they wanted to hear what they missed. Some would borrow the book and read it themselves, but most wanted to come in at lunch so I could read it to them. (These were not young children—they ranged in age from 13 to 19.) They couldn't wait to hear what happened next. They were eager to find out what our next story would be.

Near the end of the year, one of my students, a tall, gangly young man, came in to see me. He was 19 years old and fighting a crystal meth addiction. He was trying to raise his young son, since the baby's mother abandoned him in favor of drugs. He had an uphill battle, as did his infant son. In spite of his challenges, he made it to school most days, and kept off drugs. He thanked me for being a great teacher and helping him. He told me that my reading to them was wonderful and he really enjoyed it. He also told me that no one had ever read aloud to him—I was the first. And he promised he would read aloud to his son.[25]

Chapter 4

The Dos and Don'ts of Read-Aloud

The first and conceivably the most important instructor in composition is the teacher, parent, or older sibling who reads aloud to the small child.

—Clifton Fadiman,
*Empty Pages: A Search for Writing
Competence in School and Society*

Dos

♦ Begin reading to children as soon as possible. The younger you start them, the easier and better it is.
♦ Use Mother Goose rhymes and songs to stimulate an infant's language and listening. Begin with simple black-and-white illustrations at first, and then boldly colored picture books to arouse children's curiosity and visual sense.
♦ With infants through toddlers, it is critically important to include in your readings those books that contain repetitions; as they mature, add predictable and rhyming books.
♦ During repeat readings of a predictable book, occasionally stop at one of the key words or phrases and allow the listener to provide the word.
♦ Read as often as you and the child (or students) have time for.
♦ Set aside at least one traditional time each day for a story.
♦ Remember: the art of listening is an acquired one. It must be taught and cultivated gradually—it doesn't happen overnight.
♦ Start with picture books that have only a few sentences on the page;

then gradually move to books with more and more text, fewer pictures, and build to chapter books and novels.

♦ Vary the length and subject matter of your readings, fiction and non-fiction.

♦ To encourage involvement, invite the child to turn pages for you when it is time.

♦ Before you begin to read, always say the name of the book, the author, and the illustrator—no matter how many times you have read the book.

♦ The first time you read a book, discuss the illustration on the cover. Ask: "What do you think this is going to be about?"

♦ As you read, keep listeners involved by occasionally asking, "What do you think is going to happen next?"

♦ Follow through with your reading. If you start a book, it is your responsibility to continue it—unless it turns out to be a bad book. Don't leave the child or students hanging for three or four days between chapters and expect interest to be sustained.

♦ Occasionally read above children's intellectual levels and challenge their minds.

♦ Picture books can be read easily to a family of children widely separated in age. Novels, however, pose a challenge. If there are more than two years (and thus social and emotional differences) between the children, each child would benefit greatly if you read to him or her individually. This requires more effort on the part of the parents, but it will reap rewards in direct proportion to the effort expended. You will reinforce the specialness of each child.

♦ Avoid long descriptive passages until the child's imagination and attention span are capable of handling them. There is nothing wrong with shortening or eliminating them. Prereading helps to locate such passages, and they can then be marked with pencil in the margin.

♦ If the chapters are long or if you don't have enough time each day to finish an entire chapter, find a suspenseful spot at which to stop. Leave the audience hanging; they'll be counting the minutes until the next reading.

♦ Allow your listeners a few minutes to settle down and adjust their feet and minds to the story. If it's a novel, begin by asking what happened when you left off yesterday. Mood is an important factor in listening. An authoritarian "Now stop that and settle down! Sit up straight. Pay attention" doesn't create a receptive atmosphere.

♦ If you are reading a picture book, make sure the children can see the pictures easily. In school, with the children in a semicircle around you, seat yourself just slightly above them so that the children in the back row can see the pictures above the heads of the others.

♦ In reading a novel, position yourself where both you and the children are comfortable. In the classroom, whether you are sitting on the edge of your desk or standing, your head should be above the heads of your listeners for your voice to carry to the far side of the room. Do not read or stand in front of brightly lit windows. Backlighting strains the eyes of your audience.

♦ Remember that everyone enjoys a good picture book, even a teenager.

♦ Allow time for class and home discussion after reading a story. Thoughts, hopes, fears, and discoveries are aroused by a book. Allow them to surface and help the child to deal with them through verbal, written, or artistic expression if the child is so inclined. Do not turn discussions into quizzes or insist upon prying story interpretations from the child.

♦ Remember that reading aloud comes naturally to very few people. To do it successfully and with ease you must practice.

♦ Use plenty of expression when reading. If possible, change your tone of voice to fit the dialogue.

♦ Adjust your pace to fit the story. During a suspenseful part, slow down, and lower your voice. A lowered voice in the right place moves an audience to the edge of its chairs.

♦ The most common mistake in reading aloud—whether the reader is a seven-year-old or a forty-year-old—is reading too fast. Read slowly enough for the child to build mental pictures of what he just heard you read. Slow down enough for the children to see the pictures in the book without feeling hurried. Reading quickly allows no time for the reader to use vocal expression.

♦ Preview the book by reading it to yourself ahead of time. Such advance reading allows you to spot material you may wish to shorten, eliminate, or elaborate on.

♦ Bring the author to life, as well as his book. "Google" the author's name to find a personal Web page, and always read the information on your book's dust jacket. Either before or during the reading, tell your audience something about the author. This lets them know that books are written by people, not by machines.

♦ Add a third dimension to the book whenever possible. For example, have a bowl of blueberries ready to be eaten during or after the reading of Robert McCloskey's *Blueberries for Sal*; bring a harmonica and a lemon to class before reading McCloskey's *Lentil*.

♦ Every once in a while, when a child asks a question involving the text, make a point of looking up the answer in a reference book with the child. This greatly expands a child's knowledge base and nurtures library skills.

♦ Create a wall chart or back-of-the-bedroom-door book chart so the child or class can see how much has been read; images of caterpillars, snakes, worms, and trains work well for this purpose, with each link representing a book. Similarly, post a world or U.S. wall map on which small stickers can be attached to locations where your books have been set.

♦ When children are old enough to distinguish between library books and their own, start reading with a pencil in hand. When you and the child encounter a passage worth remembering, put a small mark—maybe a star—in the margin. Readers should interact with books, and one way is to acknowledge beautiful writing.

♦ Encourage relatives living far away to record stories on audiocassettes that can be mailed to the child.

♦ Reluctant readers or unusually active children frequently find it difficult to just sit and listen. Paper, crayons, and pencils allow them to keep their hands busy while listening. (You doodle while talking on the telephone, don't you?)

♦ Follow the suggestion of Dr. Caroline Bauer and post a reminder sign by your door: "Don't Forget Your *Flood* Book." Analogous to emergency rations in case of natural disasters, these books should be taken along in the car or even stored like spares in the trunk. A few chapters from "flood" books can be squeezed into traffic jams on the way to the beach or long waits at the doctor's office.

♦ Always have a supply of books for the babysitter to share with the child and make it understood that "reading aloud" comes with the job and is preferable to the TV.

♦ Fathers should make an extra effort to read to their children. Because the vast majority of primary-school teachers are women, young boys often associate reading with women and schoolwork. And just as unfortunately, too many fathers would rather be seen playing catch in the driveway with their sons than taking them to the library. It is not by chance that male school scores have taken a dramatic downturn in the last three decades. A father's early involvement with books and reading can do much to elevate books to at least the same status as sports in a boy's estimation.

♦ Arrange for time each day, in the classroom or in the home, for the child to read by himself (even if "read" only means turning pages and looking at the pictures). All your read-aloud motivation goes for naught if time is not available to put the acquired motivation into practice.

♦ Lead by example. Make sure your children see you reading for pleasure other than at read-aloud time. Share with them your enthusiasm for whatever you are reading.

+ When children wish to read to you, it is better for the book to be too easy than too hard, just as a beginner's bicycle is better too small rather than too big.
+ Encourage older children to read to younger ones, but make this a *part-time,* not a full-time, substitution for you. Remember: the adult is the *ultimate* role model.
+ Regulate the amount of time children spend in front of the television. Research shows that after about ten TV hours a week, a child's school scores begin to drop. Excessive television viewing is habit-forming and damaging to a child's development.
+ When children are watching television, closed-captioning should be activated along with sound. For older children who know how to read but are lazy about it, keep the captioning on and turn the volume down.

Don'ts

+ Don't read stories that you don't enjoy yourself. Your dislike will show in the reading, and that defeats your purpose.
+ Don't continue reading a book once it is obvious that it was a poor choice. Admit the mistake and choose another. Make sure, however, that you've given the book a fair chance to get rolling; some, like *Tuck Everlasting,* start slower than others. (You can avoid the problem by pre-reading at least part of the book yourself.)
+ If you are a teacher, don't feel you have to tie every book to class work. Don't confine the broad spectrum of literature to the narrow limits of the curriculum.
+ Don't overwhelm your listener. Consider the intellectual, social, and emotional level of your audience in making a read-aloud selection. Never read above a child's emotional level.
+ Don't select a book that many of the children already have heard or seen on television. Once a novel's plot is known, much of their interest is lost. You can, however, read a book and view the video afterward. That's a good way for children to see how much more can be portrayed in print than on film.
+ In choosing novels for reading aloud, avoid books that are heavy with dialogue; they are difficult for reading aloud *and* listening. All those indented paragraphs and quotations make for easy *silent* reading. The reader sees the quotations marks and knows it is a new voice, a different person speaking—but the listener doesn't. And if the writer fails to include a notation at the end of the dialogue, such as "said Mrs. Murphy," the audience has no idea who said what.

♦ Don't be fooled by awards. Just because a book won an award doesn't guarantee that it will make a good read-aloud. In most cases, a book award is given for the quality of the writing, not for its read-aloud qualities.

♦ Don't start reading if you are not going to have enough time to do it justice. Having to stop after one or two pages only serves to frustrate, rather than stimulate, the child's interest in reading.

♦ Don't get too comfortable while reading. A reclining or slouching position is most apt to bring on drowsiness. A reclining position sends an immediate message to the heart: slow down. With less blood being pumped, less oxygen reaches the brain—thus drowsiness.

♦ Don't be unnerved by questions during the reading, particularly from very young children in your own family. If the question is obviously not for the purpose of distracting or postponing bedtime, answer the question patiently. There is no time limit for reading a book, but there is a time limit on a child's inquisitiveness. Foster that curiosity with patient answers—then resume your reading. Classroom questions, however, need to be held until the end. With twenty children all deciding to ask questions to impress the teacher, you might never reach the end of the book.

♦ Don't impose interpretations of a story upon your audience. A story can be just plain enjoyable, no reason necessary, and still give you plenty to talk about. The highest literacy gains occur with children who have access to discussions following a story.

♦ Don't confuse quantity with quality. Reading to your child for ten minutes, with your full attention and enthusiasm, may very well last longer in the child's mind than two hours of solitary television viewing.

♦ Don't use the book as a threat ("If you don't pick up your room, no story tonight!"). As soon as your child or class sees that you've turned the book into a weapon, they'll change their attitude about books from positive to negative.

♦ Don't try to compete with television. If you say, "Which do you want, a story or TV?" they will usually choose the latter. That is like saying to a nine-year-old, "Which do you want, vegetables or a donut?" Since *you* are the adult, *you* choose. "The television goes off at eight-thirty in this house. If you want a story before bed, that's fine. If not, that's fine, too. But no television after eight-thirty." But don't let books appear to be responsible for depriving the children of viewing time.

Chapter 5

Sustained Silent Reading: Reading Aloud's Natural Partner

> An unread story is not a story; it is little black marks on
> wood pulp.
>
> —Ursula LeGuin

AMONG the many purposes of reading aloud, a primary one is to motivate the child to read independently for pleasure. In academic terms, such reading is called SSR—sustained silent reading. Take a book, a newspaper, a magazine, and enjoy it! No interruptions for questions, assessments, or reports; just read for pleasure. The concept operates under a variety of pseudonyms, including DEAR (drop everything and read), DIRT (daily individual reading time), SQUIRT (sustained quiet uninterrupted reading time), and FVR (free voluntary reading).

This chapter will be devoted to SSR in school as well as at home. I'll also examine a variety of topics associated with silent reading: reading incentive programs (like Accelerated Reader and Reading Counts), teachers' reading habits, junk reading, and "summer setback."

Because we adults have done this thing called reading for so much of our lives, we take many of its facets for granted. Children do not, as evidenced by the story told to me by Lee Sullivan Hill, of Clarendon Hills, Illinois. One day her young son Colin came upon her reading silently to herself and asked, "What are you doing?"

"Reading," she answered.

"Then why aren't you making any noise?"

So she explained how people read *to themselves* as well as to others, like when she reads to him. Hearing that, the light dawned for Colin. "So *that's* what Daddy does!" recalling when he had seen his father reading silently to himself—in fact, practicing SSR. Until it is explained, silent reading is sometimes a mystery to young children. Apparently, it's also a mystery to some school administrators. Here is the exact wording from an evaluation done by the principal of an eighth-grade language arts teacher who had included a forty-minute SSR period in her students' weekly schedule (as prescribed by the school improvement plan): "I see a great deal of free reading taking place in your classroom. I realize the students are working on assigned reading, however I feel that much of the reading taking place in the classroom could take place out of the class. This would allow you more time to interact with the students. Decisions as to how class time is used must be sound if our students are going to be successful later on."

Here's how would I respond to that principal:

1. SSR works as well as any other method and the research proves it (see page 83).
2. It's almost impossible to interact with students about literature they haven't read—so they're reading it.
3. The students who are the least likely to read outside school are the ones who either hate reading and/or come from homes where there is the least space and quiet for solitary reading; my classroom is a clinic where such reading ills can be cured.
4. There is a natural fall-off in recreational reading during adolescence due to the hormonal and social conflict inflicted on their twenty-four-hour day; this is most often reflected in how badly they use their out-of-school time, so I'm providing structured time for reading.
5. My classroom may be the *only* place where some of them ever see other people reading silently to themselves, and it might be the *only* place they ever see an adult reading for pleasure and not just for work. My classroom is a laboratory for positive role modeling.

But Didn't the National Reading Panel Condemn SSR or Independent Reading?

"Condemn" is a little harsh, but the panel didn't exactly give an unqualified endorsement to it, and that bumped the practice from some districts afraid of losing federal funds. In a nutshell, here's the scoop on the NRP versus SSR.

The National Reading Panel's 2000 report noted that there wasn't sufficient scientific evidence to support SSR's use in school, especially if it is being used as the *only* method of instruction.[1] Now, I know of no one in their right mind who is advocating that SSR be the *only* way to teach reading, any more than I would advocate that the only way to learn a foreign language is by doing workbook exercises and taking tests. There needs to be some instruction, but you also need to get out and speak the language with others—which is the equivalent of what SSR does for the reader. How can anyone imagine students could get better at reading without reading and reading a lot?

The NRP study subgroup deemed only fourteen short-term studies worthy of their disputed[2] "medical-scientific" standards and found insufficient evidence among them to support SSR, even though SSR students performed the *same* as ten of the control groups and surpassed the control groups in the four remaining studies. Not a negative SSR performance in their fourteen "scientific" studies, but this was not convincing enough for the NRP.

As the good folks at Merck Pharmaceuticals will tell you these days, short-term studies are far less reliable than long-term studies, especially when dealing with things "medical-scientific." Which brings us to Stephen Krashen, the leading proponent for inclusion of independent reading in the classroom schedule. This professor emeritus from the University of Southern California has thoroughly refuted the NRP's claims, as have a host of other qualified reading authorities.[3] Krashen examined not fourteen short-term SSR studies, as the NRP did, but a total of fifty-three studies, long ones and short ones. The chart below shows the results when broken down by study duration; overwhelmingly the results favor SSR, especially for yearlong studies. As you can see, the only three negative results for SSR were in short-duration studies, compared to twenty-five positive results. If that were a baseball or football score (25–3), could it be more decisive?

Sustained Silent Reading (SSR) Study Results

DURATION	Positive	No Difference	Neg.
Less than 7 mos.	8	14	3
7 mos.–1 year	9	10	
Greater than 1 yr.	8	2	

SOURCE: Stephen Krashen, *The Power of Reading*

Where do these negative SSR feelings come from? Perhaps from the wonderful folks who make all those workbooks, textbooks, and score sheets that wouldn't be bought and used in class during the time students were lounging around reading books, magazines, and newspapers and getting so good at reading they might need even fewer of those sheets next year.

SSR is based upon a single simple principle: Reading is a skill—and the more you use it, the better you get at it. Conversely, the less you use it, the more difficult it is.[4]

In 2002, the OECD, an international organization that for decades has helped its thirty-two governments monitor school achievement worldwide, issued a report called *Reading for Change,*[5] in which it examined the reading literacy of 250,000 fifteen-year-olds in the thirty-two countries. In every country, those who read the most read the best regardless of income level (see chart on page 95). A decade earlier, a similar study by the International Association for the Evaluation of Educational Achievement (IEA) compared the reading skills of 210,000 students from thirty-two different countries; it found the highest scores (regardless of income level) among children:[6]

♦ Who were read to by their teachers daily
♦ Who read the most pages for pleasure daily

Moreover, the frequency of SSR had a marked impact on scores: Children who had it daily scored much higher than those who had it only once a week. American NAEP assessments found the identical pattern for the nearly thirty-five years the NAEP has been testing hundreds of thousands of U.S. students.[7] The evidence for reading aloud to children *and* SSR is overwhelming—yet most children are neither read to nor experience SSR in the course of a school day.

During several years at the end of the 1990s, I surveyed 2,887 teachers from approximately thirty states, in every region of the country. These teachers averaged fourteen years' experience, and 95 percent taught elementary grades—the most critical years for reading. Among the questions I asked: Does their school have any form of SSR in place as a matter of school policy? The response was 60 percent no, 40 percent yes. Considering the overwhelming evidence in favor of SSR for ten to fifteen minutes a day, how can two-thirds of educators ignore it and still expect scores to rise?

Is SSR a New Idea?

Originally proposed in the early 1960s by Lyman C. Hunt Jr., of the University of Vermont, SSR received some of its most important support from the research of reading experts Robert and Marlene McCracken.[8] After experimenting with a variety of techniques and schools, the McCrackens recommend the following structures for SSR programs:

1. Children should read to themselves for a *limited* amount of time. Teachers and parents should adapt this to their individual class or family and adjust it with increasing maturity. Ten or fifteen minutes is the common choice for the classroom.
2. Each student should select his own book, magazine, or newspaper. No changing during the period is permitted. All materials must be chosen before the SSR period begins.
3. The teacher or parent must read also, setting an example. This cannot be stressed too strongly.
4. No reports are required of the student. No records are kept.

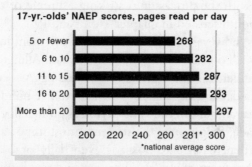

Those who read the most, read the best.

Source: U.S. Department of Education, NAEP, 2004, *Long-Term Trend Reading Assessment.*

The single most interesting and comprehensive study ever done on SSR is Stephen Krashen's *The Power of Reading.*[9] It is inconceivable that anyone could read this book and *not* resolve to incorporate SSR into the school day. If I could require one professional book to be read by all teachers and librarians, *The Power of Reading* would be my choice.

What Are the Exact Benefits of SSR?

The benefits vary with the individual, but in its simplest form SSR allows a person to read long enough and far enough that the act of reading becomes automatic. If one must stop to concentrate on each word—sounding it out and searching for meaning—then fluency is lost along with meaning. It is also fatiguing. Being able to do it automatically is the goal.[10] To achieve this, the Commission on Reading (in *Becoming a Nation of Readers*) recommended two hours a week of independent reading. Where do you find that time? The commission recommended less time be spent on skill sheets and workbooks.[11]

Because it is supposed to be informal and free of grades, SSR also provides students with a new perspective on reading—as a form of recreation. Judging from educated adults who come home each evening and think they can only relax by watching television, there is a critical need for such lessons in childhood.

On the secondary level, SSR may not cause an immediate or short-term change in student skills (no "quick fix"), but it can result in positive changes in attitude toward the library, voluntary reading, assigned reading, and the importance of reading. This affects the amount students read and thus their facility with the process.[12] A striking example of this is Lewenberg Middle School, discussed in chapter 1 on page 19.

Younger readers, however, show significant improvement in both attitude and skills with SSR. "Poor readers," points out Richard Allington,[13] a leading researcher and president of the International Reading Association, "when given ten minutes a day to read, initially will achieve five hundred words and quickly increase that amount in the same period as proficiency grows."[14]

By the third grade, SSR can be the student's most important vocabulary builder, more so than basal textbooks or even daily oral language. The Commission on Reading noted: "Basal readers and textbooks do not offer the same richness of vocabulary, sentence structure, or literary form as do trade books. . . . A diet consisting only of basal stories probably will not prepare children well to deal with real literature."[15] Indeed, about half of the three thousand most commonly used words are not even included in K–6 basals.[16] As shown in the chart on page 16, printed material introduces three to six times more rare words than conversation does.

What Would Cause SSR to Fail?

The McCrackens report that most instances where SSR fails are due to:

- ◆ Teachers (or aides) who are supervising instead of reading
- ◆ Classrooms that lack enough SSR reading materials

The McCrackens cite the teacher as a critical role model in SSR, reporting widespread imitation by students of the teacher's reading habits.[17]

Students in one class noticed the teacher interrupting her reading to look up words in the dictionary and began doing the same. When a junior high teacher began to read the daily newspaper each day, the class began doing the same.

Here's an example of an entire nation that practiced SSR successfully for four decades and then ran into a snag. As a reading model, Japan has been unrivaled in the world. Its citizens consume enormous amounts of print, and lead the world in newspaper readership (64 percent of Japanese adults read a daily newspaper, compared to 23 percent in the United States).[18] Few outsiders, however, understand the reason behind the Japanese numbers: time. No, they get the same twenty-four hours everyone else gets, but they get them in different doses.

Japan's highway tolls have long been among the highest in the world. A U.S. toll of $14 would be $47 in Japan, unless there's a bridge to cross, and then it jumps to $97. The result is that almost everyone in Japan takes public transportation to work, commutes that often average an hour each way.[19] This allows for 120 uninterrupted daily minutes of either reading or napping. All that time and all that reading put Japan at the top of book, magazine, and newspaper consumption—that is, until the mid-1990s.

That's when Japanese readership began to drop, and it continues to drop.[20] The cause was the arrival of what they call the "thumb tribe"—commuters with computer games, e-mail, cell phones, and laptops. In short, distractions.

The more distractions confronting a nation, a family, or a class, the less reading is accomplished. If you really want to get more reading done, then take control of your distractions: needless trips to the mall, land phones and cell phones, multiple televisions, DVD players, e-mail, computer games—each calling for immediate attention or multitasking. The "thumb tribe" is flourishing in America as well.

What About Summer-School Reading Programs?

Further proof of SSR's benefits is found in the research on "summer setback." Many parents, especially those whose children are having difficulty with school, see summertime as a school vacation and take it literally: "Everyone needs a vacation, for goodness' sake. He needs to get away from school and relax. Next year will be a new start." That attitude can be extremely detrimental, especially to a poor reader.

There is an axiom in education that "you get dumber in the summer." A two-year study of three thousand students in Atlanta, Georgia, attempted to see if it was true. They found that *everyone*—top students and

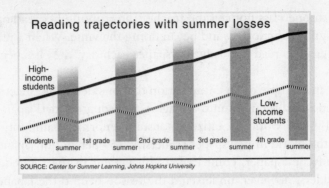

Reading trajectories with summer losses

High-income students

Low-income students

Kindergtn.   1st grade   2nd grade   3rd grade   4th grade
summer   summer   summer   summer   summer

SOURCE: *Center for Summer Learning, Johns Hopkins University*

poor students—learns more slowly in the summer. Some, though, do worse than slow down; they actually go into *reverse,* as you can see in the figure above.[21]

Top students' scores rise slightly between the end of one school year and the beginning of the next. Conversely, the bottom 25 percent (largely urban poor) lose most of what they gained the previous school year. Average students (the middle 50 percent) make no gains during the summer but lose nothing either—except in the widening gap between themselves and the top students. Projected across the first four years of school, the "rich-poor" reading gap that was present at the start of kindergarten has actually widened.

Many factors cause the loss. The affluent child's summer includes: a family of readers who model that behavior and offer quiet spaces conducive to reading; a home that is print-rich with books, magazines, and newspapers; visits to the mall with stops at the bookstore or library; a family vacation or summer camp out of town in which new people, places, and experiences extend background knowledge and offer new vocabulary; and a high probability that educational or informational TV and radio will be seen and heard.

Conversely, the at-risk child's summer includes: a home *without* books, magazines, or newspapers, and without adults who read avidly; no car by which to leave a dangerous neighborhood; no bookstores or convenient library; a daily routine in which the child seldom meets new people, new experiences, or new vocabulary, thus no growth in background knowledge; and little likelihood that educational or informational TV or radio will be seen or heard.

The adage "If you don't use it, you lose it" proves true for children who live these kinds of summers. Without printed material and without new experiences, the reading skills grow rusty and atrophy.

How can you prevent the traditional summer reading gap? The research gives little support to traditional summer school but a great deal to summer *reading*—reading *to* the child and reading *by* the child. Jimmy Kim's study of 1,600 sixth-graders in eighteen schools showed that the reading of four to six books during the summer was enough to alleviate summer loss. He further noted that when schools required either a report or essay to be written about a book read during the summer or that parents verify the student had read one summer book, this greatly increased the chances of its being read.[22]

Most libraries have summer reading incentive programs, so make sure your child is enrolled and participates. And take your child on field trips— even if you just visit local places like a fire station, the museum, or the zoo—and talk and listen. One of the most original solutions I've heard is this one from Paul E. Barton, senior associate in the Policy Evaluation and Research Center at Educational Testing Service (ETS), and someone who has researched and written extensively on the subject of poverty and schooling from preschool to prisons.[23] Barton knows full well the scarcity of books in the lives of poor children, and it provoked him to tell *USA Today* that at-risk communities should be making bookmobiles or traveling libraries "as ubiquitous as the Good Humor man."[24]

Will SSR Work in the Home as Well?

The same SSR principles apply in the home as in the classroom. Indeed, considering that by the end of eighth grade, a child has spent only 9,000 hours in school compared to 95,000 outside school, it behooves parents to involve themselves in home SSR before they challenge a teacher on "why Jesse isn't doing better in reading this year." On page 107 in chapter 6, you will find a testimonial letter from a mother and classroom teacher, Teresa Heitmiller Olea, who put SSR to work with her reluctant remedial-reader son.

But remember, if the classroom teacher is pivotal, so, too, is the parent; don't tell your child to go read for fifteen minutes while *you* watch television. You can, of course, tailor SSR to fit your family. For children who are not used to reading for more than brief periods of time, it is important at first to limit SSR to ten or fifteen minutes. Later, when they are used to reading in this manner and are more involved in books, the period can be extended—often at the child's request. As in the classroom, it is important to have a variety of available material—magazines, newspapers, novels, picture books. A weekly trip to the library can do much to fill this need. Three decades of NAEP research along with a thirty-two-nation study of 250,000 teens showed that the more kinds of reading material in a home, the higher the child's reading scores in school (see figure on page 95).[25] I should also note that the Three Bs (books, book baskets, and bed lamps) I mentioned earlier are invaluable to the success of family SSR.

The time selected for family SSR is also important. Involve everyone in the decision, if possible. Bedtime seems to be the most popular time, perhaps because the child does not have to give up any activity for it except sleeping—and most children gladly surrender that. But some children are too tired to read with engagement, so you need to take that into account as well.

Won't Requiring Children to Read Eventually Turn Them Off?

When I'm doing a parent program, I ask: "How many of you have ever *forced* a child to do something—like pick up his room or brush his teeth?" The question receives a positive response from 90 percent of the audience.

I continue, "We can all concede that it's easier for everyone involved if the child can be *enticed* instead of forced into doing those things, but sometimes we haven't the time, choice, or patience. Now let's take it further: How many of you think you should ever force a child to *read*?" Far fewer hands go up.

The reason parents avoid forcing reading is fear that the child will grow to hate reading and eventually stop. How true is that? Take ten-year-olds who are forced to brush their teeth or change their underwear—do they stop doing those things when they grow up? No. So why do we think forcing children to read will kill the love of reading?

Of course, the better word to use here is *require,* as opposed to *force.* Nearly all children are *required* to attend school, and all adults are *required* to observe the speed limit, but few end up hating it because of the requirement. The way to take the sting out of the "requirement" is to make the requirement so appealing and delicious that it becomes a pleasure—and that's where reading aloud comes into play.

In chapter 9, I share the story of Sonya Carson, a single parent who required her two sons to obtain library cards and read two books a week. Today one is an engineer and the other is a preeminent pediatric brain surgeon. Dr. Michael DeBakey, the man who invented the Mobile Army Surgical Hospital (MASH) and led the crusade to create the National Library of Medicine, now the world's greatest medical archive, was required to read a book a week as a child.

Children don't have a chance for higher levels of achievement without high-level reading skills. Where nothing is asked, usually nothing is received. In offices where punctuality is not required, people seldom arrive on time. So how to require reading and keep it pleasure-oriented? First, remember that pleasure is more often caught than taught (that means—read aloud to them). Next:

- Make sure you, the adult role model, are seen reading daily. It works even better if you read at the same time as the child.
- For young children, looking at the pictures in books and turning pages qualifies as "reading."
- Allow children to choose the books they wish to read to themselves, even if they don't meet your high standards.
- Set some time parameters, short at first and longer as children get older and read more.
- Newspapers and magazines should count toward reading time.

The self-selection, self-interest factor is important here. Let children read what interests them. Those school summer reading lists require them to read what interests the faculty.

If this idea of a reading requirement still puts you off, think about this: if you require a child to pick up his room or brush his teeth but *don't* require him to read, then it's obvious you think household and personal hygiene are more important than the child's brain.

What About Those Computerized "Reading Incentive" Programs?

Twenty-five years ago when *The Read-Aloud Handbook* was first published, the idea of computerized reading-incentive/reading management programs would have sounded like science fiction. Today it is one of the most hotly debated concepts among both educators and parents: Should children read for "intrinsic" rewards (the pleasure of the book) or should they be enticed to read for "extrinsic" rewards—prizes or rewards (or grades)?

Advantage Learning System's Accelerated Reader and Scholastic's Reading Counts, the two incentive industry leaders, work this way: The school library contains a core collection of popular and traditional children's books, each rated by difficulty (the harder the book, the more points it has). Accompanying the books is a computer program that poses questions after the student has read the book. Passing the computer quiz earns points for the student reader, which can be redeemed for prizes like school T-shirts, privileges, or items donated by local businesses. Both programs strongly endorse SSR as an integral part of their program and require substantial library collections. Both Accelerated Reader and Reading Counts have expanded their scope beyond "incentives" to include substantial student management and assessment tools, with Accelerated Reader having the largest customer base nationally.

Before going forward with this subject, I must note, in the spirit of full disclosure, that I have been a paid speaker at three Accelerated Reader national conventions. I spoke on the subjects of reading aloud, SSR, and home/school communication problems, topics I have addressed at conventions for nearly all the major education conferences, from the International Reading Association (IRA) and the American Library Association (ALA) to the National Association for the Education of Young Children (NAEYC).

I have written and spoken both favorably and negatively about these computerized programs, but in recent years I've grown increasingly uneasy with the way they are being used by districts. Too often these days I see them being abused in ways similar to basketball, for example. In its original form, Dr. James Naismith was trying to create a form of "indoorsy" exercise that would have an "outdoorsy" flavor to it. He invented basketball less than three miles from the home I'm sitting in right now. A century later, some people still use it as a form of exercise, some a form of sport, and then others take it to another level and turn it into a local obsession— maybe even a form of legalized child abuse—while warping the original intention of the sport. I don't have to spell out those towns, cities, and states.

When I survey my seminar audiences nationally, I am meeting an increasing number of dedicated educators and librarians who are alarmed by the way these programs are being used. The original design was a kind of "carrot-on-a-stick"—using points and prizes to lure reluctant readers to read more. For a while the big complaint from critics was about these points or incentives. But I didn't have a problem with that as long as the rewards didn't get out of hand (and some have). As for incentives, my family's been benefiting from those frequent traveler "point programs" for decades. Every professional athlete, every CEO, and most sales reps have incentive clauses in their contracts. Who says this is bad business?

The real problem, as I see it, arrived when districts bought the programs with the idea that they would *absolutely* lift reading scores. "Listen," declares the school board member, "if we're spending fifty grand on this program that's supposed to raise scores, then how can we allow it to be *optional*? You know the kids who'll never opt for it—the ones with the low scores, who drag everyone else's scores down. No—it's gotta be mandatory participation." And to cement it into place, the district makes the point system 25 percent of the child's grade for a marking period. Oooops! They just took the "carrot" off the stick, leaving just the stick—a new grading weapon. Do you see the basketball connection now?

Here is a scenario that has been painted by more than a few irate librarians (school and public) in affluent districts that are using the computerized programs:

> The parent comes into the library looking desperately for a "seven-point book."
>
> "What kind of book does your son like to read?" asks the librarian.
>
> The parent replies impatiently, "Doesn't matter. He needs seven more points to make his quota for the marking period, which ends this week. Give me anything."

In cases like that, we're just back to same ol' same ol': "I need a book for a book report. But it's due on Friday—so it can't have too many pages."

The only time the incentives really work on attitudes is when participation is voluntary. It's the equivalent of the difference between "enlistees" in the Army and "draftees." There's a big difference in their attitudes: one is in for a career, the other is in for as little time and work as possible.

As for the research supporting the computerized programs, that's hotly contested with no long-term studies with adequate control groups. True, the students read more, but is that because the district has poured all that money into school libraries and added SSR to the daily schedule? Where's the research to compare twenty-five "computerized" classes with twenty-five classes that have rich school and classroom libraries and daily SSR in the schedule? So far, it's not there.[26]

Believe it or not, high reading scores have been achieved in communities without computerized incentive programs, places where there are first-class school and classroom libraries, where the teachers motivate children by reading aloud to them, give book talks, and include SSR/DEAR time as an essential part of the daily curriculum. And the money that would have gone to the computer programs went instead to building a larger library collection. Unfortunately, such instances are rare. Where the scores are low, often so is the teacher's knowledge of children's literature, the library collection is meager to dreadful, and drill and skill supplant SSR/ DEAR time. (Consider the blight of empty bookshelves in urban and rural schools noted in chapter 7.)

Are There Any Other Negatives Associated with These Computerized Programs?

Here are some serious negatives to guard against:[27]

♦ Some teachers and librarians have stopped reading children's and young adult books because the computer will ask the questions instead.
♦ Class discussion of books decreases because a discussion would give away test answers, and all that matters is the electronic score.
♦ Students narrow their book selection to only those included in the program (points).
♦ In areas where the "points" have been made part of either the grade or classroom competition, some students attempt books far beyond their level and end up frustrated.

Before committing precious dollars to such a program, a district must decide its purpose: is it there to motivate children to read more or to create another grading platform?

My Daughter Is Very Much into Magazines. Do They Count?

I'm sorry to be the first to tell you this, ma'am, but your daughter is "engaged." But not the way you're thinking. "Engagement" is one of the hot new terms in reading research these days. Reading engagement includes asking: How deeply involved is the student in reading? How often does the student read? For how long? Which kinds of text are read—books? magazines? newspapers? comics? How much pleasure (if any) does the student find in it or is it always done as work? Taken collectively, these offer a very accurate gauge of how "engaged" the student is in reading. Metaphorically speaking, it's the "want to" factor in reading, unmeasured by standardized testing but a giant impetus for voluntarily reading in the 7,800 annual hours outside school. The psychological term for this is "flow," and the athletic term is "zone"—when individuals are so immersed in what they're doing they forget the time and seem to be floating in space.[28]

The OECD's 2002 study of fifteen-year-olds in thirty-two countries measured the effect of student engagement on reading literacy: the higher the engagement, the higher the scores; the lower the engagement, the lower the scores.[29] What parts of the engagement formula were important? The best readers read from the widest variety of texts and read longest from the deepest material—books—that require (and nurture) longer attention spans. Those who read less fiction but lots of comic books, newspapers, and magazines didn't finish at the top but were a close second. Thus all kinds of reading count (fiction being highest), as long as it is done often. The greater the variety of print in the home, the higher the student score (and vice versa). A larger number of *books* also led to higher scores and to more reading diversity and greater interest.

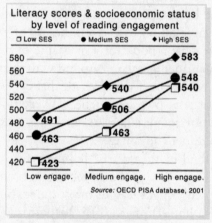

As "engagement" levels increase,
so also do reading scores, even for
students at the lowest income levels.

As seen in the figure above, students from lower income families tended to have lower scores, but when they were highly engaged (motivated) readers, they scored higher than students from the highest income levels who were poorly engaged readers and very close to the most engaged middle income students. Thus, high reading engagement is capable of vaulting the lowest SES student to significantly higher scores and overcoming family culture. Motivation (which pushes frequency) is therefore a critical factor in elevating the at-risk readers.

How Can Reading a Newspaper or Magazine Make You Smarter?

Back in the 1980s, Dr. Max Cowan, a world-renowned neurobiologist, was invited to speak with some congressional aides about the structure of the brain. Figuring most of them had never seen an actual brain, he grabbed a postmortem specimen, wrapped it in plastic, and headed off to Capitol Hill. However, when security opened his briefcase and came across the brain, there was considerable alarm. When Cowan patiently explained that it was just a brain, the guards asked warily, "What are you going to do with it?"

"It's like this," he explained. "My colleagues here come from sophisticated places like Boston and New York. I come from the Midwest . . . I feel I need all the help I can get, so I always carry a spare."[30]

Beyond the humor of that situation, an extra brain would certainly give a person an advantage, especially if you could hand-pick the brain. Imagine how helpful it would be in taking a test. If only there were a way to carry a spare brain, not too large, mind you, about the size of a—paperback book!

And that's exactly what a book (or a magazine or newspaper) amounts to: a spare brain. The reader is walking around with the brain of the author stuffed into a back pocket or a purse. With that arrangement, you're no longer limited to just your own experiences. Every time you read, you're tapping into the author's experiences, tomorrow a different author, a different brain. It's the reader's advantage.

My mother was fond of the adage "Tell me who your friends are and I'll tell you who you are." She used it to caution her four sons against associating with people who might lead us into trouble. But it also works in a positive way. I have a librarian friend, Jan Lieberman, who, when I'm in her company, leaves me exhaustingly stimulated about books and theater and food and music and libraries. Each of us is a product of the people we "hang around with," and if we make room in our lives for people who are smarter than we are, we make ourselves better.

The easiest self-improvement is through reading. On average, I spend one hour a day reading the *New York Times* and *USA Today*. In so doing, I'm hanging around with some of the most knowledgeable people in journalism. These reporters, in turn, are hanging around with some of the most knowledgeable people in their respective circles, and I'm allowed to eavesdrop on their conversations—about politics and war and sports and theater and movies and books. All for about two dollars a day. Is that great or what? (I should add that associating with this crowd can be very humbling; every day I'm reminded how little I know about a great many things.

But it means there's more to learn and more incentive to read! Even as a grown-up!)

And one of the best parts of being able to "hang out" with smarter people is that the experience is entirely *portable*. When I'm standing in line at the bank or sitting in a coffee shop, out comes a book. The people in the next booth at a restaurant in Union City, California, might have thought I was eating alone that February night in 2005, but they were wrong. I was dining with Carl Erskine, the old Brooklyn Dodgers pitcher, who was telling me how Jackie Robinson helped him cope when a Down syndrome child entered his family.[31] The folks in the next booth couldn't see Erskine and Robinson, but I could—they were right there on the newspaper page in front of me. In twenty-five years of traveling the lecture circuit, I've never dined alone, as long as I had a book, magazine, or newspaper—my personal mental health spa.

The frequent-flyer programs I mentioned earlier are a perfect analogy for SSR. Much of the at-risk student's improvement (see figure on page 95) is attributable to a kind of frequent-reader program. As a student finds more pleasure in reading, he reads more frequently—which increases the student's reading scores. All the while the accrued time on task (mileage points) earns him a free trip (out of his neighborhood). Through his readings, the student is meeting and hanging out with a more educated crowd. This helps vocabulary, background knowledge, and attitudes, which further lifts reading scores. If you're keeping score at home, this is more beneficial than an airline mileage program.

How Do I Stop Them from Reading "Junk" During SSR?

I will address part of the "junk" issue in chapter 8 with the issue of "series" books, but there is another aspect that fits into SSR—what Krashen calls "lite" reading. Series books usually fit this category because they're accessible, having both simple sentence structure and simple plots.

With that in mind, Krashen and graduate student Kyung-Sook Cho decided to try series books with adults for whom English is a second language (ESL).[32] They selected four immigrant women, three Korean and one Hispanic, whose ages were thirty, twenty-three, thirty-five, and twenty-one. Their average residency in the United States was 6.5 years. The oldest of the four was a thirty-five-year-old Korean who had majored in English in college and had taught it for three years in a high school. None of them, however, felt confident enough with English to speak it unless it was required, and most did little or no recreational reading in English.

Wishing to combine the women's low reading levels with interesting text, the researchers chose the grade-two level books in the Sweet Valley High series, called Sweet Valley Kids (seventy pages each). After being given some background information about the series and characters, the women were simply asked to read the books during their free time for several months. Occasional discussions took place between one of the researchers and the women, to answer any questions they might have, but for the most part they were comprehending what they read.

The response was just as anticipated. "All four women became enthusiastic readers. Mi-ae reported she read eight Sweet Valley Kids books during one month; Su-jin read eighteen volumes in two months; Jin-hee (the English major) read twenty-three in a little less than a month; and Alma (Hispanic) read ten volumes over a two-week period. Two of the women read as many words per month as would a native-born student."

All became very fond of the series. "This is the first experience in which I wanted to read a book in English continuously," said one woman. The one who had taught English in high school said, "I read the Sweet Valley series with interest and without the headache that I got when reading *Time* magazine in Korea. Most interestingly, I enjoyed reading the psychological descriptions of each character." She went on to read thirty Kids volumes, along with seven of the Twins series and eight of the Sweet Valley High books. All of the women reported an involvement with the characters in the books that served to bring them back for more.

All displayed greater proficiency not only in their reading but in speaking English as well. And all demonstrated increased vocabulary development.

Krashen and Cho noted: "Our brief study with these four women also supports the value of 'narrow' reading—reading texts in only one genre or by only one author—for promoting literacy development. Narrow reading allows the reader to take full advantage of the knowledge gained in previously read text."

This study is one of many that demonstrate the powerful role that recreational "lite" reading—series books and comic books—plays in developing good and lifetime readers. Is it classic literature? Of course not. Does it have a better chance of creating fluent readers than the classics would? Definitely. And can it eventually lead to the classics? Yes, and certainly sooner than would *The Red Badge of Courage*.

My Son Loves Comic Books—Is That Good or Bad?

Comic books are a frequent childhood choice of people who grow up to become fluent readers.[33] The reasons for their popularity and success are the same as for series. And anyone questioning their success in creating readers should consider this: In the IEA assessment of more than two hundred thousand children in thirty-two countries, Finnish children achieved the highest reading scores. And what is the most common choice for recreational reading among Finnish nine-year-olds? Fifty-nine percent read a comic almost every day.[34]

I am not recommending comic books as a steady diet for reading aloud, but as an introduction to the comic format. Young children must be shown how a comic "works": the sequence of the panels; how to tell when a character is thinking and when he is speaking; the meaning of stars, question marks, and exclamation points.

In recent years, with the arrival of the *manga* mode from Japan, along with the graphic novel, comic books have experienced a revival and revolution, one that sometimes includes heavy strains of sex and violence. (Need I say this is not peculiar to comics? Books and film have similar situations.) So the days of giving a child the money for a comic book and sending him or her off to the corner convenience store are a thing of the past. As with television, videos, and books, responsible adults must stay aware and awake.

On the basis of my personal experiences and the research available, I would go so far as to say if you have a child who is struggling with reading, connect him or her with comics.

As a child, I had the largest comic book collection in my neighborhood, as did Stephen Krashen, Cynthia Rylant, John Updike, and Ray Bradbury. And there is this reflection from a Nobel Peace Prize winner, South Africa's Bishop Desmond Tutu: "My father was the headmaster of a Methodist primary school. Like most fathers in those days, he was very patriarchal, very concerned that we did well in school. But one of the things I am very grateful to him for is that, contrary to conventional educational principles, he allowed me to read comics. I think that is how I developed my love for English and for reading."[35]

If you're looking to challenge a child's mind and vocabulary with comics, then I suggest *The Adventures of Tintin*. If you looked closely at Dustin Hoffman while he was reading to his son in *Kramer vs. Kramer*, you would have noticed he was reading *Tintin*. Or if you read the list of favorite read-alouds offered by historian Arthur Schlesinger Jr. in the *New York Times Book Review*, you would have found Hergé's *Tintin* between *Huckleberry Finn* and the Greek myths.[36]

Begun as a comic strip in Belgium in 1929, *Tintin* now reaches, in comic book form, thirty countries in twenty-two languages and is sold only in quality bookstores. The subject is a seventeen-year-old reporter (Tintin) who, along with his dog and a cast of colorful and zany characters, travels around the globe in pursuit of mad scientists, spies, and saboteurs.

Two years were spent researching and drawing the seven hundred detailed illustrations in each issue. But *Tintin* must be *read* in order to be understood—and that is the key for parents and teachers. Each issue contains eight thousand words. The beautiful part of it is that children are unaware they are reading eight thousand words. (See *Tintin in Tibet* in the picture book section of the Treasury, where you will also find a selection of good books in the comic mode.)

If Adults Are Supposed to Be Role Models, How Much Should Teachers Read?

Throughout this book I've offered research showing the impact of parent role models on children's reading habits. Though they have less impact than parents, teachers should be reading role models as well—especially for those children whose parents cannot or will not do the job. The trouble, however, is that most teachers are seldom seen reading for pleasure. Reading for work, from the text, from lesson plans, yes. But sitting back and savoring a book for its own sake or talking about a book they read last night? Seldom.

Research about teachers shows that in schools where their administrators talk about books and professional journals, the teachers read more on their own.[37] So why wouldn't the same be true for students if *their* instructional leaders talked more about books? In other words, the teacher stands before the class and daily gives mini book talks based on the classroom library.

The fly in this ointment is that book talks work only when the person talking has actually read the book. And the harsh reality here is most teachers don't read much.

That's not a speculative comment but one based on both research and personal experience. One study of 224 teachers pursuing graduate degrees showed they read few or no professional journals that included research.[38] (Suppose your doctor read only *Prevention* magazine?) More than half said they had read only one or two professional books in the previous year, and an additional 20 percent said they had read nothing in the last six months or one year. What did they read beyond professional material?

+ Twenty-two percent read a newspaper only once a week.
+ Seventy-five percent were only "light" book readers—one or two a year.
+ Twenty-five percent were "heavy" readers (three to four books a month). This means that teachers don't read any more often than adults in the general population.[39]

More recently (1998), in a national survey of 666 academic high school teachers, almost half reported not reading one professional journal or magazine. The 51 percent who did such reading regularly were also more apt to belong to professional associations linked to their teaching area. The survey group averaged fifteen years of teaching, with 63 percent holding graduate degrees. Science teachers led all disciplines, with 61.8 percent reading at least one journal, while social studies trailed the faculty at 36.4 percent.[40]

There are only two practical ways to get words into the human brain: through the ear and through the eye. If the child comes from a home where there is a dearth of spoken language and little or no print, the only remaining way for the child to acquire good vocabulary is through the eye—that is, by reading. And here's where the classroom teacher plays a pivotal role.

If a teacher approaches reading in a rote manner (drill-and-teach-the-test), the student will never be inspired to read outside school, where he spends the largest amount of time (7,800 hours a year). On the other hand, if the student child enters a school or library and meets a clone of America's number one reading teacher, then the kid has a chance.

That number one reading teacher is Oprah Winfrey. In the last decade, she's inspired more people to read more pages in more good books than anyone in American history. Now *that's* a reading teacher! (See chapter 8 for more on Oprah.) So if the child walks into a classroom or library that has an Oprah clone in it, he's far more likely to be inspired to start reading the particular author or book she talked about. Now the kid is reading and reading a lot—outside school; he's reading on the bus, he's reading in bed, on the toilet, and at the breakfast table. And through all those pages, he's accumulating the vocabulary words he never hears at home or from family.

In order for that to happen, however, the teacher or librarian has to be an avid reader like Oprah. You can't talk about a book you haven't read, any more than you can talk about a movie you haven't seen. When I do teacher seminars, at this juncture I walk over to a teacher, pick up her bottle of water, and say, "You know, you and I could share this bottle today, we could share a cell phone, even a pen, and you can't catch a cold from me today. Because I don't have a cold. In the same way, if a teacher or librarian doesn't have the love of reading, the class can't catch it from her. And half the teachers don't have the love—which is a big problem for half the kids in the country, especially the ones coming from homes where the parents don't have it either."

When someone becomes a teacher, they're also opening up a dating service, with a specialty in blind dates. She's like the matchmaker in *Fiddler on the Roof*. All year long she's trying to entice students to go out on dates with authors—that is, to pick up this book or that book and spend twenty minutes with the author, someone they've never met. The better she knows her students and authors or books, the more successful will be the "match-making." But the teacher (or librarian) who doesn't read much will fail for sure.[41]

When My Students Encounter Unknown Words, Shouldn't They Look Them Up in the Dictionary?

Holy St. Brendan on a bicycle! You're talking "word skipping" here, a reading felony! It's the very thing they invented "guided reading" to prevent—to *guide* children into the books on their own reading level. This is also one of the points that the National Reading Panel frets about—students left on their own to just *read*. The fact is, if you're an average person, you're going to be encountering unknown words for the rest of your life. You won't live long enough to learn them all, but you will learn some—a lot, if you read a lot. But when you first meet them, you don't know them. Here are a couple of research facts on vocabulary and comprehension.

In order to understand what's transpiring on a page, one needs to know about 90 percent of the words. If you've got that, you can pretty much figure out what's going on from the way the unknown words are used in the sentences. If the unknown amount is larger than 10 percent, then your understanding of the text itself will be seriously flawed.

As for those words in the text you don't know, most people need repeat encounters to know and remember them. I always tell my parent audiences that the only words children learn having heard them only once are the words you wish you had never said in front of them. The rest of the words we need to encounter multiple times. How many times, to be exact? The research shows that four encounters with an unknown word does little or no good, but twelve meetings enhances comprehension.[42]

So those teachers are wrong when they assume the child is missing something in not knowing each word. What is happening is that all those close encounters with the unknowns are getting him or her closer to the twelfth time when it finally clicks and becomes embedded in the comprehension and memory banks.

Guided reading is a good concept if not taken too far. There are schools and libraries that set that concept in stone and God help you if you're caught reading a book above your level. This completely ignores the role of motivation. Let me give you a personal example.

Back in 1985, I decided to buy an Apple computer and force myself to leave the familiar world of DOS. I took a few basic lessons at the store, and then bought *Macworld* magazine. I remember reading the magazine that night and understanding *nothing*. I might as well have been reading Swahili. In the ensuing days, I played around with the computer, and tried reading the magazine again. I probably read through the magazine three times that month. This pattern went on for months, and each month I found myself understanding more and more of the articles, and applying the knowledge to my computer. It was repeat-readings that helped the most, coupled with the motivation to master the Mac system. Today, I'm still a passionate Mac guy and one who understands almost everything in my monthly computer magazines.

When a child is passionately interested in a subject (the Red Sox, Mars, salamanders, etc.), the worst thing you can do is "guide" him away from printed material about that subject. Instead, guide him to material on his own level but let him know the harder stuff is available as well. It's amazing what levels we can reach with a passionate interest. Only a parent, a teacher, or a librarian can recognize this passion in a student. Computerized programs haven't a clue.

Chapter 6

In Their Own Words

Experience, the universal Mother of Sciences.
—Miguel de Cervantes

DESPITE all the research included in this book, nothing rings truer than real-life personal testimony. With that in mind, I offer a small collection of correspondence from parents and teachers who have allowed me to share their personal stories. Most share a common theme—that one person, one comment, or one conversation can make a difference in literacy.

Dear Jim:

My name is Schelly Solko and I teach kindergarten in Bakersfield, California. I read to my students every day and know that it pays off. When I taught older students, I did silent reading (SSR) with them but I was sure it would never work with kindergartners. So for the last 12 years I read and they listened. Not bad, but not enough, I know now.

This fall, with all the talk about standards, etc. I decided my 5-year-olds could handle silent reading. Well, Jim, I tell you, they love it! And so do I. With less than 10 minutes a day, five times a week, I've read to myself the newest edition of your *Read-Aloud Handbook*, *Chicken Soup for the Soul*, and *Fish* while the children were doing their reading—and they were wonderful. There is an occasional wiggle and giggle, but, for the most part, it is so successful. Here's how I know:

We decided to wear our pajamas to school the day we studied the letter "P-p." We ate pancakes, did math pizza, etc. They were so hyped for a week that I knew silent reading could never happen. Was I ever wrong. We'd been doing silent reading since the third week of September and now it was the first week of January. I told them that they didn't have to have *silent* reading that day, but they had to have "still reading" (expecting some noise and chatter). They got their books, I got mine, I gave the signal, and I began to read my book. I couldn't believe my ears. I heard nothing! I carefully looked around the room. Every child was reading—it was incredible! I thought all the day's distractions—pajamas, etc.—would interfere, but the training and habits they had formed won out. I continued to read and so did they.

On another subject, your *Handbook* inspired the five kindergarten teachers here at school to revamp the homework program we have had "since dirt." Kindergartners had never been "allowed" to check out books from the school library. When we questioned this, nobody had an answer. So now, once a week, each child checks out a book, takes it home, and has someone read it to him or her. In twelve years teaching at this school, I have never had a higher homework return-rate. The parents are reading to them and the kids love it.

—Schelly Solko,
Bakersfield, California

Dear Jim:

In October 2002, I heard you speak to our PTA in Cincinnati, Ohio. When you said "reading fathers" were your pet project, I decided to write you about my husband, Bill McMahan, who, in his mid-fifties, discovered the immense pleasures of reading aloud. As a "fifth-time" father, Bill has experienced healing through reading to our son nightly for the last five years. Our son is now 12 and the two of them continue to find great pleasure in reading together (no plans to stop!).

Let me start by saying that I'm an English professor who has always loved books. When I had my first (and only) child, Gabe, I surrounded him with books and read to him. I taught him finger-plays, read to him daily, kept a "print-rich" home, etc. In spite of all these efforts Gabe reached third grade complaining, "I hate to read."

Then Bill decided to get involved. As a child, my husband was an unmotivated student who never enjoyed reading, probably because of undiagnosed learning disabilities. He discovered a few favorite writers while in Vietnam, yet never developed a passion for reading. Ours is his second marriage; with his first four children, he worked long hours and didn't understand the value of reading aloud.

Bill McMahan and son Gabe formed a special bond when Bill began reading aloud to his son.

When our son, Gabe, was seven, someone gave him an Animorph action figure, and Bill decided to check out the Animorph series by K. A. Applegate. He began reading an Animorph book to Gabe and soon discovered they both liked the kooky humor and the science embedded in these sci-fi stories about kids with a mission to save the earth from the Yeerks—kids who could morph into animals. Soon Bill and Gabe were curling up every night at bedtime to read for an hour or longer about the Animorphs' adventures.

Eventually the Animorph series led to Harry Potter and later to Lloyd Alexander's fantasy books and the Deltora Quest series. Over the past five years, Bill has read aloud more than three hundred books to Gabe, some of them more than once! Reading has created a huge bond between them and greatly expanded their imaginations.

Gabe is now 12 and I can happily look back over five years of the two of them reading together in bed 30 to 60 minutes almost every night—thousands of pages (at least 30,000 pages). Most nights I fall asleep to the blessed sound of my husband reading aloud to my son. I serve as their vocabulary resource—we often pause to talk about word connotations. (They keep a dictionary handy, too.)

Books have become a huge bond between my son and his father. Characters like Hermione and the Weasley family (from Harry

Potter) are like members of our own family! In time, Gabe began to read more willingly on his own; he has reread most of the same books that Bill reads to him. Gabe's now in seventh grade and despite a diagnosis of ADHD, he consistently excels in language arts and independent reading and tested in the ninety-ninth percentile in language arts in national proficiency tests (I hate those tests). Gabe sees himself as a smart kid because he's a reader; he no longer shies away from thick books; and his vocabulary is more advanced than most of my college students.

An equally amazing change has come in Bill. Once a reluctant reader, in his fifties he developed a missionary zeal for reading aloud to kids. He often tells friends and family members the storylines of the books he and Gabe are reading; to other dads, he extols the pleasures of reading aloud. For a while, Bill and I published a school newsletter called "The Fourth-Grade Booklovers' News." He also became a school volunteer who conferenced with kids about their "independent reading" (SSR in grades 3–5), steering them toward great books. In addition, the sci-fi interest has motivated Bill to read some college-level textbooks on biology, physics, and chemistry, which, in turn, have led to conversations about black holes and the archaebacteria around the dinner table! Of course, living with Bill and Gabe has pushed me to broaden my own reading tastes beyond the Newbery winners.

All this reading has been motivated by pure pleasure, not by "shoulds." Although Gabe has other hobbies, including sports and art, I feel confident that nothing in his life has opened his heart and soul as much as reading aloud with his dad!

    —Trudelle Thomas, author of *Spirituality in the Mother Zone*
    (Paulist Press) and professor of English, Xavier
    University, Cincinnati, Ohio

For some strange reason today's culture has convinced itself that requiring a child to do something is inherently damaging to the child's well-being. Oh, it's perfectly acceptable to force them to pick up their rooms and wash their necks, but heaven forbid you require them to read. This parent/teacher offers an insight into "requirements."

Dear Jim:

As background, I have a master's degree in education and have taught for about 20 years. Presently, I am a resource specialist. I enjoy reading and enjoy reading aloud to others. My husband is very respectful of my education and love for reading, but reading does not come easy for him. (He calls himself dyslexic, as his reading is very labored.) He only reads in the subject area of his work.

Our oldest (of two), Stephen, was conceived in 1991. (It was probably a few days later that I began reading to him in utero!) I bought children's books to fill our shelves and knew he would love books, because I was going to do everything "right."

After he was born, I read to him. That wasn't easy to do when he grew into a toddler because he was such an active little guy—he wouldn't sit in my lap for very long.

At the end of preschool, his teacher suggested we retain him, that he was not ready for kindergarten. As a teacher and a parent, I knew she was wrong, that he was brilliant and ready for kindergarten. He was and is brilliant, but he continued to be a below-grade-level student in kindergarten and first grade. During a student study team meeting in second grade, it was decided that he should be tested for a learning disability. As a result of this assessment, he was assessed to have an auditory processing challenge, but he did not qualify for special education.

Since he did not have a disability that would affect his ability to be a reader, we continued to plug along, but he still hated reading and performed below grade level in language arts. By fourth grade he was only reading at second grade level and all areas of school that required reading were very difficult for him. This was a very stressful time for me, as my ego was so involved. How could I, as a "good" mom and educator, have a child working below grade level? I was not working outside the home at the time and devoted a lot of energy to tutoring him and staying in close contact with the school.

His teachers in all four grades had sent home reading logs, which he was to complete and I was to sign after he read aloud or to himself—the assignment was 15 minutes of reading per day. He is a compliant boy and did what was asked of him, even though he did not enjoy it. I did not want to turn him off to reading, so I never dreamed of making him read for longer than the required 15 minutes per day. It was too painful for me to make him read, since he disliked it so intensely.

In January of 2001, on the advice of the reading specialist at his school (Stephen was in fourth grade), I attended your presentation at Sierra College in Rocklin, California. During the presentation, I heard you say that it is OK to force or require a child to read, that the only way to become proficient at any worthwhile task is to practice. I was in *shock*.

The entire presentation hit me very hard and I realized that I had failed my son. He had been "forced" by his parents to learn to ride a bike. It was a good thing! We did not put his bike away after his first fall with the training wheels and say, "Oh, honey, that's so hard for you! Let's just try riding a few minutes a day." No, we stayed with him, holding on to the back of his seat, until he was able to ride. Then, once able to stay up for a while on his own, he rode and rode and rode. When he fell, he got up again, and rode some more. When he was finally able to ride without training wheels, we called the grandparents (long-distance) and bragged! We videotaped him! We took photos! We wrote in his baby book!

So the next day at dinner, the Momma Bear in me came out and I asked for everyone's attention. I told them things were going to change around our house. I retold the explanation that we only improve by practicing. We were going to be a family that reads for the purpose of becoming better readers, etc. I don't actually recall my exact words, but my family all had that "deer in the headlights" look from the tone of my voice and the expression on my face.

Prior to speaking with them, I looked at our daily schedule and came up with a plan, which I shared at that dinner. Stephen left for school at 8:30 A.M. and arrived home at 3:30 P.M. The new plan was that he and I would read for 30 minutes in the morning after his little sister left for school. He would earn a stripe on his "stripe chart" for every 30 minutes of reading. (When he completed the chart, he earned a trip to buy Legos.) At night, after homework and dessert, he and I would read for another 30 minutes. The tone of my voice and the tears in my eyes told my family that this was going to happen. My husband agreed to read aloud to my daughter, while Stephen and I read silently. (Not being a "reader," this was wonderful for my children to see—their daddy reading.)

For approximately two months, I sat next to Stephen with my book. I was available to help him with difficult words in his book, but because he was reading at his own reading level, we were able to read independently for the majority of the time. He started with the Captain Underpants series, which was a thrill for him because it was a *chapter book*! When the 30 minutes were over, we would compare notes on our books and brag about how many pages or chapters we had read. In those two short months, he gained confidence and pleasure in reading. It was like a miracle.

I told Stephen that prior to the new reading program at home, he had been reading an hour and 15 minutes a week. Now he was reading 6 *hours* a week. He could visually comprehend it because his "stripe chart" filled up so quickly. It made a huge difference. He is now in 5th grade and I am thrilled to share that he is reading at grade level. He still struggles with auditory processing and still does not choose to read for pleasure, but when he reads it is pleasurable. He tells me about the books he is reading without me asking. He has crossed that bridge from the boy who hated to read to a boy who finds pleasure in books and the magic they hold.

When you do the math, you see that Stephen went from a second-grade level to fifth-grade level *in one year.*

—Teresa Heitmiller Olea,
Granite City, California

From time to time my wife reminds me that there's a fine line between being enthusiastic and being obnoxious. I've sometimes had a hard time keeping my enthusiasms to myself. So when I fell in love with reading to my kids, I wanted everyone else to feel that too, sometimes even a stranger.

Dear Jim:

I don't expect that you will remember me, but twenty years ago, I was a 25-year-old manager of a Radio Shack computer center across the street from your employer, the Springfield Newspapers. You purchased a computer from me and I went to your home to install it. While there, we had a great conversation regarding the importance of reading to your children. I was the father of a six-month-old son at the time.

When you heard a six-month-old, you immediately asked, "Do you read to him?"

My response was, "No, not yet—he's only six months old." You said he was not too young and that I should start immediately. Eight months later, my wife and I had a daughter and a few years later another son and then another daughter. I have read countless books to them. By third or fourth grade, we were reading books together, taking turns reading, and rewarding our accomplishments by watching the movie version of the stories. For example, we would read *The Incredible Journey* and then watch *Homeward Bound.*

I am probably one of the few 45-year-old men who has read *Little Women*—twice! I understood the value of reading from an educational perspective, but the quality family time was an added bonus that may be obvious to you but looking back now, it was some of the most cherished time I've had with my kids.

I then decided to become more involved in their formal education.

When my son started kindergarten, I ran and was elected to the school committee, where I served until he was in high school. I left for a few years and I am now back on the school committee in my community.

I wanted to personally thank you for your influence 20 years ago in the basement of your home. Please know that the work you do had a profound effect on at least four kids in Rehoboth, Massachusetts.

—Don Nokes,
Rehoboth, Massachusetts

Sometimes all a person needs is a little nudge. There were a thousand kindergarten teachers in the crowd that day, but the only one who counted for me is this woman.

Dear Jim:

A few weeks ago I saw you speak at the California Kindergarten Conference in San Francisco and I wanted to thank you for inspiring me to do something I have always been nervous about doing. I have two children, a son age eight and a daughter age 6. Our house is full of books and our whole family reads a lot. I've read to my children since they were tiny babies and started reading chapter books to my son when he was four. Both my children love books and school, and are doing well academically. However, there has been a difference in how I read to my children.

My daughter is profoundly deaf and we use American Sign Language (ASL) to communicate with her. Fortunately, I knew a little sign language and was able to "read" to my daughter as soon as we learned she was deaf. I could at least point to a picture of a shoe in a book and sign "shoe." We have taken classes in ASL almost continuously for the last 5 years and our signing has improved.

This brings me to my "thanks." I had never read a chapter book to my daughter since I did not think I could sign it. But listening to you talk that Saturday morning I knew that I not only could, but I had to try. I came home and dug out a copy of *Charlotte's Web*. I read a paragraph silently to myself and then I signed it to her. It's a slow process, but we are both enjoying it. She carries the book around, kissing it, and signing "I love this book!" So thank you, Jim Trelease.

—Kathy Jackson,
Fremont, California

The next letter is from rural Nisswa, Minnesota (population 2,000). I hear politicians proclaim that throwing money at education problems is like throwing it

down the drain. "What you really need to do," they say, "is run it like a business."
Nisswa demonstrates what happens when a business works to help schools instead of
just making money off them.

Dear Jim:

As background for this letter, I'm the general manager of one of
the premier golf and family resorts in the Midwest, Grand View
Lodge, located in Nisswa, Minnesota. That plays a little part in what
I'm going to tell you.

In 1996, when our daughter Pammy was in the second grade
(she's now in twelfth), my wife, Patricia, and I decided we'd like to
do something for her classroom. Something in the way of a gift—a
science experiment, hamsters, a new video unit—something fun or
educational but not in the budget.

I asked Pammy's teacher what she wanted, and she immediately
replied, "Books."

I thought to myself: Right—you must have an entire library here,
what on earth do you need with more books? So I said, "OK, why
don't you think about it and I'll get back to you." Two weeks passed
and I made another inquiry and received the same answer: "Books."

I was starting to get the message. Off I went to the school library,
looked around, and thought, What a crummy collection. I also noticed what has now become my pet peeve: the library was being
overtaken by the "media center." All the money, space, and attention was going to the computer lab that was taking up a large portion in the library.

So I stopped at the local bookstore and the owner, Suzy Turcotte,
a wonderful supporter, recommended that, inasmuch as I was now
interested in elementary and early childhood reading, I should read
The Read-Aloud Handbook by Jim Trelease. I read the book and became a believer, adamant that our school would put the emphasis
on reading and *that the resources would be there to get the job done.*

With that in mind, I founded NERF (Nisswa Enhanced Reading
Foundation) to fund it, an idea that had to have come from above
because it was too good to come from me. Our funding for NERF
comes from four sources.

1. At Grand View Lodge we've always used gift certificates to
   promote the lodge down in Minneapolis, giving them to nonprofits to use in fundraisers like silent auctions and charity golf
   tournaments. Now we ask the nonprofit group to find a spon-

sor for the gift certificate who will make a donation to NERF in the amount of approximately 40 percent of the face value of the certificate. It's a winning situation in that Grand View Lodge gives away the same number of certificates as previously, the nonprofits in Minneapolis love it because it provides a very nice prize for them, and our foundation benefits. (We do not have the affluent population in Nisswa that exists in the metro area, so we basically get them down there to fund us up here.)

2. Private parties and foundations give us grants.
3. We sell golf passes for $20 to play a couple of courses here that normally cost $80 or more. The course gets $10 and the foundation gets $10, and they're restricted to a couple of days where the course knows the tee times would go unsold. We sell about 200 of these a year.
4. We hold a large book sale in the conference center at Grand View Lodge with 15 percent of the proceeds going to the book foundation.

In all, we raise about $20,000 annually and as much as $35,000 in our best years. From day one, money has never been a problem. It's amazing how many books you can accumulate with $15,000 to $25,000 a year. Here are some programs NERF has supported:

1. *Beautiful Books:* A read-aloud opportunity where we send home beautiful but very expensive books. This is a program for kindergarten and first grade. We send two books in a bag and ask that they be returned in a couple of days. If they are not returned we buy more.
2. *Classroom libraries:* Each teacher is given $250–$300 per year to purchase books for their classroom to ensure easy access to age-appropriate titles.
3. *The incentive reading room:* A room with hundreds of paperbacks; eligible students may choose a book to keep. My theory is: If it's a reward, it must be valuable. Kids can get a couple of books per year and they really like it. We've been doing it for nine years.
4. *March Madness:* In March, every other year, we set a goal for out-of-school reading minutes. If the goal is met, every student gets a book to keep. I actually had a mother tell me, *"My son comes home and does not turn on the TV until he gets his minutes*

in, without any prompting." We do it for a month, with the idea that anything you do for a month can become a habit.

5. *Rainy Day Bookstore:* At the local bookstore down the street from school, we keep money on account in case a teacher needs a book—they just go buy it. No questions, no paperwork, no permission needed. This is one of the teachers' favorite programs. We also offer mini-grants of several hundred dollars that teachers can apply for to fund a reading idea.

6. *New teacher book fund:* We increase the amount of in-classroom library money for teachers in their first teaching job.

NERF is now in its tenth year and here are a few of our statistics:

+ $250,000.00 raised and spent on books and programs;
+ Approximately 6,000 books added to our library collection;
+ 1,500 books given away to students as incentives for having read or for having done something that needs rewarding;
+ 1,000 books added to individual classroom libraries

But our pride and joy is the Julia Thorpe Cote Nisswa Children's Library. This $750,000 project is funded in large part by the Cote Foundation (the private foundation of the owners of Grand View Lodge). This library is unlike any library you've ever seen. In fact, our theme for it was "This ain't your mama's library." It's attached to the Nisswa Elementary School and serves the community's children year-round.

Jim, you probably won't be surprised that middle school teachers often say they can pick out the students from Nisswa Elementary—they're the best readers. Forgive me for bragging, but our daughter Pammy just got a perfect score on the reading and critical thinking portion of the SAT.

—Mark Ronnei,
Nisswa, Minnesota

One of the areas where the "business" model falls short in schools is in its failure to recognize that children are not like planes and trains—they all don't arrive or depart on time. Some need a little more time than others, kids like Brad. It's possible you have a Brad in your house. But does your house have a mom like Brad's?

Dear Jim:

When we met in Leeds, Alabama, I promised to send you the story of my family and reading aloud. First of all, besides being the proud mother of two sons, I am an educator with 35 years of experience in elementary education and library media, with four degrees in elementary education, and one in library and information studies. I know firsthand how important parental involvement is in the lives of children.

When my first son, Matt, was four years old he got a little brother. By this time Matt knew all the letters of the alphabet, recognized beginning and ending sounds, and was reading signs and some words. In kindergarten he was one of the first to read, and loved every minute he was reading.

My younger son, Brad, was more active. He enjoyed running, jumping, attacking, and was rarely still. We tried reading with Brad, but after a few pages he lost interest and wanted to "get down and play." I would have been worried, but when he was two and a half, to my husband's and my amazement, he pointed out all the letters of the alphabet on his educational toy, the one that said the letter of the alphabet when the string was pulled. He could randomly identify all the letters, so we just knew he would read early and eventually enjoy it as much as his brother.

When Brad was almost five, he came to Mother's school to take the standardized entrance test for kindergarten. Imagine my horror and chagrin when I found he did not score high enough to be placed in the regular class. I felt like a failure as a mother and teacher.

As I was discussing my disappointment with my friend, the teacher of the gifted resource class Matt was in, she asked me point-blank, "Do you read aloud to him?" I had to admit that with my taking graduate classes for my education specialist degree, and after helping Matt with his homework, I was just too tired to battle with Brad, getting him to be still to listen to me read. She sternly told me, "Well, try!"

After that, I tried—and tried. At first his father or I had to bodily hold him down to read to him, or forcefully hold him as Matt read to him. Then I had the bright idea of asking what he wanted me to read. Surprisingly enough, he wanted *The Wizard of Oz*. We read the whole set as he learned to be still and listen. At first I only read a few pages, but he gradually listened to a chapter at a time, then two.

When Brad entered kindergarten, he was not at the top of his class in reading but he managed to keep up. At the end of the year he was beginning to read in a pre-primer. During first grade he made good progress, but his scores on the standardized test taken in the spring showed that, although he was way above average in math and spelling, he was high average in reading comprehension, just average in reading vocabulary, and below average in listening skills.

By the time Brad was in the third grade, he was the first to learn his multiplication facts. On the standardized test taken in the spring, he was in the 99th percentile in math, 94th percentile in language, but his vocabulary skills were still too low. However, we were still reading aloud nightly, taking turns reading.

At the end of Brad's fourth grade, his brother had been accepted at the district's high school for gifted students and this became Brad's dream. Although he continuously scored well above the 90th percentile on his achievement tests in all areas except vocabulary skills, he just couldn't get past the final screening for admittance into the gifted program, a prerequisite for entrance into the magnet high school. By this time he was putting undue pressure upon himself and trying too hard.

When Brad was in eighth grade, he asked to be tested again. This time, instead of the district's diagnostician, we decided to let an expert from the local university test him and this time he passed. Four years later, through hard work, perseverance, and yes, reading aloud, Brad, the former failure on the kindergarten pretest, became valedictorian of his high school class. In 2005, *Newsweek* ranked that high school the best in the U.S.

Now when I teach a children's literature or library media class for the University of Alabama, I tell Brad's story. I emphasize the importance of reading aloud to students, as well as having parents read aloud to their children. Matt and Brad were both full scholarship students in college, graduating summa cum laude in engineering; but that was not always the way things were. No one said reading aloud would be easy, but it is oh, so important!

—Susan Nelson,
McCalla, Alabama

Chapter 7

The Print Climate in the Home, School, and Library

Few forms of theft are quite as damaging to inner-city children as the denial of a well-endowed school library.

—Jonathan Kozol

TWENTY-TWO years ago, in the midst of a great political campaign, one candidate painted America as a "shining city on a hill." And he was right. And then the opposition speaker declared that America was really "a tale of two cities." And he was right, too. It depended on your vantage point.[1]

And the same arguments can be made about American books. There are places in America where they have so many books, in a manner of speaking, they throw them out on the lawn on weekends to get rid of them. (I'll introduce you later to some people who live in such places.) And in the same country, under the same government, there are homes, schools, and communities that scarcely have seen a new book in forty years. (We'll go there, too.)

To put it all into perspective, let's change the word "reading" to "rodeo." For the sake of discussion, let's say the nation's leaders suddenly decided that rodeo was the most important subject in our schools' curriculum. (This is not as far-fetched as you might think: if the price of gas keeps going skyward, some people are going to be looking very differently at horses.) There would suddenly be new courses created around horsemanship, saddles and equipment would have to be ordered, riding coaches credentialed, and mandatory riding and roping classes begun in rodeo lab classes. All of this would culminate in mandatory grade-level rodeos (including "exit rodeos" for the high school seniors) to ensure that "no rider was left behind."

And sure as the sun sinks in the west, there would be states that excel and those that fail. In fact, to show this idea isn't all that wacky, the list is already available! To find it, set your browser for the professional rodeo circuit's world standings. It doesn't really matter which event you look under, so let's check the standings for bareback riding, a very difficult event. You can see the top twenty money winners for that event in the list below. Now focus on where the competitors come from. See anyone from New Jersey? Rhode Island? How about Delaware or New York? Already we can easily predict which states are going to be on the "failing schools" list—the places that have the fewest horses. It's tough to get good at rodeo if you're missing a horse.

Rodeo Standings

Rank	Name	State
1	Monte Downare	Colo.
2	Micky Downare	Colo.
3	Heath Ford	Colo.
4	Jason Havens	Ore.
5	Mike Outhier	Texas
6	Zach Dishman	Texas
7	Cody Jessee	Ore.
8	Ryan Gray	Wash.
9	Royce Ford	Colo.
10	Bobby Mote	Ore.
11	Tim Shirley	Colo.
12	C. Gerke	Colo.
13	Chad Klein	La.
14	Lance Kelly	Aust.
15	Daron Lacina	N.D.
16	Kelly Timberman	Wyo.
17	Kyle Bowers	Alberta
18	Travis Whiteside	Alberta
19	Trever Roosevelt	Wash.
20	Rowdy Buechner	Ida.

Professional rodeo standings indicate the states that have the most and fewest horses, just as reading scores reflect which states have the most and fewest books.

And it's just as difficult to get good at reading if you're short of books. No Child Left Behind ensures that children who are behind in reading are entitled to after-school tutoring and extra help with phonics. Nice. But giving phonics lessons to kids who don't have any print in their lives is like giving oars to people who don't have a boat—you won't get very far.

Let me repeat a portion of the table[2] from the introduction, the part that characterizes the print climate in the homes of two kinds of kindergartners: those with high interest in print and those with low interest.

Home Information	High Interest in Books (%)	Low Interest in Books (%)
Number of books in home	80.6 books	31.7 books
Child owns library card	37.5	3.4
Child is taken to library	98.1	7.1
Child is read to daily	76.8	1.8

Before I go any further, allow me to state that the great disparity in the American print climate—home and school—is entirely fixable. Price is not a problem. If we can rebuild Afghanistan and Iraq at a cost of $200 billion, we can fix all the urban school and public libraries in America. Easy. All we have to do is believe that it's worth it. If we have to, we can build a strong case that it would come under Homeland Security. Today's desperate fifteen-year-old semiliterate in South-Central LA is tomorrow's unemployed homegrown terrorist. If you doubt it, ask the people in Oklahoma City.

I've got four people waiting in the wings of this chapter who will show us what can be done on just a shoestring, so there's no end to possibilities if we had funding. Everything these four have done can be done in your city, town, or state.

Just as climate affects sports scores, the same connection can be made between climate and reading scores. The last two decades of research by respected researchers like Neuman,[3] Duke,[4] Krashen,[5] McQuillan,[6] Allington,[7] and Lance[8] unmistakably connect access to print with high reading scores and, conversely, lack of access with lower scores. It's a shame the education experts haven't figured this out yet, even when one of the best researchers (Neuman) was an assistant secretary of education in Washington. Instead, they blame the teachers, curriculum, or students for the low scores, which is like the governor of Maine complaining his state hasn't had a horse in the Kentucky Derby since God knows when.

When the NAEP reading assessments were measuring the amount of print in the home, they found a positive connection between large amounts of print in the home and more independent reading, which led to higher scores.[9] International studies have drawn the same conclusions,[10] and Elley's 1992 study of 210,000 students found the larger the school and classroom libraries, the higher the students' reading scores.[11]

More than thirteen states have produced research connecting a stronger library program to higher student scores,[12] including Baughman's research on the Massachusetts MCAS exam that showed a higher ratio of "books-per-pupil" and a full-time librarian meant an eleven-point advantage, and that a higher percentage of the student body visiting the library per week accounted for a twelve-point advantage. Both factors proved true at every grade level and would be a clear advantage for children at lower socioeconomic levels attending schools with good library programs.[13]

The most dramatic example of the impact of the print climate on entire school districts is the one involving three California communities, twenty and forty miles apart on the map but worlds apart in other ways. Krashen and colleagues at USC did a print inventory of homes, classrooms, and libraries in the three communities—Beverly Hills, Watts, and Compton.[14] In Beverly Hills, high scores send 93 percent of its high school students to college, while relatively few go to college from Watts and Compton. In 1999, Compton's state-appointed administrator reported that barely one in ten students was performing at grade level. One look at the chart below clearly shows the print desert surrounding urban children, versus the print "rain forest" surrounding others.

Average Print Climate in Three California Communities

	Books in Home	Books in Class	Books in School Library	Books in Public Library
Beverly Hills	199	392	60,000	200,600
Watts	4.5	54	23,000	110,000
Compton	2.7	47	16,000	90,000

Krashen's evidence[15] was presented to a state commission revising California's language-arts curriculum in the 1990s after the state tied Louisiana for last in the nation in reading. With the state holding one of the nation's largest child-poverty populations, and lowest support for school and public libraries, California politicians responded with $195 million for more phonics instruction.[16] How effective has that been? Last in the nation in 1996, even with the increased phonics funding the state's students still ranked at the bottom by 2004.[17] Not that the legislature was completely deaf to the school library crisis: in the late 1990s, they committed to an annual $28 per pupil expenditure for libraries, but by 2005 that had shriveled to less than $1 a pupil.[18] All of this provoked the following response from a *Los Angeles Times* writer: "The state's long neglect of school libraries is a scandal. California is dead last among the states in the ratio of credentialed librarians to students; it has 1 librarian for every 5,036 students, more than five times worse than the national average of 1 to 953. Even the state's adult prison system does better, with 1 librarian to 4,283 inmates."[19]

Since school is supposed to make up for any home deficits, one would expect at-risk children to meet good classroom libraries—or some semblance of *no child left without a good library*. Instead, Nell Duke found the same deficits as in the home when she spent a year studying twenty first-grade classrooms—ten suburban and ten urban—in Massachusetts. Despite having teachers with an average eighteen years' experience, the urban students were more restricted in how often they could use the classroom library, the library selections were older and of a poorer grade, their class reading time was spent on less complex text, they spent more time copying and taking dictation, their teachers read to them less often and from simpler texts, and the books-per-pupil ratio was half that of the high SES classrooms.[20] Additionally, seven of the advantaged classes were read to from chapter books while only two of the low SES classes heard chapter books.

The inequities worsen in the higher grades. Let's test that thesis in the epicenter of America's literacy efforts—Washington, D.C., boasting more literacy organizations per square mile than any other place in America ("Google" "literacy" + "Washington, DC" for a sampling). Despite all those government literacy offices, D.C. public schools' reading scores rank at the bottom with nonstates Guam and the Virgin Islands. In poverty, the District of Columbia's citizens again rank at or near the bottom. With that in mind, let's drop by the John Philip Sousa Middle School in D.C.

In 1950, John Philip Sousa Middle School was one of the five all-white schools denying entrance to African American students in what became a single case before the Supreme Court called *Brown v. Board of Education*. Because of that, Sousa is listed as a National Historic Landmark.

Historic it may be, but fifty years later it's not a school most people, white or black, would want their children to attend. What was an all-white state-of-the-art junior high in 1950 is now 99 percent black, with students drawn from some of the poorest homes in Washington, D.C., and holding some of the lowest scores in the nation. In recent years teachers and students complained about the thirty- and forty-year-old books in the library, but the book gripes finally ceased. By the time the nation was observing the fiftieth anniversary of *Brown v. Board of Education*, the library was closed, used only when a sewage pipe leaked into a math class.[21]

If Government Won't Recognize the Print Problem, What Can Anyone Do?

First of all it's not all government's fault. Part of the problem is a family and school situation—people who think the purpose of a book is to learn to read. "Once you learn, who needs to read? Everything you need is on TV or the computer." A national awareness campaign like the one I mentioned in the introduction could help enlighten some of those minds. There is also a secret government program that puts the equivalent of a *free* daily newspaper or weekly news magazine into the home of 99 percent of American homes, yet most people don't know about it. What makes it even more extraordinary is that it's associated with the most successful reading scores in the world. See page 169 in chapter 9 for details.

Short of wringing our hands in frustration until government wakes up, we have to find a way to get books into the lives of poor urban and rural children. Let me introduce you to four people who, largely unknown to each other, successfully took on that challenge. Here are two men and two women who have lived George Bernard Shaw's expression "Some men see things as they are and ask why? I dream things that never were and ask why not?"

Let's start with Danny Brassell. Back in 1995, Brassell was struggling to keep his head above water as a beginning teacher in a district so dysfunctional the state of California was forced to take it over: Compton Unified, located twenty-six freeway miles north of "The Magic Kingdom." One of the first things Brassell noticed was the lack of books in his classroom and school. Considering the students were coming from homes that suffered the same deficiency, this was intolerable.

California's antagonistic relationship with books and libraries, however, was an old story to the twenty-three-year-old Brassell. He remembered how the 1978 passage of the state's famous Proposition 13 had reduced property taxes statewide and, in the process, devastated state and school libraries, costing his librarian-father his job in San Diego and forcing a family move out of state. In light of that, if you were making a movie about this, you might describe what Danny did next as "The Revenge of the Librarian's Son."

Danny Brassell.

First, he created his own classroom library, including bound autobiographies his students wrote that fired their enthusiasm for reading. When the superintendent dropped in for a visit, he asked if Brassell needed anything.

"Sure," he replied, "a reading carpet." Despite a positive response, it never arrived. So Brassell went scavenging at a local carpet store, told them what he needed, and they agreed to give him any decent stuff they ripped out of people's houses when they were laying new rugs. What they actually delivered was enough to carpet Brassell's whole school and two more besides. "This told me that lots of times all you have to do is ask—ask and make sure you write a thank-you note," he said to me. "In fact, once you identify yourself as a teacher, most people want to give you a discount."

The next task was to create the school's library. Contacting some friends at a private school brimming with celebrities' kids in the wealthy Brentwood section of Los Angeles, Brassell asked if they could get the kids to donate the books they had outgrown. Bingo—two thousand books! Next he created a nonprofit organization called Assignment Books, bent on rebuilding or creating Compton school libraries. "One thing I learned the hard way: Unless you have the principal on board, you're dead before you know it. After I raised ten thousand books for one Compton school library, a new principal came in and turned the library into a study hall."

Besides convincing affluent friends and schools to donate their used children's books (or money, if they chose), Brassell was driving all over Southern California in his Ford Escort ("I could squeeze 1,000 books into it.") and stopping at every Salvation Army thrift shop he could find. "My father told me once, 'Whenever you come across an old book, page through it. In the old days, folks mistrusted banks and stored cash in their books.' Sure enough—$300 in a book at the Salvation Army. After I turned it in to the major, I had the greatest relationship you could imagine with that shop." In three years of scavenging, Brassell collected 84,000 books for Compton school libraries. Meanwhile, up in the state capital, Sacramento, the legislature was debating the sorry state of California reading scores and scrounging around for $195 million for more phonics materials.

For the moment, we leave Danny Brassell teaching his class and trawling suburbia for books, and move fifty miles north to Agoura Hills, where one day in 1998, eight-year-old Brandon Keefe was home from school with a cold and tagged along with his mother who had a board meeting at a local residential treatment center for children. She'd been a volunteer and board member there for twenty-five years but something was going to happen that day that would change her life. While playing with his video game in the corner that day, Brandon also was aware of what the grown-ups were discussing—the difficulties in creating an adequate library for the facility's children, with most of the talk centering on the expense.

Back in his third-grade classroom the next day, the subject of community service came up and Brandon's teacher asked if anyone had any sugges-

Brandon Keefe.

tions. Brandon's response was "My mom's orphanage needs books." Soon a plan was devised: Since most of his affluent classmates had an abundance of books they'd either outgrown or never intended to read, why not a book drive to collect them for kids who had no books? Soon Brandon was speaking at morning assemblies and in classrooms, organizing and promoting the campaign.

Just before winter break, Brandon's mom went to pick him up at school and instead of meeting a little boy with his backpack, she found a little entrepreneur surrounded by cartons containing 847 books he and his classmates had collected. "Merry Christmas, Mom!" he said.

Afterward, Robin Keefe, a strong advocate for volunteerism, kept thinking to herself, If these children could achieve this, others could as well. The sense of pride and accomplishment shouldn't be theirs alone. Why not offer other children the same opportunity? With that in mind, she and Brandon formed a nonprofit organization called BookEnds whose purpose was to connect individual volunteer schools with needy ones, but from there, all the work, organizing, and distributing would be student-driven.

The result has been extraordinary. To date, more than 120,000 students have donated and distributed one million books to 240,000 needy students in greater Los Angeles schools, while creating eighty-two school and youth center libraries. Community reaction has been positive enough to draw a few big-name donors out of the woodwork to offer financial support, names like Verizon, Eisner, Boeing, Toyota, American Express, Disney, and Coca-Cola.

Maybe the lesson for adults in this is: the next time a boardroom of grown-ups is vexed by a problem, go out and find a kid with a video game, sit him in the corner, and let him listen in.

It was inevitable that the Keefes and Danny Brassell should meet, see their common goals, and join forces. Today Brassell is an assistant professor in the teacher education department at California State University–Dominguez Hills and board member of BookEnds; Robin Keefe is president of Book-

Ends; and Brandon is a senior at UCLA, majoring in clinical science and accounting, and a public spokesperson for BookEnds.

Brigid Hubberman.

Across the continent in Ithaca, New York, Brigid Hubberman was encountering similar problems with some of the families she was working with at WIC sites (Women, Infants, and Children, a federal assistance program). While families were in the WIC waiting rooms, it was Brigid's part-time job to demonstrate the reading of books and how to interact with them. Even with children as young as one and a half years of age, she could tell if the child had any book experience and most had not. When she asked the school district what percentage of incoming students had essentially no book experience, the response was 20–25 percent. Worth noting is the fact that Ithaca is the home of Cornell University, an Ivy League institution, yet nearly a quarter of the community was "at-risk" for literacy. Soon Hubberman became adamant that every child in the community, not just the ones at WIC sites, deserved a healthy book start.

In 1995, she convinced a local bank, Tompkins Trust Company, to fund a book for every newborn in the county, something they continue to do to this day. The following year, she saw the holidays as another opportunity to get books into the homes of at-risk children. She secured funding for new books that WIC parents could choose and have gift-wrapped at the site that could be taken home as gifts.

In 1997, various county community agencies had a brainstorming day and Hubberman asked for a breakout session on how to create a community-wide "culture of literacy"—connecting every family and every child to print in a pleasurable way. "Hey," someone suggested in the session, "what about free bus tokens for families going to the library?" The eight committee members soon grew to thirty and became the Family Reading Partnership. Ideas and projects began to flow.

One member, Jim Crawford, noted, "People who use libraries use them, not because they don't have books but because they do have them and want even more." In other words, the book you own is a kind of seed that leads to more. This concept became the Bright Red Bookshelves. Collection crates were sprinkled at twelve sites (like Wegman's grocery stores) throughout Ithaca, where people could drop off lightly used books. These were collected, cleaned, and divested of annotations, and then placed on bright red bookshelves in centrally located sites for social services, even police stations and juvenile courts.

Soon a community-wide Literacy Vision Day was convened with representatives from every sector—schools, police, social services, hospitals, and librarians. Another local bank began contributing enough funds to give every incoming kindergartner (1,400) a free book at registration at the start of school.

A decade old now, the Family Reading Partnership (FRP) resides rent-free in a school district building; the model has been adopted by two neighboring counties; the New York State family court system has incorporated the Bright Red Bookshelf idea in its locations; FRP is used as the coordinator to deliver books to various social agencies that use books to connect with families in counseling; it also funds books so every pediatrician (thirty) in the county can distribute a book at wellness visits. A visitor to Ithaca, New York, cannot remain oblivious for long that reading is a community-wide habit: billboard-size banners hang from buildings and rooftops, reminding adults to "Read to me—any time, any place."

Leaving Brigid Hubberman's campaign, we drive east to North Adams, Massachusetts, where one day in 2000, David Mazor was visiting his daughter at Massachusetts College of Liberal Arts. Mazor had been an independent film distributor for twenty years and now resided in Amherst, the town he grew up in. He'd also been doing some writing on the subject of futurism and now, finished with the subject, he looked around for someone who might be able to use one of the brand new books he'd used in his research. He wondered if the college's library could use them.

"Absolutely," declared the librarian. "We haven't been able to buy a new book in two years because of budget cuts. All the money goes for online periodicals." And thus was sparked an idea that became a consuming fire in Mazor's mind.

"If you want books, I'll get you books," Mazor told him. And he meant it. "I was living in Amherst, surrounded by all these professors from five colleges—Amherst, Smith, UMass, Hampshire, and Mount Holyoke—

*Like his childhood hero Bill Russell,
David Mazor began to "visualize"
his problem: how to help the book-
neediest places in America.*

people who have more books than they know what to do with," he explained to me one day. He ended up collecting so many books the college had to send a truck to collect them.

And then one night Mazor thought, if a state college in a state like Massachusetts is short of books, what about elementary and high schools? He "Googled" "poorest county in the poorest state" and came up with Durant, Mississippi (population 3,000, average income $19,600). "I was so excited about the idea, I could barely sleep. In the morning, I called Durant High School and asked if they needed books. The librarian told me they hadn't been able to buy a book in forty years. All their funds went to repair the building. So when they built the new school in 1960, if they brought over the books from the old school, most are still there and not much has been added. She told me if a kid wanted to read a book on the Apollo moon mission, it would be impossible in that library.

"Books aren't like basketball backboards," Mazor explains. "If the backboard breaks, the school runs out and fixes it because they've got a game scheduled in the gym for Friday night. But when a book is lost or damaged, it doesn't get replaced because there's nothing coming Friday night that requires it."

At this point Mazor's mind was doing something he learned to do back in high school. He grew up in a family of readers, his father a law professor and his mother a social worker, and there were books everywhere. But one book stood out then and still does. It was a little paperback—*Go Up for Glory,* the autobiography of basketball great Bill Russell. It transported Mazor from his privileged circumstances in Amherst to Russell's segregated Louisiana and left an indelible impression. And there was another point in the book, a section in which Russell described his psychological breakthrough—when he started to "visualize" game situations before they happened and then how he would respond in the game. By the 1990s, this concept would be a staple of sports psychologists.

"Even as a kid, I got the point immediately and it shaped my life," he recalls. "All these years later, I'm thinking, if that book could make that big an impression on me as a kid, what about the book that's supposed to bring some kid to the far reaches of the world, the book he's never going to see because it's not in his school library. Somewhere there's a kid who's never seen a Van Gogh or a Michelangelo, but if he reads a biography there's a chance his life could change. The right book . . . the right kid." And all this time, Mazor is doing his Bill Russell thing, visualizing possibilities.

"I live in this community where we have all these books that no one's read since junior was in fourth grade. So out to the yard sale go the books on a weekend. If nobody buys them, they get *thrown out*. It's like having all these oil wells in your backyard. 'What a nuisance! How are we going get rid of all this excess oil?' Books in affluent homes don't get reread or worn-out." Mazor began to network in an area that had as many educators and books per square mile as any place in America. Soon he no longer had to hit the yard sales; cartons were being dropped off at his house and his garage was overflowing.

He now had boxes of books for Durant and was "Googling" through the South, Indian reservations, colleges, high schools, and elementaries. Here was a roadmap for his dream. Talking with librarians at various sites, he began to tailor the shipments: "What kinds of books do you need most? Listen, if you find a kid who is really interested in a particular subject and you haven't got a book on it, e-mail me and I'll get it." One school asked for children's books in English and Bengali—he got them!

He was soon supplying ten to fifteen schools around the country, and not just with single shipments. "I realized this was becoming too important to be a hobby. So I sold my business, formed a nonprofit called Reader to Reader, Inc., and Amherst College donated space in the religious life center." By 2005, he was supplying 160 schools in twenty-seven states from Maine to Mississippi, and he had more than a dozen volunteers cleaning, sorting, and packing—including a retired college admissions officer. A grant from Daimler-Chrysler paid for all his shipping costs, special purchases, and wish lists for one year. Cash and check donations began to pour in along with books. The local Barnes & Noble asked customers to donate a book when they bought one at Christmastime and it brought in 1,500 books. As of 2006, Reader to Reader had shipped 200,000 books to some of the book-neediest places in America.

Danny Brassell, Robin and Brandon Keefe,[22] Brigid Hubberman,[23] David Mazor[24]—four people who saw things as they were and asked why, four people who dreamed things that never were and asked why not? Forget the debates about cloning dogs and sheep—clone these people and you could change America.

With the Internet in Place, What's the Role of Libraries?

As I note in chapter 8, the Internet's unrestrained growth and unverifiable offerings are a *long* way from replacing libraries. I once said that the biggest threat to libraries was—libraries. Their unwillingness to recognize that their role was changing in school and community posed a far bigger threat than the Internet. Fortunately, they've seen the light and we're witnessing a library revolution in many cities and schools. Not that they did it willingly. It was very much a desperation move—caught as they were between a rock and a hard place: mega-bookstores on one end and the digital revolution on the other. It was a whole lot more comfortable for the patron to either go to a bookstore with a café or stay home and surf the net. Who wants to sit on those rock-hard maple chairs at the library, anyway? Given a choice of life or death, the libraries chose to act like bookstores.

Twenty-five years ago, while the culture critics were announcing the death of reading in America as a new video store popped up on every other corner and the number of cable channels was mushrooming, the mega-bookstore was being born. Gone were the "No Food and Beverage" signs on the door! Instead of discouraging people from sitting around reading the goods, they'd offer them cushions, couches, and soft rugs. Hungry? Have a snack in the café. Tired of the bandbox mall store with a narrow selection of books? Try our mega-inventory of everything under the sun. And there's no need to hurry—we don't close until 11 P.M.

The *New York Times Magazine* described the new atmosphere this way: "The . . . superstore is to this generation's avid readers what an Andrew Carnegie Library was to those of an earlier era: community center, reading room and, of course, repository of thousands of books. The carefully calculated lounge-and-browse ambiance is so relaxing—so free from petty distractions of commerce—that a Manhattan customer died at the Broadway and 82nd Street branch, nestled in an overstuffed chair and left to slumber undisturbed until closing."[25]

At a time when reading was supposed to be dead, the bookstores made themselves "user-friendly" and, in effect, woke the dead. Someone finally publicly admitted that we humans like to sit comfortably when we read and often prefer to nibble and sip while we do so. The booksellers sensed that if you build it comfortable and tasty, "they will come." And come they did, in numbers that made librarians envious. Within a decade they had their architects on the phone and the demarcation lines between store and library were blurring. These days it's getting harder and harder to tell if you're in the mall or the reference room. The shining example is the Salt Lake City Public Library, which debuted in 2003.

Built with $65 million of public bond money, SLCPL holds: a plush art gallery; more than 150 computers (including some for games); a rooftop garden; a book collection in eighty-eight languages; a children's department that includes a cave and "Grandma's Attic" room with rafters, pillows, and a trunk for dress-ups; the now ubiquitous snack bar; a cantina with a big-screen TV; and music (including rock) piped throughout the building. True, the noise level is a little higher than it used to be—and that's the way most patrons like it. In fact, the librarians wear buttons labeled "No Shh!" How did this go over with the sedate Salt Lake City crowd? Patronage numbers tripled in less than a year.

Public libraries aren't just mimicking the brick and mortar look of the stores. Those that can't afford renovations settle for imitating the social experience. For example, the busiest community public library in America (500,000 visitors) is the Queens Borough Public Library in New York. Its secret: thirty thousand events a year in the library.[26] There are cruise ships that can't compete with the event calendar of that library.

While high school and elementary libraries haven't had the funding for makeovers (too busy fulfilling all those No Child Left Behind requirements), colleges have been turning themselves inside out to change.[27] *Out* are the isolationist carrels and *in* are conference tables and group study rooms. With cafés as ubiquitous as bottled water machines and computers, campus libraries resemble "intellectual gathering places" where tomorrow's thinkers try out their ideas. As a Columbia University librarian put it, "[The library] is moving from being a warehouse to a workshop." They come for the intellectual and social jousting they can't have alone online or in dormitory rooms.

Actually, I always thought it was inevitable they'd return to the library. After all, there's only room for so much downloaded music either in your life or on your laptop. Sooner or later, one of them had to reach capacity. And we've renovated the libraries to welcome them home. Nice.

How Do I Make My School Library More Successful on a Limited Budget?

You can start by taking a hard look at your local grocery store. In 1996, the *New York Times* ran an article on supermarkets and the keys to their success.[28] The author noted that there originally was only one rule for supermarkets:

Put the milk at one end of the store and bread at the other—to get people to walk through the entire store. That rule still applies: The more they see, the more they buy. But the shopper surveys and Universal Price Code scanner offer other insights, including some we might apply to libraries:

- Only 31 percent of grocery patrons bring a shopping list (more than half of adult library patrons arrive without a book in mind; even more so for children).
- Two-thirds of purchases are unplanned (very similar to book choices).
- Products placed at the optimum level (15 degrees below eye level) sell 8 percent better (clear or weed spaces at eye level for displaying books).

Few grocery customers know that food companies pay $9 billion for shelf space ("slotting fees"), accounting for one-half of stores' annual profits. In simple terms, they're renting shelf space. Paying that kind of money, the manufacturer makes sure its product is displayed on the shelf to its best advantage—that is, face out. This visibility is so connected to sales, the low-paying companies receive the worst seats in the house—the top and bottom shelves.[29]

The reason companies want each product face out is simple: It's the cover that most often influences our choices—the picture of the cookie, cereal, cake, or magazine. Any magazine editor can tell you immediately the names of the persons whose images will immediately boost newsstand sales (once it was Diana, then it was Oprah, now it's Brad or Britney).

Unlike grocery stores, too many libraries haven't discovered that face-out marketing enhances circulation.

Compare that successful marketing approach with what we do with books and children. I often get the feeling that if most children's librarians were brought in as consultants for the grocery industry, the first thing they'd suggest would be to turn all the boxes and bags sideways to squeeze more of them onto the shelf.

What does the spine of the book tell you? The title, author, publisher, and Dewey decimal number. Since 60 percent of the people going into a bookstore or library don't have a particular book (or author or publisher) in mind, it's the cover that will move the book, not the spine. The majority of public and school libraries I see in my travels are clueless when it comes to these principles. Some don't have a single book shelved with the cover facing out. An amazing number have them face out but beyond the reach of children who could read them. The power of putting books face out works even at the lowest levels of literacy. When researchers observed a kindergarten classroom library for one week, 90 percent of the books that children chose had been shelved with the covers facing out.[30] The photograph on the previous page of the children's room of a public library is typical of what I find in 90 percent of libraries (school and public) around the United States. (Yes, I know there are exceptions to this rule, and the reason they stand out is because they're *exceptions*.)

Where Do I Get the Library Shelf Space for Face-Out Books?

I'm not talking about positioning *every* book face out. Bookstores don't place every book face out, but the ones they really want to move—the new arrivals, the bestsellers—always go face out. Unlike most educators and librarians, publishers know that the cover sells the book, so not only do they work extra-hard designing the right cover, many pay the book chains as much as $750 a month per book to have the cover showing.[31] *That's* how important the cover is.

Nonetheless, classroom teachers have even less room than libraries for this approach. In response to the space challenge, a few years ago a teacher (whose name I wish I had jotted down) told me how she'd solved the problem by installing rain gutters in the dead spaces throughout her classroom: the space between the chalk ledge and the floor, the two-foot space between the closet and the chalkboard. Then another teacher sent me photographs of the rain gutters she'd installed.

The rain gutters they were talking about were purchased at the local hardware store for about three dollars per ten-foot strip, and were made of enameled, reinforced plastic. As plastic, they were easily cut to any size and were supported by plastic brackets that could be screwed into almost any wall, including concrete blocks (see photo). And they hold a *lot* of books—face out.

After I mentioned the concept at an all-day teacher workshop, Mike Oliver, then the principal of Alma Elementary in Mesa, Arizona,[32] approached me at the break. "We could do this at my school!" he exclaimed with great enthusiasm. "We could do it in every classroom. I know we could." I could see the images dancing in his head as he spoke to me. I could also see an inner-city principal who understood that reading is more than just teaching the basics, more than drill and skill.

That summer, Oliver spent nearly $3,000 on rain gutters (I call him the Martha Stewart of rain gutters!). Recruiting volunteers from parents and faculty, he installed the shelving throughout the school, including his own office. Since then, Mesa has asked him to open two new schools (Barbara Bush Elementary and then James Zaharis Elementary), with each bearing

Photo by Larry LaPrise.

At a cost of just $3 for ten feet, plastic rain gutter turns dead wall space into an attractive opportunity for face-out book marketing.

his unique imprint for literacy: Children will come to love books if surrounded by quality instruction, a rich print environment, a caring, reading faculty, and rain gutters.

Good ideas like rain gutter bookshelves are highly contagious, fortunately. As soon as other principals and librarians saw Mike Oliver's school site, copycats sprang up all over the area. The photo on the previous page is one example, from Peralta Trail Elementary in nearby Gold Canyon, Arizona. In Chattanooga, Tennessee, businessman Bill Thurman has led a community-wide campaign to blanket childcare centers and children's wards in local hospitals with the rain gutters.

Rain gutters alone aren't going to solve a school or community's reading problems. They're merely a piece of a marketing strategy. But without marketing, few products get off the ground, no matter how good their design.

How Do I Find Out About Good New Children's Books?

What children read is less important than *that* they read, but most adults want the best for their money. This handbook, with its list of a thousand read-alouds in the Treasury, should solve at least part of the problem of what to buy; the list is also updated monthly at my Web site, www.trelease-on-reading.com. If you are fortunate enough to have in your community a bookstore that specializes in children's books (or a general bookstore that gives more than cursory attention to children), by all means tap them as a resource. Many have free newsletters to keep you abreast of new titles in children's books.

In addition, your neighborhood library subscribes to several journals that regularly review children's books, including *The Horn Book, Kirkus Reviews, Booklist, Book Links,* and *School Library Journal.* It may also provide you with the annual lists of books designated as "notable" by the American Library Association. The modern public library fully recognizes the limitations of today's parents, many of whom were not readers as children but now want better for their children. To help in that area, libraries like Salt Lake City's make booklists available for parents and children. A quick look at their Web site (www.slcpl.lib.ut.us/index.jsp) shows a button for "Booklists" that links to categories containing thousands of titles arranged and chosen by professional librarians—all for free.

Here are some more resources:

- In 1999, the National Education Association (NEA), the nation's largest teacher organization, conducted an online survey for teachers' favorite books for children. The top hundred choices are about as good a list as you'll ever find. It's free for the downloading at the NEA Web site at www.nea.org/readacross/resources/catalist.html. The page also includes a link to the children's own hundred choices, also excellent.

- The American Library Association and its national board of reviewers offer an extensive listing each year that includes the best of children's books, videos, and audios. The lists can be found at your local public library or on the Web at www.ala.org/ala/alsc/awardsscholarships/childrensnotable/Default1888.htm.
- Publishers annually ask ten thousand students and teachers to vote on their favorite books published in a given year, tabulating the votes into lists called "Children's Choices." There are three components to the vote: children (elementary), young adults (teens), and teachers. More information and the lists can be found on the Web at www.reading.org/resources/tools/choices.html.
- A complete list of all the books used on the hundreds of *Reading Rainbow* episodes can be found at its Web site, http:gpn.unl.edu/rainbow/booklist/booklist.asp.
- The Center for the Study of Books in Spanish for Children and Adolescents, directed by Isabel Schon, Ph.D., is at California State University–San Marcos, San Marcos, CA; Web site, http:www.csusm.edu/csb/.

If you are just looking for a guide to good books, not necessarily new ones, your child's teacher (if she regularly reads to classes) may have a list of choices she can't possibly get to in the course of the year. At your next parent-teacher conference, ask for recommendations. Your community children's librarian also can be a good resource.

How Can I Find a Copy of a Favorite Book from My Childhood?

It used to be that in order to find that long-lost favorite children's book, you had to have the name of either the book or the author. Not anymore. Today, Book Stumpers comes to the rescue. Run by Loganberry Books, a used-and-rare bookstore, Book Stumpers allows you to post a description of your book online (for $2). Each day, librarians from all over the country (who obviously have some time on their hands) visit the Web site (www.logan.com/loganberry/stump.html) and take the postings as personal challenges. Last year they had a better than 70 percent success rate.

Stanley Woodworth's problem wasn't in remembering the title or author. He just couldn't locate a copy. Growing up in Massachusetts during the Depression, Woodworth spent long hours devouring childhood classics like *The Merry Adventures of Robin Hood* and *Treasure Island,* but none had the hold on him of *Porto Bello Gold* by Arthur D. Howden Smith—an obscure volume intended as a prequel to *Treasure Island*.

Somewhere between childhood and adulthood, Woodworth and his beloved book parted company. Perhaps it was lost, maybe worn out—he never knew. But he did remember it fondly and often found himself searching for his old friend on the dusty shelves of used book stores—to no avail. For forty years Woodworth taught ancient and foreign languages, English, and philosophy at the Cate School in Carpinteria, California, living on the school grounds and becoming a beloved campus figure. All the while, he built his personal library.

And then one day he was browsing the shelves of Bart's Books, a legendary used book store in nearby Ojai, and there it was—*Porto Bello Gold*, for $2.50. "I was so excited," he said later, "I would have paid $250 for it." And yet, when he got it home, he was afraid to open it, never mind read it, for fear it would be too much of a disappointment after sixty years. But finally he did, and what he found was beyond even his wildest expectations. There, following the title page, was a child's scribbled signature— *Stanley Woodworth*.

What he'd found was the original volume from his childhood shelf. The boy and his book finally had been reunited.[33]

Mr. Woodworth died a few years short of the Internet revolution and the miracles it performs for book searches. No longer do you have to plod wearily between used book stores searching in vain for that special title. Just go online to sites such as Bookfinder.com, Abebooks.com, or Alibris.com and begin your search. Each of those sites is linked to thousands of booksellers across the continent. For example, today I plugged *Porto Bello Gold* into www.bookfinder.com and came up with 140 existing copies, ranging in price from $4.45 to $75. Of course, to determine if your signature is inside the book, you'd need to (1) e-mail each bookseller, and (2) have some spare time.

Chapter 8

Lessons from Oprah, Harry, and the Internet

Computers are incredibly fast, accurate and stupid; humans are incredibly slow, inaccurate and brilliant; together they are powerful beyond imagination.

—Albert Einstein

THERE are days when I honestly think I'm living in a parallel universe where during the last ten years Oprah Winfrey has had millions of people of every race and income level gladly reading books they'd normally never choose for themselves and the Harry Potter books have inspired millions of kids to read seven-hundred–page books, while in the *other* universe, the education bureaucrats were trying to improve children's reading by testing them more than any nation on earth.[1]

Oprah never gives a test, yet her "students" rushed out and bought almost nine hundred thousand copies of *Anna Karenina* when she selected it for her club. The first six Potter books contained a total of 3,365 pages (more pages than Dickens's four longest novels) and not one page contained a quiz question. Since Oprah and Harry have been so successful, wouldn't you think the school folks would borrow a page or two from their methods and procedures? Instead, they do the complete opposite but expect to get the same results. You couldn't *make up* stuff like this!

So while we're waiting for the bureaucrats to drop by our universe, let's see what can be learned by looking at Ms. Winfrey's lesson plans (we'll look at Harry next and then the Internet).

Four Lessons from Oprah

How Did Oprah Make TV into a "Pro-Reading" Experience?

Television has long had a parasitic relationship with print, stealing many of its early reporters and analysts from newspapers and magazines. Local and network news departments still swipe a large amount of their material from daily newspapers, put a new tread on it, and peddle it a few hours or days later as their own. For decades, authors and writers have been mainstays on television as guests on the *Today Show, Good Morning America, Larry King Live,* and other daily talk shows. Television almost never gave to print what print offered to TV.

Then along came Oprah Winfrey. In 1996, after ten years of sleaze and self-help as a show menu, her staff tentatively suggested that she do a "book club." Oprah herself was a big reader and had been since age five. Reading three books in a weekend (her normal diet) would give her an enormous advantage over nearly everyone in the television industry, as well as most teachers, who don't read that many books in two months (see page 100 in chapter 5).

It has been Oprah's reading appetite that drives the curriculum of her book club. There is no supervisor or syllabus telling her what she should like or not like. This formula will only work in schools if the teacher is a devoted reader, like Oprah—the Queen of Read.

Lesson No. 1: Oprah's Book Club could never have succeeded if she herself hadn't been an avid reader. You can't give someone a cold if you don't have one, and you can't give a child the love of reading if you yourself don't have it.

What Does Oprah's Book Club Have to Do with a Class of Fifth-Graders Who Hate to Read?

Let's look at who is watching television at ten in the morning or two in the afternoon, when Oprah's show is aired in a lot of places: not the valedictorians or honors graduates or the former gifted and talented students. They're all working. Oprah's "class" often consists of the laid-off, the laid-back, and the lying-down crowd, many people who hadn't read a book in twenty years, people who quit reading because they got tired of reading dead poets they couldn't understand back in high school.

It should also be noted that Oprah and her producers were smart enough at the very start not to use the word I used in the previous paragraph: "class." They knew very well the connotations carried by that word with many in their audience: requirements, demands, and tests. So they used the word "club," which suggests belonging, membership, and invitation.

Lesson No. 2: Book Club works better than Book Class.

If Oprah's Audience Is So Reluctant, How Did She Motivate Them?

Having selected a book, Oprah simply walks out to her audience of twenty-two million in 119 countries and talks about the book she's selected. She talks about the book animatedly, passionately, and sincerely. No writing, no tests, no dumb dioramas to make, just good, old-fashioned enthusiasm for something she's read.

Above everything else, this is the key to Oprah's book success—she recognized what too many educators have forgotten: we're an oral species. We define ourselves first and foremost orally. When we see a good movie, a good ball game, a great concert—the first thing we want to do afterward is talk about it. When my wife and I see a good movie, do you think we rush out to the car, pull some napkins out of the glove compartment, and write down the main idea? "Honey, what do you think was the *theme*?"

What can we apply from this to our work with children? Well, let's eliminate not all but much of the writing they're required to do whenever they read. ("The more we read, the more we gotta write, so let's read less and we can work less, right?") We adults don't labor when we read, so why are we forcing children to? It hasn't created a nation of writers *or* readers.

On the other hand, look what Oprah's created: when she began her book club there were 250,000 discussion groups nationally. Today there are more than 500,000 such groups,[2] including a nationwide series called One Book, One City, initiated by Nancy Pearl and Chris Higashi at the Washington Center for the Book, and certainly helped by the climate Oprah had created.

Lesson No. 3: More talk, less writing; more open discussion without right or wrong answers.

Can the Oprah Lessons Be Applied in the Home?

One of the first to recognize the "home" potential of Oprah's club was Shireen Dodson, assistant director of the Center for African American

History and Culture at the Smithsonian Institution and the mother of an eleven-year-old daughter. In 1996, Dodson founded a book discussion group that eventually led to the publication of a popular handbook on the subject: *The Mother-Daughter Book Club: How Ten Busy Mothers and Daughters Came Together to Talk, Laugh and Learn Through Their Love of Reading* (Harper). Along with bringing the mother–daughter relationships closer, the club provoked greater class participation by the girls, broadened their reading interests, and provided platforms for open discussion of issues both parent and child had avoided previously.[3]

As soon as Margie McPartland of Greenwich, Connecticut, saw Dodson's book in 1997, she knew she had to start a mother-son book club. Many of her mom friends were anxious about their sons starting middle school, so she had no trouble collecting a dozen mothers with eleven-year-olds in tow for two hours a week (usually a Saturday or Sunday, depending on sports schedules). "Our first book was Lois Lowry's *The Giver* and we almost fell off our chairs at the discussion that ensued," McPartland told me.

The McPartland club eventually became a model for other moms in the area, including Brenda Chapman and some friends in Ridgefield, Connecticut. Their boys were starting fourth grade when they launched their group. As Brenda explained it to me:

> Each month a different mother/son combo picked a book to read. The boy who picked the book comes to the next meeting with some questions about the book. That boy will be the facilitator for the question part and then the discussion opens up to whatever else is on their minds about the story. They usually talk on the subject for about an hour and sometimes longer. We meet on the second Saturday morning of the month at 8 A.M. This is the time least likely to interfere with sports. We meet in my husband's little office that is located in the center of town. Since he's a real estate appraiser with nothing but county maps on the walls, we joke that it's a low stimulation environment so the boys aren't distracted. After the talk, the boys play in the empty parking lot and the moms debrief on the topics brought up that morning and plan the next month's meeting. No one brings food or drink, it's totally no-frills, but it seems to work.
>
> When we started, the boys were fourth-graders and most of them had the same teacher, Julie Droller, in third grade. This very dynamic teacher introduced book groups to her class and gave our boys a great start into the world of discussion around literature.
>
> Unfortunately, the following year this same teacher was having

trouble getting her class to get the gist of what a book discussion should entail. After a couple of conversations, we asked our boys to model a discussion for the third-graders. It was a wonderful success. All the children read the same text. It was Cynthia Rylant's short story "Slower Than the Rest." Our book group boys divided into three small groups. They sat in circles as they would for our regular meeting and the third-graders formed a circle around the outside of each group. The boys had their discussion and the third-graders listened. After the discussion wound down, about thirty minutes later, the third-graders asked the boys questions related to the book and to being in a regular book group.[4]

Julie asked her class to notice how the discussion was similar to or different from the kinds of discussions they had been having themselves. At the end, the older boys answered questions about our group and how they felt about it. They all said it was fun to meet with your friends outside school. Some said that there were books they wouldn't have chosen themselves but read for the group and ended up liking. They also expressed how they liked just reading and talking about the book without any other work attached.

The beauty of our group meeting outside of school is that we have control over the material. We (meaning both mothers and sons) seem to gravitate toward topics that will lead to discussions outside our regular comfort zone. The moms still leave 90 percent of the discussion to the boys, but we do manage to put our two cents in, value wise, at the end of the meeting. It seems to be particularly potent when a sensitive issue is addressed in the third person through a character. As moms, we feel like we've gotten to know our sons better and hear what they're thinking about, and even struggling with, socially and morally. Personally, I've learned a lot about my peers and their parenting style. I think we have a great support system in place as we enter middle school and are faced with decisions on some of those tough social issues.

Whether you're contemplating a book discussion club for your family or class, my current favorite guide is *Deconstructing Penguins* (Ballantine) by Lawrence and Nancy Goldstone. Simply put, it's a manual on how to "dig a tunnel" into the heart and soul of a book. (Disregard both the title and the cover of the book—they're awful.) You can find other discussion guides online at: Book Discussion Groups for Kids at Multnomah County Library (www.multcolib.org/talk/guides.html) and the Washington Center for the Book, in Seattle (www.spl.org/default.asp?pageID=collection_discussiongroups).

Lesson No. 4: The love of reading is more caught than taught and best caught in groups.

Six Lessons from Harry Potter

Back in 1998, when the first Harry Potter book (*Harry Potter and the Sorcerer's Stone*) came across the sea, the arrival went largely unnoticed by educators and government because they were so busy ranting about the lack of reading being done by children. At the same time, children's editors were telling their authors, "Please don't send me a four-hundred-page manuscript. Today's kids will *not* read thick books!" Back in the library, the librarians were trying to cope with yet another load of "series" trash. "We just got rid of the Babysitters Club and Sweet Valley High books, and now the Goosebumps arrive! What's that you say? There's a hot new title? *Harry* what? Please don't tell me it's another series."

It was a series, of course, and in changing the world of children's reading it offered some valuable lessons about what and why children read.

How Is Harry Potter Different from Other "Series" Books?

There are two kinds of series books:

1. The quick-and-easy commercial kind, such as Nancy Drew, Goosebumps, and The Babysitters Club.
2. The more sophisticated series, such as Cleary's Ramona books, Lewis's Chronicles of Narnia, Banks's Indian in the Cupboard, and Rowling's Harry Potter.

The quick-and-easy series are often mass-produced, sometimes written by more than one author, and churned out at a pace of more than one a year; the books in a more sophisticated series are always written by one person, published a year or more apart, and characterized by richer text, plot, and characterization.

Along with its excellent imagery, what immediately sets Harry Potter books apart from nearly all others is the amount of text. Consuming that many words, students are getting prodigiously better at reading—many for the first time—and enjoying it. When the 2004 NAEP reading scores were announced, the folks in Washington were ecstatic over the seven-point rise by the fourth-graders, the largest increase in thirty-three years, and were trumpeting that it proves the effectiveness of all those Reading First tests. Really now? Did anyone stop to think that maybe a certain young wizard had something to do with the magical elevation? After all, this was the first generation of NAEP test-takers to have grown up with Harry, to have lived all their known lives in a culture awash in 100 million copies of his books. How about a nod to J. K. Rowling and her little wizard for the impact they might have had on vocabulary and comprehension?

I'm not talking about literary style or imagery, not even emotional levels—just the number of words a child must traverse in order to reach the end. Here's a word count I did for some books, including a few classics:

Goosebumps: 8 words per sentence; 22,450 words in book.
Heidi: 19.6 words per sentence; 93,600 words in book.
The Hobbit: 18 words per sentence; 97,470 words in book.
The Hunchback of Notre Dame: 15 words per sentence; 126,000 words in book.
Harry Potter and the Order of the Phoenix: 13.5 words per sentence; 214,536 words in book.

Lesson No. 1: Harry Potter has children willingly reading books that are nine times longer than *Goosebumps* and twice as long as *Heidi*.

Why Are the Potter Books So Popular?

The fantasy is rich and the cheeky humor is very appealing, but there's something else, too. Shortly after Harry's initial success, and while many adults were pondering his fortune, a Texas library professor made a simple but insightful observation: The Harry Potter books are entirely "plot-driven."

This isn't to say such a condition is good or bad, but it may account for many children's reactions to the series. When we adults want to enjoy ourselves with print, relax on the beach or in front of a roaring fire on a winter afternoon, many of us choose a novel that will have us turning pages, forgetting what time it is, and reading into the wee hours. In such circumstances we don't want issue-driven novels or complex studies of human character. We want a good, old-fashioned, plot-driven book that we can read for pleasure.

But what do the adults foist on students? Issue- or character-driven novels, awarded prizes for their complexity and character study. This is not to say such volumes are either bad or ill-chosen, but where in the name of

Uncle Newbery are the plot-driven books on the award lists? (I might point out, the most popular Newbery winners are the ones with strong plot lines.)[5] It's okay for adults to read thrillers, but children should be reading for learning, enrichment, and insight—not for the pure pleasure of finding out what happens next. As Harry might say, "Oh, those stupid Muggles!"

Lesson No. 2: Children want page-turners, just like grown-ups do.

Are the Potter Books Really a Threat to Children's Souls?

The writer Anna Quindlen once wryly observed, "There is nothing so wonderful in America that someone can't create a Calvary out of it." So when thirty-five million children lay down their Walkmans, cell phones, remotes, and Gameboys to read four-hundred- to eight-hundred-page books (Harry Potter), the doomsayers shout, "It's the Devil wearing the Messiah's clothes!"

Anything new, popular, or magical becomes the anti-Christ—which is not peculiar to our time or place. The furor over the Potter books mimicks a similar one in 1847, when Sir James Young Simpson introduced pain-killing anesthetics to the maternity ward in the same Scottish city (Edinburgh) where the first Harry Potter book would be written 147 years later. Simpson was immediately accused by church leaders of circumventing God's will. (If God imposes pain in childbirth, who is man to nullify it?) Today, Simpson's practices are commonly used in both Christian and secular hospitals throughout the world.

While we are on the subject of hospitals and children: Two researchers monitored children's admissions to British hospital emergency rooms during a three-year period, including the two weekends in which books five and six in the Potter series were released. According to their report in the December 2005 issue of the *British Medical Journal,* admission rates for children ages seven to fifteen were down by almost one half on those two weekends. Apparently, reading is good for the body as well as the mind.

The issue of censorship and children's books is greater than we have space for here (see my essay at www.trelease-on-reading.com/censor1.html), so for now, suffice it to say: In the nearly ten years since the arrival of the Potter books, school crime was down,[6] teen pregnancies declined,[7] and teen smoking and drug use dropped.[8] Additionally, the thousands of midnight Potter publication parties in bookstores were marked by nothing but orderly, good-humored behavior on the part of nearly one million children and their parents—something that probably couldn't have been said about similar gatherings of children and parents at a thousand midnight Little League games. If, indeed, there were all those satanic connections to the Potter books, where is the evidence of the devil's work upon tens of millions of children's souls in the last decade?

If you are a school district or library being challenged on the Harry Potter books, you might wish to call up support from two Christian (one Protestant and one Catholic) resources: *Looking for God in Harry Potter* (Reed Elsevier) by John Granger, a home-schooling Christian father of seven; and Father Roderick Vonhögen, a Catholic priest of the Archdiocese of Utrecht (The Netherlands), who has explored the positive classical and biblical origins of all the Harry Potter books in his popular podcasts.[9] And by all means, visit the American Library Association's Web site for support materials.[10]

Lesson No. 3: In all religious censorship arguments, it's good to recall the words of the legendary Yale chaplain William Sloane Coffin, who said, "Christ came to take away our sins, not our minds."[11]

What's Wrong with "Series" Books in the First Place?

That question is best answered by the award-winning research of Dr. Catherine Sheldrick Ross, acting dean of graduate studies and professor of library and information science at the University of Western Ontario, Canada.[12]

Ross found "series books" to be the uncontested favorite of young readers for the last one hundred years, but acknowledges they have long been objects of scorn among the cultural gatekeepers—teachers and librarians. That antagonism is worth exploring if you wish to understand children's reading patterns.

According to Ross, around the time of the Civil War and coinciding with significant revolutions in printing and delivery services (like the railroads), there appeared a new kind of reading material: cheap fiction called the "story papers" and "dime novels." Printed on inexpensive pulp paper, these stories of adventure-bound heroes and heroines appealed to the servant and labor classes—the very people ignored by traditional publishers.

With their "blood and thunder" tales of cowboys and Indians, pirates, outlaws, and triumphant orphans, the story papers and dime novels were published biweekly, became national sensations, and were denounced by social critics who predicted disaster.

The offspring of the dime novel was the "series book" for young readers, conceived by Edward Stratemeyer in the late 1890s. Aimed at the preteen and teen reader, the series books eventually included Nancy Drew, The Hardy Boys, The Bobbsey Twins, The Motor Boys, The Rover Boys, Tom Swift, and The Outdoor Girls. The stories were adventure- or family-oriented, written nonstop by a large syndicate of writers, all using pseudonyms.

The elitists were so certain Nancy Drew would corrupt girls' minds (as sixty years later they thought Goosebumps would turn every child into a serial killer), H. W. Wilson Company, the largest U.S. manufacturer of library supplies, refused to print Nancy Drew index cards for the card catalog, and even published a list of nearly sixty authors who should not be circulated by libraries, all of them authors of series like Tom Swift and The Bobbsey Twins.

Coupled with the elitism was the widely held belief that fiction was something to be fed to children in only small, controlled doses. They believed children only learned from facts; therefore, fiction was useless. And the worst fiction of all would be the sensational fiction of series books. Here's a quote from 1850: "No part of education . . . is of greater importance than the selection of proper books. . . . No dissipation can be worse than that induced by the perusal of exciting books of fiction . . . a species of a monstrous and erroneous nature."[13]

What made the series books especially evil for children was that they were "addictive." Children weren't content to read just one; they'd read the first, then the second, then the third, and so on. Unfortunately, moaned the experts, the whole time they're reading that junk, they're not reading the wonderful nonfiction book on sponges that just arrived in the library!

Lesson No. 4: The fear that series books (or Harry) will corrupt the soul is at least as old as The Bobbsey Twins and a close relative of Y2K paranoia.

Do Series Books Actually Do Any Good or Just Take Up Kids' Time?

Certainly series books make a "pleasure connection" with the child. As we saw in chapter 1, humans seldom do something over and over unless it brings repeated pleasures. Pleasure is the "glue" that holds us to a particular activity.

How much damage these mindless adventure stories might do was hotly debated, but not by young Jacques, who was fresh off the boat from France in 1920 and soaking up every Frank Merriwell sports novel he could find. Nor was he ashamed years later to admit the profoundly positive influence the books played in his reading development and acclimation to America, except by then he was well on his way to becoming America's best-known humanities scholar—Jacques Barzun (who turned ninety-six in 2000 and celebrated by producing a best seller on the history of world culture).[14] On page 97, we saw Krashen's research on the effectiveness of using series books with ESL students.

In 1926, the American Library Association asked 36,750 students from thirty-four cities to name their favorite books. Ninety-eight percent listed one of the mass-produced Stratemeyer series books (The Rover Boys, The Motor Boys, Tom Swift, and The Bobbsey Twins), with the high-IQ students reading twice as many of the series books.[15]

And finally, Ross points to the large chunks of reading done by the series reader as examples of what Margaret Meek called "private lessons." That is, these daily readings teach the child the rules about skimming and inferring, about where one must slow down to decipher the clues, about the importance of chapter titles or of character and setting.[16] The adage that "the more you read, the better you get at it" is not only true, it should also be the slogan of series books.

Over a five-year period during the 1990s I surveyed 2,887 teachers, with an average of fourteen years' teaching experience. When asked to name their favorite childhood books, 30 percent named a series book as their personal favorite. Since a 1999 study shows teachers' literacy skills to be the equal of their college classmates', and 50 percent of the teachers' skills exceed 80 percent of the general population's,[17] it should be obvious that series books do not impede literacy.

The most conclusive evidence of series books' ability to produce better readers can be found in the thirty years of research done by Professor G. Robert Carlson. Each semester he asked his graduate students to write their "reading autobiographies," recollections of their early years with reading—what they loved and what they hated. As he reported in *Voices of Readers: How We Come to Love Books*, the majority of those students had strong relationships with series books in their early years. Did it stunt their intellectual growth? Well, if they made it all the way to graduate school, apparently not.[18]

Lesson No. 5: Series books are avidly read by the best readers, without impeding their skills.

Why Do They Always Ruin a Book Like *Harry Potter* with a Movie?

I sympathize with the teacher or librarian trying to interest a student in a book, only to hear the response, "I already saw the movie." I concede that a book's "dramatic tension" or plot can be seriously impaired if the film is seen first. Fortunately books outnumber films by 300 to 1, so why not focus on "unfilmed" books?

Part of the language arts curriculum should be to teach the difference between cinema and literature, that they are not the same, any more than a photograph of a buffalo is the same as a painting or sculpture of a buffalo. The best way to teach that difference is to read the book together, view the film afterward, and explore the differences.

Often the child who uses the film as an excuse for not reading a book isn't an avid reader in the first place. The problem is not with the film but in our failure to build a pleasure bridge between that child and print. As for claims that a movie drains book interest, everyone who thinks Cecil B. De-Mille ruined Bible sales when he made those epic Charlton Heston films, please raise your hand.

We can and should use a popular film to jump-start student interest in prequels, sequels, or other books by the author. The first Harry Potter movie debuted four years after the first book appeared yet it pushed the first volume back to the number one spot on the best-seller lists and boosted sales of the three sequels. Three months before Peter Jackson unveiled his *Lord of the Rings* film, the attendant publicity increased sales of the book by 400 percent, without even a movie tie-in attached to the cover. Even more remarkable, as a result of movie interest *The Hobbit* had its best sales year since its debut in 1937, an increase in sales of 500 percent. So it was no surprise to see the Narnia book sales jump 630 percent with the movie.

Purists are often dismayed by the fact that the movie draws a bigger audience than the book, even though the book is better. That's entirely understandable: the original book probably had $20,000 in advertising behind it and the film had $50 million. If you spent $50 million promoting *Gray's Anatomy,* you'd get a pretty big readership (though the subject matter may not be what some readers had in mind when they saw the ads).

Lesson No. 6: Film and literature are not mutually exclusive; use the movie to promote other books by the author or sequels.

Five Lessons from the Internet

With the firm arrival of the Internet to most homes, offices, and schools, many educators are wrestling with how to squeeze both books and bytes into their budget, and parents are wrestling with dosage-time questions. The technocrats say the world's children can be turned into millions of hitchhikers on the "information highway," who surf their way to achievement heights beyond anyone's estimation. The traditionalists point out books are more permanent, portable, and far more verifiable than computer bytes. Somewhere there's a rational land of comfort between the doomsayers and irrepressible optimists.

If doomsayers had a patron saint I think it would be Plato who warned in his *Phaedrus* that if people turned to reading and writing, it would spell the end of memorization.

The optimists would be represented by Thomas Edison who predicted in 1922 that "the motion picture is destined to revolutionize our education system and . . . in a few years will supplant, largely, if not entirely, the use of textbooks."

So let's see if we can find a happy medium. For what it's worth, I confess my biases right up front: By some people's standards, I'm a media freak; I own five Apple Macs, built my Web site myself, and use the Internet all day long for research, news, entertainment, and shopping (mostly for books). I just clicked on the folder containing the PDF research files I've downloaded for this edition of *The Read-Aloud Handbook*: there were 111 documents totaling 3.4 gigabytes of space—and those are just the PDFs. This morning I downloaded thirty-five minutes of a radio readings from the BBC and fifty minutes from NPR, both of which I'll listen to either on my iPod or in the car. (More on that on page 173 in chapter 9.) Google could be the best thing to happen to the inquisitive mind since Gutenberg, or as one writer put it: "Historians will have a common term for the period prior to the appearance of Google: the Dark Ages."[19] So I'm a fan. But not a blind one.

Does a Computer in the Home or Classroom Improve Students' Scores?

One can play at a computer as well as work at it. What you do with it determines the size of the benefits, if any.

Nate Stulman was a sophomore at Swarthmore College when he decided to monitor how his classmates were using their computers.[20] Despite the fact that Swarthmore is one of the five top-ranked small colleges and universities in the United States, Stulman discovered its students were using their computers in the same way millions of others do at lesser schools: they were playing games, e-mailing boyfriends and girlfriends, killing time in chat rooms, and uploading and downloading music. Endlessly. Writing for the *New York Times* op-ed page, Stulman concluded that many students are too immature to handle the distractions and temptations of the Internet, a fact largely unaddressed by those who think the "goof-off machines" will make books obsolete. This is reassuring to me when I look back on my own immature behavior in college. Kids are kids, and sophomores behave sophomorically, even when there is DSL or Wi-Fi.

In a 2003 study of 1,680 school-aged children's time diaries and home computer use, researchers found "moderation" to be a key factor in students' scores.[21] Those who used computers for less than eight hours weekly had scores that were a few points higher "on measures of letter-word recognition, reading comprehension, and mathematics calculation problems than children without computer use." They also found this amount of use did not reduce those students' reading time (whereas the same amount of TV use lowered reading time). Indeed, the computer users had more reading time than did noncomputer users. This doesn't mean the computer use caused the high scores; the cause could easily be from all the reading they were doing. What it does show, however, is that eight hours a week of computer use does not damage children's school achievements.

Conversely, those with more than eight hours' home use had scores that were no different from noncomputer users' but they weighed an average of twelve pounds more than their nonuser peers.

How the computer is used and how often it is used often determines students' scores.

An international study of fifteen-year-olds in thirty-two countries found achievement negatives connected to excessive computer access. With home usage, researchers found the more computers in the home, the lower the math and reading scores. This suggests multiple computers become more of a distraction or hindrance than a help for the student. When the study moved to classroom use, there was no negative impact as long as usage was for educational or communication purposes. Overuse in school was associated with lower scores, while moderate use showed no negatives.[22]

Simply put, the presence of something that can be used as a toy means it will be used as a toy when it is more readily available. Adults need to moderate the usage to prevent it from becoming a distraction to other kinds of learning and physical well-being. Page 165 in chapter 9 contains information about an inexpensive commercial product that can limit child use of computers to x hours a week.

Lesson No. 1: Wiring the home or school is a long way from wiring the brain. Kids will be kids.

Why Do We Need Print If We Have the "Information Highway"?

Growing at a rate of 10 million pages a day, the Internet is now estimated to contain more than 550 *billion* pages, of which the search engines have catalogued about 25 percent. And while those billions of pages contain some of the most useful information known to man, much of it amounts to the mindless minutiae you find stuck on a refrigerator.[23]

An essential part of the Internet superstructure is its "links" system, those underlined words connecting you to subjects related to your present location. When school board members argue in behalf of the information highway instead of the library, they don't realize that the shelf life of Web pages can be a lot shorter than that of books because of "link rot." When you click on a link and receive a "Not Found 404" message or something similar, you've hit a dead end. The page has either moved or been taken down.

How common is "link rot"? According to two professors who did a 27-month study tracking 515 links to educational material on the Web, one-third of them were dead in 2.25 months and half were dead in five years.[24] Are half the books in a library completely out of date in five years? Hardly. Internet "link rot" amounts to having half the exit ramps on American highways ceasing to exist in five years but no one told the mapmakers.

As for "Googled" information supplanting that in books, here's a letter to the *New York Times* from a political science professor after the paper ran a story on books versus bytes:

To the Editor:
True, the Internet and digitized materials quickly bring great quantities and many kinds of information to our fingertips. But does this approach also bring deeper insight and wisdom?
Reviewing the term papers for classes in "Nationalism in Post-Soviet Eurasia" and "Negotiation in World Affairs" this spring, I

have found an almost direct correlation between the best grades and whether students used books as well as materials accessible by computer.

Even though students were instructed to use and cite several required books in their papers, some chose to rely entirely on sources that begin http//. This group of papers benefited from the latest reports on demonstrations in Kiev and Bishkek, but they lacked the depth and long view acquired by spending a few hours with a real book.

Last but not least, there is the problem of evaluating sources. Many seem to regard the Wikipedia online encyclopedia as no worse than a standard, hard-copy encyclopedia. One of my students thought he had discovered the truth about Russia from a Trotskyite newspaper he found on the Web. Who was Trotsky? He did not know or care.[25]

Having said all of that, there are some excellent resources for family Internet usage. Two of the best are:

1. *Great Web Sites for Kids* from the American Library Association;[26]
2. *The Virtual Middle School Library,* maintained by a retired professional librarian, and it's an Internet treasure chest.[27]

Lesson No. 2: The Internet cannot and should not replace a good school or public library for reference and research. They should coexist compatibly.

Isn't There Important Information on the Web?

Yes, but most students are unwilling to dig for it. A 2002 study by Google showed that 85 percent of search-engine users never go beyond the first page's results.[28] The late Stephen Jay Gould used to complain that his Harvard students were unwilling to go deeper than the first level when searching for information on the Web.[29]

Let me give you a simple but fictitious example of the "digging" often necessary when researching via the Internet. Let's say you've chosen to write a paper on hair growth and one day in your recreational reading you stumble across a newspaper article stating that new research shows that people who use computers five or more hours a day have greater hair growth. The research project is not named but one of the scientists involved is quoted by name. A Google search of that name turns up his university bio page—in fact, two university pages. *Click.* The first one is from ten years ago, before he did the research, and now outdated. *Click.* Back to the original Google page. *Click* on the other bio page. Yes, it's the current university bio, different university now, which contains a link to a list of his published research. *Click*. The list includes the hair growth study and lists either a PDF file for downloading or a link to the journal that published it. *Click*. You're finally at the original source. It did, however, require some digging and clicking. In other words, the information highway is seldom a speedway. But I do love traveling it, and, with experience, you become more intuitive and successful in using it, especially in determining if the information is academic (peer-reviewed, professional research) or commercial (sponsored by a hair-growth company).

Lesson No. 3: The information highway only works for those with the drive to complete the journey.

What About All the Reading the Kids Do Online and the PowerPoint Projects They Now Produce?

Reading and comprehension are more difficult when done from a monitor than from a book. Screen reading is 25 percent slower because computer screens use a technology that renders lettering at a resolution of 72 dpi (dots per inch), compared to 600 dpi for most books. This makes the computer screen six times less clear than book text.[30] In a comparative study of college undergraduates reading from both a computer screen and printed material, the comprehension level was significantly lower from the computer screen.[31] Students admitted to printing out Web material because of the difficulty both in reading it and comprehending text on the screen. No less an authority than Microsoft's Bill Gates has stated, "Reading off a screen is still vastly inferior to reading off of paper. . . . When it comes to something over four or five pages, I print it out and I like to have it to carry around with me and annotate."[32]

While educators and critics decry the state of student writing, many schools are busy adopting a computer program almost *designed* to hide writing deficits: PowerPoint, a favorite for corporate presentations (no wonder we're using it in the schools as we try to make them more business-like). These presentations contain slides with built-in charts, animated graphics, and sound effects—just like video games. Needless to say, classmates and parents are quite impressed. In suburbia, PowerPoint is replacing the traditional book report and diorama as the presentation of choice.

The downside is that content often takes a backseat to bells and whistles. As one principal told the *Wall Street Journal*, "You can make a pretty crappy presentation look good." Writing becomes sentence fragments with bullets and sound effects, without much depth. Still, the program has its advocates who argue that this is a new age and the computer will bring out skills in children who might not be adept at making a shoebox diorama. Another principal extolled PowerPoint's virtues, saying it requires teamwork, technology know-how, and public speaking—the skills required in today's job market.[33]

Another skill the principal might have mentioned is *counting*, which is what someone did while one district's superintendent was being mesmerized. "When I was working in a school technology department, I watched eighth-grade students present PowerPoint projects to an obviously proud superintendent. Curious, I counted the number of words that each student had actually written. On average, each eighth-grade student had spent two weeks writing 77 words."[34]

(This is not to say that all charts or visuals are distractions. Where we could really use an occasional chart or visual is the notoriously dull presidential address to the nation. Be he Democrat or Republican, none seems to have grasped the visual concepts of the business world and applied it to the citizenry. Remember: visual receptors in the brain outnumber auditory receptors by a ratio of thirty to one.)

Lesson No. 3: (a) Reading from a computer screen is slower and less efficient than reading from paper, and (b) Bells and whistles camouflage shallow content.

Won't All the E-mail Use Help to Improve Writing?

Most of what passes for e-mail is the equivalent of conversation at the drinking fountain or voice-mail messages—short, disjointed, and shallow. Would anyone recommend that as a model for elocution lessons? Just because kids are doing more talking on their cell phones does not ensure that their diction or grammar is going to improve.

No research shows an improvement in writing, grammar, or imagination since professional writers began using computers or word processors instead of typewriters or pens. Spelling has improved, and the writing and editing are faster, but faster is not better. Does eating a meal faster make it taste better?

Lesson No. 4: Garbage in, garbage out, just like a typewriter.

Isn't It Better for My Child to Be in Front of a Computer Than in Front of a TV?

Anything can be overdone—food, basketball, gambling, religion, even books. When such overuse interferes with a person's meeting with other persons in a meaningful way—especially for children whose social skills are still unformed—then the medium can become addictive. It is extremely easy to become addicted to the instant gratification of pushing a single computer key. For the introverted child (or adult), the computer offers an escape from reality, and that can lead to social dysfunction.

We must remember that all the creativity claims now linked to computer use were also laid out for *Sesame Street* three decades ago, and as Clifford Stoll, a renowned computer security expert, observed, "So where's that demographic wave of creative and brilliant students now entering college?"

As we know, there's been no marked improvement in either creativity or reading scores since *Sesame Street* arrived. Stoll sees strong parallels between *Sesame Street* and computers. "Both are pervasive, expensive and encourage children to sit still. Both display animated cartoons, gaudy numbers and weird, random noises. . . . Both give the sensation that by merely watching a screen, you can acquire information without work and without discipline."[35]

Nor should any of this be considered a diatribe against computer games. My grandsons play computer games on my computer when they visit but dosages are controlled. Most computer games are predictable and children reach their saturation points fairly early. And because the experience is addictive, it requires vigilance and moderation.

Lesson No. 5: As the Greeks said, moderation in all things, which means, in this case, parents must remain involved and in control.

What's with Boys and Computers? My Son Loves the Computer but Hates Books.

You could do a whole book on just the issue of males and computers in our culture, so there isn't enough space to do justice to it here, but this *is* a book on reading and we have a serious male/boy problem there. The international study of fifteen-year-olds in 2000 showed male readers finishing significantly behind their female peers in *all* thirty-two nations.[36] Along with the sports culture factor I noted in the introduction, other factors may be at work, including the fact that at-risk boys often come from families where there either isn't an adult male at home or that male does not read *to* the child or *in front* of him. Coupled with the fact that most elementary teachers and librarians are female, the question arises whether boys perceive early on that "reading is for girls."

When the University of Winnipeg's Herb Katz and Laura Sokal investigated such assumptions, they found both good news and bad.[37] Studying seventy-two diverse second-grade boys (the age at which the knowledge of gender difference is fully understood), there was no correlation between whether the students saw reading as feminine and how much they liked reading. That was encouraging. What did raise concerns was that as early as second grade, fully 25 percent had developed a negative attitude about reading—"That's for weird kids." If allowed to persist, this would be the group that did the least amount of reading in the future, had the lowest scores, and did the most to lower overall reading averages.

The researchers offered two solutions:

1. Supply more positive reading role models that boys can identify with (dads, male teachers, and community leaders).
2. Allow them to choose books that are decidedly "in-group" for males.

The latter selections are usually the ones that basal reading series and school collections frown upon as inappropriate but that most avidly reading males indulge in at home: comic books, *Calvin & Hobbes, Mad Magazine, Sports Illustrated for Kids,* and books like *Uncle John's Bathroom Reader for Kids Only.* Although some adults still refer to this as "vomitrocious" reading fare, the research by people like Krashen[38] and Carlson and Sherill[39] clearly shows this kind of reading often leads to better and more sophisticated material later on. (See the write-ups in the anthology section of the Treasury for details on *Guys Write for Guys Read* and *Uncle John's Bathroom Reader for Kids Only.*

If it's any consolation, boys' reading woes are not entirely peculiar to our time. In the 1700s, Samuel Johnson offered this as a solution: "I am always for getting a boy forward in his learning, for that is sure good. I would let him at first read any English book which happens to engage his attention; because you have done a great deal when you have brought him to entertainment from a book. He'll get better books afterwards."[40]

What boys will read avidly may not always be the preference of girls or adults.

Chapter 9

TV, Audio, and Technology: Hurting or Helping Literacy?

I believe television is going to be the test of the modern world, and that in this new opportunity to see beyond the range of our vision we shall discover either a new and unbearable disturbance of the general peace or a saving radiance in the sky. We shall stand or fall by television—of that I am quite sure.

—E. B. White,
"Removal from Town"
Harper's (October 1938)

W ITH electronic media now the dominant force in a child's life outside of family (and for some, even larger than the family), it must be included in any book or discussion about literacy. Does it help literacy or is it all harm? In reading the previous chapter, you saw the positive impact of Oprah's televised message. A big plus there. Recall the positive role TV played in raising public awareness during the Vietnam War, the Civil Rights struggle, and, more recently, the aftermath of Hurricane Katrina. Big pluses there, too. In chapter 5, I alluded to a mechanical "tutoring" device widely used by the children in Finland, now boasting the world's highest reading scores. Sounds to me like a good use of technology. We'll explore that and more in this chapter.

In a page or two, you'll also see negatives that counterbalance some of those positives, but first, a hopeful message: media is very much like the medications in your medicine cabinet. Helpful as they might be, they definitely need parental oversight and controls. Can that be done with today's media? In response, I share the story I've offered to all of my parent audiences for fifteen years.

It begins with a woman named Sonya Carson trying to raise two sons in inner-city Detroit as a single parent. One of twenty-four children, Mrs. Carson had only a third-grade education. A hardworking, driven woman, she worked as a domestic and child's caregiver for wealthy families—sometimes working two or three jobs at a time to support her sons. Sometimes she worked so hard that she had to "get away to her relatives for a rest." Only years later did her sons discover that she was checking herself into a mental institution for professional help for depression.

Her sons, on the other hand, were not working themselves into any kind of frenzy. Both were on a slow boat to nowhere in the classroom. Bennie, the younger one, was the worst student in his fifth-grade class. As if raising two sons in one of the most dangerous cities in America was not enough, Mrs. Carson now faced the challenge of the boys' grades. She met it head-on.

> "Bennie—you're smarter than this report card," she declared, pointing to his math score. "First thing, you're going to learn your times tables—every one of them!"
>
> "Mom, do you know how many there are? It would take me a whole year!" he replied.
>
> "I only went through the third grade and I know them all the way through my twelves," his mother answered. "And furthermore, you are not to go outside tomorrow until you learn them."
>
> Her son pointed to the columns in his math book and cried, "Look at these things! How can anyone learn them?"
>
> His mother simply tightened her jaw, looked him calmly in the eye, and declared, "You can't go out until you learn your times tables."

Bennie learned his times tables—and his math scores began to climb. His mother's next goal was to get the rest of his grades up. Her intuition pointed to the television that never seemed to be off when the boys were home. "From now on, you can only watch three television programs a week!" A week! (What Sonya Carson lacked in book sense she made up for with common sense that would be vindicated nearly thirty years later when major research studies showed a powerful connection between "over-viewing" and "underachievement.")

She next looked for a way to fill the free time created by the television vacuum. She said, "You boys are going to the library and checking out *two* books. At the end of each week you'll write me a report on what you've read." (Only years later did the boys discover she couldn't read well enough to understand any of the reports.)

They didn't like it, of course, but they didn't dare refuse. And in reading two books a week, then talking about them with his mother, Bennie raised his reading scores. And because the entire curriculum was tied to reading, the rest of his report card began to improve. Each semester, each year, the scores rose. And by the time he was a senior in high school he was third in his class, scoring in the ninetieth percentile of the nation.

Dr. Ben Carson concedes his medical career could have been undone by the wrong dosage of TV when he was a child.

With colleges like West Point, Yale, and Stanford waving scholarships in his face, but with only ten dollars in his pocket for application fees, Bennie let his choice fall to whichever school won the College Bowl television quiz that year (Yale). He spent four years there majoring in psychology, then went on to the medical schools at the University of Michigan and Johns Hopkins. Today, at age fifty-five, Dr. Ben Carson is one of the world's premier pediatric brain surgeons. When Johns Hopkins named him head of pediatric neurosurgery, he was, at age thirty-three, the youngest in the nation.

Ask Dr. Carson to explain how you get from a fatherless inner-city home and a mother with a third-grade education, and from being the worst student in your fifth-grade class, to being a world-famous brain surgeon with a brother who is an engineer. Again and again, he points to two things: his mother's religion (Seventh-Day Adventist) and the pivotal moment when she limited their television viewing and ordered him to start reading. (For the "complete" story, read *Gifted Hands: The Ben Carson Story* by Ben Carson.)

I have people in my audiences with three times the education of young Mrs. Carson and ten times her income—but not half her common sense and courage when it comes to raising children. They can't bring themselves to "raise" children—they can only "watch them grow up," and most of the watching occurs from the couch in front of a television set.

There are two important things to remember from the Carson family's story: (1) Mrs. Carson didn't trash the set—she *controlled* it, and (2) with high expectations of her children, she demanded appropriate behavior from them. In controlling the dosage of TV, Mrs. Carson averted disaster. Dosage determines the impact of anything—from hurricanes and aspirin to reading and television.

What Exactly Is So Wrong with Television?

Until recently, the answer was "nothing." It was the abuse of the set that caused the problem. TV was just an innocent bystander to parent neglect or irresponsibility. At least, that's what many experts felt. New research, however, is getting closer to identifying TV as more of an accomplice. But even if the research fails to completely indict TV, all of the research points to the dangers of over-viewing among all age groups, with the youngest being the most prone to danger. Let's start with that age group and work upward.

1. When the television viewing habits of 2,500 children were tracked and examined by researchers at Seattle's Children's Hospital, the doctors concluded that for each hour of daily TV viewed by the child before age three, the risk of attention deficit hyperactivity disorder (ADHD) by age seven increased by 10 percent.[1] (ADHD is now the most common childhood behavioral disorder.)

   In light of that finding, the Kaiser Family Foundation's most recent media research[2] offers statistics that don't bode well for future classrooms:

   ◆ Among children age two or younger, 59 percent watch TV daily and 42 percent watch DVDs or videos.
   ◆ Among children age two or younger, average daily screen time is two hours and forty-eight minutes (TV plus DVD/video).
   ◆ Televisions are a permanent part of the bedroom for 30 percent of children by age three and 43 percent of children by age six.
   ◆ In homes with children age six or younger, the TV is left on at least 50 percent of the time, even if no one is watching, and 30 percent have the set on "almost all" or "most" of the time.
   ◆ Among families with children under age six, only 34 percent subscribe to a newspaper.

Today's young parents, awash in their ambitions to keep their child one step ahead of the neighbors' child, are buying into an electronic culture that is one big suede shoe operation. Remember the hucksters who used to push their snake oil products off covered wagons and then moved to late-night infomercials? They just encamped in the nursery, promoting a series of toys, DVDs, videos, and gadgets that will make your child into an infant Einstein. But considering the unhappy childhood of Einstein, who would want it? Apparently millions of parents, all of them ignorant of comments like this from the director of child research at one of the nation's biggest toy companies: "There is no proof that this type of toy helps children become smarter."[3] Child development experts caution against the do-all toys intended to boost IQ. As one critic explained, "The most useful toy is the one that requires the most activation on the part of a young child. The more they have to use their minds and bodies to make something work, the more they are going to learn." There is ample research, however, to substantiate the claim that "There's a sucker born every minute." That could easily be amended to "sucker-parent."

2. Once children are in school, the impact of heavy viewing is reflected in student achievements in both reading and math. In a study of 348 ethnically diverse third-graders from six California schools, the presence of a television set in the child's bedroom was significantly associated with lower math, reading, and language arts scores.[4] (See the chart below.) Kaiser media studies show bedroom TVs always correlate to more viewing hours.[5]

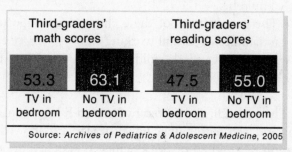

A TV in the child's bedroom spells more viewing and lower scores.

Third-graders' math scores		Third-graders' reading scores	
53.3	63.1	47.5	55.0
TV in bedroom	No TV in bedroom	TV in bedroom	No TV in bedroom

Source: *Archives of Pediatrics & Adolescent Medicine*, 2005

By age eight, 60 percent of children not only lived in a home with three televisions but also had a TV in their bedroom.[6] Kaiser found that children with TVs in their bedrooms watched ninety more minutes daily (ten hours more weekly). If a video game is in the bedroom, the child plays thirty-two minutes more daily, and the availability of a bedroom computer doubles the usage when compared with a child who doesn't have it in the room (ninety minutes versus forty-seven minutes).

Nor is it just an academic problem. In 1999, sleep researchers working with parents and teachers of 495 students, kindergarten through fourth grade, found that those with televisions in their bedrooms were far more apt to have difficulty falling asleep and woke up more often during the night. This made them more prone to sleepiness during the day, impeding their school performance. The researchers strongly urged the rooms be cleared of both TVs and computers, especially if there are sleeping problems.[7]

3. Like the elephant in the room that no one wanted to talk about, the black-white reading gap smoldered for decades before federal requirements forced everyone to break down their scores demographically. The ensuing uproar brought outcries and attention to the problem. As evidenced in the first three chapters of this book, poverty plays a significant role in that gap. But when poverty was accounted for and still black scores were low, researchers began digging for other causes. Among other things, there was a definite TV connection. The case in point was the study of an academically oriented high school in the middle-class white-black community of Shaker Heights, Ohio.[8]

In this situation, black children of parents with at least one graduate degree still scored 191 points below their white counterparts in similar family circumstances. Among the reasons offered:

♦ Their parents were the first generation of high education (college) achievers and may not be seen studying or reading as often as they should be.
♦ The grandparents of these children (an important support group in families) were still working class.
♦ Middle-class black children watched twice as much TV as their white counterparts.

The research, conducted by Ronald F. Ferguson, an African American and lecturer in public policy at Harvard, showed that this first generation of children of black achievers watched *twice* as many hours of TV as their white classmates: three hours a day compared to one and a half hours. The Kaiser Family Foundation study in 2000[9] showed national results almost identical to Ferguson's study, but also found that black children were far more likely to have TVs, including ones with premium cable services, in their bedroom.

Black syndicated newspaper columnist Derrick Z. Jackson, a finalist for the Pulitzer Prize in 2001, associates some of the black community's more pronounced social ills with excessive television habits. When national obesity reports linked heavy viewing with obesity, Jackson noted that the rate of overweight African American children was double that of white children. Jackson saw the persistent black-white reading gap mirrored in TV viewing: 42 percent of black fourth-graders watch six or more hours daily, compared with 13 percent of white students and 8 percent of Asian American children. Jackson wrote: "It is hard to believe that a people so full of energy and purpose 40 and 50 years ago would literally sit out the fruits of their labor. Rosa Parks and others changed this nation by sitting down. African Americans must change it again by sitting down with a book instead of a television."[10] Blunt, but I'd say it's long past time for bluntness. And Bill Cosby agrees.

When I hear black leaders asking for more black representation on TV, I wonder: Wait a minute—won't that inspire even *more* viewing in the black community? Is someone missing the math here? Never mind multiplying the TV faces—multiply the reading scores!

4. We now have a long-term study that links dosage to higher education, based on records of daily childhood viewing. In 2005, New Zealand researchers published results of a twenty-six-year study of 980 children born between 1972 and 1973. The group included full representation of every socioeconomic level.

Data were obtained from the families at ages five, seven, eight, eleven, thirteen, and fifteen, while interviews were used at age twenty-six to determine each member's educational achievement level. Adjusting for IQ, socioeconomic status, and childhood behavioral problems, the children's schooling level by age twenty-six was consistently directly related to how much they viewed TV throughout childhood (see chart below). Children who viewed less than one hour a day were the most likely to achieve a college degree. The researchers noted, "These findings indicate that excessive television viewing is likely to have a negative impact on educational achievement. This is likely to have far-reaching consequences for an individual's socioeconomic status and well-being in adult life."

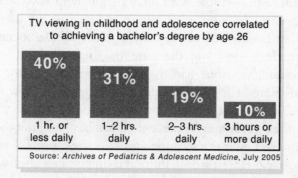

TV viewing in childhood and adolescence correlated to achieving a bachelor's degree by age 26

1 hr. or less daily	1–2 hrs. daily	2–3 hrs. daily	3 hours or more daily
40%	31%	19%	10%

Source: *Archives of Pediatrics & Adolescent Medicine*, July 2005

Is There an Amount of TV That
Is Not Harmful to Children?

Before looking at the recommended dosage, it's important to understand that the greatest academic damage done may not be by the content of the shows viewed but by what is *not being done* during those twenty-eight hours a week of sitting inertly in front of the TV: the games not played, the chores not done, the drawings not drawn, the hobbies not worked, the friends not made or played with, the homework not done, the bikes or skateboards not ridden, the balls not caught, the books not read, and the conversations not held. I hear parents call it "my babysitter"—but if there were a babysitter who did that much damage to your kid's mind, you'd be at the police station in a heartbeat.

The average child is watching twenty eight hours a week, almost three times the dosage recommended by the American Academy of Pediatrics (AAP). The AAP calls for ten hours a week, and no TV for children under two. This was based on a research analysis of twenty-three TV-learning studies of 87,025 children in England, Japan, Canada, and five areas of the United States between 1963 and 1978.[11] The findings showed no detrimental effects on learning (and some positive effects) from TV viewing up to ten hours a week; however, after that, the scores begin to decline.

When more than three hundred pediatricians were surveyed about parent response to the AAP's TV limits and recommendations, 51 percent expressed frustration at parents' total lack of interest. So I ask you: whose job is it in this country to wake up comatose parents? Someone better do it soon because knowing television's potential for harm and keeping the knowledge to ourselves instead of sharing it with parents amounts to covering up a land mine on a busy street.

Presidents, schools, and religious institutions are among the biggest offenders in this regard—those with bully pulpits who have failed to sound the alarm, perhaps because so many are addicted to the medium themselves. The last twenty years have seen a parade of Democratic and Republican presidents decrying the state of education and extolling the virtues of testing, yet none had the courage to say, "As for you parents watching this State of the Union address, I happen to know from the research that 63 percent of you are watching television while you and your families eat dinner. Another 54 percent of you have no limits on your children's viewing, yet by every measure available, the more TV your children watch, the lower their test scores. Putting it simply: Parents, have you completely lost your minds?" I may not live long enough to see a president with that kind of courage, but how about the clergy?

What can a school district or church or synagogue do to publicize the dangers in over-viewing? You could start with this chapter. Share it with parents. The American Academy of Pediatrics' Web site[12] offers an assortment of helpful papers for parents on everything from children and the Internet to using TV wisely in the family. They'll be happy to grant you permission for distribution.

I can also tell you what many schools in Hawaii are doing to turn the tide of both reading and TV viewing. Back in 1999, a local businessman named Jed Gaines created the nonprofit Read Aloud America[13] to deliver an evening program called RAP (Read Aloud Program) that is bent on changing student and parent attitudes about reading and television viewing. While students are being read to by volunteers and faculty, the RAP staff reads to parents, talks to them about the links between too much TV and low school scores, reads to them some more, and answers questions about parenting issues. Afterward there is dinner and door prizes. Initially kids put the pressure on parents to come to the event because it's so much fun, but once the parents arrive and find it's nonthreatening (no tests, no embarrassments) and discover how much they enjoy the readings and group learning, they're ready and willing to return for the remaining five sessions during the semester. It's a unique and amazingly successful concept that to date has reached 94,000 parents at meetings of as many as 1,000. Imagine for a minute if every state had three or four such units in operation. If you follow the right formula, there are proven ways to get parents to attend such functions in large numbers.[14] And parents are the missing ingredient in education.

Can't You See How Hard It Is to Monitor or Limit Children's TV or Gaming Hours?

As a matter of fact, it's never been easier to control it! The same technology that has flooded the airwaves with 1,352 weekly hours of children's programming (up from twenty-seven hours in 1965) now allows us to control it, and I don't mean that facetiously. Having had to play the TV policeman in our house, I know the pain (more on that later in this chapter). So here's something to ease the pain, with side effects that are nothing but wonderful. It's called the Time-Scout Monitor[15]—a commercial product (less than $100) that limits how much time family members can spend on

TV, videos, PlayStation, or computers. It would have made my life as a parent a lot easier thirty-five years ago.

About the size of a Walkman, the monitor comes with three account cards on which the parent loads time, and a set of parent control cards. Let's say you want your child (or children) to watch only eight hours of TV a week. At week's start, you set the child's card for eight hours. Your TV is plugged (and locked) into the Time-Scout Monitor. To turn the set on, you or the child must swipe the card through the Time-Scout; this activates the set and thirty minutes are subtracted from the child's eight-hour total. At the end of that thirty minutes, the set (or whatever electrical device is being operated) turns off. Another swipe (and thirty-minute loss) is required to begin operation again.

Time-Scout works just like a debit card, limiting how much time a family spends with TV, DVDs, or computers.

Since the set of parent cards includes several that allow you to add or subtract time, or even shut down the entire device until further notice, you have the option of using the device for behavior modification: "Kiernan, you've done a wonderful job on your homework this week, so I'm adding an extra hour to your Time-Scout card for this weekend."

One of the side effects of this "pain-killer" is that it fosters family harmony. Siblings who haven't spoken civilly to each other in years are suddenly best friends and bringing new meaning to the term "time-sharing."

As good as the product is, if you have three televisions or two computers in the home and you want to limit children's time, you've got a problem. The Time-Scout works on only one machine at a time (unless you buy more than one). But there's a solution to this too. If you wanted to lose weight and had four bowls of candy spread around the house, the first step would be to reduce the number of bowls. Once you're down to one TV or one computer, then the Time-Scout will manage it for you. But first *you* have to manage the total.

One cautionary note: on computers, the Time-Scout should be used only on the monitor, not the hard disk, since a sudden shutdown at the thirty-minute mark would prevent correct shutdown procedures and thus cause loss of data.

If the Time-Scout price tag is too steep for you, there is a cheaper device for controlling the set. It's called "TVB-Gone" ($14.99), a keychain device sold at stores like Target. It will turn off any television set within range, so if you think your children have reached their TV-saturation point, simply click it (openly or secretly) and the set shuts down: "Oh-oh—I think it's over-heated, kids. Better go outside and play for a few hours while it cools down."

Still on the subject of controls and dosage, the single best organization for combating TV excess is the TV-Turnoff Network, a nonprofit group bent on promoting less TV viewing (www.tvturnoff.org). Founded in 1994, the TV-Turnoff Network is "dedicated to the belief that we all have the power to determine the role that television plays in our own lives."

The organization offers two yearly events: (1) TV-Turnoff Week, and (2) More Reading, Less TV—the latter intended to fill the void with printed pages. The Turnoff Week has been approved by sixty-five national organizations, including the American Medical Association, the National Education Association, and the American Academy of Pediatrics. Since 1995, more than twenty-four million schoolchildren and their families have partici-pated in the campaign, with the network providing an abundance of materials for organizing the event with families, including "fact sheets" they hope will startle parents into involvement. Every school in America should be enrolled.

If You Didn't Have a Mechanical Device, How Did You Manage Your Family's Viewing?

Our restricted viewing began in 1974, at about the time I'd begun to no-tice a growing television addiction in my fourth-grade daughter and kindergarten-age son. (They are now forty-one and thirty-seven.) Even our long-standing read-aloud time each night had begun to deteriorate be-cause, in their words, it "took too much time away from the TV."

One evening while visiting Marty and Joan Wood of Longmeadow, Massachusetts, I noticed that their four teenage children went right to their homework after excusing themselves from the dinner table.

I asked the parents, "Your television broken?"

"No," replied Marty. "Why?"

"Well, it's only six forty-five and the kids are already doing homework."

Joan explained, "Oh, we don't allow television on school nights."

"That's a noble philosophy—but how in the world do you enforce it?" I asked.

"It is a house law," stated Marty. And for the next hour and a half, husband and wife detailed for me the positive changes that had occurred in their family and home since they put that "law" into effect.

That evening was a turning point for my family. After hearing the details of the plan, my wife, Susan, agreed wholeheartedly to back it. "On one condition," she added.

"What's that?" I asked.

"You be the one to tell them," she said.

After supper the next night, we brought the children into our bedroom, surrounded them with pillows and quilts, and I calmly began, "Jamie . . . Elizabeth . . . Mom and I have decided that there will be no more television on school nights in this house—forever."

Their reaction was predictable: They started to cry. What came as a shock to us was that they cried for four solid months. Every night, despite explanations on our part, they cried. We tried to impress upon them that the rule was not meant as a punishment; we listed all the positive reasons for such a rule. They cried louder.

The peer group pressure was enormous, particularly for Elizabeth, who said there was nothing for her to talk about during lunch at school since she hadn't seen any of the shows her friends were discussing. There was even peer pressure on Susan and me from neighbors and friends who thought the rule was needlessly harsh.

As difficult as it was at first, we persevered and resisted the pressure on both fronts. We lived with the tears, the pleadings, the conniving. And after three months we began to see things happen that the Woods had predicted. Suddenly we had the time each night as a family to read aloud, to read to ourselves, to do homework at an unhurried pace, to learn how to play chess and checkers and Scrabble, to make plastic models that had been collecting dust in the closet for years, to bake cakes and cookies, to write thank-you notes to aunts and uncles, to do household chores and take baths and showers without World War III breaking out, to play on the parish sports teams, to draw and paint and color, and—best of all—to talk to one another, ask questions, and answer questions.

Our children's imaginations were coming back to life again.

For the first year, the decision was a heavy one, but with time it grew lighter. Jamie, being younger, had never developed the acute taste for television that Elizabeth had over the years, and he lost the habit fairly easily. It took Elizabeth longer to adjust.

Over the years the plan was modified until it worked like this:

1. The television is turned off at suppertime and not turned on again until the children are in bed. Monday through Thursday.
2. Each child is allowed to watch one school-night show a week (subject to parents' approval). Homework and chores must be finished beforehand.
3. Weekend television is limited to any two of the three nights. The remaining night is reserved for homework and other activities. The children make their selections separately.

We structured the diet to allow the family to control the television and not the other way around. Perhaps this particular diet won't work for your family, but any kind of control is better than none. Unfortunately, "none" is the norm in 54 percent of American families.

Don't Kids Need the Entertainment Break That Electronic Media Offer?

Everyone needs a break. But when you're talking about 1,460 hours a year (that's the total hours of TV, video, and DVD for the average child), that's a little more than a break. That's the equivalent of watching *Gone With the Wind* 392 times a year. Give *me* a break!

In his autobiography, *A Life in the Twentieth Century,* the Pulitzer Prize–winning historian Arthur Schlesinger Jr. writes that he read 598 books by the age of fourteen and viewed 482 movies between ages fourteen and nineteen.[16] If the latter sounds outrageous, it's not. It amounts to one and a half movies a week or 90 minutes, compared to 1,680 minutes of weekly entertainment for most American children today. So it's not the entertainment that softens the mind, but the dosage.

What About the Mechanical Reading Tutor You Mentioned Earlier?

For the moment, I'm going to call the device "CC," and I want to introduce you to it via the place that has achieved the highest performance with it.[17]

As I pointed out in chapter 1, Finland's children don't start formal schooling until age seven, yet they achieve the highest reading scores in the world.[18] Finnish children use the CC device and they use it *often*. Even more astounding, these high-scoring children also watch fairly large amounts of television—far more time than they spend reading books. Their daily viewing is about two-thirds of what American children watch, which is the highest in the world.[19]

The CC device used to be pretty expensive in the United States ($250), but the price has dropped since 1993—when it went to *zero* dollars. Free. In fact, it comes built into every television set in America. It's the closed-captioning chip you access through your remote device.

Almost half of all Finnish TV shows are our old sitcoms like *Gilligan's Island, Bonanza, The Brady Bunch, The Partridge Family,* and *Hogan's Heroes*— so many shows that the Finns can't afford to dub Finnish into all the soundtracks, so they just run them in English with Finnish closed-captioning or subtitles.

This means that almost half of everything a nine-year-old Finn wants to watch is going to be in a foreign language. In order to understand it, he'll have to be able to read Finnish and be able to read Finnish *fast!* In chapter 1 I wrote about "motivation" as a missing ingredient in the National Reading Panel's report, but it's not missing among Finnish children. Whereas motivation propels American teens to learn to drive a car, it pushes kids in Finland to learn to read.

It stands to reason that reasonable doses of captioned television can do no harm, and most likely it can help greatly with reading. There is enough research to indicate significant gains in comprehension and vocabulary development (especially among bilingual students) when receiving instruction with educational television that is captioned.[20]

In 2003, a first-grade teacher told me about a young girl entering her class in September. "On the first day of school, she was already reading on a third-grade level. That's always unusual, but what made it more so was that her parents were both deaf. Normally the hearing child of deaf parents is language deficient and therefore behind—but this child was three years ahead. I could hardly wait to conference with the parents. They beamed when I told them of their daughter's achievement and they explained that she'd had closed-captioning all her life."

There are several other factors that make closed-captioning so effective as a reading tutor. Earlier I wrote about the thirty to one ratio of visual receptors over auditory receptors in the brain. Also note that while adults have learned to tune out various distractions in our environment (like captioning), children have not. Everything registers with them, including the connections between what is being said and what is being shown at the bottom of the screen. There's that sponge effect again.

Now recall the observations in chapter 7 about the print climate of at-risk children. I mentioned there was a government program that puts the equivalent of a daily newspaper or weekly news magazine in the home—for free. Can you see what's coming? The number of words flowing across the screen (closed-captioning) in the course of three hours is more than the average adult would read in a daily newspaper or a weekly news magazine. Enabling the TV's closed-captioning is the equivalent of a newspaper subscription, but, unlike the subscription, it costs nothing.

As for toddlers and preschoolers who are unable to read the words on the screen, as well as the words in the books and magazines in the house, those items help acclimate the child to print and sounds and meaning. The same thing happens with closed-captioning. In fact, you could easily argue that the characters on the show are reading aloud the closed-captioning to the child.

Considering what we know about captioning, in addition to the emphasis a succession of presidents has placed on reading skills, it seems a little weird that we've not heard a word from them about the importance of parents turning on that "tutoring device." It's especially weird when you realize it was Bill Clinton's good friend and George W.'s father who signed the legislation that put the free closed-captioning chip in all TV sets in the first place—President George H. W. Bush.

Do Audiobooks Count as Reading?

Depending on what you're looking at or listening to, technology and literacy are not mutually exclusive. It all depends on the person in charge—you. When parents ask me if stories on tape are okay, I respond: "If they're used as a full-time substitute for a literate parent, no, they're not okay. But if used to supplement your readings or used by children whose parents are illiterate or unavailable, they are excellent!"

As Americans spend more and more time in their cars, audio recordings have become a major player in the publishing industry, especially with the average round-trip commute lasting fifty minutes. Why not use the time to enlarge your horizons beyond the freeway? The recorded book is a perfect example of how technology can be used to make this a more literate nation.

For family or classroom use, audio recordings are a big plus. And while they lack the immediacy of a live person who can hug and answer a child's questions, recorded books can fill an important gap when the adult is not available or is out of breath. Even when used as background noise while a child is playing, their verbal contents are still enriching his vocabulary more than television would with its abbreviated sentences. So by all means begin building your audio library with songs, rhymes, and stories. Community libraries and bookstores now have a growing assortment for all ages. You should definitely consider recording the stories yourself and encouraging distant relatives to do the same and send them as gifts. What could be more personal and last as long? And might I add, for long family car trips, audiobooks are the greatest "peacekeepers" short of the UN.

Forty years ago, you had to be blind in order to get a recorded book in America. With the arrival of audiocassettes and portable tape decks, a new industry was born. One of the early fears was that audiobooks would make readers "print lazy," similar to Plato's anxiety that print would shrivel our memory muscles. As it turned out, the fears of audiobooks diminishing our wits were baseless; in fact, the opposite proved to be true. The heaviest users are among the most literate people in America, according to a national survey.[21] Among the study's findings:

- Seventy-five percent were college graduates and 41 percent had advanced degrees.
- Eighty percent had an annual family income of $51,000 or higher.
- Eighty-six percent read at least one newspaper daily.
- Twenty-one percent read at least twenty-five books a year.

Your local library can be your cheapest resource for audiobooks and will search area libraries for titles it doesn't have. My personal preference for unabridged audiobooks is Recorded Books, Inc. (for both children's and adult titles) because of its huge catalog of titles and its superior stable of readers and narrators. The ultimate success of an audiobook is determined by the reader and Recorded Books has cornered the best.

The recent addition of the DVD player to family transportation does nothing but deprive the child of yet another classroom: conversation with parents or the shared intellectual experience of listening to an audiobook communally. Unlike the DVD, audio recordings are experienced by those in both the front *and* back of the car. This allows the parent to stop a tape or disc and ask, "Why do you think he did that? What do you think he meant by that?" That doesn't happen with a DVD. Another home learning advantage is lost in the rush to adopt the latest techno gadget.

While on the subject of listening while traveling: when you run out of audiobooks, consider old-time radio dramas. Some are commercially available through such places as Cracker Barrel restaurants and RadioSpirits.com for about $3 a show, and there is also a Web site, www.otrcat.com/all.htm, that offers thousands of these old shows as MP3 files burned to a CD for as little as twenty cents a show. It's one of the best bargains on the Web. These old dramas keep children focused, nurture listening skills, and exercise their imaginations far better than any video or DVD.

Computer technology now includes the option to download audiobooks to your computer or MP3 player, services currently offered by Audible.com, the New York Public Library, and a growing number of other sources.

There is, however, a vast ocean of information and entertainment that sits undetected by the general public: Internet radio, and I don't mean the podcasts that many shows are making available, which are wonderful. While most users know it's there, few realize Internet radio can be turned into a wireless portable audiobook. To give you an idea of its size, almost everything broadcast by public radio in the United States for the last five years has been archived in huge sound vaults that can be listened to at any hour of the day. The collection is searchable, so if you remember a former advertising executive being interviewed about the tricks the industry uses to get people to buy stuff they really don't need, and you think it would be ideal for a middle school class you're teaching on advertising, you can find it easily in the NPR archives.[22] Much of the material in the archives is not listed by Google. For an example of how the Internet can be used to augment almost any book you read aloud to students, check out the supplementary material listed with the novel *Roll of Thunder, Hear My Cry* in the Treasury (page 268).

To use an interview like the one with the advertising man in your classroom or library, you don't need NPR's permission—as long as you're going directly from the Internet to your class. If you record it first, then you're supposed to get permission, which is seldom a problem for nonprofit circumstances (although NPR sells its own recordings and prefers that you buy those). While most of NPR's offerings fall in the news and information categories, along with excellent interviews by the likes of Diane Rehm and Leonard Lopate, there is next to nothing in the way of drama or readings. (I'll return to NPR's best attributes in a minute.) The BBC (British Broadcasting Corporation), however, offers seven hours a day of such broadcasts, including chapters from a half-dozen children's novels that are posted as they appear on air. Unlike NPR, the BBC stores most of its shows for only seven days and then erases them. (Look, it's a small island.) A current listing of the BBC children's readings can be found at www.bbc.co.uk/bbc7/bigtoe/books/.

BBC readings and dramatizations are usually suitable for teens and adults. To find a listing of the present offerings, go to www.bbc.co.uk/radio/. At the first page, click on the "Arts & Drama" button under "Speech" and you'll have a full plate.

Now here's the tricky part of this trove of sounds. Nearly everything you would like to listen to comes through your computer as "streaming audio," using the free RealAudio plug-in (a few use Microsoft's media player). Because streaming audio only appears as sound, there is no file to turn into an MP3 file or burn as a CD. But those clever little nerds in the back room have come up with inexpensive applications (less than $35) that allow you to save any sound file playing through your computer, even converting it into multiple little MP3 files if you wish. With the file saved to your hard disk, you can burn a CD or download it into your iPod for travel. A list of the various PC and Mac applications that allow this saving can be found at my Web site at www.trelease-on-reading.com/npr-search.html. Keep in mind, these recordings should be made for personal use only.

Now to return to public radio offerings (NPR daily listeners now outnumber the *combined* circulation of the thirty-five largest newspapers in America)[23]: Some of the excellent interviews done at NPR's affiliate stations aren't listed in the master NPR archive or Google but are listed at the local sites like KQED (San Francisco), WNYC (New York), KPCC (Pasadena), MPR (Minneapolis), and WAMU (Washington, D.C.). So each week, I visit these sites in search of either author or education-oriented interviews. When I find a good one, I list it with a link at my Web site. So if you're looking for a great source of education-related interviews, check out www.trelease-on-reading.com/npr-interview-list.html. To give you an idea of what is waiting to be heard, here are descriptions of three great interviews:

From Poverty to Carnegie President: For more than twenty years he's been one of America's premier cultural leaders: from classical scholar to leading the world's busiest library (New York Public) out of near bankruptcy to president of Brown University to president of the Carnegie Foundation. Few realize the humble beginnings of Vartan Gregorian's journey from childhood impoverishment in Iran. His story is one of inspiration and courage, trademarks of American immigration. And his grandmother ought to be in a Grandparents Hall of Fame. Listen to his interview with Gail Harris of Boston Public Radio's *The Connection*, May 12, 2003, at www.theconnection.org/shows/2003/05/20030512_b_main.asp.

From Chauffeur to President's Counselor: He was the only black male in his college class. His college summers were spent as a chauffeur-butler for an aristocratic Southern family that was shocked that he could read. Yet Vernon Jordan would become a young lawyer helping to integrate the University of Georgia, president of the Urban League, survivor of an assassin's bullet, and counsel not only to the president of the United States but also to some of the most powerful leaders in corporate America. Listen as he tells his life story to Diane Rehm at www.wamu.org/programs/dr/ 01/11/02.php, including his description of the frank exchange between father and son when his unlettered parents delivered him to college, knowing his reading scores were lower than those of his classmates.

From Refugee Camp to Harvard: The most selective college in America is Harvard University. To gain acceptance there, even via the privileged suburbs, is a major achievement, but to reach it from a Thailand refugee camp by way of a New York City hardware store is almost inconceivable. Listen to twenty-four-year-old Van Tran tell his story to NPR's Scott Simon on NPR's *Weekend Edition* at www.npr.org/rundowns/ segment.php?wfId=1939783.

You'll find links at my Web site to hour-long radio interviews with authors Avi, Kate DiCamillo, Walter Dean Myers, Chris Van Allsburg, J. K. Rowling, and Lois Lowry.

In summary, the technology is here to stay. Whether it wreaks wonders or havoc will largely depend on whether we allow it to work *on* us or work *for* us. Some people use a commute as downtime; others use it to waste time; and still others see it as smart time, leaving themselves fifty minutes more knowledgeable than when they began the commute. Your choice.

Treasury of Read-Alouds

How to Use the Treasury

AN essential element in reading aloud is what you choose to read. Not everyone reading this book is familiar with children's literature, either yesterday's or today's. Some readers are new parents or teachers, and others are veterans to the experience; some are looking for standards, and others are seeking newer titles. To meet that diversity, I've tried to strike a balance between old and new in compiling this list.

I recognize the danger in compiling any book list. Some will see it as exclusive ("If it's not mentioned in *The Read-Aloud Handbook*'s Treasury, it can't be any good!"), and that's a mistake. Others may be insulted that their all-time favorite has been ignored. Only a thousand-page volume could do justice to the many titles that deserve mention, and a book that size would be out of the reach of nearly everyone. Rather than being comprehensive, this list is intended as a starter and time-saver. One thing to keep in mind as you look through the list is that these are *read-aloud* titles, which eliminates some books that are difficult to read aloud or, because of the subject matter, are best read silently to oneself—like Robert Cormier's *The Chocolate War* (subject) or Mark Twain's *Tom Sawyer* (dialect).

There are nine categories and all books in the respective categories are listed alphabetically by title (the author/illustrator index to the Treasury at the end of the book will also help you locate books):

♦ Picture Books (p)
♦ Short Novels (s)
♦ Novels (n)
♦ Poetry (po)
♦ Anthologies (a)

With each major title, I've included a listening level. Thus when you read "K–2," that refers to the grade level (kindergarten through second grade) at which the child could hear and understand the story; it is not the reading level of the book (see page 36 for a discussion of reading versus listening levels). In the book's summary section, related titles are sometimes listed and if they have their own listing in the Treasury, I've added an annotation such as (n) beside the title to indicate where each can be found in the Treasury (see abbreviations listed above). Therefore, when "*My Father's Dragon* (s)" appears as a related title, the "(s)" indicates that a full description of that book can be found in the Short Novel section of the Treasury.

I have tried to limit my selections to just those that are still in print, mindful of how frustrating it is to have someone recommend a book only to find that it's out of print (OP). However, OP is far less of a problem today than it was before used book stores went online. It is nearly impossible to come up empty searching for any book published in the last forty years (see page 136 for further details). Nonetheless, restricting myself to in-print titles is one way of keeping this book from growing too cumbersome.

Happy reading!

Treasury Contents

Wordless Books

These books contain no words; the story is told entirely with pictures arranged in sequence. Wordless books can be "read" not only by prereaders and beginning readers, but also by adults (even illiterate or semiliterate) who want to "read" to children. They can "tell" the book, using the pictures for clues to the emerging plot. Books marked with a ★ are described at length in the Picture Book section of the Treasury.

Ah-Choo! by Mercer Mayer (Dial, 1976)
Ben's Dream by Chris Van Allsburg (Houghton Mifflin, 1982)
A Boy, a Dog, and a Frog by Mercer Mayer (Dial, 1967)
Deep in the Forest by Brinton Turkle (Dutton, 1976)★
Frog Goes to Dinner by Mercer Mayer (Dial, 1974)
Frog on His Own by Mercer Mayer (Dial, 1973)
Frog, Where Are You? by Mercer Mayer (Dial, 1969)
Good Dog Carl by Alexandra Day (Green Tiger, 1985)
Peter Spier's Rain by Peter Spier (Doubleday, 1982)
Sector 7 by David Wiesner (Clarion, 1997)
The Silver Pony by Lynd Ward (Houghton Mifflin, 1973)★
The Snowman by Raymond Briggs (Random House, 1978)
Time Flies by Eric Rohmann (Crown, 1994)
Tuesday by David Wiesner (Clarion, 1991)

Predictable Books

These picture books contain word or sentence patterns that are repeated often enough to enable children to predict their appearance and thus begin to join in on the reading.

Are You My Mother? by P. D. Eastman (Random House, 1960)
Brown Bear, Brown Bear, What Do You See? by Bill Martin Jr. (Henry Holt, 1983)★
The Cake That Mack Ate by Rose Robart (Atlantic, 1986)
Can I Help? by Marilyn Janovitz (North-South, 1996)
Chicka Chicka Boom Boom by Bill Martin Jr. and John Archambault (Simon & Schuster, 1989)
Chicken Soup with Rice by Maurice Sendak (Harper, 1962)
Do You Want to Be My Friend? by Eric Carle (Putnam, 1971)

Drummer Hoff by Barbara Emberly (Prentice-Hall, 1967)

Duck in the Truck by Jez Alborough (Harper, 2000)

The Flea's Sneeze by Lynn Downey (Henry Holt, 2000)

Goodnight Moon by Margaret Wise Brown (Harper, 1947)★

Hattie and the Fox by Mem Fox (Simon & Schuster, 1987)

The House That Jack Built by Jeanette Winter (Dial, 2000)

If You Give a Moose a Muffin by Laura Numeroff (Harper, 1991)

If You Give a Mouse a Cookie by Laura Numeroff (Harper, 1985)★

I Know an Old Lady Who Swallowed a Pie by Alison Jackson (Dutton, 1997)

The Important Book by Margaret Wise Brown (Harper, 1949)

I Went Walking by Sue Williams (Harcourt Brace, 2005)

Is It Time? by Marilyn Janovitz (North-South, 1994)

Let's Go Home, Little Bear by Martin Waddell (Candlewick, 1993)

The Little Old Lady Who Was Not Afraid of Anything by Linda Williams (Crowell, 1986)

Millions of Cats by Wanda Gag (Putnam, 1977)

Mrs. McNosh Hangs Up Her Wash by Sarah Weeks (Harper, 1998)

My Little Sister Ate One Hare by Bill Grossman (Crown, 1996)

The Napping House by Audrey Wood (Harcourt Brace, 1984)★

Oh, Look! by Patricia Polacco (Philomel, 2004)

Over in the Garden by Jennifer Ward (Rising Moon, 2002)

Over in the Meadow by Olive Wadsworth (Viking, 1985)

Owl Babies by Martin Waddell (Candlewick, 1992)★

Pierre: A Cautionary Tale by Maurice Sendak (Harper, 1962)

The Pig in the Pond by Martin Waddell (Candlewick, 1992)

Rolie Polie Olie by William Joyce (Harper, 1999)

Simpkin by Quentin Blake (Viking, 1994)

Snip Snap! What's That? by Mara Bergman (Greenwillow, 2005)★

This Is the Bear by Sarah Hayes (Candlewick, 1993)

This Is the House That Was Tidy and Neat by Teri Sloat (Henry Holt, 2005)

This Is the Van That Dad Cleaned by Lisa Campbell Ernst (Simon & Schuster, 2005)

Tikki Tikki Tembo by Arlene Mosel (Holt, 1968)★

The Very Hungry Caterpillar by Eric Carle (Philomel, 1969)★

We're Going on a Bear Hunt by Michael Rosen (Atheneum, 1992)★

The Wheels on the Bus by Maryann Kovalski (Little Brown, 1987)

Reference Books

How Animals Live: The Amazing World of Animals in the Wild
BY BERNARD STONEHOUSE AND ESTHER BERTRAM; JOHN FRANCIS, ILLUS.
Grades K and up   *96 pages*
Scholastic, 2004
This amounts to a Whitman's Sampler box of short but fascinating informational text about wildlife—including mammals, reptiles, birds, insects, and fish. It offers strange but true facts in single paragraphs about how they are born and how they parent, cooperate, fight, defend, and hide themselves. Typical is the description of the unique relationship between the courser bird and crocodiles. The coursers serve as flossing agents by picking the meat from between the teeth of crocodiles. In turn, the crocs recognize the good dental plan offered by the birds and refrain from eating them.

Merriam-Webster's Primary Dictionary
Grades PreS–2   *624 pages*
Merriam-Webster, 2005
There's something to be said for having a real dictionary close to your dinner table or reading area. When a child asks the meaning of a word, running over to the computer will not carry the same meaning as turning pages. This is especially true if you're trying to raise a reader. Besides, little of what you will find online will be on a child's dictionary level. On the other hand, this volume will be right on target with its 32,000 entries and six hundred full-color illustrations by one of America's premier illustrators, the late Ruth Heller. Merriam-Webster has been the American standard since 1847 and with good cause. Also in the series: *Merriam-Webster's Primary Dictionary* (Grades 3–5); *Merriam-Webster's Intermediate Dictionary* (Grades 6–10); and *Merriam-Webster's Collegiate Dictionary* (Grades 11 and up).

New Dinos
BY SHELLEY TANAKA; ALAN BARNARD, ILLUS.
Grades 1–5   *49 pages*
Atheneum, 2002
Technology like CT (CAT) scans is giving us new insights into the dinosaur world and forcing us to reconsider many earlier beliefs. In short but informative sections (about two to four paragraphs in length) accompanied by outstanding illustrations, we find the latest in dinosaur discoveries, written by a leading nonfiction writer for children. Also by the author: *Discovering the Iceman; Aboard the Titanic; Secrets of the Mummies;* and *Graveyards of the*

Dinosaurs. Related titles: *The Dinosaurs of Waterhouse Hawkins* (p); *Dinosaurs before Dark* (s); and *Scholastic Dinosaurs A to Z: The Ultimate Dinosaur Encyclopedia* by Don Lessem.

Scholastic Children's Encyclopedia

Grades 2–6   710 pages
Scholastic, 2004

There are more than six hundred entries with two thousand photographs, diagrams, charts, and maps. In addition, "Key Facts," "Did You Know?" and "Amazing Facts!" boxes offer information in bite-size but entertaining chunks. An excellent single-volume encyclopedia for preschool through first grade is *DK First Encyclopedia* with seven hundred photos and descriptions (166 pages).

Picture Books

Aesop's Fables

BY JERRY PINKNEY
Grades 2–5   85 pages
North-South, 2000

Aesop's fables offer us not only wisdom but also an introduction to the characters, ideas, and images that turn up again and again in the literary tradition. This volume includes more than sixty of Aesop's most famous tales. The most economical collection is *Aesop's Fables,* selected and adapted by Jack Zipes. Good smaller collections include *Anno's Aesop: A Book of Fables by Aesop* by Mitsumasa Anno, and *Fables* (contemporary) by Arnold Lobel. *Aesop and Company* by Barbara Bader includes historical background information on Aesop and his times.

Alexander and the Terrible, Horrible, No Good, Very Bad Day

BY JUDITH VIORST; RAY CRUZ, ILLUS.
Grades K and up   34 pages
Atheneum, 1972

Everyone has a bad day once in a while, but little Alexander has the worst of all. Follow him from a cereal box without a prize to a burned-out nightlight. Sequels: *Alexander Who Used to Be Rich Last Sunday,* and *Alexander, Who's Not (Do you hear me? I mean it!) Going to Move.* Also by the author: *If I Were in Charge of the World and Other Worries* (po). Related books: *Are You Going to Be Good?* by Cari Best; *Once Upon an Ordinary Day* by Colin McNaughton.

All About Alfie (series)

BY SHIRLEY HUGHES
Grades PreS–1   *128 pages*
Lothrop, 1998

This collection features preschooler Alfie in four of his most popular stories (published individually over the years). Though set in England, the stories radiate the feeling of children everywhere—from facial expressions and clothing to the crises that really matter to young children (birthday party companions). With spare text and glorious illustrations, the plots easily hold young children's attention. Other books about Alfie's family: *Annie Rose Is My Little Sister* and *The Big Alfie and Annie Rose Storybook*. Also by the author: *Dogger* and, for older children, *Ella's Big Chance: A Jazz-Age Cinderella* (p).

Arthur's Chicken Pox (series)

BY MARC BROWN
Grades PreS–1   *28 pages*
Little, Brown, 1994

Long before he was discovered by PBS, there was Arthur in print, a series of wildly popular stories about an aardvark family's warm and often hilarious adventures at home, at school, and in the neighborhood. There are numerous books to choose from, and children can relate to Arthur. In this adventure, he's got a case of chicken pox, along with all its lifestyle complications for the entire family.

Aunt Minnie McGranahan

BY MARY SKILLINGS PRIGGER; BETSY LEWIN, ILLUS.
Grades K–2   *30 pages*
Clarion, 1999

Everyone in the small Kansas farm town thought Aunt Minnie had lost her mind when she took in nine orphaned nieces and nephews in 1920. Based on the true story of one of the author's relatives, the tale describes Minnie's sometimes whimsical adventures with the children as they adjust to farm life and she adjusts to all of them. Related book: *Saving Sweetness* (p).

Baby Brains

BY SIMON JAMES
Grades PreS–1   *24 pages*
Candlewick, 2004

This is a wonderful send-up of the super-baby syndrome that afflicts too many parents, but, on another level, it's also a funny story for children. Mr.

and Mrs. Brains do "everything right." Before this baby is born they read to him, play music and foreign language tapes, even watch the news with the sound turned up. Thus, days after Baby Brains is born, he's sitting up reading the newspaper when his parents come down for breakfast. After breakfast he announces he'd like to go to school tomorrow, which he does, and heads the class! It's not long before he joins the astronauts for a trip into space and that's where it all comes apart—but in a good way. In the sequel, *Baby Brains Superstar,* the wee wizard is back as a musical prodigy and rock 'n' roll star. Related book: *A Fine School* by Sharon Creech.

Baby in a Basket

BY GLORIA RAND; TED RAND, ILLUS.

Grades K–2   *36 pages*

Dutton, 1997

With the winter of 1917 approaching Fairbanks, Alaska, Marie Boyer bids good-bye to her postmaster husband, bundles her three-year-old and four-month-old daughters in fur skins, and boards a large sleigh for the ten-day trip to warmer and safer Seattle. But a ferocious winter storm strikes the travelers, spooking the horses and dumping the sleigh's contents into the snow and river. How they survive and the miraculous river rescue of the baby in the basket make this true story a great read-aloud. Related books: *The Bear That Heard Crying* by Natalie Kinsey-Warnock; *Mailing May* (p); and *The Year of Miss Agnes* (n).

The Biggest Bear

BY LYND WARD

Grades K–3   *80 pages*

Houghton Mifflin, 1952

Johnny adopts a bear cub fresh out of the woods and its growth presents problem after problem—the crises we invite when we tame what is meant to be wild. Also by the author: *The Silver Pony* (p). Related books: *Capyboppy* by Bill Peet; *Harry's Pony* by Barbara Ann Porte; *The Josefina Story Quilt* by Eleanor Coerr; and *Rikki-Tikki-Tavi* (p).

Big Jabe

BY JERDINE NOLEN; KADIR NELSON, ILLUS.

Grades 1–4   *30 pages*

Lothrop, 2000

Some saw him as a Moses figure, others as John Henry, but everyone agreed that Big Jabe did wondrous things on the plantation—things no other slave ever dreamed of doing, including saving many of his people. The illustrator, Kadir Nelson, is the single best talent I've seen in children's books in the last ten years and this book radiates with his art. Also by the author: *Harvey Potter's Balloon Farm; Hewitt Anderson's Great Big Life;* and *Plantzilla.*

The Book of Beasts

BY E. NESBIT, ABRIDGED AND ILLUSTRATED BY INGA MOORE
Grades K–2   *54 pages*
Candlewick, 2001
E. Nesbit was one of the great storytellers for children, and Moore has slightly abridged one of her most charming short stories for this volume and illustrated it magnificently. It's the story of young Lionel, who is suddenly summoned to the palace where, to his amazement, he's crowned king to replace his late great, great, great, great, great grandfather. Although he's warned by court counselors not to open *The Book of Beasts* in the library, he does so, thus freeing from its pages a fierce dragon that sets about devouring the countryside. Is there something in the book that might save the kingdom from the dragon? Dare he open it again? Related books: *Do Not Open* by Brinton Turkle; *Matthew's Dragon* by Susan Cooper; *The Minpins* (p); *My Father's Dragon* (s); *Saint George and the Dragon* retold by Margaret Hodges; *The Reluctant Dragon* (s); and a chapter book, *The Dragonling* by Jackie French Koller.

Brave Irene

BY WILLIAM STEIG
Grades K–5   *28 pages*
Farrar, Straus & Giroux, 1986
When Irene's dressmaker mother falls ill and cannot deliver the duchess's gown for the ball, Irene shoulders the huge box and battles a winter storm to make the delivery. Also by the author: *Sylvester and the Magic Pebble* (p). Related books on courage: *The Butterfly* (p); *High as a Hawk: A Brave Girl's Historic Climb* (p); *Mirette on the High Wire* (p); and *When Jessie Came Across the Sea* (p).

Bridget and the Gray Wolves

BY PIJA LINDENBAUM
Grades PreS–K   *36 pages*
R&S Books, 2001
Take a fussy, bossy preschooler, mix in a field trip on which she gets lost,

add a pack of gray wolves in the deep woods, and what do you have? A
sure fire read-aloud winner, both humorous and suspenseful. Little Bridget
soon takes charge of the pack, organizing them into games and feeding
them mud soup. A highlight for any young audience will be the nap time
scene when the wolves must first retreat to their "pee trees." Related book:
The Gunniwolf (p).

Brown Bear, Brown Bear, What Do You See?

BY BILL MARTIN JR.; ERIC CARLE, ILLUS.
Grades PreS–K   *24 pages*
Henry Holt, 1983
This classic predictable book follows the question through various animals
and colors. Sequel: *Polar Bear, Polar Bear, What Do You Hear?* Also by the author: *Barn Dance; Chicka Chicka Boom Boom;* and *The Ghost-Eye Tree.* For
other predictable books, see list on page 179.

Captain Abdul's Pirate School

BY COLIN MCNAUGHTON
Grades 1–5   *32 pages*
Candlewick, 1994
Hoping to toughen up their children, parents send them off to pirate
school—something like a contemporary military or prep school. With
tongue-in-cheek humor (some of it scoundrel-crude), the kids shape up
and then turn against the pirates. Prequel: *Jolly Roger and the Pirates of Captain Abdul.* Sequel: *Captain Abdul's Little Treasure.* Also by the author: *Here
Come the Aliens* (p). Other pirate books: *How I Became a Pirate* by Melinda
Long; *Maggie and the Pirates* by Ezra Jack Keats; and *Pirate Diary: The Journal
of Jake Carpenter* by Richard Platt.

A Chair for My Mother

BY VERA B. WILLIAMS
Grades K–3   *30 pages*
Greenwillow, 1982
This is the first book in a trilogy of tender stories about a family of three
women: Grandma, Mama, and daughter Rosa (all told in the first person
by the child). In this book, they struggle to save their loose change (in a
glass jar) in order to buy a chair for the child's mother—something she
can collapse into after her waitressing job. In *Something Special for Me,*
the glass jar's contents are to be spent on the child's birthday present. What
an important decision for a little girl to make! After much soul-searching,
she settles on a used accordion. In *Music, Music for Everyone,* the jar is

empty again. With all the loose change going for Grandma's medical expenses now, little Rosa searches for a way to make money and cheer up her grandma.

Chato and the Party Animals

BY GARY SOTO; SUSAN GUEVARA, ILLUS.

Grades K–2   *28 pages*

Putnam, 2000

When Chato, the original party animal (cat), discovers that his friend Novio Boy came from the pound and thus doesn't even know his own birthday, he decides to schedule one for him and invites everyone in the barrio. The problem: he forgets to invite Novio Boy. When he doesn't show up and can't be found, everyone assumes he's died or been kidnapped. When he finally shows up, there is a great *pachanga*. An excellent celebration of Latino culture. Other books in the series: *Chato's Kitchen* and *Chato Goes Cruisin'*. Also by the author: *Baseball in April* (s).

Chewy Louie

BY HOWIE SCHNEIDER

Grades PreS–K   *32 pages*

Rising Moon, 2000

My three-year-old grandson never laughed so hard at a book as he did with this one, the tale of a new puppy with a gigantic need to chew. Louie devours everything in sight, from food bowls, tables, chairs, toys, and the vet's pants, to the family car. Will they have to give Louie up to save their home? And then comes the wonderful ending! As much as he understands dogs, Schneider also understands kids and where their funny bones are. Related book: *The Best Pet of All* by David LaRochelle. Also by the author: *Wilky the White House Cockroach*.

Cloudy with a Chance of Meatballs

BY JUDI BARRETT; RON BARRETT, ILLUS.

Grades PreS–5   *28 pages*

Atheneum, 1978

In the fantasy land of Chewandswallow, the weather changes three times a day, supplying all the residents with food out of the sky. But suddenly the weather takes a turn for the worse; instead of normal-size meatballs, it rains meatballs the size of basketballs, and pancakes and syrup smother the streets. Something must be done! Sequel: *Pickles to Pittsburgh*. Also by the author: *Animals Should Definitely Not Act Like People* and *Animals Should Definitely Not Wear Clothing*.

The Complete Adventures of Peter Rabbit

BY BEATRIX POTTER

Grades PreS–1   *96 pages*

Warner, 1982

Here are the four original tales involving one of the most famous animals in children's literature—Peter Rabbit. Children identify with his naughty sense of adventure, and then thrill at his narrow escape from the clutches of Mr. MacGregor. Although all the Potter books come in a small format that is ideal because young children feel more comfortable holding that size (3" × 5"), this larger volume is the most affordable choice and still retains the Potter illustrations. The original story of Peter was contained in a get-well letter Potter wrote to a child; the story of that child and his letter is explored in the picture book *My Dear Noel* by Jane Johnson and can be used as low as kindergarten level. Author study: a children's biography, *Beatrix Potter*, by Alexandra Wallner. There is a wealth of Potter information on the Web, beginning with www.peterrabbit.co.uk/.

Corduroy

BY DON FREEMAN

Grades PreS–2   *32 pages*

Viking, 1968

In this beloved story, a teddy bear searches through a department store for a friend. His quest ends when a little girl buys him with her piggy-bank savings. Also by the author: *A Pocket for Corduroy* and *Beady Bear*. For related books, see *Ira Sleeps Over* (p).

A Day's Work

BY EVE BUNTING; RONALD HIMLER, ILLUS.

Grades K–4   *30 pages*

Clarion, 1994

A young Mexican-American boy seeks work for his newly arrived grandfather who speaks no English. In persuading a man that his grandfather knows how to garden, the boy tells a small lie that ends up causing them twice as much work. The lesson in truthfulness is apparent, but just as important is the tender relationship of the child with an old man who needs help in a frightening new land. Related title: *The Paperboy* by Dav Pilkey.

Deep in the Forest

BY BRINTON TURKLE

Grades PreS–2   *30 pages*

Dutton, 1976

A wordless book reversing the conventional Goldilocks and the Three Bears tale. This time the bear cub visits Goldilocks's family cabin, with hilarious and plausible results. Also by the author: *Thy Friend, Obadiah* and *Do Not Open*. For a list of other wordless books, see the list on page 179. For a list of other fairy tale parodies and sequels, see page 290.

Dinosaur Bob and His Adventures with the Family Lazardo
BY WILLIAM JOYCE
Grades PreS–4 · 30 pages
Harper, 1988

In this dinosaur fantasy book, the Lazardo family brings a dinosaur home from Africa and it proves to be the ultimate pet for home and community—after some initial misgivings by the police department. Also by the author: *George Shrinks; Rolie Polie Olie;* and *Santa Calls.*

The Dinosaurs of Waterhouse Hawkins (nonfiction)
BY BARBARA KERLEY; BRIAN SELZNICK, ILLUS.
Grades 1 and up 48 pages
Scholastic, 2001

In 1856, artist and naturalist Waterhouse Hawkins, collaborating with a leading scientist, earned an extraordinary commission: to build a dinosaur park. Think *Jurassic Park* in Queen Victoria's time. On an island outside London, Hawkins began building his giant models. And giants they were. Just one of the creatures required thirty tons of clay, six hundred bricks, fifteen hundred tiles, and thirty-eight casks of cement. The finished product would astonish Victorian England and lead him to the United States, where he was invited to build more models, this time in Central Park. Unfortunately, in the middle of his work, the henchmen of the infamous (and jealous) Boss Tweed vandalized the project beyond recovery. To this day, shattered pieces from the original models are still buried beneath the soil in Central Park. One could easily say that everything that has been done with dinosaurs since then—from plastic models and cereal prizes to movies and fantasy books like *Jurassic Park*—began with this one man's vivid imagination. It is a tale as fantastic as the creatures themselves. Related book: *Mammoth* by Patrick O'Brien.

Eddie, Harold's Little Brother
ED KOCH AND PAT KOCH THALER; JAMES WARHOLA, ILLUS.
Grades 1–3 28 pages
Putnam, 2005

Eddie idolized his older brother, not just because he was older but also because he was the best athlete in the neighborhood. Everyone wanted Harold on their team. The one they didn't want was Eddie. Harold insisted Eddie be chosen for one side or the other but eventually even he tired of Eddie's clumsiness. There was one skill that Eddie did have—he could talk about almost anything. When he talked about his brother's games, the boys were spellbound. So when a notice appeared about a public speaking contest, Harold was certain this was meant for Eddie and convinced him to give it a try. So Eddie wrote his speech, rehearsed it in front of the team, and entered the contest. What followed eventually led the never-at-a-loss-for-words Ed Koch to the mayor's office of New York City. For other picture book biographies, see *My Brother Martin* (p).

Ella's Big Chance: A Jazz-Age Cinderella

BY SHIRLEY HUGHES
Grades 1–4   *46 pages*
Simon & Schuster, 2004
Of the hundreds of Cinderella versions through the ages, this is my current favorite, with exquisite art, a flapper Jazz-Age setting, and an original and touching ending. Related titles: *Adelita: A Mexican Cinderella Story* by Tomie dePaola; *The Egyptian Cinderella* by Shirley Climo; *Yeh-Shen: A Cinderella Story from China* by Ai-Ling Louie; and for older readers-listeners, the novel *Ella Enchanted* by Gail Carson Levine.

Encounter

BY JANE YOLEN; DAVID SHANNON, ILLUS.
Grades 3–7   *30 pages*
Harcourt Brace, 1992
In observance of the five hundredth anniversary of Columbus's arrival in the Western Hemisphere, Yolen viewed the arrival through the eyes of a Taino Indian boy on San Salvador who has a foreboding dream about the newcomers—portrayed in hauntingly beautiful illustrations. But the boy's warnings are rejected by the tribe's elders. A thought-provoking book on imperialism and colonialism. Related reading: *Time* article, "Before Columbus," October 19, 1998, pages 76–77, detailing recent archeological discoveries about the Taino tribe in Caribbean digs. An interesting companion book: *Me, All Alone, at the End of the World* (p).

Erandi's Braids

BY ANTONIO HERNANDEZ MADRIGAL; TOMIE DEPAOLA, ILLUS.
Grades PreS–2   *30 pages*
Putnam, 1999

It was once the custom for women in poor Mexican villages to sell their hair, which was then used for wigs and fancy embroidery. In this tale, Erandi's mother has decided to sell her hair in order to pay for a much-needed fishing net. The barber refuses, saying hers is too short, but that he would gladly take the child's braids. It is now the child's difficult decision to make. Related books: *The Legend of the Bluebonnet* (p) and *The Babe and I* by David A. Adler.

The Everything Book

BY DENISE FLEMING
Inf–Tod   *64 pages*
Henry Holt, 2000
After Mother Goose, all new parents should have this terrific book about everything important to a child—animals, shapes, colors, rhymes, finger games, food, faces, letters, traffic, and toys. The art is a rainbow feast for the eyes, but is done in a style very young children can easily absorb. Related book: *My First Word Book* by Jane Yorke.

The Foot Book

BY DR. SEUSS
Tod–PreS   *28 pages*
Random House, 1968
Most of Dr. Seuss's books are aimed at kindergarten and older, but here is one of the more accessible ones for toddlers, mainly because the subject is so near (eighteen inches away) to the child's heart: feet! No plot but lots of repetition, rhyme, and Seussian illustrations. For more information about the author, see *If I Ran the Zoo* (p).

Froggy Gets Dressed (series)

BY JONATHAN LONDON; FRANK REMKIEWICZ, ILLUS.
Grades PreS–K   *32 pages*
Viking, 2000
Young Froggy is so excited about the first snowfall, he rushes outside to play with his friends before realizing he's forgotten to get dressed! He's out of breath and back outside after all that dressing, when his mother shouts to remind him he's forgotten his long underwear! This popular series includes: *Froggy's Best Christmas; Froggy's Day with Dad; Froggy Eats Out; Froggy's First Kiss; Froggy Goes to Bed; Froggy Goes to the Doctor; Froggy Goes to School; Let's Go Froggy; Froggy's Halloween; Froggy Learns to Swim; Froggy Plays Soccer; Froggy Plays in the Band;* and *Froggy's Baby Sister.*

Full, Full, Full of Love

BY TRISH COOKE; PAUL HOWARD, ILLUS.

Grades PreS–K   *24 pages*
Candlewick, 2003

This book is like sitting down to dinner with a very happy family. When little Jay Jay is dropped off at his grandmother's, he helps her prepare the big Sunday family dinner. Gran's home is full of love and kisses, but there's lots of work to be done, so Jay Jay will need to feed the fish, put out dishes, pick up the spilled candy, and be patient. And when everyone finally sits down for the meal, it is a very full one, filled with love and family, one that all children should have access to.

Goin' Someplace Special

BY PATRICIA MCKISSACK; JERRY PINKNEY, ILLUS.

Grades 2–5   *34 pages*
Atheneum, 2001

In the segregated 1950s, a young African American girl takes her first bus trip into downtown Nashville, to go to her "special place." En route with her new sense of maturity (traveling alone for the first time), she must endure a series of racial indignities that nearly wear her down. Her spirit is resurrected, however, by the etched lettering above the door of that special place—"Public Library: All Are Welcome." Jerry Pinkney's authentic watercolor illustrations create the perfect tapestry for this story of human struggle. The author continues this tale in a series of short novels set in 1960 when a ten-year-old witnesses the Nashville lunch counter sit-ins five years before the Civil Rights Act was passed, starting with *Abby Takes a Stand: Scraps of Time*. Related books: *Delivering Justice* by Jim Haskins; *Leon's Story* (s); *More Than Anything Else* by Marie Bradby; and *Freedom on the Menu: The Greensboro Sit-ins* by Carole Boston Weatherford.

Good Job, Little Bear (series)

MARTIN WADDELL; BARBARA FRITH, ILLUS.

Tod–K   *32 pages*
Candlewick, 2002

The last line of this book, "I'll be there when you need me—always," sums up what this entire series is about: the relationship between parent and child (big bear and little bear). Each volume explores the warm interactions between the two, in their cave and in the forest, making the series the epitome of "cozy" and an ideal bedtime companion. Other books in the series: *Can't You Sleep, Little Bear?; Let's Go Home, Little Bear; You and Me, Little*

Bear; and *Sleep Tight, Little Bear.* Related books: *Where's My Teddy?* (p) and *You Can Do It, Sam* (p).

Goodnight Moon
BY MARGARET WISE BROWN; CLEMENT HURD, ILLUS.
Inf–Tod   *30 pages*
Harper, 1947
This classic is based on a bedtime ritual, sure to be copied by every child who hears it. Also by the author: *The Important Book; The Runaway Bunny;* and *Sailor Dog.* Related bedtime books for infants and toddlers: *Can't You Sleep, Little Bear?* by Martin Waddell; *Good Night, Gorilla* by Peggy Rathman; *How Do Dinosaurs Say Good Night?* (p); *Kiss Good Night* by Amy Hest; *Max's Bedtime* by Rosemary Wells; *The Napping House* (p); *Shhhhh! Everybody's Sleeping* (p); and *Sleep Tight, Little Bear* by Martin Waddell.

Grandma's Bears
BY GINA WILSON; PAUL HOWARD, ILLUS.
Grades PreS–1   *34 pages*
Candlewick, 2004
Imagine a sleepover at Grandma's in which she has five bears living with her: bears that are warm and cuddly, bears that play hopscotch on the kitchen floor, eat too many donuts, get soap in their eyes, and hug you like a warm towel when you get out of the tub. And they're real! This is one great "grandmother-bedtime book" with the marks of a classic. Related books: *Are You Going to Be Good?* by Cari Best; *Grandma Summer* by Harley Jessup; *Ira Sleeps Over* (p); and *Sleep Tight, Little Bear* by Martin Waddell.

The Great Fuzz Frenzy
JANET STEVENS AND SUSAN STEVENS CRUMMEL
Grades PreS–1   *56 pages*
Harcourt Brace, 2005
This whimsical tale was born the day the authors watched a tennis ball roll into prairie-dog town. What would the dogs think it was? So they put themselves into the mind of those underground dogs confronted by a round lump of fuzz and just imagined. The result is a delightful romp that has many applications to human behavior—copycatting, greed, even early-warning signals. The large fold-out pages (which are not text-heavy) and brightly colored illustrations will make this a read-aloud standard for years. Try to have a tennis ball nearby when reading this book.

The Gunniwolf

BY WILHELMINA HARPER; BARBARA UPTON, ILLUS.

Grades PreS–K   *30 pages*

Dial, 2003

For many years, this was a read-aloud standard at library story hours. It is now back with glorious illustrations that breathe new life into the tale of a well-intentioned little girl who ignores her mother's cautions about a wolf in the woods, a gentler first-cousin to "Little Red Riding Hood" but without Grandma. After tense moments (and lots of wordplay between wolf and child), she escapes, never to disobey her mother again. Don't miss this! For a list of fairy tale parodies, see page 290.

Harry in Trouble (series)

BY BARBARA ANN PORTE; YOSSI ABOLAFIA, ILLUS.

Grades K–2   *48 pages*

Greenwillow, 1989

This Harry easy-reader series is about people as real as the folks next door—grade-schooler Harry, his widower father, and their relatives, neighbors, friends, and teachers. In this book, Harry loses his library card for the third time. Also in the series: *Harry's Dog; Harry's Mom; Harry Gets an Uncle; Harry's Visit;* and *Harry's Pony.*

Harvesting Hope: The Story of Cesar Chavez

BY KATHLEEN KRULL; YUYI MORALES, ILLUS.

Grades 1–4   *48 pages*

Harcourt Brace, 2003

This is a stunning biography of the man who made some of the richest people in America listen to some of the poorest. Despite the limitations of a picture book, the author and illustrator are able to create a multidimensional image of a man who walked so proudly in the footsteps of Gandhi and Martin Luther King Jr., faced down the rich and powerful, and changed America. The book spans his childhood in the Arizona desert and the bitter loss of his family's farm to the backbreaking harvest years and the blossoming of his labor movement for indigent farm workers. For other picture biographies, see *My Brother Martin* (p).

Heckedy Peg

BY AUDREY WOOD; DON WOOD, ILLUS.

Grades K–5   *30 pages*

Harcourt Brace, 1987

A determined mother outsmarts a witch who has captured and bewitched her seven children. Also by the author: *A Cowboy Christmas* and *The Napping House* (p). Related books: *The Widow's Broom* by Chris Van Allsburg and *The Whingdingdilly* (p).

Henry and the Kite Dragon
BY BRUCE EDWARD HALL; WILLIAM LOW, ILLUS.
Grades K–2   *36 pages*
Philomel, 2004
Set in New York's Chinatown in the 1920s, an elderly Chinese grandfather's hobby, kite making, puts him at the center of two warring groups of neighborhood boys—one Italian and one Chinese. The Italians' hobby was homing pigeons, which are endangered by the large Chinese kites. Because neither side talks to the other, their conflict grows into a stone-throwing confrontation until a giant dragon kite forces them to resolve the dispute.

Here Come the Aliens!
BY COLIN MCNAUGHTON
Grades PreS–2   *26 pages*
Candlewick, 1995
A spaceload of horrific-looking aliens is en route to earth, and they're loaded down with McNaughton's usual helping of "gross" appetites, noises, and faces. Earthlings are forewarned to beware. And then the hideous creatures catch a glimpse of what awaits them on earth and they retreat into space. What frightened them? The class picture from a preschool group of four-year-olds!

High as a Hawk: A Brave Girl's Historic Climb
BY T. A. BARRON: TED LEWIN, ILLUS.
Grades 1–3   *30 pages*
Philomel, 2004
Famed mountain guide Enos Mills successfully led the campaign to create the Rocky Mountain National Park. His friends and correspondents ran from Teddy Roosevelt and Kit Carson to Helen Keller and Booker T. Washington. But of the more than 250 trips he made as a guide to the top of the park's highest ridge, he claimed the most memorable was the one he made in 1905 with a determined eight-year-old girl named Harriet Peters, the youngest ever. This is the true story of their memorable journey to 14,255 feet, illustrated in the lush watercolors of the great Ted Lewin.

The House on East 88th Street

BY BERNARD WABER

Grades PreS–3   *48 pages*

Houghton Mifflin, 1962

When the Primm family discovers a gigantic crocodile in the bathtub of their new brownstone home, it signals the beginning of a wonderful picture book series. As soon as the Primms overcome their fright, they see him as your children will—as the most lovable and human of crocodiles. Sequels (in this order): *Lyle, Lyle, Crocodile; Lyle and the Birthday Party; Lyle Finds His Mother; Lovable Lyle; Funny, Funny Lyle; Lyle at the Office;* and *Lyle at Christmas.* Also by the author: *Ira Sleeps Over* (p); *The Mouse That Snored;* and *Evie & Margie.*

How Do Dinosaurs Say Good Night?

BY JANE YOLEN; MARK TEAGUE, ILLUS.

Grades PreS–K   *30 pages*

Scholastic, 2000

In this popular bedtime book for little dinosaur fans, the author uses different dinosaurs as humorous examples of good and bad bedtime behavior. Other books in this excellent series: *How Do Dinosaurs Get Well Soon?; How Do Dinosaurs Clean Their Rooms?; How Do Dinosaurs Count to Ten?;* and *How Do Dinosaurs Eat Their Food?* Related fiction books on dinosaurs: *Can I Please Have a Stegosaurus, Mom? Can I Please?* by Lois G. Grambling and *Little Grunt and the Big Egg: A Prehistoric Fairy Tale* by Tomie dePaola.

Humphrey, Albert, and the Flying Machine

BY KATHRYN LASKY; JOHN MANDERS, ILLUS.

Grades K–3   *32 pages*

Harcourt Brace, 2004

In one of the very best parodies of the traditional fairy tale, Lasky gives us an irrepressible pair of brothers who accidentally are caught in the curse of the "100-year sleep" cast upon the princess and her castle. They're the first to awaken (and they do their hilarious best to awaken everyone else—with no luck!), and then recall the part in the story about a "handsome prince" waking the sleeping princess with a kiss. They want no part of that but slash their way through the vines and into town to set up a casting call in which the winner is a world-class, real-life inventor. For a list of fairy tale parodies, see page 290.

If You Give a Mouse a Cookie

BY LAURA NUMEROFF; FELICIA BOND, ILLUS.

Grades PreS–K   *30 pages*

Harper, 1985

In a humorous cumulative tale that comes full circle, a little boy offers a mouse a cookie and ends up working his head off for the demanding little creature. Sequels: *If You Give a Moose a Muffin; If You Give a Pig a Pancake;* and *If You Take a Mouse to the Movies.* For other cumulative stories, see Predictable Books on page 179.

If I Ran the Zoo

BY DR. SEUSS

Grades PreS–4   *54 pages*

Random House, 1950

Little Gerald McGrew finds the animals at the local zoo pretty boring compared with the zany, exotic creatures populating the zoo of his imagination (just like a little lad imagined things while walking to and from school in Seuss's first book for children, *And to Think That I Saw It on Mulberry Street*). Dr. Seuss's father ran the zoo in Springfield, Massachusetts, for thirty-one years. Seuss author studies: "Oh, the Places You've Taken Us: RT's Tribute to Dr. Seuss," in the May 1992 issue of *Reading Teacher;* a children's biography, *Dr. Seuss: Young Author and Artist*, by Kathleen Kudlinski (Aladdin, 2005); and two adult biographies, *The Seuss, the Whole Seuss, and Nothing But the Seuss: A Visual Biography of Theodore Seuss Geisel* by Charles D. Cohen, and *Dr. Seuss and Mr. Geisel* by Judith and Neil Morgan, the definitive book on his personal life. Fans of Dr. Seuss also will enjoy the books of Bill Peet—see *The Whingdingdilly* (p). Listen to Philip Nel, author of *Dr. Seuss: American Icon,* dissect the creative mind of Dr. Seuss on the 100th anniversary of his birth, via the Internet (*Midmorning*, Minnesota Public Radio, March 11, 2004) at: www.publicradio.org/tools/media/player/news/midmorning/2004/03/11_midmorn2.

Ira Sleeps Over

BY BERNARD WABER

Grades K–6   *48 pages*

Houghton Mifflin, 1972

This is a warm, sensitive, and humorous look at a boy's overnight visit to his best friend's house, centering on the child's quandary of whether or not to bring his teddy bear. It makes for lively discussion about individual sleeping habits, peer pressure, and the things we all hold on to—even as grown-ups.

In the sequel, *Ira Says Goodbye,* the two best friends experience a childhood pain when one moves away. Waber is also the author of the popular *Lyle the Crocodile* series that begins with *The House on East 88th Street* (p) and *Evie & Margie,* about two female best friends. Related books: *Corduroy* (p); *I Lost My Bear* by Jules Feiffer; *Mirabelle* (p); and *Where's My Teddy?* (p).

The Island of the Skog

BY STEVEN KELLOGG

Grades PreS–2   *32 pages*

Dial, 1973

Sailing away from city life, a boatload of mice discover the island of their dreams, only to be pulled up short by the appearance of a fearful monster already dwelling on the island. How imaginations can run away with us and how obstacles can be overcome if we'll just talk with others are central issues in this tale. Also by the author: *The Mysterious Tadpole* (p).

I Stink!

BY KATE AND JIM MCMULLAN

Grades PreK– 2   *32 pages*

Harper, 2002

More than sixty years ago, Virginia Lee Burton created a series of picture books that introduced children to the civic lives of their cities and towns: *Katy and the Big Snow* and *Mike Mulligan and His Steam Shovel* (p). Now comes *I Stink!* Quite a contrast, but still successful. Let's face it, times change. They don't write children's books today the way Washington Irving wrote 'em in the old days, and that's a good thing, in my view. The McMullans give us not only an inside look at the mechanics of the modern garbage truck (something that'll fascinate most children), but also a taste of what life would be like without it. Jim McMullan's flamboyant use of mashed-up, exploding, slithering, rumbling, and dripping typefaces lends both amusement and texture to the tale. Also by the authors: *I'm Mighty!* (a tugboat).

Johnny on the Spot

BY EDWARD SOREL

Grades 1–4   *28 pages*

Simon & Schuster, 1998

Young Johnny and his adult neighbor accidentally invent a radio that broadcasts events one day in advance. The conflict arises when Johnny is sworn to secrecy and forbidden to interfere with the future—even if he knows a calamity is about to occur. Created by one of America's premier political artists, the story is both adventure and morality tale. Related titles: *A Day's Work* (p) and *The Real Thief* by William Steig.

The Last Princess: The Story of Princess Ka'iulani of Hawai'i
BY FAY STANLEY; DIANE STANLEY, ILLUS.
Grades 2–6   *36 pages*
Simon & Schuster, 1991
The story of the last princess is also the story of America's last state—Hawaii. It is a tragic but important tale, showing the proud heritage of the Hawaiian people and one of the dark chapters in American history. Related book: *Encounter* (p).

The Legend of the Bluebonnet
RETOLD BY TOMIE DEPAOLA
Grades PreS–4   *30 pages*
Putnam, 1984
Here is the legend behind the bluebonnets that blanket the state of Texas—the story of the little Comanche Indian orphan who sacrificed her only doll in order to end the drought that was ravaging her village. Related books: *The Legend of the Indian Paintbrush* by Tomie dePaola; also *Erandi's Braids* (p) and *The Lost Children* (p). A complete listing of books by Tomie dePaola can be found at: http:www.tomie.com/. Recently, he has written a series of autobiographical chapter books (in order): *26 Fairmont Street; Here We All Are; On My Way;* and *What a Year.* For author studies: *Tomie dePaola: His Art and His Stories* by Barbara Elleman.

Lilly's Purple Plastic Purse
BY KEVIN HENKES
Grades PreS–1   *30 pages*
Greenwillow, 1996
Few writers for children have as firm a grip on the pulse of childhood as does Kevin Henkes. His mice-children experience all the joys and insecurities of being a kid, but he manages to maintain a light touch throughout his stories. In this case, Lilly loves school and her teacher—until the day her antics distract the class and the teacher must temporarily confiscate her precious new plastic purse. Shattered, she's uncertain how to handle this small rebuke and seeks ways to show her hurt. With the help of her family, Lilly overcomes her embarrassment and hasty behavior, writes an apology, and soars on the good feelings that come from doing the right thing. Lilly also stars in: *Lilly's Big Day; Chester's Way;* and *Julius, the Baby of the World.* Related book: *Rotten Teeth* (p).

The Little House

BY VIRGINIA LEE BURTON
Grades PreS–3   40 pages
Houghton Mifflin, 1942

This Caldecott Medal winner uses a little turn-of-the-century house to portray the urbanization of America. With each page, the reader/listener becomes the little house and experiences the contentment, wonder, concern, anxiety, and loneliness that the passing seasons and encroaching city bring. Many of today's children who daily experience the anxieties of city life will identify with the little house's eventual triumph. Other books by the author: *Mike Mulligan and His Steam Shovel* (p). Related books: *Farewell to Shady Glade* and *Wump World* by Bill Peet.

The Little Old Lady Who Was Not Afraid of Anything

BY LINDA WILLIAMS
Grades PreS–1   28 pages
Harper, 1988

Walking through the dark woods toward home, the little old lady is approached by a succession of scary articles of empty clothing—gloves, hat, shoes, trousers, etc. She refuses to allow them to frighten her until she encounters the last one—which sets her running. In the end, however, she solves the problem by making all the items into a scarecrow. Other scary but nonthreatening books for young children: *Here Come the Aliens!* (p); *There's a Nightmare in My Closet* by Mercer Mayer; *Snip Snap! What's That?* (p); and *The Squeaky Door,* retold by Margaret Read MacDonald.

Little Red Riding Hood

RETOLD BY TRINA SCHART HYMAN
Grades PreS–3   32 pages
Holiday, 1983

It's hard to imagine a better illustrated version of this famous tale. The artist has given us a child and grandma who are every child and grandmother and a texture so rich you can almost smell the woods. Related books: *Flossie and the Fox* by Patricia McKissack (African American version) and *The Gunniwolf* (p). See page 290 for more parodies and fairy tales.

The Lost Children

RETOLD BY PAUL GOBLE
Grades 1–5   30 pages
Simon & Schuster, 1993

This is the Blackfoot cautionary tale about six boys who were neglected by their family and village. In despair, the boys left the earth and became bunched stars in the heavens—what we call the Pleiades—and their lights today are reminders that children are the Great Spirit's greatest gift, to be treasured always. Other books by Paul Goble include: *Crow Chief; Death of the Iron Horse; Dream Wolf; The Girl Who Loved Wild Horses; Iktomi and the Berries; Iktomi and the Boulder;* and *Star Boy.*

Other American Indian books: *Annie and the Old One* by Miska Miles; *The Boy Who Lived with the Seals* by Rafe Martin; *The First Strawberries: A Cherokee Story* by Joseph Bruchac; *Knots on a Counting Rope* by Bill Martin Jr. and John Archambault; *The Legend of the Bluebonnet* (p); and *The Rough-Face Girl* by Rafe Martin (Indian Cinderella).

Mirabelle

BY ASTRID LINDGREN; PIJA LINDENBAUM, ILLUS.
Grades PreK–1   *24 pages*
R&S Books, 2003
Originally published in 1949 and now back with new illustrations, the author wastes no time: "I'm going to tell you about the strangest thing that has ever happened to me. It was two years ago, when I was just six. Now I am eight." We never learn the youngster's name, which is only fair since she represents all children who dream of dolls or toys that come to life. In this child's case, more than anything else she wishes for a doll, something her farm family's meager finances cannot afford. One evening while her parents are in town and she is alone at the farm, she meets an old man in a wagon. When she kindly offers assistance, he rewards her with a pretty gold seed and says that if she plants and waters it, she'll find a surprise. What she grows is her heart's desire—a doll, though not an ordinary one. Also by the author: *Pippi Longstocking.* Related book: *Betty Doll* by Patricia Polacco.

Madeline (series)

BY LUDWIG BEMELMANS
Grades K–3   *30 pages*
Viking, 1939
This series of six books features a daring and irrepressible girl named Madeline and her eleven friends, who all live together in a Parisian boarding school. The author's use of fast-moving verse, daring adventure, naughtiness, and glowing color keep it a favorite in early grades year after year. Other books in the series: *Madeline and the Bad Hat; Madeline and the Gypsies; Madeline in London; Madeline's Rescue;* and *Madeline's Christmas.*

Mailing May

BY MICHAEL O. TUNNELL; TED RAND, ILLUS.

Grades PreS–2   *36 pages*

Greenwillow, 1997

The year is 1914 and five-year-old May wants to visit her grandmother in Idaho. All that stands between them is seventy-five miles of treacherous, roadless mountains and the exorbitant cost of a train ticket. Her wish is finally fulfilled when she agrees to let her parents mail her to Idaho. Posted with stamps, she boards the train's mail car and heads for Grandma's. Based on a true story. Related books: *Baby in a Basket* (p) and *Marvin of the Great North Woods* (p).

Make Way for Ducklings

BY ROBERT MCCLOSKEY

Grades PreS–2   *62 pages*

Viking, 1941

In this Caldecott award–winning classic, we follow Mrs. Mallard and her eight ducklings as they make a traffic-stopping walk across Boston to meet Mr. Mallard on their new island home in the Public Garden. Also by the author: *Blueberries for Sal; Burt Dow, Deep-Water Man; Lentil;* and *One Morning in Maine.* Be sure to check out *Make Way for McCloskey: A Robert McCloskey Treasury,* a single-volume anthology containing six of his best works. Related books: *Chibi: A True Story from Japan* by Julia Takaya and Barbara Brenner; *John Philip Duck* by Patricia Polacco; and *Micawber* (p).

Marven of the Great North Woods

BY KATHRYN LASKY; KEVIN HAWKES, ILLUS.

Grades K–4   *36 pages*

Harcourt Brace, 1997

In 1918, one of history's worst flu epidemics was sweeping across the world, killing tens of thousands. The Lasky family believed their ten-year-old son's chances of escaping the plague would be greater if he spent the winter far from the city of Duluth, Minnesota. So they packed Marven's bags and sent him by train to a logging camp in the great North Woods. A true story of courage, history, and the warm friendship between a small Jewish city boy and a French-Canadian giant. Related book: *Mailing May* (p) by Michael O. Tunnell.

Max

BY BOB GRAHAM

Grades PreS–K   *26 pages*

Candlewick, 2000

Little Max is the son of two superheroes, Captain Lightning and Madam Thunderbolt, but he's a late bloomer at flying—not quite ready for prime-time heroics, can't even hover. As an ordinary kid in superhero clothes, he worries his folks and amuses his classmates. Finally, when the occasion warrants—a baby bird falling from its nest—Max flies. Here is a heroic triumph for young listeners. Related book: *Leo the Late Bloomer* by Robert Kraus.

Me, All Alone, at the End of the World

BY M. T. ANDERSON; KEVIN HAWKES, ILLUS.
Grades 2 and up   34 pages
Candlewick, 2005

As used here, "End of the World" means "end of the road"—far from the noise and distractions of civilization. That's where the boy lives happily all by himself. And then a businessman discovers the beautiful setting, deems it too good to be left to a solitary boy, and builds an amusement park and grand hotel. Now the boy has friends—something he likes very much—but he's lost something, too. Can he live without it? This is a beautifully il-lustrated book that may contain as many meanings as there are readers in an age when every inch of ground is meant to be occupied and profited from. The "friends" in this book could be seen as the money used to loosen the reluctance of communities to allow the "big box" people to build nearby. I suspect it's a book Wal-Mart will not be stocking. Also by the author: *Handel, Who Knew What He Liked* and *The Serpent Came to Gloucester.* Related book: *Dreamland* by Roni Schotter.

Micawber

BY JOHN LITHGOW; C. F. PAYNE, ILLUS.
Grades PreK–2   24 pages
Simon & Schuster, 2002

In this delightful picture book, brilliantly illustrated by C. F. Payne, we meet a squirrel named Micawber in New York's Central Park whose fa-vorite haunt is the Metropolitan Museum of Art—to be more exact, the skylight on the museum's roof where he can gaze with rapture at the works of Rembrandt, Titian, and Rubens. One day he sees an aspiring artist set up her easel and canvas in the gallery and begin to copy the masters. Sud-denly a light dawns for Micawber. So this is how they make those pictures! In flawless, witty, rhyming verse we follow the squirrel as he follows the artist home to her apartment and borrows her paints each night while she sleeps to paint his own canvases. In the end, we open two double-page spreads to see the result of his nightly labors. Lithgow is one of the very few celebrities whose work is deservedly published; most of the others would never see print if they had a noncelebrity name on the book.

Mighty Jackie (nonfiction)
BY MARISSA MOSS; C. F. PAYNE, ILLUS.
Grades 1–4   36 pages
Simon & Schuster, 2004
In March 1931, Jackie Mitchell's dream was finally going to come true: Jackie would get a chance to show the world's greatest hitters that a seventeen-year-old could throw a mighty mean curveball. All those barnyard practice throws would finally come to something, and not just against any team—against the mighty New York Yankees, led by Babe Ruth and Lou Gehrig, coming through Tennessee on a spring barnstorming tour. So when Jackie Mitchell struck out Babe and Lou in succession while pitching for the Chattanooga Lookouts, there was considerable excitement— and not just because Jackie was seventeen years old. The bigger story was that Jackie Mitchell was a girl! In this wonderful retelling, Moss and C. F. Payne bring to life a little-known but true story in American sport. How it remained buried all these years is a wonder. Related books: *Girl Wonder* by Deborah Hopkinson; *Mama Played Baseball* by David A. Adler; and *Players in Pigtails* by Shana Corey.

Mike Mulligan and His Steam Shovel
BY VIRGINIA LEE BURTON
Grades K–4   42 pages
Houghton Mifflin, 1939
This is the heartwarming classic about the demise of the steam shovel and how it found a permanent home with driver Mike. Also by the author: *Choo-Choo; The Emperor's New Clothes; Katy and the Big Snow;* and *The Little House* (p). Related books: *Man on the Moon* by Simon Bartram and *Pop's Bridge* by Eve Bunting.

The Minpins
BY ROALD DAHL; PATRICK BENSON, ILLUS.
Grades K–4   47 pages
Viking, 1991
This is one of Dahl's final and most sensitive and dramatic works. When a small boy disobeys his mother and enters the dark forest, he meets not only the monster she predicted but also tiny matchstick-size people who inhabit all the trees. The tiny creatures enable his escape and help destroy the mon-

ster. Related books: *The Book of Beasts* (p) and *Do Not Open* by Brinton Turkle.

Mirette on the High Wire

BY EMILY ARNOLD MCCULLY

Grades K–2   *30 pages*

Putnam, 1992

One hundred years ago in a small boardinghouse in Paris, there appeared a stranger seeking solitude. He was the Great Bellini, a daredevil tightrope walker who had lost his confidence. In the weeks that followed, the innkeeper's daughter became enchanted with rope walking and was able to restore the man's lost confidence while becoming a star herself. Winner of the Caldecott Medal, the book was followed by *Starring Mirette and Bellini* and *Mirette & Bellini Cross Niagara Falls*. Also by the author: *The Bobbin Girl.* Related books: *Brave Irene* (p) and *The Man Who Walked Between the Towers* by Mordicai Gerstein.

Miss Nelson Is Missing (series)

BY HARRY ALLARD; JAMES MARSHALL, ILLUS.

Grades PreS–4   *32 pages*

Houghton Mifflin, 1977

Poor, sweet Miss Nelson! Kind and beautiful as she is, she cannot control her classroom—the worst-behaved children in the school. But when she is suddenly absent, the children begin to realize what a wonderful teacher they had in Miss Nelson. Her substitute is wicked-looking, strict Miss Viola Swamp, who works the class incessantly. Wherever has Miss Nelson gone and when will she return? Sequels: *Miss Nelson Is Back* and *Miss Nelson Has a Field Day.*

Molly Bannaky (nonfiction)

BY ALICE MCGILL; CHRIS K. SOENTPIET, ILLUS.

Grades 3–8   *32 pages*

Houghton Mifflin, 1999

Benjamin Banneker was one of the first black American scientists, wrote the first black almanac, and was part of the federal panel that planned Washington, D.C., but the story behind the man was his grandmother. She came to America as a white indentured servant, having narrowly escaped the English gallows by proving she could read the Bible. In America, she served her seven years of servitude, later bought a farm, and then bought a newly arrived slave, whom she grew to love and married. For the story of her famous grandson, see *Dear Benjamin Banneker* by Andrea D. Pinkney.

Molly's Pilgrim

BY BARBARA COHEN
Grades 1–4   *41 pages*
Morrow, 1983
Molly, an immigrant child and target of her classmates' taunts, discovers she is more a part of America's Thanksgiving tradition than anyone in the class. This book was the basis for the 1985 Academy Award–winning best short film of the same title. Related books: *An Outlaw Thanksgiving* by Emily Arnold McCully; *Thanksgiving at the Tappletons'* by Eileen Spinelli; and *Thank You, Sarah: The Woman Who Saved Thanksgiving* (p).

My Brother Martin: A Sister Remembers (nonfiction)

BY CHRISTINE KING FARRIS; CHRIS SOENPIET , ILLUS.
Grades 1–5   *30 pages*
Simon & Schuster, 2003
One unfortunate aspect of heroes and icons is that we put them on such high pedestals that they're out of children's reach; thus children can find little of themselves in our heroes, which is not a good thing. Along comes Christine King Farris, older sister of Martin Luther King Jr., who regrets the loss of both her brother and those things that made him human. Thankfully, she has put her memories down in this fine little narrative—the events of one family's childhood years that molded, inspired, entertained, and sometimes frightened its three children, the human things we seldom find in the history books but that make heroes real to readers. Related books: *The Boy Who Drew Birds: The Story of John James Audubon* by Jacqueline Davies; *Eleanor* (Eleanor Roosevelt) by Barbara Cooney; *Harvesting Hope: The Story of Cesar Chavez* (p); *Joe Louis: America's Fighter* by David A. Adler; *Major Taylor: Champion Cyclist* by Lesa Cline-Ransome; *Roberto Clemente* by Jonah Winter; and *You're on Your Way, Teddy Roosevelt* by Judith St. George.

The Mysterious Tadpole

BY STEVEN KELLOGG
Grades PreS–4   *30 pages*
Dial, 1977
When little Louis's uncle in Scotland sent him a tadpole for his birthday, neither of them had any idea how much havoc and fun the pet would cause in Louis's home, classroom, and school swimming pool. The tadpole

turns out to be a direct descendant of the Loch Ness monster (but what a cuddly monster this is!). Also by the author: *Island of the Skog* (p). Related books: *The Best Pet of All* by David LaRochelle; *The Serpent Came to Gloucester* by M. T. Anderson; and *The Water Horse* (s).

The Napping House

BY AUDREY WOOD; DON WOOD, ILLUS.
Tod–PreS   28 pages
Harcourt Brace, 1984
One of the cleverest bedtime books for children, this simple tale depicts a cozy bed on which are laid in cumulative rhymes a snoring granny, a dreaming child, a dozing dog, and a host of other sleeping characters—until a sudden awakening at daybreak. The subtle lighting changes in the double-page illustrations show the gradual passage of time during the night and the clearing of a storm outside. Also by the author: *Heckedy Peg* (p).

The Neighborhood Mother Goose

PHOTOGRAPHED BY NINA CREWS
Inf–PreS   64 pages
Dutton, 1989
Nina Crews took her camera into urban America and coupled Mother Goose with children of every hue, making it a rainbow's worth of traditional nursery rhymes peopled by children who have been traditionally excluded from such volumes. Other Mother Goose collections: *The Everything Book* (p); *Lucy Cousins' Book of Nursery Rhymes* by Lucy Cousins; and *Pio Peep! Traditional Spanish Nursery Rhymes* selected by Alma Flor Ada and F. Isabel Campoy.

Niccodini's Song

BY CHUCK WILCOXEN
Grades PreS–2   32 pages
Dutton, 2004
In the long ago before space shuttles and jumbo jets, there was a kindly night watchman who worked in the rail yards. One night, a sleepless locomotive asks him to sing a lullaby. Before long, all the engines want the same. Eventually the mothers of the town, walking their crying babies, overhear the song and regularly make their way to the fence near the rail yard. When a windstorm disturbs the sleep of every baby in town, the mothers come to the yard in hopes Mr. Niccodini will sing them back to sleep. But how will he ever be heard over the wails of hundreds of babies?

Nora's Ark

BY NATALIE KINSEY-WARNOCK; EMILY ARNOLD MCCULLY, ILLUS.
Grades K–3 32 pages
Harper, 2005
In this heartwarming true story of the great Vermont flood of 1927, the author celebrates the unbreakable ties of family and neighbors as they descend on one farmhouse to escape the floodwaters. To complicate matters, they also bring their chickens, cows, pigs, and horses, but Grandma Nora is not the least disturbed, as long as she can find Grandpa, who left twenty-four hours earlier on a rescue mission. Also by the author: *The Bear That Heard Crying.* Related books: *Aunt Minnie McGranahan* (p); *The Bravest of Us All* by Marsha Diane Arnold; and *Miss Ida's Front Porch* by Sandra Belton.

Odd Boy Out: Young Albert Einstein (nonfiction)

BY DON BROWN
Grades 2–7 30 pages
Houghton Mifflin, 2004
In this simple but insightful biographical picture book on the life of the great scientist, the author offers hope for every child who marches to a different drummer, who doesn't blossom on time, who isn't good at sports, who believes in daydreaming about things that no one else can even imagine, and who is the class outsider. And for those who think they know the story already, that Einstein worked on the atom bomb—wrong. He was barred from working on it because his pacifist leanings prevented him from receiving a security clearance. This is picture book biography at its very best, from the author-illustrator whose work places him at the very front of the field. Also by the author: *American Boy: The Adventures of Mark Twain; Uncommon Traveler: Mary Kinsley in Africa; Rare Treasure: Mary Anning and Her Remarkable Discoveries; Alice Ramsey's Grand Adventure;* and *Ruth Law Thrills a Nation.* For other picture book biographies, see *My Brother Martin* (p).

An Orange for Frankie

BY PATRICIA POLACCO
Grades K and up 40 pages
Philomel, 2004
It is books like this that make Polacco one of the great picture book storytellers of our time; her body of work should outlast that of most of her contemporaries. We start with a family of nine, Christmas Eve, a father missing in a snowstorm, a boxcar of hungry and freezing hobos, one missing sweater, and a lost Christmas orange—all of it neatly tied into a happy holiday ending. Based on the author/artist's family history, this is as good

as holiday stories get! Related books: *Mim's Christmas Jam* by Andrea Davis Pinkney and *A Cowboy Christmas* by Audrey Wood.

The Paperboy

BY DAV PILKEY

Grades PreS–K   *30 pages*

Orchard (paperback), 1999

Talk all you want about the "loneliness of the long distance runner"— what about the loneliness of the hard-pedaling paperboy? Long before dawn breaks, a young black boy leaves his warm bed, folds his papers, and begins the dark ride from house to house, returning in the end to a still-warm bed and the satisfaction of a lonely task accomplished. A fine tribute to a vanishing breed of child laborers. Related book: *A Day's Work* (p).

Pink and Say

BY PATRICIA POLACCO

Grades 3 and up   *48 pages*

Philomel, 1994

Based on an incident in the life of the author–illustrator's great-great grandfather, this is the tale of two fifteen-year-old Union soldiers—one white, one black. The former is wounded while deserting his company; the latter has been separated from his black company and stumbles upon the left-for-dead white soldier. The pages that follow trace this sad chapter in American history about as well as it's ever been told for children, beginning with a visit to the black soldier's mother, who is living on a nearby plantation ravaged by the war. There the wounded boy is nursed to both health and full courage, while discovering the inhumanity of slavery. Related title: *Thunder at Gettysburg* by Patricia Lee Gauch.

Please, Baby, Please

BY SPIKE AND TONYA LEWIS LEE; KADIR NELSON, ILLUS.

Inf–Tod   *28 pages*

Simon & Schuster, 2002

This talented husband-and-wife author team offers a witty but very true-to-life picture of a rambunctious toddler's day, following her many moods from daybreak to bedtime. Toddlers will love seeing themselves in this young lady, especially in her more mischievous moments. Illustrator Kadir Nelson has imbued this child with the essence of a happy childhood. With the recurring use of "please," the meaning of that lovely word has a better chance of being learned and instilled than by any other means. Sequel: *Please, Puppy, Please.*

The Poppy Seeds

BY CLYDE ROBERT BULLA
Grades K–2   *34 pages*
Puffin, 1994

A selfish old man who scorns the friendship and needs of his neighbors is finally reached through the kindness of a Mexican child who attempts to plant poppies in the man's yard. Related book: *I, Doko: The Tale of a Basket* by Ed Young.

Regards to the Man in the Moon

BY EZRA JACK KEATS
Grades PreS–3   *32 pages*
Four Winds, 1981

When the neighborhood children tease Louie about the junk in his backyard, his father shows him how imagination can convert rubbish into a spaceship that will take him to the farthest galaxies. The next day, Louie and his friend Susie hurtle through space in their glorified washtub and discover that not even gravity can hold back a child's imagination. Related book: *Man on the Moon* by Simon Bartram. The settings for Ezra Jack Keats's books are largely the inner city, but the emotions are those of all children. *Keats's Neighborhood: An Ezra Jack Keats Treasury* is an excellent anthology containing ten of Keats's best, including *The Snowy Day; Goggles!; Whistle for Willie; Peter's Chair;* and *Apt. 3*. Included is an excellent essay on Keats by Anita Silvey.

Richard Wright and the Library Card (nonfiction)

BY WILLIAM MILLER; GREGORY CHRISTIE, ILLUS.
Grades 2–5   *32 pages*
Lee & Low, 1999

Growing up in segregated Mississippi in the 1920s, young Richard Wright had an insatiable hunger for print that only a library card could satisfy. Unfortunately, his skin color prevented him from owning one. So as a young janitor, the future author of *Native Son* and *Black Boy* conspired with a white man to beat the system. Related book for younger students: *Tomás and the Library Lady* by Pat Mora, the childhood story of Tomás Rivera, the son of migrant workers who became a university chancellor.

High-Scoring Sports Picture Books

America's Champion Swimmer:
  Gertrude Ederle by Terry
  Widener
The Babe and I
  by David A. Adler
Baseball Saved Us
  by Ken Mochizuk
Casey at the Bat
  by Ernest Thayer
  (C. F. Payne, Illus.)
Eddie, Harold's Little Brother
  by Ed Koch and Pat Koch
  Thaler
The Greatest Skating Race
  by Louise Borden
Joe Lewis: America's Fighter
  by David A. Adler
*Jump! From the Life of Michael
  Jordan* by Floyd Cooper
Major Taylor: Champion Cyclist
  by Lesa Cline-Ransome

Mighty Jackie
  by Marissa Moss
Mudball
  by Matt Tavares
Oliver's Game
  by Matt Tavares
Players in Pigtails
  by Shana Corey
Roberto Clemente
  by Jonah Winter
Satchel Paige
  by Lesa Cline-Ransome
Shoeless Joe & Black Betsy
  by Phil Bildner
Shooting for the Moon
  (Annie Oakley)
  by Stephen Krensky
Teammates
  by Peter Golenbock
Play Ball!
  by Jorge Posada

Rikki-Tikki-Tavi

BY RUDYARD KIPLING; ADAPTED AND ILLUSTRATED BY JERRY PINKNEY
Grades K–4   *44 pages*
Morrow, 1997
Rikki is a fearless mongoose adopted by a family in India to protect their child. In no time, he is tested by the cunning cobra snakes that live in the garden. Made famous by Kipling a century ago, this tale features a ferocious fight between the mongoose and snakes and is not for the timid.

Rocks in His Head (nonfiction)

BY CAROL OTIS HURST; JAMES STEVENSON, ILLUS.
Grades 2 and up   *30 pages*
Greenwillow, 2001
Like all children, the author's father as a child had a dream of what he wanted to do when he grew up—anything to do with rocks. Throughout

his childhood, he dug, polished, and saved them. When the Depression wiped out the family business, he ended up as the nighttime janitor at the local science museum (in Springfield, Massachusetts, just a few blocks from where a certain kid named Teddy Geisel was growing up dreaming of "cats in hats"). Eventually, his consuming love for rocks and science and earned him the title of curator of mineralogy and then museum director. This heartwarming memoir can serve as a springboard for students and families to share their own family stories of dreams pursued and achieved. Related books: *Pop's Bridge* by Eve Bunting and *My Brother Martin* (p).

Rotten Teeth

BY LAURA SIMMS; DAVID CATROW, ILLUS.

Grades K–3   *30 pages*
Houghton Mifflin, 1998

Melissa is the smallest, quietest person in first grade. And she's never brought anything for show and tell—until today! Direct from her father's dental lab comes a bottle of rotten teeth, extracted from her father's patients. To the disgusted astonishment of her teacher, Melissa puts a rotten tooth on each classmate's desk. No one has ever brought anything like this for show and tell, and suddenly Melissa is a class star!

Other fun books about school: *100th Day Worries* by Margery Cuyler; *Author Day* by Daniel Pinkwater; *A Fine, Fine School* by Sharon Creech; *The Frightful Story of Harry Walfish* by Brian Floca; *Lost and Found* and *The Secret Shortcut,* both by Mark Teague; and *The Recess Queen* by Alexis O'Neill.

The Secret Knowledge of Grown-ups

BY DAVID WISNIEWSKI

Grades 6 and up   *48 pages*
Morrow, 1998

The author has taken standard rules of behavior imposed by adults—Eat your vegetables! Don't blow bubbles in your milk with your straw!—and offers the "top secret" intricate, humorous, and mind-boggling reasons behind the rules. This book is the perfect launching pad for readers and listeners to devise further send-ups of family and school rules; for example, the real reason they don't want you to run in the hallways at school is. . . . Sequel: *The Secret Knowledge of Grown-ups: The Second File.*

The Secret Shortcut (series)

BY MARK TEAGUE

Grades PreS–K   *32 pages*
Scholastic, 1996

Wendell and Floyd are in trouble with their teacher for being late for school every day. She doesn't understand how hard they're trying: every shortcut they take to save time is a turn for the worse. They meet pirates one day, a plague of frogs the next, even spacemen. It's their last secret shortcut—the jungle route—that turns out to be the best and muddiest of all. Sequels: *Lost and Found* and *One Halloween Night*.

The Seven Silly Eaters
BY MARY ANN HOBERMAN; MARLA FRAZEE, ILLUS.
Grades K–3   *38 pages*
Harcourt Brace, 1997
There are seven children in the Peters family and, unfortunately, each has a different favorite food that must be specially prepared or the child will not eat. Mrs. Peters is at her wits' end and worn to a frazzle trying to cook these specialties three times a day. When her birthday arrives, she's certain her children won't remember it—but she's wrong. They're up all night scheming, and their birthday present accidentally solves her cooking dilemma forever. Also by the author/poet: *A House Is a House for Me*.

The Silver Pony
BY LYND WARD
Grades PreS–4   *176 pages*
Houghton Mifflin, 1973
A classic wordless book (and the longest published for children), this is the heartwarming story of a lonely farm boy and the flights of fancy he uses to escape his isolation. His imaginative trips take place on a winged pony and carry him to distant parts of the world to aid and comfort other lonely children. Also by the author: *The Biggest Bear* (p). List of other wordless books on page 179.

Snip Snap! What's That?
BY MARA BERGMAN; NICK MALAND, ILLUS.
Grades PreK–K   *30 pages*
Greenwillow, 2005
This is a happy mix of *We're Going on a Bear Hunt* (p), *The Little Old Lady Who Was Not Afraid of Anything* (p), and *There's a Nightmare in My Closet* by Mercer Mayer. An alligator comes calling at the children's door. As it and they move from room to room, the question is asked, "Were they afraid?" eliciting the response (louder and louder each time), "You bet they were!" Until they gather their courage and turn on the creature, driving him out.

Jim's Favorite Friendship Books

Chester's Way
  by Kevin Henkes

A Cowboy Christmas
  by Audrey Wood

Danitra Brown, Class Clown
  by Nikki Grimes

A Day's Work
  by Eve Bunting

Eddie, Harold's Little Brother
  by Ed Koch and Pat Koch Thaler

Erandi's Braids
  by Antonio H. Madrigal

Evie & Margie
  by Bernard Waber

The Friend
  by Sarah Stewart

Me, All Alone, at the End of the World
  by M. T. Anderson

Mr. Lincoln's Way
  by Patricia Polacco

Mutt Dog
  by Stephen M. King

Nora's Ark
  by Natalie Kinsey-Warnock

The Recess Queen
  by Alexis O'Neill

The Reluctant Dragon
  abridged by Inga Moore

Somebody Loves You, Mr. Hatch
  by Eileen Spinelli

The Sugar Child
  by Monique de Varennes

Teammates
  by Peter Golenbock

Wallace's Lists
  by Barbara Bottner and Gerald Kruglik

Was he scared? This is great fun with a group or class. Related book: *The Squeaky Door*, retold by Margaret Read MacDonald.

Somebody Loves You, Mr. Hatch

BY EILEEN SPINELLI; PAUL YALOWITZ, ILLUS.
Grades K and up   *30 pages*
Simon & Schuster, 1991
A definitive book on friendship, it introduces us to a lonely little man, Mr. Hatch, who has no friends. And then one day a box of Valentine chocolates is delivered to him by mistake, changing his life forever. For more friendship books, see list above.

The Story of Little Babaji

BY HELEN BANNERMAN; FRED MARCELLINO, ILLUS.
Grades Tod–K   *68 pages*
Harper, 1996

Reset in India (where it originally was written in 1899), redrawn with Indian characters (instead of the African grotesques it degenerated into), and with the offending names removed, this is nearly word-for-word the original story of *Little Black Sambo.* The original version rightly fell from favor in the 1950s, but this retelling corrects the earlier offenses and allows children to enjoy the battle of wits between the child and the boy-eating tigers. Related book: *The Tale of Peter Rabbit* by Beatrix Potter.

The Story of Ruby Bridges (nonfiction)
BY ROBERT COLES; GEORGE FORD, ILLUS.
Grades 1–5   26 pages
Scholastic, 1995
From the pen of a Pulitzer Prize–winning research psychiatrist comes the true story of six-year-old Ruby Bridges, one of four black children selected by a federal judge to integrate the New Orleans public schools in 1960. Escorted to the school doors by federal marshals, Ruby had to pass through a gauntlet of curses and spittle. Whispering prayers and backed by her parents' love, the child withstood the daily attacks without bitterness. Rarely can we teach American history using a six-year-old; usually history is peopled by adults—explorers, kings, queens, generals, and inventors. Here is a powerful exception. Ruby Bridges herself expands on Coles's work in *Through My Eyes,* updating the story, including photographs taken during and after the integration conflict. For related books, see listings with *Roll of Thunder, Hear My Cry* (n).

Sylvester and the Magic Pebble
BY WILLIAM STEIG
Grades PreS–4   30 pages
Simon & Schuster, 1969
In this contemporary fairy tale and Caldecott Medal winner, young Sylvester finds a magic pebble that will grant his every wish as long as he holds it in his hand. When a hungry lion approaches, Sylvester wishes himself into a stone. Since stones don't have hands, the pebble drops to the ground and he can't reach it to wish himself normal again. The subsequent loneliness of both Sylvester and his parents is portrayed with deep sensitivity, making all the more real their joy a year later when they are happily reunited. Also by the author: *The Amazing Bone; Brave Irene* (p); *Doctor De Soto; Pete's a Pizza; The Toy Brother;* and *Zeke Pippin.*

Thank You, Sarah: The Woman Who Saved Thanksgiving (nonfiction)

BY LAURIE HALSE ANDERSON; MATT FAULKNER, ILLUS.

Grades K–3   40 *pages*

Scholastic, 2002

By the middle of the 1800s, only New England states were observing Thanksgiving, to the chagrin of Sarah Hale, widowed mother of five and the editor of America's most popular women's magazine. So she began a campaign to make the day a national holiday, an effort that fell on the deaf ears of four straight presidents. Hale had not only written them letters but also urged her readers to do the same—and they did, by the tens of thousands, all to no avail. They couldn't vote, so no president had to listen to them. Then came the fifth president, a man carrying a great sorrow in his heart but still aware of how much he and we should be grateful for—Abraham Lincoln. Related books: *Molly's Pilgrim* (p) and *Milly and the Macy's Parade* by Shana Corey, which uses a fictionalized young girl to uncover the origins of the famous Macy's Thanksgiving Day Parade. Based on a true anecdote, the tale revolves around a thousand Macy's employees who are recent immigrants and homesick for lands where costume parades and street festivals are the norm.

Thomas' Snowsuit

BY ROBERT MUNSCH; MICHAEL MARTCHENKO, ILLUS.

Grades PreS–4   24 *pages*

Annick, 1985

Thomas hates his new snowsuit, much to the dismay of his mother, his teacher, and his principal—all of whom find him a most determined fellow. But children will find the situation just plain funny! Robert Munsch is as popular with Canadian children as Shel Silverstein (see *Where the Sidewalk Ends* [po]) is in the United States. Also by the author: *The Boy in the Drawer; David's Father; 50 Below Zero; I Have to Go! Moira's Birthday; Mortimer;* and *The Paper Bag Princess.*

Tikki Tikki Tembo

BY ARLENE MOSEL; BLAIR LENT, ILLUS.

Grades PreS–3   40 *pages*

Henry Holt, 1968

This little picture book tells the amusing legend of how the Chinese people stopped giving their first-born sons incredibly long first names and started giving all children short names. Related books with Asian settings: *Beautiful Warrior: The Legend of the Nun's Kung Fu* by Emily Arnold McCurry; *Blue*

Willow by Pam Conrad; *The Boy Who Drew Cats* retold by Arthur A. Levine; *Crow Boy* by Taro Yashima; *The Emperor and the Kite* by Jane Yolen; *Kamishibai Man* by Allen Say; and *The Voice of the Great Bell* by Lafcadio Hearn.

Tintin in Tibet (comic book)

BY HERGÉ
Grades 2–4   *62 pages*
Little, Brown, 1975

When you've been in print for more than sixty years, translated into twenty-two languages, and praised in the *New York Times,* you must be special. Tintin is just that. He's the boy detective who hopscotches the globe in pursuit of thieves and smugglers. Loaded with humor, adventure, and marvelous artwork (seven hundred pictures in each issue), *Tintin* has special appeal for parents who want to assist their child in reading: each *Tintin* contains more than eight thousand words. Having heard *Tintin* read aloud, children will want to obtain his other adventures and read them by themselves, oblivious to the fact that they are reading so many words in the process. Because of the size of the pictures, *Tintin* is best read aloud to no more than two children at a time. Furthermore, a comic book should be read aloud to the child only a few times—to show the child how a comic book works. This is similar to the concept of a model train: the parent shows the child how, then turns it over to the youngster to use.

Beginning in 1994, *Tintin's* American publisher began issuing hardcovers, three comics to a volume. The single best *Tintin* resource: *Tintin: The Complete Companion* by Michael Farr, the world's leading authority on all things *Tintin*. Related books in comic format: *Bone #1: Out of Boneville* (series) by Jeff Smith; *Moby Dick* retold by Lew Sayre Schwartz and illustrated by Dick Giordano; an excellent series of stories told in comic format, selected and edited by Art Spiegelman and Françoise Mouly; *Little Lit: Folklore & Fairy Tale Funnies; Strange Stories for Strange Kids;* and *It Was a Dark and Silly Night.*

The True Story of the Three Little Pigs

BY JOHN SCIESZKA; LANE SMITH, ILLUS.
Grades K and up   *28 pages*
Viking, 1989

For two hundred years we've taken the word of the three little pigs as "gospel truth." But when the author presents the infamous wolf's side of the story, we get an implausible but entertainingly different point of view. This book began a wave of fairy tale parodies by other authors, many of which are listed on page 290.

The Truth About Poop (nonfiction)
BY SUSAN E. GOODMAN; ELWOOD H. SMITH, ILLUS.
Grades K–3   *40 pages*
Viking, 2004
This is an example of informational text that not only isn't boring, it also pro-
vokes a greater interest and respect—despite the awkwardness of the title and
subject matter (fecal material). Using clever humor (rather than crude), the
author explores the history and science of waste while holding the interest
with weird facts (for example, camel poop is completely dry because camels
cannot waste the moisture in the desert). A few more science books like this
and we'd have a lot more kids majoring in science. Related titles: *Grossology:
The Science of Really Gross Things* by Sylvia Branzei; this book is a little more
sophisticated and wider in its scope, including spit, mucus, urine, dandruff,
scabs, bad breath, body odor, etc., along with household or class experiments.

The Ugly Duckling
BY HANS CHRISTIAN ANDERSEN; ROBERT INGPEN, ILLUS.
Grades 1 and up   *34 pages*
Penguin, 2005
It is a special book that unites one of the world's great storytellers with one
of the world's great illustrators, and that's what this classic volume does
brilliantly in a traditional telling of the ugly duckling ridiculed by his
brothers and sisters who leaves home in search of beauty and finds it within
himself. Related books: *Eleanor* (Eleanor Roosevelt) by Barbara Cooney;
The Ugly Truckling by David Gordon; and Jane Yolen's picture book biography, *The Perfect Wizard: Hans Christian Andersen,* author of the original
ugly duckling. Also: *Thumbelina,* adapted by Brad Sneed.

Uncle Jed's Barbershop
BY MARGAREE K. MITCHELL; JAMES RANSOME, ILLUS.
Grades K–4   *30 pages*
Simon & Schuster, 1993
In the segregated South of the 1920s, Uncle Jed was the only black barber in
the county, riding horseback from one sharecropper to the next. His dream
was to own a barbershop, but every time he had enough money saved, an-
other neighbor's crisis proved more worthy of the money. Finally his dream
comes true! Related books: *Freedom on the Menu: The Greensboro Sit-ins* by
Carole Boston Weatherford; *The Friend* by Sarah Stewart; *From Miss Ida's Porch*
by Sandra Belton; *Goin' Someplace Special* (p); *Leon's Story* (s); *My Brother
Martin: A Sister Remembers* (p); *Rocks in His Head* (p); *The Story of Ruby
Bridges* (p); and the novel *Roll of Thunder, Hear My Cry* (n).

The Very Hungry Caterpillar

BY ERIC CARLE

Grades Tod–1   *38 pages*

Philomel, 1969

What an ingenious book! It is at once a simple, lovely way to teach a child the days of the week, how to count to five, and how a caterpillar becomes a butterfly. First, this is a book to look at, with bright, bright pictures. Then it is something whose pages beg to be turned—pages that have little round holes in them made by the hungry little caterpillar. And as the number of holes grow, so does the caterpillar. Other books by the author: *The Grouchy Ladybug; Mister Seahorse; The Very Busy Spider; The Very Clumsy Click Beetle;* and *The Very Lonely Firefly.*

Wagon Wheels

BY BARBARA BRENNER; DON BOLOGNESE, ILLUS.

Grades K–2   *64 pages*

Harper (paperback), 1993

In four short chapters, this story can be read either as a long picture book or as an introduction to chapter books. Three young black brothers follow a map to their father's homestead on the western plains. The trio braves storms, fires, and famine to reach their goal. For other historical fiction and nonfiction picture books, see page 68.

We're Going on a Bear Hunt

BY MICHAEL ROSEN; HELEN OXENBURY, ILLUS.

Grades Tod–K   *32 pages*

Atheneum, 1992

A family hunts a bear through field, river, swamp, forest, snowstorm (with predictable, appropriate sounds and movement). When they find him, he hunts them back home via the same route and sounds. See list of predictable/cumulative books on page 179. For an affectionate look at bears: *Good Job, Little Bear* (p) and *Grandma's Bears* (p).

When Jessie Came Across the Sea

BY AMY HEST; P. J. LYNCH, ILLUS.

Grades 1–5   *32 pages*

Candlewick, 1997

The courageous and bittersweet story of American immigration is told in the story of a Jewish orphan girl from Eastern Europe who receives a one-way ticket to America from the village rabbi. This great opportunity is tempered by the fact she must leave her grandmother—the only relative she has in the world. The girl's courage in the New World and her eventual reunion with her grandmother make this an inspiring story. Related book: *Street of Gold,* retold by Rosemary Wells.

Where the Wild Things Are

BY MAURICE SENDAK

Grades K–3   *28 pages*

Harper, 1963

This is the 1963 Caldecott winner that changed the course of modern children's literature. Sendak here creates a fantasy about a little boy and the monsters that haunt and fascinate children. The fact that youngsters are not the least bit frightened by the story, that they love it as they would an old friend, is a credit to Sendak's insight into children's minds and hearts. Also by the author: *In the Night Kitchen.*

Where's My Teddy? (series)

BY JEZ ALBOROUGH

Grades PreS–K   *24 pages*

Candlewick, 1997

Alborough has created three popular books in this series about little Eddie and the giant bear who lives in the park. In their first encounter (*Where's My Teddy?*), Eddie mistakenly ends up with the bear's teddy and the bear has his. Though each is equally afraid of the other, they both finally end up with the right teddy. In the second book (*It's the Bear!*), Eddie's mother is a nonbeliever until she and the bear come face-to-face (reminiscent of Robert McCloskey's *Blueberries for Sal*). In the third book (*My Friend Bear*), their fear of each other is happily resolved when each realizes how much they have in common—including a needless fear of each other and a love of their teddies. Related books: *Good Job, Little Bear* (p) and *Grandma's Bears* (p).

Where's Waldo? (series)

BY MARTIN HANDFORD

Grades PreS–4   *26 pages*

Little, Brown, 1987

Waldo is a hiker on a worldwide trek who plays hide-and-seek with the reader-viewer, who has to find him as he threads his way through thousands of people populating a dozen different landscapes. Children will spend hours searching the pages for Waldo and the list of more than three hundred items checklisted at the end of the book. Also note that in each scene Waldo loses one of his twelve personal items. Books like this stretch children's attention spans while polishing visual discrimination. (They should also be required equipment for anyone taking a child under six to a restaurant or church.) Sequels: *The Great Waldo Search; Where's Waldo? The Fantastic Journey;* and *Where's Waldo? In Hollywood.*

The writer/photographer team of Jean Marzollo and Walter Wick offer a similar challenge with the I Spy photo book series, including: *I Spy Extreme Challenger!; I Spy Gold Challenger!;* and *I Spy Year-Round Challenger!* Walter Wick created a less challenging series of "search and find" books for younger children, called Can You See What I See. Other books containing visual puzzles: *Imagine a Day* and *Imagine a Night,* both by Sarah L. Thomson and Rob Gonsalves (who is an M. C. Escher for kids), and *The Mysteries of Harris Burdick* by Chris Van Allsburg.

The Whingdingdilly

BY BILL PEET
Grades PreS–5   *60 pages*
Houghton Mifflin, 1970
Bill Peet should be declared either a national treasure (along with Dr. Seuss) or a modern Aesop. Using animals to make his points, he has explored the human condition in a way that has helped us all to better understand each other. Typical is this book: Discontented with his life as a dog, Scamp envies all the attention given to his beribboned neighbor—Palomar, the wonder horse. But when a backwoods witch changes Scamp into an animal with the feet of an elephant, the neck of a giraffe, the tail of a zebra, and the nose of a rhinoceros, he gets more attention than he bargained for: He ends up a most unhappy circus freak. But all ends well, and tied into the ending is a subtle lesson for both Scamp and his readers: Be yourself!

Among Peet's most popular titles are: *Big Bad Bruce; The Caboose Who Got Loose; Eli; Encore for Eleanor; Farewell to Shady Glade; Fly, Homer, Fly; How Droofus the Dragon Lost His Head; Kermit the Hermit; Randy's Dandy Lions;* and *Wump World.* Also, *Bill Peet: An Autobiography* is a 180-page autobiography (Caldecott Honor winner) with an illustration on every page.

The Wolf Who Cried Boy

BY ROB HARTMAN; TIM RAGLIN, ILLUS.
Grades K–3   *30 pages*
Putnam, 2002
In this clever takeoff on the traditional "boy who cried wolf," we meet Little Wolf, a stubborn cub with an appetite for junk food like "chipmunks and dip." His parents, on the other hand, insist that he eat the nourishing foods they serve, like three-pig salad. They do concede, however, that in the good

old days before Little Wolf was born, when shepherd boys were plentiful, there was nothing as tasty as boy chops, baked boy-tato, and boys-n-berry pie!

All of this whets both Little Wolf's appetite and his imagination, so the next day he sounds the alarm that he's spotted a boy. By the time his parents finish a long and fruitless search, their dinner is burned and they must content themselves with junk food. Which is just what Little Wolf wanted in the first place! So he tries it again the next day—and we all know what's coming: a Boy Scout! For a list of other parodies, see page 290.

The Wretched Stone

BY CHRIS VAN ALLSBURG

Grades 2–7   *30 pages*

Houghton Mifflin, 1991

When the crew of a clipper ship sailing tropical seas discovers a deserted island, they also find a large gray stone, luminous and with one smooth side. When it is brought on board, an eerie change begins to envelop the ship. Fascinated by the rock, the crew gradually deserts its work and leisure activities, spending more and more time gazing in silent numbness at the rock—despite the protestations of their captain. In the hands of one of today's most important and thought-provoking author-illustrators for children, this is a powerful allegory about the effects of television on society. Related books: *Kamishibai Man* by Allen Say and *When Charlie McButton Lost Power* by Suzanne Collins.

Van Allsburg's other books include: *Ben's Dream; The Garden of Abdul Gasazi; Jumanji; Just a Dream; The Mysteries of Harris Burdick; The Polar Express; The Stranger; The Sweetest Fig; Two Bad Ants; The Widow's Broom; The Wreck of the Zephyr;* and *The Z Was Zapped* (an unusual alphabet book). Listen to a one-hour interview with Van Allsburg (*Midmorning Show,* Minnesota Public Radio, November 30, 2004), online at: http:news.minnesota.publicradio. org/programs/midmorning/listings/mm20041129.shtml.

You Can Do It, Sam (series)

BY AMY HEST

Grades Tod–PreK   *28 pages*

Candlewick, 2003

If ever a picture book series deserved the adjective "cozy," this is it. In this, the third book in the series, Mrs. Bear and her cub Sam are baking little cakes together, licking bowls, packing the cakes, and finally driving through the snow to deliver them as surprises to neighbors. The title comes from Sam's concern over whether he can carry each package all the way to the doorstep *all by himself.* Also in the series: *Kiss Good Night* and *Don't You Feel*

Well, Sam? Amy Hest is also the author of these outstanding books: *The Purple Coat* and *In the Rain with Baby Duck* and, for older children, *When Jessie Came Across the Sea* (p).

Short Novels

Baseball in April
BY GARY SOTO
Grades 6 and up   *107 pages*
Harcourt Brace, 1990
A product of the Latino community in Fresno, California, Soto grew up with a cement factory across the street, a junkyard next door, and a raisin factory at the end of the street. This collection of eleven short stories is largely based on his early teen years, filled with the bittersweet laughter and tears found in all adolescent lives. Also by the author: *Chato and the Party Animals* (p) and the short story collections *Living Up the Street; Local News;* and *Help Wanted.*

The Bears' House
BY MARILYN SACHS
Grades 4–6   *82 pages*
Dutton, 1987
A perfect vehicle for a classroom discussion of values, this novel portrays a ten-year-old girl whose mother is ill and can no longer care for her family after the father deserts them. The girl decides to tend to the family while suffering the taunts of classmates because she sucks her thumb, wears dirty clothes, and smells. To escape, she retreats to the fantasy world she has created in an old dollhouse in her classroom. Sequel: *Fran Ellen's House.* Related book: *The Great Gilly Hopkins* by Katherine Paterson and *The Hundred Dresses* (s).

The Best Christmas Pageant Ever
BY BARBARA ROBINSON
Grades 2–6   *80 pages*
Harper, 1972
What happens when the worst-behaved family of kids in town comes to Sunday school and muscles into all the parts for the Christmas pageant? The results are zany and heartwarming; a most unusual Christmas story. Sequels: *The Best School Year Ever* and *The Best Halloween Ever.* There is also

an excellent CD recording of the three novels, narrated by Broadway's Elaine Stritch: *The Best Barbara Robinson CD Audio Collection Ever.*

Jim's Favorite Kindergarten Novels
(in order of difficulty)

Two Times the Fun
  by Beverly Cleary
Chibi: A True Story from Japan
  by B. Brenner and J. Takaya
Junie B. Jones and the Stupid
  Smelly Bus
  by Barbara Park
The Chalk Box Kid
  by Clyde Robert Bulla
My Father's Dragon
  by Ruth Stiles Gannett
Chocolate Fever
  by Robert Kimmel Smith

Dinosaurs Before Dark
  by Mary Pope
  Osborne
The Reluctant Dragon
  adapted by Inga Moore
The Stories Julian Tells
  by Ann Cameron
The Water Horse
  by Dick King-Smith
Wolf Story
  by William McCleery
James and the Giant Peach
  by Roald Dahl

A Blue-Eyed Daisy
BY CYNTHIA RYLANT
Grades 4–8   *99 pages*
Simon & Schuster, 1985
This is about a warm yet bittersweet year in the life of an eleven-year-old girl and her family in the hills of West Virginia as she experiences her first kiss, has a brush with death, comes to understand her good but hard-drinking father, and begins to grow into the person you'd love to have as a relative. Related books: *Because of Winn-Dixie* (n) and *Ida Early Comes Over the Mountain* (n).

Cam Jansen and the Mystery of the Dinosaur Bones (series)
BY DAVID ADLER
Grades 1–3   *56 pages*
Puffin, 1997
Thanks to Cam Jansen's photographic memory, little escapes her notice in this easy mystery series that now comprises more than twenty books. You might say she's a grade-school Nancy Drew, but with far fewer pages per book. In this volume, when Cam's class visits the museum's dinosaur room,

she quickly notes that three of the skeleton's bones are missing! This is an excellent introduction to the mystery genre.

Chocolate Fever

BY ROBERT K. SMITH
Grades 1–3   *94 pages*
Dell, 1978
Henry Green doesn't just like chocolate—he's crazy about it. He even has chocolate sprinkles on his cereal and chocolate cake for breakfast. He thus is a prime candidate to come down with the world's first case of "chocolate fever." Funny, with a subtle message about moderation. *Jelly Belly,* also by the author, uses humor and insight to describe the self-image problems of an overweight child. In *Jelly Belly,* as well as in *The War with Grandpa,* Smith paints a powerful picture of the relationship between child and grandparent.

Dinosaurs Before Dark (Magic Tree House series)

BY MARY POPE OSBORNE
Grades K–2   *76 pages*
Random House, 1992
In this first book of the popular time-travel series (with three- to four-page chapters), young Annie and Jack discover a treehouse that transports them back in time to the age of dinosaurs. The journey is filled with fantasy adventure while exploring scientific, cultural, or historic places and events.

The Friendship

BY MILDRED TAYLOR
Grades 4 and up   *53 pages*
Dial, 1987
The Logan children (from *Roll of Thunder, Hear My Cry*) witness the searing cruelty of bigotry during this story set in 1933 in rural Mississippi, where two men (one white, one black) see their onetime friendship destroyed by violence when the black man dares to call the other by his first name. Readers should be aware of racial epithets in the context of the story. For other books by the author and related titles, see listing with *Roll of Thunder, Hear My Cry* (n).

Frindle

BY ANDREW CLEMENTS
Grades 3–6   *105 pages*
Simon & Schuster, 1996

This book will have you laughing out loud by paragraph five and wanting to adopt the main character (a fifth-grade boy) by the end of the first chapter, nodding in affirmation of its wisdom throughout, and wiping the tears away at its end. The story is what education, family, and relationships are supposed to be about, never mind what a good book can do for the reading appetite. And—it's fall-down funny. Oh, yes, it's about the dictionary, too. It was overlooked for the Newbery Award but it keeps winning kids' votes in the state awards. No author rivals Clements in capturing the soul of the American classroom. Also by the author: *The Jacket; The Janitor's Boy; The Landry News; The Last Holiday Concert; Lunch Money; The Report Card;* and *A Week in the Woods.* (See also page 73.)

The Half-a-Moon Inn

BY PAUL FLEISCHMAN
Grades 2–6   *88 pages*
Harper, 1980
A chilling fantasy-adventure story about a mute boy separated from his mother by a blizzard and later kidnapped by the wicked proprietress of a village inn. Fast-moving, white-knuckle reading.

Out-of-Print Novels Too Good to Miss

Used copies are available at
www.bookfinder.com or www.alibris.com.

SHORT NOVELS:
  Four Miles to Pine Cone by Jon Hassler (Grade 6 and up)
  Stargone John by Ellen Kindt McKenzie (Grades 2–4)
  Wingman by Manus Pinkwater (Grades 2–5)
FULL NOVELS:
  The Button Boat by Glendon and Kathryn Swarthout (Grades 3–5)
  The December Rose by Leon Garfield (Grade 6 and up)
  The Dog Days of Arthur Cane by Ernesto Bethancourt (Grades 4–7)
  The Hero from Otherwhere by Jay Williams (Grades 4–7)
  Holding Me Here by Pam Conrad (Grade 6 and up)
  Rasmus and the Vagabond by Astrid Lindgren (Grades 2–5)
  Run by William Sleator (Grades 5–7)
  Stars in My Crown by Joe David Brown (Grade 5 and up)

Herbie Jones (series)

BY SUZY KLINE

Grades 1–4   95 pages

Putnam, 1985

Third-grader Herbie and his irrepressible pal Raymond meet the challenges and trials of third grade—from escaping the bottom reading group to escaping the girls' bathroom. All of it is done with a blend of sensitivity and humor, topped off with some side-splitting "gross-outs." Also by the author: *Herbie Jones and the Birthday Showdown; Herbie Jones and the Class Gift; Herbie Jones and the Dark Attic; Herbie Jones and the Monster Ball; Herbie Jones and Hamburger Head;* and *What's the Matter with Herbie Jones?* For younger readers, see Kline's Horrible Harry series.

Hoofbeats: Katie and the Mustang (series)

BY KATHLEEN DUEY

Grades 3–5   134 pages

Dutton, 2004

When nine-year-old Katie loses her parents and sister to fever in 1844, it looks as though no one will take her in—until Mr. and Mrs. Stevens do. The unsmiling childless couple wasn't looking for a daughter as much as they wanted live-in help for their Iowa farm, so Katie becomes their servant-girl. Her lone friend is a beautiful mustang Mr. Stevens has bought but cannot tame. As the Stevenses sour on farm life and Katie, she overhears their plans to travel west, shoot the mustang, and deposit Katie at an orphanage. But that's not Katie's plan; hers will carry her away and into the night. The following three books in the Mustang series focus on her own journey with the mustang toward Oregon and the only relative she thinks she has. The pages are small and compact, making for a short novel experience and one packed with believable characters and a rich historic setting. The series begins with four books and then moves to a new series, time period, and setting. The second series begins with *Hoofbeats: Lara and the Gray Mare,* set in medieval times in Ireland. Related books: *A Family Apart* (n) and *Riding Freedom* by Pam Muñoz Ryan.

The Hundred Dresses

BY ELEANOR ESTES

Grades 3–6   78 pages

Harcourt Brace, 1944

Wanda Petronski comes from the wrong side of the tracks and is the object of class jokes until her classmates sadly realize their awful mistake and cruelty. But by then it's too late. Though written more than a half century ago, the book has a message about peer pressure that has lost none of its power or relevance.

The Iron Giant: A Story in Five Nights
BY TED HUGHES
Grades 1–4   *58 pages*
Harper, 1987
The excellent children's movie of the same name was loosely based on this science fiction–fantasy, a modern fairy tale, but the book is more nuanced. It describes an invincible iron giant—a robot without a master—that stalks the land, devouring anything made of metal. Suddenly the earth faces a threat far greater than the giant when an alien creature lands—forcing the iron man into a fight for his life. The sequel, *The Iron Woman,* doesn't match the original.

Junie B. Jones and the Stupid Smelly Bus (series)
BY BARBARA PARK
Grades K–1   *70 pages*
Random House, 1992
Don't be put off by the title of this book, part of a wonderfully funny series (more than thirty books to date). Junie B. is Ramona, Little Lulu, and Lucy all rolled into one determined kindergartner. No one in children's publishing approaches Barbara Park when it comes to children's humor, and her 22 million copies sold in the Junie series is proof positive. Park's other books, like *Mick Harte Was Here* (s) and *Skinnybones* (s), are aimed at older students and demonstrate why she's consistently a state award winner with children.

Keeper of the Doves
BY BETSY BYARS
Grades 3–6   *121 pages*
Viking, 2002
This could be among the best work of this author's distinguished career. Like one of those old Kodak prints that are remarkably sharp but tiny, Byars's novel is small in size (121 pages and almost palm size), yet this 1897 family lives and breathes large as life when enlarged into our minds by the author. The family (five daughters, one son, mother, father, a maiden aunt, a liberated grandmother, and one simple-minded recluse cared for by the father) is so believable that when the book ends, you're inclined to protest, "Hey! Don't go. Come back, I'm still here."

The bulk of the tale focuses on a precocious girl named Amen (the last of the five daughters), and follows her from birth to age eight. There is much humor, thanks to the mischievous twins assigned to "raise" Amen. They are just two years older and prone to exaggeration and great flights of fancy. Always lurking in the background is the mysterious Mr. Tominski, the wild-eyed recluse who saved Amen's father's life when the latter was a boy, thus earning him a place of refuge with the family but not exemption from the torment of the twins. And when their ill-considered words about him possibly cause his accidental death, Amen and the reader have much to think about: how little we really know about the people we talk about and how easy it is for words to be transformed from "blessings" into "weapons." For other books by the author, see *The Midnight Fox* (n).

Lafcadio, the Lion Who Shot Back

BY SHEL SILVERSTEIN
Grades 2–6   *90 pages*
Harper, 1963
Lafcadio decides he isn't satisfied being a lion—he must become a marksman and man-about-town and painter and world traveler and. . . . He tries just about everything and anything in hope of finding happiness. If only he'd try being himself. A witty and thought-provoking book, it's Silverstein's first for children; for his other titles, see *Where the Sidewalk Ends* (po).

Leon's Story (nonfiction)

BY LEON WALTER TILLAGE
Grades 2–6   *105 pages*
Farrar, Straus & Giroux, 1997
For years, the custodian spellbound the children at his Baltimore school with his story of growing up in segregated North Carolina, how families and community managed to survive, and then the tumultuous civil rights years when they unleashed the dogs. This is his amazingly simple but powerful true story. Related books: *From Miss Ida's Porch* by Sandra Belton and *Uncle Jed's Barbershop* (p).

A Lion to Guard Us

BY CLYDE ROBERT BULLA
Grades K–4   *117 pages*
Crowell, 1981
In a simple prose style that is rich in character and drama, one of America's best historical writers for children offers a poignant tale of the founding fathers of the Jamestown colony and the families they left behind in England.

Here we meet a plucky heroine named Amanda who is determined to hold fast to her brother and sister despite the grim agonies of their mother's death, poverty, and shipwreck. All the while she clings to the dream that someday she will find the father who left them all behind. Also by the author: *The Chalk Box Kid; Ghost Town Treasure; Pirate's Promise; The Poppy Seeds* (p); and *Shoeshine Girl* (s).

The Littles (series)
BY JOHN PETERSON
Grades 1–4   *80 pages*
Scholastic, 1970
Children have always been fascinated by the idea of "little people"—from leprechauns to Lilliputians, from Thumbelina to hobbits. Unfortunately, much of the famous fantasy literature is too sophisticated for reading aloud to young children. The Littles series is the exception—fast-paced short novels centering on a colony of six-inch people who live inside the walls of the Bigg family's home and have dramatic escapades with gigantic mice, cats, gliders, and telephones. There have been eleven books in the series. Related books: *The Minpins* by Roald Dahl and, for older students, *The Borrowers* by Mary Norton; *The Indian in the Cupboard* (n); and *Stuart Little* (n).

Mick Harte Was Here
BY BARBARA PARK
Grades 3–5   *88 pages*
Knopf, 1995
This is Barbara Park at her serious best. Told through the eyes of an angry, grieving, yet plucky and funny thirteen-year-old sister, it's the story of her younger brother's death from a bike accident, which would have ended otherwise had he been wearing a helmet. Park fills it with warm and often hysterically funny recollections of this terrific boy, who could unnerve anyone with his creative antics. Far from maudlin, it has won numerous children's-choice state awards. See also *Skinnybones* (s).

Minnie and Sophie: All Around the Town
BY MIRIAM COHEN; THOMAS F. YEZERSKI, ILLUS.
Grades Pre–K   *68 pages*
Farrar, Straus & Giroux, 2004
In six anecdotal stories, we follow two sisters (ages five and seven) through their Brooklyn neighborhood during the Great Depression. These stories about an outing to the amusement park, clothes, treasure hunts, and games

with playmates will strike universal chords with today's children while offering a peek at a far tamer and gentler world of the 1930s. Prequel: *Minnie and Sophie*.

The Monster's Ring (Magic Shop series)
BY BRUCE COVILLE
Grades 2–4   *87 pages*
Pantheon, 1982
Just the thing for Halloween reading, this is the Jekyll-and-Hyde tale of timid Russell and the magic ring he buys that can turn him into a monster—not a make-believe monster but one with hairy hands, fangs, and claws, one that roams the night, one that will make short order of Eddie the bully, and one that will bring out the worst in Russell. An exciting fantasy of magic gone awry. This is part of the Magic Shop series, which includes: *Jeremy Thatcher, Dragon Hatcher; Jennifer Murdley's Toad;* and *The Skull of Truth*.

My Father's Dragon (series)
BY RUTH S. GANNETT
Grades K–2   *78 pages*
Knopf, 1948
This is the little fantasy novel that has stood the test of time—surviving in print for more than a half century. So it must be good! The three-volume series is bursting with hair-raising escapes and evil creatures. The tone is dramatic enough to be exciting for even mature preschoolers but not enough to frighten them. The narrator relates the tales as adventures that happened to his father when he was a boy. This is an excellent transition series for introducing children to longer stories with fewer pictures. The rest of the series, in order: *Elmer and the Dragon* and *The Dragons of Blueland*. All three tales are combined in a single volume, *My Father's Dragon: 50th Anniversary Edition*. Related dragon books for young readers: *The Best Pet of All* by David LaRochelle; *The Book of Beasts* by E. Nesbit, abridged by Inga Moore; *The Serpent Came to Gloucester* by M. T. Anderson; and *The Reluctant Dragon* (s).

On My Honor
BY MARION DANE BAUER
Grades 5–9   *90 pages*
Clarion, 1986
When his daredevil best friend drowns in a swimming accident, Joel tells no one and returns home to deny the reality and truth of the tragedy. This

gripping drama of conscience and consequences is also a story of choices—the ones we make and those we refuse to make. Related book: *A Taste of Blackberries* (s).

Owls in the Family

BY FARLEY MOWAT
Grades 2–6   108 pages
Little, Brown, 1961
No child should miss the author's reliving of his rollicking boyhood on the Saskatchewan prairie, where he raised dogs, gophers, rats, snakes, pigeons, and owls. It is an era we will never see again. Mowat would grow up to become a world-famous writer and naturalist (author of *Never Cry Wolf,* book and film). Also by the author: *Lost in the Barrens.* Related books: *Capyboppy* by Bill Peet; *Gentle Ben* (n); and *My Side of the Mountain* (n).

The Reluctant Dragon

BY KENNETH GRAHAME, ABRIDGED AND ILLUSTRATED BY INGA MOORE
Grades 1–4   52 pages
Candlewick, 2004
The author of the classic *Wind in the Willows* gives us here a simple boy-and-dragon story. The dragon is not a devouring dragon but a reluctant one who wants nothing to do with violence. The boy is something of a local scholar, well-versed in dragon lore and torn between his desire to view a battle between the dragon and St. George and the desire to protect his friend the dragon. Inga Moore has done a slight but sensitive abridgement here of Grahame's original text, and she offers large and brilliantly colored illustrations to complement the tale. No one captures the English countryside like Moore. The original version is available from Holiday House publishers. Related books: *The Book of Beasts* and *The Book of Dragons,* both by E. Nesbit; *My Father's Dragon* (s); *Saint George and the Dragon,* retold by Margaret Hodges; and *The Story of Ferdinand* by Munro Leaf.

The Rifle

BY GARY PAULSEN
Grades 6 and up   104 pages
Harcourt Brace, 1995
This short biography of a weapon, from its artistic birth on the eve of the Revolutionary War to the present time, offers a moving portrait of the many people whose paths intersect with the rifle during its 230-year history. Although the weapon is always at the center of this tale, American history shares much of the stage as the rifle's role changes with the social

structures of the times. Also by the author: *Hatchet* (n). Related book: *Gun-stories: Life-Changing Experiences with Guns* by S. Beth Atkin.

Rip-Roaring Russell (Russell and Elisa series)
BY JOHANNA HURWITZ
Grades K–2   *96 pages*
Morrow, 1983
In this delightful introduction to chapter and series books, we follow little Russell, his younger sister, Elisa, and their family and friends through preschool, kindergarten, and primary grades. Hurwitz understands children and families. No one can resist loving the characters in her books. After this first book, the series reads in this order: *Russell Sprouts; Russell Rides Again; Russell and Elisa; E Is for Elisa; Make Room for Elisa; Ever Clever Elisa; Elisa in the Middle;* and *Elisa in the Summer.*

Shipwrecked: The True Adventures of a Japanese Boy (nonfiction)
BY RHODA BLUMBERG
Grades 3–7   *80 pages*
Harper, 2003
This volume proves "truth is stranger than fiction." It's 1836, and a nine-year-old Japanese boy (Manjiro) becomes the sole support of his mother and siblings. At age fourteen, he's working on a fishing ship and becomes marooned for four months on a deserted island with four crewmates. When rescued by an American whaling ship, the five could not be returned to Japan because of that country's laws that "outsiders" must be captured and killed. The crewmates choose to be put ashore in Hawaii but the boy joins the American crew and later becomes the first Japanese person to enter the United States. After attending a one-room schoolhouse in Massachusetts, he joins a merchant ship and eventually is returned to Japan where he's imprisoned and tried eighteen times for being contaminated by foreigners. But when Admiral Perry enters the bay in Tokyo, Manjiro is sent for as an interpreter/advisor for the Japanese government and is instrumental in the subsequent treaty between the United States and Japan. Related books: *Baseball Saved Us* by Ken Mochizuk (a story from the Japanese internment camps); *Hiroshima: The Story of the First Atom Bomb* by Clive A. Lawton; *Kensuke's Kingdom* (n); and *The True Adventure of Daniel Hall* by Diane Stanley.

Shoeshine Girl
BY CLYDE ROBERT BULLA
Grades 1–4   *84 pages*
Harper, 1989

A spoiled ten-year-old girl, having driven her parents to the edge, is sent to spend the summer with her aunt. Immediately she's in trouble for conning a neighboring child into a loan. Determined to have spending money, she lands a job at a local shoeshine stand and there she receives a maturing dose of reality and responsibility. Related books: *Bud, Not Buddy* (n) and *The Pinballs* (n).

Skinnybones

BY BARBARA PARK
Grades 3–5   *112 pages*
Knopf, 1982
One of the funniest voices writing for middle-grade children, Park creates characters who may not always be lovable, but they are remarkably alive and interesting as they deal with losing ball games, moving, camp, or sibling rivalries. Best of all, they are funny—not cutesy or caustic, but genuinely and interestingly funny. Typical is Alex Frankovitch of *Skinnybones*, who is an uncoordinated smart aleck who throws tantrums; he's also a laugh a minute. Sequel: *Almost Starring Skinnybones*. Also by the author: *Junie B. Jones and the Stupid Smelly Bus* (s) and *Mick Harte Was Here* (s).

The SOS File

BY BETSY BYARS, BETSY DUFFEY, AND LAURIE MYERS
Grades 1–3   *72 pages*
Henry Holt, 2004
Placing a folder at the front of the classroom, the teacher gives his students a chance for extra credit: all they have to do is write an essay or story about a traumatic moment—a time they had to call 911 or were so frightened they could barely speak or walk. Each of his eleven students accepts the challenge, writing tales that are entirely believable for primary-grade students. Some raise the hairs on the neck (like the pair who meet a black bear on their hike), some make you laugh (like the student with the ungoverned appetite who ate the candy bars instead of selling them for fund-raising), and several are quite poignant (like the student attempting to find the traveling salesman who discovered her in a Dumpster when she was one day old). Each tale runs an average of three pages and they are excellent examples of short narrative.

Soup (series)

BY ROBERT NEWTON PECK
Grades 4–6   *96 pages*
Knopf, 1974

Two Vermont pals share a genius for getting themselves into trouble. The stories are set in the rural 1930s when life was simpler and the days were longer. But the need for a best friend was just as great then as now. There are a dozen books in the series. For older readers: *A Day No Pigs Would Die* (n).

Stone Fox
BY JOHN R. GARDINER
Grades 1–7   *96 pages*
Crowell, 1980
Here is a story that, like its ten-year-old orphan hero, never stands still. Since it has sold more than one million copies in twenty-five years with little or no corporate advertising, there must be great word-of-mouth out there for this book about the love of a child for his grandfather and the loyalty of a dog for his young master. Based on a Rocky Mountain legend, the story recounts the valiant efforts of young Willy to save his grandfather's farm by attempting to win the purse in a local bobsled race. For a list of other dog stories, see page 246.

The Stories Julian Tells (series)
BY ANN CAMERON
Grades K–3   *72 pages*
Pantheon, 1981
The author takes six short stories involving Julian and his brother and weaves them into a fabric that glows with the mischief, magic, and imagination of childhood. Though centered on commonplace subjects like desserts, gardens, loose teeth, and new neighbors, these stories of family life are written in an uncommon way that will both amuse and touch young listeners. Sequels: *Julian's Glorious Summer; Julian Secret Agent; More Stories Julian Tells;* and *The Stories Huey Tells.*

The Stray
BY DICK KING-SMITH
Grades 1–4   *139 pages*
Dell, 2002
One day, on a nearly deserted beach, an old woman (Henny Hickathrift) who had walked away from her old age home and hopped a train to the seaside, took her cane and wrote in the sand: "I am a stray old woman." That inscription soon leads five red-headed siblings to the old woman. It's Henny's seventy-fifth birthday and the children insist she come home with them to celebrate in style. The afternoon visit stretches into a week, then a

month, and finally becomes permanent as the family falls in love with her. In the style the author has made his trademark in books like *Babe: The Gallant Pig,* this is a warm celebration of family and aging. Also by the author: *The Invisible Dog; A Mouse Called Wolf; Pigs Might Fly; The School Mouse;* and *The Water Horse* (s).

A Taste of Blackberries
BY DORIS B. SMITH
Grades 4–7   *52 pages*
Crowell, 1973
In viewing death from a child's point of view, the author allows us to follow the narrator's emotions as he comes to terms with the death of his best friend, who died as a result of an allergic reaction to bee stings. The sensitivity with which the attendant sorrow and guilt are treated makes this an outstanding book. It blazed the way for the many other grief books that quickly followed, but few have approached the place of honor this one holds. Related books about death: *Bridge to Terabithia* (n); *A Day No Pigs Would Die* (n); and *On My Honor* (s).

Two Times the Fun
BY BEVERLY CLEARY
Grades PreK–K   *92 pages*
Harper, 2005
Beverly Cleary raised a set of twins, so she knows the breed well. Couple that with her witty insight into the workings of family life and you've got everything that makes this collection of four stories work so well. Jimmy and Janet are four-year-olds with two distinct approaches to things like dog biscuits, new boots, holes in the ground, and personal possessions. Originally separate picture books, these four tales work perfectly in the short novel category for preschoolers.

The Water Horse
BY DICK KING-SMITH
Grades K–2   *120 Pages*
Dell Yearling, 2001
When eight-year-old Kirstie and her five-year-old brother, Angus, discover a purse-size object washed up on the Scottish coast after a storm, they thinks it's some kind of egg and needs to be saved in the bathtub. Their guess is more than correct. With the head and neck that look somewhat like a horse's, the body of a turtle, and the tail of a crocodile, the creature

is about the size of a newborn kitten. But it won't stay that size for long. What they have inadvertently hatched is the future Loch Ness monster.

Dick King-Smith, author of the popular *Babe: The Gallant Pig,* gives us not a monster story here but an affectionate look at what might have been if there really was a Loch Ness monster and if it had been raised by two affectionate children, a cooperative mom, a seafaring father, and a once grumpy but now knowledgeable grandfather. Each short chapter deals with the increasing challenges faced by the family as the creature grows larger, requires increasing amounts of food, and needs to learn that not all people are its friends. But how to train a "monster"? Also by the author: *Stray* (s).

When the Soldiers Were Gone

BY VERA W. PROPP
Grades 2–5   *101 pages*
Putnam, 1999
World War II and the German occupation of the Netherlands are over, and life is returning to normal. That is when a young schoolboy is turned over to a man and woman who are his mother and father. But years earlier he had been taken in by another Dutch couple to be sheltered during the occupation. Having lived with them for so long, he has forgotten they are not his real parents and that he is, in fact, Jewish, not a Christian. While the author has reduced the terrors of the war to the believable scale of an eight-year-old, she neither traumatizes the reader-listener nor trivializes the war because, as a classroom teacher for twenty-five years, she truly understands children. It is a heartwarming but powerful tale. Related titles: *The Butterfly* by Patricia Polacco; *The Greatest Skating Race* by Louise Borden; *The Little Riders* by Margaretha Shemin; and *Twenty and Ten* by Claire H. Bishop.

The Whipping Boy

BY SID FLEISCHMAN
Grades 3–6   *90 pages*
Greenwillow, 1986
The brattish medieval prince is too spoiled ever to be spanked, so the king regularly vents his anger on Jeremy, a peasant "whipping boy." When circumstances lead the two boys to reverse roles, à la *The Prince and the Pauper,* each learns much about friendship and sacrifice. Painted with Fleischman's broad humor, this is a fast-paced Newbery-winning melodrama with short, cliff-hanger chapters.

Wildfire!

BY ELIZABETH STARR-HILL

Grades K–3   *66 pages*

Farrar, Straus & Giroux, 2004

This is a multilayered adventure novel for beginning chapter book listeners. The adventure part involves two young boys caught in a wildfire with a runaway dog. A second layer describes the loving relationship one of the boys, Ben, enjoys with the grandparents who have raised him in their rural Florida hamlet since his parents died when he was four (he's now ten).

A third layer is devoted to the peer pressure applied to Ben by one particular boy who has been quietly belittling Ben and his family. In their small town, the Fourth of July is the only holiday of the summer and the town has always tried to make the most of it. This year, however, a drought has made the surrounding woodland too dry for fireworks. When Ben casually mentions to his peers that his grandfather had bought him a supply of fireworks before they announced the ban, peer pressure is applied to secretly take them and light them anyway.

Full-Length Novels

Adam Canfield of The Slash

BY MICHAEL WINERIP

Grades 5–8   *326 pages*

Candlewick, 2005

If you had to summarize this book in one sentence, it would be: "Woodward and Bernstein meet Joe and Frank Hardy." Better make that "Jo" Hardy, because half of this intrepid duo is an African American female named Jennifer, the bright, level-headed co-editor of Harris Elementary/ Middle School's student newspaper, the *Slash*. The role of Frank falls to co-editor Adam Canfield, a bright but *un*level-headed eighth-grader. Instead of Bayport, author Michael Winerip (a Pulitzer Prize–winning education writer for the *New York Times*) has placed his co-editors in wealthy Tremble, suburbia brimming with over-scheduled kids too busy to play, school administrators and real estate agents too focused on test scores, and a husband-wife team that owns both the cable company and the local newspaper and is thus able to slant news and views as they wish.

True, Jennifer and Adam use methods only an experienced adult investigative reporter would know, but they retain a child's view of the world.

Super-kids, but still kids at heart. The nucleus of the novel is a contest of wills between the ill-tempered principal, Mrs. Morris, and the two editors. This is a superb introduction to modern journalism and to some contemporary issues the author has dealt with as a reporter. Related book: *The Landry News* by Andrew Clements.

The Adventures of Pinocchio

BY CARLO COLLODI; ROBERTO INNOCENTI, ILLUS.
Grades 1–5   *144 pages*
Knopf, 1988

Unfortunately, most children's familiarity with this 1892 classic comes from the emasculated Disney or TV versions. Treat your children to the original story of the poor woodcarver's puppet who faces all the temptations of childhood, succumbs to many, learns from his follies, and gains his boyhood by selflessly giving of himself for his friends. The Knopf edition, the most lavishly illustrated ever, is the real *Pinocchio*.

Bambi

BY FELIX SALTEN
Grades 2–5   *191 pages*
Aladdin, 1988

Don't be misled by the Disney version of this tale. Salten's original forest is far deeper than the film. Intended as a protest against hunting, the story follows the young roe deer from birth to the arrival of danger—man. This is an accessible classic for children, but also for experienced listeners. If you insist upon an abridged version, then use Janet Schulman's (Atheneum).

The Bad Beginning (series)

BY LEMONY SNICKET
Grades 2–4   *162 pages*
Harper, 1999

Contrary to the title, this is a splendid beginning to an enormously popular series that follows the "riches-to-rags" tale of three resilient orphans who no sooner overcome one Dickensian misfortune and villain than even darker ones appear. The children must and do resist these threats with determined quick wits. Sending up the moralistic Victorian adventure tales of a century ago, as well as old-time Saturday movie serials, the author's asides to the reader-listener are humorous, helpful, and enlightening (especially with vocabulary). The series now runs to at least eleven books, and hopefully the first movie will be the last (awful!).

Because of Winn-Dixie

BY KATE DICAMILLO
Grades 2–5   *182 pages*
Candlewick, 2000
Ten-year-old Opal Buloni is not only the new kid in town, she's also a preacher's kid. And she is one of the most refreshing characters to come to children's literature in a dog's age. She picks up a stray dog at the neighborhood Winn-Dixie grocery (that's how it got its name) and charms her daddy into letting her keep him. She also charms everyone she meets, collecting the weirdest assortment of cast-off grown-ups and kids you'll ever meet and grow fond of. Also by the author: *The Tale of Despereaux*. Related books: *A Blue-Eyed Daisy* (s); *Ida Early Comes over the Mountain* (n); *Lilly's Crossing* (n); and *Riding Freedom* by Pam Muñoz Ryan.

Black Beauty

BY ANNA SEWELL; CHARLES KEEPING, ILLUS.
Grades 4–8   *214 pages*
Farrar, Straus & Giroux, 1990
In this classic animal novel, and the first with an animal as narrator, the author vividly describes the cruelty to horses during the Victorian period, as well as giving a detailed picture of life at that time. Related books: *The Black Stallion* (series) by Walter Farley; *Hoofbeats: Katie and the Mustang* (series) by Kathleen Duey; *King of the Wind: The Story of the Godolphin Arabian* by Marguerite Henry; and *Riding Freedom* by Pam Muñoz Ryan.

Bridge to Terabithia

BY KATHERINE PATERSON
Grades 4–7   *128 pages*
Crowell, 1997
Few novels for children have dealt with so many emotions and issues so well: sports, school, peers, friendship, death, guilt, art, and family. This popular Newbery winner deserves to be read or heard by everyone. Also by the author: *The Great Gilly Hopkins*. Related book: *The Pinballs* (n).

Bud, Not Buddy

BY CHRISTOPHER PAUL CURTIS
Grades 4–8   *243 pages*
Delacorte, 1999
After escaping a succession of bad foster homes, ten-year-old Buddy sets out to find the man he suspects to be his father—a popular jazz musician

in Grand Rapids, Michigan. Told in the first person, this engaging Newbery winner brims with humor and compassion while offering a keen insight into the workings of a child's mind during the Great Depression.
Related books: *A Family Apart* (n); *No Promises in the Wind* by Irene Hunt;
and *Roll of Thunder, Hear My Cry* (n). Also by the author: *The Watsons Go to
Birmingham*. If you have the free plug-in RealAudio, you can hear a one-
hour interview with the author online at: http:news.mpr.org/play/audio.
php?media=/midmorning/2003/05/16_midmorn2.

Caddie Woodlawn

BY CAROL RYRIE BRINK
Grades 4–6   *286 pages*
Simon & Schuster, 1935
You take *The Little House on the Prairie;* I'll take *Caddie Woodlawn*. Ten times
over, I'll take this tomboy of the 1860s with her pranks, her daring visits to
Indian camps, her one-room schoolhouse fights, and her wonderfully be-
lievable family. Try to pick up the 1973 edition with Trina Schart Hyman's
illustrations. For experienced listeners. Sequel: *Magical Melons.* Related book:
Riding Freedom by Pam Muñoz Ryan.

The Call of the Wild

BY JACK LONDON
Grades 6 and up   *126 pages*
Viking (Whole Story edition), 1996
This 1903 dog story, set amidst the rush for gold in the Klondike, depicts
the savagery and tenderness between man and his environment in unforgettable terms. The Whole Story edition includes extensive sidebars and illustrations that add greatly to the story's setting in time and place. For
experienced listeners. Also by the author: *White Fang* (look for the edition
illustrated by Ed Young). On the Web: http:sunsite.berkeley.edu/London/.
Related books: *Jason's Gold* (n) and *Where the Red Fern Grows* (n). For a list
of great dog stories, see page 246.

The Cay

BY THEODORE TAYLOR
Grades 2–6   *144 pages*
Doubleday, 1969
An exciting adventure about a blind white boy and an old black man ship-
wrecked on a tiny Caribbean island. The first chapters are slow but it builds
with taut drama to a stunning ending. Sequel/prequel: *Timothy of the Cay.*
Also by the author: *The Bomb* (atomic); *Sniper,* an outstanding suspense

story set at a "big cat" preserve in Southern California; *Ice Drift;* and *A Sailor Returns.* Related books: *Hatchet* (n) and *Kensuke's Kingdom* (n).

Charlotte's Web: 50th Anniversary Retrospective Edition

BY E. B. WHITE; GARTH WILLIAMS, ILLUS.

Grades K–4   *213 pages*

Harper, 2002

One of the most acclaimed books in children's literature, it is loved by adults as well as children. The tale centers on the barnyard life of a young pig who is to be butchered in the fall. The animals of the yard (particularly a haughty gray spider named Charlotte) conspire with the farmer's daughter to save the pig's life. While there is much humor in the novel, the author uses wisdom and pathos in developing his theme of friendship within the cycle of life.

It took them fifty years, but E. B. White's publisher finally included something about the author. For a half century this modern classic didn't include a single sentence about the author in the hardcover edition. The only mention was his byline on the cover. With this fiftieth anniversary edition we have some information to bring the man alive for young readers: how he lived, how he wrote, and samples of his editing and concerns while he wrote. Twelve pages by Peter Neumeyer were added to this handsome oversize edition, pages that do a great writer justice. The print in this edition is half again larger than the regular hardcover and paperback, making a slightly longer book. Also by the author: *Stuart Little* (n). Beverly Gherman's *E. B. White: Some Writer!* is an excellent children's biography of the author. Related books: *Spiders!* from Time for Kids is an excellent picture book on the world of spiders; *Cricket in Times Square* by George Selden; and *Poppy* (n).

The City of Ember

BY JEANNE DUPRAU

Grades 4–7   *288 pages*

Random House, 2003

More than 240 years before the story opens, a great holocaust confronted the population of earth. To save the species, one group created a huge underground city, Ember, that would be safe from the ravages above. Because it was complete with giant storehouses of supplies and a huge generator, humanity could survive. These forefathers also conceived a means by which the inhabitants would be able to extricate themselves from their underground tomb after 200 years, estimating that by then the surface would be habitable again. Detailed instructions were given to the care of the mayor, who, in turn, would pass them to his successor. The book picks up the story almost 250 years later. Those instructions have long been misplaced and forgotten, and so has much of history. The people know only their life underground and live increasingly meager existences with dwindling supplies and energy.

But the youngest generation is chafing under the regimentation of the old order, even wondering if there might be something beyond the here and now, pondering, "What if—?" Two such people are twelve-year-olds Doon and Lina. The latter has stumbled on some strange but ancient instructions in her grandmother's closet, and the former is a born rebel and questioner but sentenced to spend the rest of his life repairing the plumbing in the bowels of the city. Together they begin the journey outward and upward that will save their civilization—if they can ever get anyone to follow them. Sequel: *The People of Sparks.* Related titles: *The Giver* by Lois Lowry; *Journey Outside* by Mary Q. Steele; and *When the Tripods Came* (n).

The Curse of the Blue Figurine (series)

BY JOHN BELLAIRS

Grades 4–8   *200 pages*

Dial, 1983

If you are looking for intelligent alternatives to the Goosebumps series, look no further than the works of John Bellairs. In this book, Johnny Dixon removes a small figurine from the basement of his church, only to be haunted by the evil spirits attached to it. Johnny and his professor friend continue their spine-tingling exploits down twisted tunnels in: *The Mummy, the Will and the Crypt; The Revenge of the Wizard's Ghost;* and *The Spell of the Sorcerer's Skull.*

Danny, the Champion of the World

BY ROALD DAHL

Grades 3–5   *196 pages*

Knopf, 1975

In what might be Dahl's most tender book for children, a motherless boy and his father—"the most wonderful father who ever lived"—go on an adventure together. Teachers and parents should explain the custom and tradition of "poaching" in England before going too deeply into the story (Robin Hood was a poacher). Also by the author: *James and the Giant Peach* (n). Related books: Try comparing the experiences of Danny with those of Leigh Botts, the boy in *Dear Mr. Henshaw* (n).

Darby

BY JONATHON SCOTT FUQUA

Grades 2–4   *240 pages*

Candlewick, 2002

To get a quick grip on this book, think of it as *To Kill a Mockingbird* for nine-year-olds—except that *Mockingbird* is narrated by a grown-up Scout who is reflecting on the events of when she was about seven; *Darby*, on the other hand, is told with the immediate feelings and words of a girl who is still nine and who hasn't achieved the wisdom that comes with hindsight. It takes us back to 1926 and the American South, specifically Marlboro County, South Carolina. And though Darby Carmichael acts as if the world revolves around her, she is beginning to notice other forces in her small universe—some of which she can't control. She is writing the book to explain the good and terrible things that happened that year in her family and community.

Truthfulness is at the heart of this novel, from the time that Darby is inspired by her best friend to become a newspaper writer. The friend (Evette) is the daughter of a black tenant farmer on Darby's father's farm. It wasn't fashionable for a white girl to have a black best friend in that time and place, but sometimes friendships grow like wildflowers. Ever since Evette told her that newspaper writers must always write the truth, Darby has been writing short articles for the local paper and has become a little celebrity in the community. Then the Carmichaels' redneck neighbor assaults a black boy he finds stealing a chicken, a beating that results in the boy's death. This opens Darby's eyes to the unfair differences between whites and blacks in her town, and she and her friend write an essay that unsettles family, friends, and community. More than a book about race, this is a morality tale about conscience and convictions, truth and justice. Readers-aloud should not be put off by the size of the book (240 pages); the page dimensions are small, and the text is double-spaced, so it's really about 140 pages in length. Related books: *Adam Canfield of The Slash* (n) and *Roll of Thunder, Hear My Cry* (n).

Dave at Night

BY GAIL CARSON LEVINE

Grades 4–8   *281 pages*

Harper, 1999

This engaging tale of childhood resilience and adventure is set in a Jewish orphan asylum in 1926. If you're familiar with Broadway musicals, you could say this is a Jewish *Annie*, without the music. Dave Caros is an eleven-year-old orphan whose noisy and rambunctious nature intimidates his relatives enough to keep them from adopting him. Thus he ends up at the HHB, the Hebrew Home for Boys in New York at the edge of Harlem. In a freezing dormitory with forty-one other boys, Dave finds the food is bad, school is awful, and the administrators are tyrants. But he soon discovers a nighttime escape route, one that allows him to roam through what we now know as the Harlem Renaissance, vibrant with authors, artists, musicians, and wealthy dowagers. A benevolent old Jewish soothsayer takes Dave under his wing and ushers him on weekly visits into this unique society, where he becomes the darling friend of a wealthy young black girl. But like Cinderella, Dave must always return before dawn to the orphanage. If the HHB is so dreadful, why does he go back? That is the heart of the tale. For related orphan books, see list with *Bud, Not Buddy* (n) and *A Family Apart* (n).

A Day No Pigs Would Die

BY ROBERT NEWTON PECK
Grades 6 and up   *150 pages*
Knopf, 1972
Set among Shaker farmers in Vermont during the 1920s, this is the poignant story of the author's coming of age at thirteen, his adventures, fears, and triumphs. As a novel of life and death, it should be read carefully by the teacher or parent before it is read aloud to children. A very moving story for experienced listeners. Sequel: *A Part of the Sky.* Also by the author: the Soup series (s).

Dear Mr. Henshaw

BY BEVERLY CLEARY
Grades 3–6   *134 pages*
Morrow, 1983
In this 1984 Newbery winner, Beverly Cleary departs from her Ramona format to write a very different but every bit as successful book—one of the finest in her long career. Using only the letters and diary of a young boy (Leigh Botts), the author traces his personal growth from first grade to sixth. We watch the changes in his relationship with his divorced parents, his schools (where he always ends up the friendless "new kid"), an author with whom he corresponds over the years, and finally the changes in himself. Along with the usual Cleary humor, there is also genuine sensitivity to the heartaches that confront the growing number of Leigh Bottses in our homes and classrooms. Sequel: *Strider.* Also by the author: *Ramona the Pest* (n). Related books: *Danny, the Champion of the World* (n) and *Thank You, Jackie Robinson* (n).

Jim's Favorite Dog Stories

Big Red by Jim Kjelgaard
Call of the Wild by Jack London
A Dog Called Kitty by Bill
  Wallace
Foxy by Helen Griffith
Hurry Home, Candy by Meindert
  DeJong
Kavik the Wolf Dog by Walt
  Morey

Lassie Come Home by Eric
  Knight
Old Yeller by Fred Gipson
Shiloh by Phyllis Naylor
Stone Fox by John Reynolds
  Gardiner
Where the Red Fern Grows by
  Wilson Rawls
Woodsong by Gary Paulsen

Deltora Quest: The Forest of Silence (series)

BY EMILY RODDA
Grades 1–5   *131 pages*
Scholastic, 2000

Here is the fantasy series for those not ready for either the complexity or length of the Harry Potter series. The author has borrowed the traditional quest motif from classical literature and coupled it with a little bit of King Arthur, The Lord of the Rings, Narnia, and even *Star Wars.* In the land of Deltora, an evil shadow lord takes over the land when the kingdom's protective stones are stolen and dispersed. To the rescue comes an unlikely trio of teen warriors (two males, one female) who set out to recover the stones and save the kingdom. Each book uncovers more stones but also enormous obstacles that block their recovery. This is followed by book two, *Dragons of Deltora,* and book three, *Deltora Shadowlands.*

A Family Apart (series)

BY JOAN LOWERY NIXON
Grades 3–7   *162 pages*
Bantam, 1987

The popular Orphan Train series is based on the years between the Civil War and the Great Depression when 150,000 homeless children were shipped west to families willing to give them shelter. Some were looking to adopt a first child, some were reaching out to enlarge their present family, and some were looking for unpaid laborers—under the guise of family. This opening book in the series follows the six Kelly children from New York City to Missouri after their widowed mother turns them over to the Children's Aid Society, which sends them to Missouri and parcels them out to farm families. Much of the book focuses on thirteen-year-old Frances and her attempts to masquerade as a boy in order to be "adopted" by the same family that takes her youngest brother. Also in the series: *Caught in the Act; In the Face of Danger; A Place to Belong; A Dangerous Promise* (Civil War); *Keeping Secrets;* and *Circle of Love.*

Other historical books about children in orphaned circumstances: *Orphan Train Rider: One Boy's True Story* and *We Rode the Orphan Trains,* both by Andrea Warren, nonfiction books with excellent photographs documenting the history of the orphan trains. Also, see Eve Bunting's picture book *Train to Nowhere,* which follows fourteen orphans through the "train" experience.

Finding Buck McHenry

BY ALFRED SLOTE
Grades 3–6   *250 pages*
Harper, 1991

Eleven-year-old Jason, baseball card collector extraordinaire, is convinced that school custodian Mr. Mack Henry is really the legendary Buck McHenry of Negro Leagues fame. Before either of them can stop it, the idea steamrolls out of control. The author creates a rich blend of baseball history, peer relationships (male and female), family, and race relations while never losing sight of a good story. Also by the author: *Hang Tough, Paul Mather* and *The Trading Game.* See also the excellent paperback series by Dan Gutman about a boy who time-travels using his baseball cards: *Jackie and Me* (Jackie Robinson); *Satch and Me* (Satchel Paige); and *Honus and Me* (Honus Wagner). See also *Thank You, Jackie Robinson* (n) and *Shadowball: The History of the Negro Leagues* by Geoffrey C. Ward and Ken Burns from the PBS documentary.

Francie

BY KAREN ENGLISH
Grades 3 and up   *199 pages*
Farrar, Straus & Giroux, 1999

Thirteen-year-old Francie Weaver is strong-willed, determined, impetuous, honest to a fault, generous, intelligent, and doesn't suffer fools gladly. This last quality made life complicated in Alabama when segregation ruled, and Francie's troubles multiply even more when she befriends an illiterate sixteen-year-old boy and begins to teach him to read. When he is accused of attempted murder, she launches a personal campaign to save him. This is a heartwarming, compelling first novel. For related books, see *Roll of Thunder, Hear My Cry* (n).

Freak, the Mighty

BY RODMAN PHILBRICK

Grades 6–9   165 pages

Scholastic, 1993

Many popular entertainment tales have involved teams—Batman and Robin, the Lone Ranger and Tonto, Luke Skywalker and Han Solo. Each member is usually of vastly different stature. In that tradition comes the team of Max and Kevin, two unlikely teenage heroes. Middle-schooler Max is gigantic, powerful, and a remedial student. The wisecracking Kevin suffers from a birth defect that limits his growth and keeps him on crutches; his body cannot grow to more than a few feet in height, but his mind has expanded to brilliant proportions. The two become fast friends and give themselves the nickname "Freak (Kevin) the Mighty (Max)." Their adventures run the gamut from escaping street bullies and outwitting school authorities, to educating Max and surviving his homicidal father. While some parts are implausible, the friendship between the two is a thing of beauty, and Max's first-person voice rings true as he painfully explores the anxieties of adolescence. Sequel: *Max, the Mighty*.

From the Mixed-up Files of Mrs. Basil E. Frankweiler

BY E. L. KONIGSBURG

Grades 4–7   162 pages

Macmillan, 1967

A bored and brainy twelve-year-old girl talks her nine-year-old brother into running away with her. To throw everyone off their trail, Claudia chooses the Metropolitan Museum of Art in New York City as a refuge, and amid centuries-old art they sleep, dine, bathe, and pray in regal secret splendor. An exciting story of hide-and-seek and a wonderful art lesson to boot. For experienced listeners. Related runaway books: a city boy hides in the wilderness in *My Side of the Mountain* (n); a city boy hides in the subway system in *Slake's Limbo* (n).

Gentle Ben

BY WALT MOREY

Grades 3–6   192 pages

Dutton, 1965

A young boy adopts a huge bear and brings to his family in Alaska all the joys and tears such a combination might invite. Though the struggle to save animals from ignorant but well-intentioned human predators is one that has been written many times over, Morey's handling of characters, plot, and setting makes this an original and exciting tale. He supports the pace of his story with many lessons in environmental science, from salmon runs to hibernation. Also by the author: *Canyon Winter; Hero; Kavik the Wolf Dog;* and *Scrub Dog of Alaska.* Related book: *The Year of Miss Agnes* by Kirkpatrick Hill.

Good Night, Mr. Tom

BY MICHELLE MAGORIAN
Grades 6 and up   *318 pages*
Harper, 1981

This is one of the longer novels listed in this Treasury; it might also be the most powerful, and adults should preview it carefully before reading it aloud. It's the story of an eight-year-old London boy evacuated during the Blitz to a small English village, where he is reluctantly taken in by a grumpy old man. The boy proves to be an abused child, terrified of everything around him. With painstaking care, the old man begins the healing process, unveiling to the child a world he never knew existed—a world of kindness, friendship, laughter, and hope. For experienced listeners. Not everyone was as fortunate as this child.

Good Old Boy

BY WILLIE MORRIS
Grades 5–8   *128 pages*
Yoknapatawpha, 1981

If Mark Twain had been writing *Tom Sawyer* in the 1940s, this is the book he'd have written. One of the South's most distinguished authors gives us the heartwarming tale of growing up in a town on the banks of the Mississippi. For experienced listeners. Sequel: *My Dog Skip,* upon which the wonderful movie was loosely based, but read the book first. Related books: *The Adventures of Tom Sawyer* by Mark Twain and *Soup* (s).

The Great Brain (series)

BY JOHN D. FITZGERALD
Grades 5 and up   *175 pages*
Dial, 1967

This is the first book in a series dealing with the hilarious—and often touching—adventures of an Irish-Catholic family surrounded by Utah Mormons in 1896, told through the eyes of a younger brother. Tom Fitzgerald is part boy-genius and part con man, but in command of every situation. The series reads well on many levels, including as a perspective of daily life at the turn of the century. For experienced listeners. Sequels (in order): *More Adventures of the Great Brain; Me and My Little Brain; The Return of the Great Brain;* and *The Great Brain Is Back.*

The Great Turkey Walk

BY KATHLEEN KARR
Grades 4–8   *199 pages*
Scholastic, 1998

Set in the time of cattle drives and the Kansas Territory, this comic-novel tall tale follows fifteen-year-old Simon Green as he journeys nine hundred miles from Missouri to Denver. But it's no ordinary journey. First, muscular but soft-headed Simon has just "graduated" from third grade after four years there. Second, he's herding a thousand turkeys. Third, he's accompanied and assisted by a recovering alcoholic and a runaway slave. En route, they encounter rustlers, Indians whose territory they've accidentally violated, Simon's no-account long-lost father who is bent on stealing the turkeys, target-hungry U.S. cavalry, and a deranged woman. And one last ingredient to make it an even tastier tale of redemption: the venture is being bankrolled by Simon's fourth-grade teacher with her life's savings. Related books: Sid Fleischman's *By the Great Hornspoon: Humbug Mountain* and *Chauncy and the Grand Rascal*.

Harry Potter and the Sorcerer's Stone (series)

BY J. K. ROWLING
Grades 2–8   *309 pages*
Scholastic, 1998

Harry is the best thing to happen to children's books since the invention of the paperback! While the series' plot is surely original, it follows in the path of C. S. Lewis's dual Narnia world, George Lucas's *Star Wars* struggles with the "dark side," and Dorothy's search for the Wizard of Oz. It is also blessed with an abundance of Roald Dahl's cheeky childhood humor.

Harry is the orphan child of two famous wizards who died mysteriously when he was very young. Rescued at age eleven from abusive relatives, he is sent to Hogwarts School (sorcery's equivalent of an elite boarding school), where he experiences high adventure as he and his friends (boy and girl) struggle with classes in potions, charms, and broom-flying, all the while battling a furtive faculty member working for the dark side.

This is not an easy read-aloud and the reader-aloud should be aware that the first two chapters of the first book are a bit complicated as they set the scene for Harry's dual world. Definitely for experienced listeners. Actor Jim Dale has done a masterful job of recording (unabridged) all of the Potter books for Listening Library/Random House and an excellent NPR interview with him can be heard online via the free RealAudio plugin at: http:www.npr.org/templates/story/story.php?storyId=4792545.

Other books to date in the series (in order): *Harry Potter and the Chamber of Secrets; Harry Potter and the Prisoner of Azkaban; Harry Potter and the Goblet of Fire; Harry Potter and the Order of the Phoenix;* and *Harry Potter and the Half-Blood Prince.*

Younger fans of Harry will also enjoy: *Deltora Quest* (n); *The Lion, the Witch, and the Wardrobe* (n); the Redwall series, beginning with *Martin the Warrior* (n); and older fans may be ready for *The Hobbit* by J. R. R. Tolkien.

Hatchet (series)

BY GARY PAULSEN

Grades 6 and up   *195 pages*
Bradbury, 1987

The lone survivor of a plane crash in the Canadian wilderness, a thirteen-year-old boy carries three things away from the crash: a fierce spirit, the hatchet his mother gave him as a gift, and the secret knowledge that his mother was unfaithful to his father. All play an integral part in this Newbery Honor survival story for experienced listeners. Sequels: *The River; Brian's Winter; Brian's Return;* and *Brian's Hunt.* Having received about four hundred letters a week with *Hatchet*-related queries, Paulsen's answered them in one book: *Guts!* the true-life events that inspired the series. Related survival books: *The Cay* and *Ice Drift,* both by Theodore Taylor; The Island (series) by Gordon Korman; *Kensuke's Kingdom* (n); *A Week in the Woods* by Andrew Clements; and *Winter Camp* by Kirkpatrick Hill. Before there was Paulsen, there was William O. Steele, who wrote outstanding outdoor historical novels, four of which have recently been reprinted (with handsome new covers): *Buffalo Knife; Flaming Arrows; Perilous Road;* and *Winter Danger.*

Other books by Paulsen include: *The Foxman* (a precursor to his later *Harris and Me*); *Mr. Tucket* (n); *The Rifle* (s); *Soldier's Heart; The Tent;* and a survival-at-sea novel, *The Voyage of the Frog.*

Paulsen also has written a memoir for children of his relationships with dogs, *My Life in Dog Years.* A Paulsen profile is available at www.trelease-on-reading.com/paulsen.html.

Holes

BY LOUIS SACHAR

Grades 4–8   *233 pages*
Farrar, Straus & Giroux, 1998

Too often, when a children's book captures a large number of prizes from adult committees (this book won the 1999 Newbery Medal, National Book Award, and *The Horn Book* Award), it turns out to be inaccessible to most children. Not so here! *Holes* is an adventure tale, a mystery, fantasy, and quest book. An important ingredient is Sachar's wit. Set in a juvenile detention station on the Texas desert, it traces the sad life of fourteen-year-old Stanley Yelnats, who has just been sentenced (mistakenly) for stealing a pair of sneakers. Not only has the friendless, hopeless Stanley been haunted all his life by a dark cloud of events, so has his family. Indeed, there is a family legend that his grandfather's long-ago selfishness in Latvia has rusted every golden opportunity for the family since then. Forced by the abusive camp police to dig holes all day long in the baking desert, he experiences an epiphany, makes his first friend, and gradually discovers courage he never knew he had. In so doing, he slowly and painfully unwinds the century-old family curse. The movie based on the book was exceptionally well received by critics and families, perhaps because the author himself wrote the screenplay. Sequel: *Small Steps.*

Sachar's acceptance speech for the Newbery (July–August 1999 issue, *The Horn Book*) offers an excellent view of how the book was created, and is reprinted with a personal profile of the author by his wife and daughter. Also by the author: *Sideways Stories from Wayside School* (n). Related book: *Maniac Magee* (n).

Homer Price
BY ROBERT MCCLOSKEY
Grades 2–5   *160 pages*
Viking, 1943
A modern children's classic, this is a collection of humorous tales about a small-town boy's neighborhood dilemmas. Whether telling how Homer foiled the bank robbers with his pet skunk or of his uncle's out-of-control doughnut maker, these six tales will long be remembered. Sequel: *Centerburg Tales.* Related books: *Good Old Boy* (n); *The Great Brain* (n); and *Soup* (s).

I Was a Rat!
BY PHILIP PULLMAN: KEVIN HAWKES, ILLUS.
Grades 3–5   *175 pages*
Dell, 2002
This is pure melodramatic parody and a slapstick adventure as only Philip Pullman can offer it. From the first chapter when a nameless and homeless boy knocks on the door of a childless couple at 10 P.M. and declares he used to be a rat, the reader-listener is hooked. And you stay that way as Pullman pulls you through a series of madcap chapters filled with threatening (but not too threatening) sewers, asylums, schools, jails, laboratories, courtrooms, and carnivals, all populated by Dickensian characters, kind and cruel. There's

a newly crowned princess (who used to be a chargirl, but reminds me a bit of a certain Diana we once knew) and the boy who used to be a rat but was recruited to be a coachman for a certain coach that used to be a pumpkin. One might say this is *Stuart Little Meets Cinderella* as written by Dickens and Roald Dahl. Other fairy tale parodies, page 290.

Ida Early Comes Over the Mountain

BY ROBERT BURCH
Grades 2–6   *145 pages*
Viking, 1980
During the Great Depression, an ungainly young woman shows up to take over the household chores for Mr. Sutton and his four motherless children. The love that grows between the children and the unconventional Ida is, like her tall tales, a joyous experience. She has been rightly described as a "Mary Poppins in the Blue Ridge Mountains." Sequel: *Christmas with Ida Early.* Also by the author: *Queenie Peavy;* three of the author's best and earliest works are back in print through the University of Georgia Press: *Skinny; Tyler, Wilkin, and Skee;* and *D.J.'s Worst Enemy.*

In the Year of the Boar and Jackie Robinson

BY BETTE BAO LORD
Grades 1–5   *169 pages*
Harper, 1984
Over the course of the year 1947, we watch a nine-year-old Chinese immigrant girl as she and her family begin a new life in Brooklyn. Told with warmth and humor and based on the author's own childhood, Shirley Temple Wong's cultural assimilation will ring true with any child who has had to begin again—culturally or socially. To know this little girl is to fall in love with her—and her neighbors and classmates. (One of the students in Bette Bao Lord's childhood classroom was the future children's novelist Avi.)

Incident at Hawk's Hill

BY ALLAN W. ECKERT
Grades 6 and up   *174 pages*
Little, Brown, 1971
An extremely timid six-year-old who wandered away from his family's farm in 1870 is adopted by a ferocious female badger, à la Mowgli in *The Jungle Books.* The boy is fed, protected, and instructed by the badger through the summer until the family manages to recapture the now-wild child. Definitely for experienced listeners. When reading this aloud, paraphrase a large

portion of the slow-moving prologue. In the sequel, *Return to Hawk's Hill,* young Ben is again missing, this time adrift in a canoe in Indian territory among the feared Cree. Related books: *Hatchet* (n) and *My Side of the Mountain* (n).

The Indian in the Cupboard (series)

BY LYNNE REID BANKS
Grades 2–6   *182 pages*
Doubleday, 1981
A witty, exciting, and poignant fantasy tale of a nine-year-old English boy who accidentally brings to life his three-inch plastic American Indian. Once the shock of the trick wears off, the boy begins to realize the immense responsibility involved in feeding, protecting, and hiding a three-inch human being from another time (1870s) and culture. Anyone concerned about the political correctness of the series may feel relieved by reading the review by Native American author Michael Dorris in the *New York Times Book Review* (May 16, 1993). Sequels: *Return of the Indian; The Secret of the Indian; The Mystery of the Cupboard;* and *The Key to the Indian.*

Inventing Elliot

BY GRAHAM GARDNER
Grades 9 and up   *181 pages*
Dial, 2004
Whenever national or corporate scandals occur, the question invariably arises, "What took so long for someone to blow the whistle?" As investigators dig deeper, they often find the corruption began not in adulthood but in adolescence. This rich and disturbing first novel describes the web that entangles a fourteen-year-old boy at an English high school. He's new, having come from another school where he'd been singled out for physical abuse by the reigning clique. At this new school, he's determined to be anonymous among the hundreds of other students. But soon he's spotted by a secret society of boys who rule the school with a reign of terror, right under the noses of a dedicated faculty. When the boys invite Elliot to join their society, he realizes this time it's "inclusion" instead of "exclusion." Joining would certainly secure his safety but it would also destroy whatever self-worth he has. This is the chasm faced every day by "whistle-blowers" in all walks of life. Without revealing the ending, I must report that it concludes on a very hopeful but suspenseful note. *Caution:* Readers-aloud should be aware there is brief sexual innuendo along with graphic violence, though not gratuitous. Related books: *Killing Mr. Griffin* (n); *Plague Year* (n); and *Scorpions* (n).

James and the Giant Peach

BY ROALD DAHL

Grades K–6   *120 pages*
Knopf, 1961

Four-year-old James, newly orphaned, is sent to live with his abusive aunts and appears resigned to spending his life as their humble servant. Then a giant peach begins growing in the backyard. Waiting inside that peach is a collection of characters that will captivate your audience as they did James. Few books hold up over six grade levels as well as this one does, and few authors for children understand their world as well as Dahl did. Also by the author: *The BFG; Danny, the Champion of the World* (n); *Fantastic Mr. Fox; Matilda; The Minpins; The Wonderful Story of Henry Sugar;* and *The Roald Dahl Treasury,* which contains the best collection of his work.

Jason's Gold

BY WILL HOBBS

Grades 4 and up   *240 pages*
Harper, 1999

One of the most promising young authors of adventure tales for young adults, Will Hobbs appears to be the heir-apparent to Gary Paulsen. In this book, Hobbs's most decorated novel to date, we follow a fifteen-year-old boy as he joins the rush for gold in the Klondike. The vivid historical and social details of the period are all there, along with an excellent blend of fictional adventure. Sequel: *Down the Yukon.* Related books: *The Call of the Wild* (n) and *White Fang* by Jack London. Also by the author: *Beardance; Bearstone; Downriver;* and *Far North.*

Journey to the River Sea

BY EVA IBBOTSON

Grades 4–7   *299 pages*
Viking Penguin, 2001

In 1910, we find Maia, a wealthy orphan girl, residing at the Mayfair Academy for Young Ladies, a setting very reminiscent of Frances Hodgson Burnett's *Sara Crewe* or *A Little Princess.* When Maia's legal guardian informs her that a worldwide search has produced her only living relatives (her father's second cousin and his family, including twin daughters her age) who live on a rubber plantation in the Amazon, her imagination takes flight. The opportunity to see the world's largest river, to explore the exotic jungles of Brazil, to spend her childhood hours and dreams with twin cousins—it's a young girl's dream come true.

Wrong, of course. The plantationed Carters are deeply in debt, the father is a leach looking for Maia's inheritance, the wife is a shrew, and the twins are nothing short of vipers. Sounds like poor Sara Crewe, right? How Maia extricates herself from this predicament, with the aid of a mysterious Indian boy with a large British inheritance, a homesick child actor, and a host of savvy natives, makes for an old-fashioned melodrama that has you rooting out loud for Maia and hissing her relatives all the way down the Amazon. Also by the author: *The Star of Kazan* (n). Related books: all of Frances Hodgson Burnett's children's novels; *Riding Freedom* by Pam Muñoz Ryan; and *Understood Betsy* (n).

Kensuke's Kingdom
BY MICHAEL MORPURGO
Grades 3–5   *164 pages*
Scholastic, 2003
Because childhood can sometimes be a case of survival, children seem to gravitate to survival books, as proven by Paulsen's success with the *Hatchet* series (n). This volume ranks with the best of that genre, with nods to *The Cay* (n) and Daniel Defoe's *Robinson Crusoe*. Like *The Cay,* it has a World War II connection and there is a tiny island with two survivors, a boy and an old man who eventually form a powerful bond. But there the similarity ends, for Morpurgo has carved a unique tale that stands on its own eight feet (if you count the dog with the two people).

The boy, Michael, is twelve years old when he and his dog are washed overboard from the family's yacht and into the Coral Sea off Australia. Clinging to the dog and a soccer ball (a touch of Tom Hanks there), the boy is washed up on a tropical island. This island, while appearing uninhabited, has a host of animals, plants, and fish that might keep him alive. It also contains one old man—a very old and very angry Japanese man named Kensuke Ogawa, a navy doctor who has been on the island since the end of World War II. Initially, Kensuke was marooned there when his ship sank, but eventually he was there by choice, more than fifty-five years after his home in Nagasaki was bombed with one of the first atomic bombs. The rest is his story and Michael's. To say the tale is inspiring is a great understatement. Entwined with the modern survival story are issues of war and peace, brotherhood, family ties, art, nature, and hope. Related books: *Baseball Saved Us* by Ken Mochizuk (a story from the Japanese internment camps); *Robinson Crusoe* by Daniel Defoe (one of the Scribner Illustrated Classics series [abridged, thank you] and illustrated by N. C. Wyeth); and three books by Gary Paulsen: *The Foxman; Hatchet;* and *The Voyage of the Frog.* Also by the author: *The Amazing Story of Adolphus Tips; Private Peaceful; War Horse;* and *The War of Jenkins' Ear.*

Morpurgo is the author of more than ninety books; in 2003 he was named Children's Laureate of Britain. BBC School Radio offers interviews with prominent British authors, with children asking the questions. The questions are available online and the author's responses can be heard via RealAudio online at: www.bbc.co.uk/schoolradio/english/meettheauthors_prog03_michael_morpurgo.shtml. More information can be found in *Dear Mr Morpingo: Inside the World of Michael Morpurgo* (Wizard Books, UK) available by ordering through www.amazon.co.uk/.

The Kid Who Invented the Popsicle (nonfiction)

BY DON L. WULFFSON

Grades 1–5   *128 pages*
Puffin (paperback), 1999

Here are the true but little-known stories behind the invention of one hundred everyday items: animal crackers, aspirin, balloons, Band-Aids, barbed wire, baseball caps, blue jeans, doughnuts, Frisbee, miniature golf, marshmallows, phonograph, ice-cream sundae, supermarkets, and yo-yos. Since none of these items takes more than a page to describe, this is the kind of book you keep in the car to bring into restaurants to read while the family is waiting for the meal; it's also perfect for brief classroom fill-ins. Sequel: *The Kid Who Invented the Trampoline* (fifty more items). Related books: In *Girls Think of Everything,* Catherine Thimmeah tells the story of fifty-nine inventions by women, from dishwashers and diapers to fire escapes and windshield wipers; *Hooray for Inventors!* by Marcia Williams; *Marvelous Mattie* by Emily A. McCully; *Odd Boy Out: Young Albert Einstein* (p); and *So You Want to Be an Inventor?* by Judith St. George.

Killing Mr. Griffin

BY LOIS DUNCAN

Grades 7 and up   *224 pages*
Little, Brown, 1978

This young-adult novel offers a chilling dissection of peer pressure and group guilt. Because of the subject matter and occasional four-letter words, care should be used in its presentation. The story deals with five high school students who attempt to scare their unpopular English teacher by kidnapping him. When their carefully laid plans unravel toward a tragic catastrophe, they find themselves unable to handle the situation. For experienced listeners. Also by the author: *I Know What You Did Last Summer* and *On the Edge* (a). Related books: *Deathwatch* by Robb White; *Inventing Elliot* (n); *On My Honor* (s); *Plague Year* (n); and *Wolf Rider* (n).

The Land I Lost

BY HUYNH QUANG NHUONG

Grades 2–6   *126 pages*

Harper, 1982

Most American children today know Vietnam only as a word associated with a bitter war that divided the nation. The author of this remembrance grew up there, one of eight children in a farming family along a river, not far from the jungle. This is the dramatic and affectionate tale of how his tiny hamlet worked together to survive the constant assaults from wild animals and a climate that would destroy lesser souls. Each of the fifteen chapters is an adventure into a long-lost world. Sequel: *Water Buffalo Days.*

Lassie Come Home

BY ERIC KNIGHT

Grades 4 and up   *200 pages*

Henry Holt, 1940

This classic dog story reads so easily, the words ringing with such feeling, that you'll find yourself coming back to it year after year. As with many dog stories, there are the usual themes of loss, grief, courage, and struggle—but here they are taken to splendid heights. Set between the Scottish Highlands and Yorkshire, England, in the early 1900s, the novel describes the triumphant struggle of a collie to return the one hundred miles to her young master. Unfortunately, Hollywood and television have badly damaged the image of this story with their tinny, affected characterization. This is the original Lassie story. For a list of dog stories, see page 246.

Lily's Crossing

BY PATRICIA REILLY GIFF

Grades 3–6   *180 pages*

Delacorte/Dell, 1997

This coming-of-age novel focuses on the summer of 1944 and one feisty yet frightened young girl in a Long Island beach community. With her beloved father shipped overseas and her best friend moved away, Lily befriends a Hungarian refugee (Albert). Together they experience the great fears and small triumphs that keep children afloat during war years. Lily, reader and future writer, learns the hard way that tall tales, spun out of control, can become dangerous lies. And Albert finds in Lily a friend who will change his life forever. This is a multiple award-winner, including Newbery Honor. Related books: *Alan and Naomi* by Myron Levoy and *Because of Winn-Dixie* (n);

The Lion, the Witch, and the Wardrobe (Narnia series)

BY C. S. LEWIS

Grades 3–6

HarperCollins, 1950

186 pages

Four children discover that the old wardrobe closet in an empty room leads to the magical kingdom of Narnia—a kingdom filled with heroes, witches, princes, and intrigue. This is the most famous (but second) of seven enchanting books called the Chronicles of Narnia, which can be read as adventures or as Christian allegory. The series in chronological order: *The Magician's Nephew; The Lion, the Witch, and the Wardrobe; The Horse and His Boy; Prince Caspian; The Voyage of the "Dawn Treader"; The Silver Chair;* and *The Last Battle. The Land of Narnia* by Brian Sibley is an excellent guide to Narnia. Many reasonable comparisons have been made between the dual world of Narnia and the Harry Potter (n) books. See also *Martin the Warrior* (n).

Listening for Lions

BY GLORIA WHELAN

Grades 3–8

Harper, 2005

194 pages

From an outstanding writer of historical fiction comes this tale set in 1919 in British East Africa where thirteen-year-old Rachel had been living an idyllic life with her medical-missionary parents until the Great Flu Epidemic struck. Suddenly orphaned, Rachel ends up in the hands of two wealthy, plotting neighbors who have lost their own daughter to the flu. Their intention had been to send their daughter back to England in hopes her visit would move the heart of her grandfather—and then loosen his purse strings (he'd disowned the girl's ne'er-do-well father years ago). Now they're manipulating the grieving Rachel into posing as their deceased daughter and sending her off to grandfather's estate with the warning that any bad news could send the old man to his grave. In England, a wonderful relationship grows between the man and child, making it all the harder for her to tell him the truth. Reminiscent of *The Secret Garden* and *Little Lord Fauntleroy*, this tale of a plucky young lady is a delightful page-turner and character study. Related title: *The Star of Kazan* (n).

Loser

BY JERRY SPINELLI

Grades 4 and up

HarperCollins, 2002

218 pages

There are Donald Zinkoffs in every neighborhood, in every classroom, and in many if not most families. They go by a variety of names: bumbler, dope, klutz, loser. As Jerry Spinelli points out in the first chapter of *Loser,* these people are largely ignored by the outside world until one day somebody notices them and labels them. Not since *The Hundred Dresses,* Eleanor Estes' timeless novel (1944) of a poor girl's trial by classroom prejudice, has anyone grabbed this subject of the odd-child-out with such force. Zinkoff is not retarded, nor is he ADHD. He's just a little out of focus, not enough to send him to special education classes but enough to leave him without a best friend.

Donald also has a giant sense of humor. His appreciative laughter and choice of clothing send early warning signals to his first grade teacher. Just as important for this story, he is the son of loving but not overbearing parents. Indeed, it is their abiding, unconditional love (along with the affection of two master teachers) that allows the boy to grow a heart that abounds in exuberant love for everything and everyone around him. Spinelli's irreverent humor will have middle-grade readers doubled over (to say nothing of the adult who tries to read it aloud). It is the humor that pulls the reader through the first half of the book, each chapter provoking you to wonder what will come next. It is this humor that also prevents the story from becoming a tale of despair.

Spinelli writes that around fourth grade, children develop their "big kid eyes," eyes that notice things they missed with "little kid eyes." Twenty-seven classmates now turn their new big kid eyes to Zinkoff, and suddenly they see things they haven't seen before. Zinkoff had always been messy and giggly and slow. But now they notice. In light of efforts to make the school climate less hate-filled and more human-friendly (in the wake of Columbine-like events), this is a novel that will succeed on more than its formidable story and character. Related book: *A Corner of the Universe* by Anne Martin.

Lupita Mañana

BY PATRICIA BEATTY
Grades 4–8   *192 pages*
Harper, 2000

After the death of her father, thirteen-year-old Lupita emigrates illegally to the United States. In slums, under cover of night, in damp freight cars, across the desert, plucky Lupita—posing as a boy—learns the meaning of fear as immigration police haunt her thoughts night and day. Here is the hope and heartbreak of poor families everywhere. Related book: *When Jessie Came Across the Sea* (p).

Maniac Magee

BY JERRY SPINELLI

Grades 5–9

Little, Brown, 1990

184 pages

One of the most popular Newbery winners ever, this is the tale of a legendary twelve-year-old runaway orphan, athlete extraordinaire, who touches countless families and peers with his kindness and wisdom. Could he be a modern Huck Finn? The book deals with racism, homelessness, and community violence in a most effective, almost allegorical manner. Also by the author: *The Library Card; Loser; Space Station Seventh Grade; Star Girl;* and *Wringer.* Author studies: Spinelli's autobiography is one of the best of its kind: *Knots in My Yo-Yo String: The Autobiography of a Kid.* Related books: *Bud, not Buddy* (n); *No Promises in the Wind* by Irene Hunt; and *The Pinballs* (n).

Martin the Warrior (Redwall Series)

BY BRIAN JACQUES

Grades 4–7

Philomel, 1994

376 pages

The Redwall series is in the tradition of *The Hobbit,* but for younger readers. Built around an endearing band of courageous animals inhabiting an old English abbey, the books describe their fierce battles against evil creatures. There is high adventure galore, cliff-hanger chapter endings, gruesome behavior by evil outsiders, and rollicking fun. For experienced listeners. *Martin the Warrior* is a prequel, going back to the founding of the abbey, and should be read first, followed by *Redwall* and then the rest of the series. Related books: *Harry Potter and the Sorcerer's Stone* (n); *The Lion, the Witch, and the Wardrobe* (n). For grade 6 and up: *The Hobbit* by J. R. R. Tolkien. Brian Jacques' official Web site is www.redwall.org/dave/jacques.html.

The Midnight Fox

BY BETSY BYARS

Grades 4–6

Viking, 1968

160 pages

From the very beginning, young Tommy is determined he'll hate his aunt and uncle's farm where he must spend the summer. His determination suffers a setback when he discovers a renegade black fox. His desire to keep the fox running free, however, collides with his uncle's wish to kill it, and the novel builds to a stunning moment of confrontation and courage. For an excellent profile of the author, see Byars's children's autobiography, *The Moon and I.* Also by the author: *Cracker Jackson; The Keeper of the*

Doves (s); *The Pinballs* (n); *The SOS File;* and *Trouble River.* On the Web: www.betsybyars.com.

The Monster Garden

BY VIVIEN ALCOCK
Grades 3–6   *164 pages*
Houghton Mifflin, 1988
Young Frances has come into possession of a tiny glob of jelly, part of a chunk stolen by her brother from their father's laboratory. While the brother's jelly is useless, his sister's is sitting on a windowsill during an electrical storm—and something untoward happens. Dad's laboratory is involved in genetic engineering, and electrical shock from the storm is enough to bring the jelly to life, though not in a form humans can recognize. To complicate matters, the girl can't bring herself to tell anyone but some friends—in secret. But secrets are almost as hard to keep as a glob that keeps growing and growing. This is an excellent exploration of social and familial relationships, as well as the very topical subject of genetic engineering. Related book: *Mrs. Frisby and the Rats of NIMH* (n).

The Mouse and the Motorcycle

BY BEVERLY CLEARY
Grades K–2   *158 pages*
Morrow, 1965
When young Keith and his family check into a run-down motel one day, the mice in the walls are disappointed. They'd hoped for young children, messy ones who leave lots of crumbs behind. What Ralph S. Mouse gets instead is a mouse-size motorcycle. He and the boy guest become fast friends and embark on a series of hallway-to-highway escapades that make this tale a longtime favorite. Sequels: *Runaway Ralph* and *Ralph S. Mouse.* Also by the author: *Ramona the Pest* (n). Related books: *Poppy* (n) and *Stuart Little* (n).

Mr. Popper's Penguins

BY RICHARD AND FLORENCE ATWATER; ROBERT LAWSON, ILLUS.
Grades 2–4   *140 pages*
Little, Brown, 1938
When you add twelve penguins to the family of Mr. Popper, the house painter, you've got immense food bills, impossible situations, and a freezer full of laughs. The short chapters will keep your audience hungry for more. Related books: *Capyboppy* by Bill Peet; *Owls in the Family* (s); *Rabbit Hill* by Robert Lawson; and *The Water Horse* by Dick King-Smith.

Mr. Tucket (series)

BY GARY PAULSEN

Grades 2–8   *166 pages*

Dell, 1997

We meet fourteen-year-old Francis Tucket just after he's been captured by
an Indian raiding party while his family was heading to Oregon via wagon
train. In typical Paulsen fashion, Francis is not going to remain captive for
long but it'll take him five books to reach his destination by way of war,
starvation, and every imaginable threat on the American frontier. The series includes (in order): *Mr. Tucket; Call Me Francis Tucket; Tucket's Ride;
Tucket's Gold;* and *Tucket's Home.* All five books have been compiled into a
single large paperback, *Tucket's Travels.* These are a little more accessible for
a younger age than is *Hatchet* (n). For more on Paulsen, see *Hatchet* (n).

Mrs. Frisby and the Rats of NIMH

BY ROBERT C. O'BRIEN

Grades 4–6   *232 pages*

Atheneum, 1971

In this unforgettable fantasy–science fiction tale, we meet a group of rats
that has become superintelligent through a series of laboratory injections.
Though it opens with an almost fairy-tale softness, it grows into a taut and
frighteningly realistic tale. Two decades after its publication, the fiction
grows closer to fact with genetic engineering; see the December 27, 1982,
issue of *Newsweek,* "The Making of a Mighty Mouse," page 67. Sequels:
Racso and the Rats of NIMH and *R-T, Margaret, and the Rats of NIMH,* both
by Jane L. Conly (Robert C. O'Brien's daughter). Also by O'Brien: *The
Silver Crown.* Related book: *The Monster Garden* (n).

My Brother Sam Is Dead

BY JAMES LINCOLN COLLIER AND CHRISTOPHER COLLIER

Grades 5 and up   *251 pages*

Simon & Schuster, 1974

In this Newbery-winning historical novel, the inhumanity of war is examined through the experiences of one divided Connecticut family during the American Revolution. Told in the words of a younger brother, the
heartache and passions hold true for all wars in all times, and the authors'
balanced accounts of British and American tactics allow readers to come to
their own conclusions.

Related Revolutionary War books: *The Fighting Ground* by Avi; *Sarah
Bishop* (n); and *Toliver's Secret* (s). Related war books: *Otto of the Silver Hand*
(n); and *The Rifle* and *Soldier's Heart,* both by Gary Paulsen.

My Side of the Mountain

BY JEAN CRAIGHEAD GEORGE
Grades 3–8   *178 pages*
Dutton, 1959

A modern teenage Robinson Crusoe, city-bred Sam Gribley describes his year surviving as a runaway in a remote area of the Catskill Mountains. His diary of living off the land is marked by moving accounts of the animals, insects, plants, people, and books that helped him survive. For experienced listeners. Sequels: *On the Far Side of the Mountain; Frightful's Mountain;* and *Frightful's Daughter.* For other survival books, see *Hatchet* (n).

Nothing but the Truth: A Documentary Novel

BY AVI
Grades 7 and up   *177 pages*
Orchard, 1991

In this Newbery Honor winner, a ninth-grader decides to irritate his teacher until she transfers him to another class. But what begins benignly soon escalates into a slanderous attack on the teacher when parents, faculty, media, and school-board members join the conflict. In the end, everyone loses. Told exclusively through documents like memos, letters, and diary entries, this is a dramatic example of how freedom of speech can be abused. Also by the author: *The True Confessions of Charlotte Doyle* (n). Related books: *Inventing Elliot* (n); *Plague Year* (n); and *Tangerine* (n).

Nothing to Fear

BY JACKIE FRENCH KOLLER
Grades 4 and up   *279 pages*
Harcourt Brace, 1991

This is a good old-fashioned historical novel that grabs you right by the heart and throat for 279 pages. Set in the Depression, it follows the travails and triumphs of a poor Irish family—especially young Danny and his mother—as they try to hold on against all odds. This is a vivid depiction of life in the 1930s, but the acts of love and courage displayed by the Garvey family are repeated daily in many families wherever poverty abides. Related books: *Bud, Not Buddy* (n) and *No Promises in the Wind* by Irene Hunt.

Number the Stars

BY LOIS LOWRY
Grades 4–7   *137 pages*
Houghton Mifflin, 1989

In 1943, as the occupying Nazi army attempted to extricate and then exterminate the seven thousand Jews residing in Denmark, the Danish people rose up as one in a determined and remarkably successful resistance. Against that backdrop, this Newbery winner describes a ten-year-old Danish girl joining forces with her relatives to save the lives of her best friend and her family. *Darkness Over Denmark* by Ellen Levine is an excellent nonfiction companion to this book, with photos of Denmark and the resistance fighters; the popular novel *Snow Treasure* by Marie McSwigan is about Norwegian children smuggling gold past the Nazis. See also *The Little Ships* and *The Greatest Skating Race*, both by Louise Borden. Author profile online at http:www.loislowry.com/. If you have the free RealAudio plug-in, you can hear a one-hour online interview with the author on the *Diane Rehm Show*, May 22, 2003: http:wamu.org/programs/dr/03/05/22.php.

Otto of the Silver Hand

BY HOWARD PYLE

Grades 5–8   132 pages

Dover, 1967

First published in 1888 and written by one of the leading figures of early American children's literature, this is an ideal introduction to the classics. Intended as a cautionary tale about warfare (and inspired by the wounded Union soldiers he saw on railroads during the Civil War), Pyle's story describes a young boy's joy and suffering as he rises above the cruelty of the world, while caught between warring medieval German tribes. Though the language may be somewhat foreign to the listener at the start, it soon adds to the flavor of the narrative. For experienced listeners. Related books: *Castle Diary* by Richard Platt, the year-long diary of a young page serving in the castle of his uncle in 1285 (a large picture book with rich text and illustrations describing everyday life), and *Matilda Bone* by Karen Cushman, about a female apprentice bonesetter in a medieval village.

Peppermints in the Parlor

BY BARBARA BROOKS WALLACE

Grades 3–7   198 pages

Atheneum, 1980

When the newly orphaned Emily arrives in San Francisco, she expects to be adopted by her wealthy aunt and uncle. What she finds instead is a poverty-stricken aunt held captive as a servant in a shadowy, decaying home for the aged. Filled with Dickensian flavor, this novel has secret passageways, tyrannical matrons, eerie whispers in the night, and a pair of fearful but plucky kids. Sequel: *The Perils of Peppermints*. Following the success of this book, the author produced four more in the same genre:

Cousins in the Castle; Ghosts in the Gallery; The Twin in the Tavern; and *Sparrows in the Scullery.*

The Pinballs
BY BETSY BYARS
Grades 5–7   *136 pages*
Harper, 1977
Brought together under the same roof, three foster children prove to each other and the world that they are not pinballs to be knocked around from one place to the next; they have a choice in life—to try or not to try. The author has taken what could have been a maudlin story and turned it into a hopeful, loving, and very witty book. Short chapters with easy-to-read dialogue. Related books: *Bud, Not Buddy* (n); *A Family Apart* (n); *Maniac Magee* (n); and *No Promises in the Wind* by Irene Hunt.

Plague Year
BY STEPHANIE S. TOLAN
Grades 7 and up   *198 pages*
Fawcett, 1991
When Bran arrives in his aunt's neatly manicured middle-class town, his clothes, hair style, and manner make him the immediate target of the high school's "jock" crowd. That he can handle, but a month later a tabloid newspaper announces his secret—that his father is about to go on trial in New Jersey as an accused serial killer. Suddenly, the town is consumed by Bran's presence and the danger this "bad seed" poses for its children, and mob mentality takes over for common sense and justice. Reading like today's headlines, it is fast-paced, thought-provoking, and offers powerful examples of all that is good and bad in school and community. Related books: *Inventing Elliot* (n); *Nothing But the Truth* (n); and *Tangerine* (n).

Poppy (series)
BY AVI
Grades K–4   *160 pages*
Orchard, 1995
A great horned owl keeps the growing deer mice population in Dimwood Forest under his fierce control like an evil dictator, eating those who dare to disobey his orders. When he kills her boyfriend, little Poppy dares to go where no mouse has gone before—to the world beyond Dimwood. Indeed, she uncovers the hoax the evil owl has perpetrated through the years and leads her frightened family to the promised land. Told with wit and high drama, this is an excellent start to the "Tales from Dimwood Forest"

that have followed: *Poppy and Rye; Ragweed; Ereth's Birthday;* and *Poppy's Return.* Older fans of this series will enjoy *Martin the Warrior* (n); younger fans *Charlotte's Web* (n).

Ramona the Pest (series)

BY BEVERLY CLEARY
Grades K–4   *144 pages*
Morrow, 1968
Not all of Beverly Cleary's books make good read-alouds, though children love to read her silently. Some of her books move too slowly to hold read-aloud interest, but that's not the case with the Ramona series, which begins with *Ramona the Pest.* The book follows this outspoken young lady, who was a forerunner of Junie B. Jones with a better grasp of grammar, through her early months in kindergarten. Children will smile in recognition of Ramona's encounters with the first day of school, show-and-tell, seat work, a substitute teacher, Halloween, young love—and dropping out of kindergarten. Long chapters can easily be divided. Early grades should have some experience with short novels before trying Ramona. The sequels follow Ramona as she grows older and, with her family, experiences the challenges of modern life: *Ramona and Her Father; Ramona and Her Mother; Ramona Quimby, Age 8; Ramona Forever;* and *Ramona's World.* Also by the author: *Dear Mr. Henshaw* (n); *The Mouse and the Motorcycle* (n); and for preschoolers: *Two Times the Fun* (s).

Roll of Thunder, Hear My Cry (series)

BY MILDRED TAYLOR
Grades 5 and up   *276 pages*
Dial, 1976
Filled with the lifeblood of a black Mississippi family during the Depression, this Newbery winner depicts the pride of people who refuse to give in to threats and harassments from white neighbors. The story is narrated by daughter Cassie, age nine, who experiences her first taste of social injustice and refuses to swallow it. Along with her family, her classmates, and neighbors, she will stir listeners' hearts and awaken many children to the tragedy of prejudice and discrimination. For experienced listeners. *Caution:* There are several racial epithets used in the dialogue. Other books in the series: *The Land* (a prequel to *Roll of Thunder*); *Let the Circle Be Unbroken; The Road to Memphis;* and four short novels, *The Friendship* (s); *Mississippi Bridge; Song of the Trees;* and *The Well.* Also by the author: *The Gold Cadillac.*

Related nonfiction titles: *Christmas in the Big House, Christmas in the*

Quarters by Patricia and Fredrick McKissack; *Delivering Justice* by Jim Haskins; *Molly Bannaky* (n); *Getting Away with Murder: The True Story of the Emmett Till Case* by Chris Crowe; *More Than Anything Else* (Booker T. Washington learns to read) by Marie Bradby; and *Rosa Parks: My Story* by Rosa Parks.

Roll of Thunder, Hear My Cry is an excellent introduction to the American Civil Rights movement, something that now can be turned into a multimedia experience. Consider the wide array of options available for *Roll of Thunder:*

Newspaper: The March 31, 1999, issue of *Education Week* carries the story of a Colorado fourth-grade class studying slavery, and how their highly publicized subsequent investigation revealed frightening modern-day slavery in "Sudan: Liberating Lesson" by Linda Jacobson, *Education Week,* pages 22–24 (www.edweek.org/ew/articles/1999/03/31/29sudan.h18.html?querystring=Linda_20Jacobson).

Video recommendations: *Once Upon a Time . . . When We Were Colored* is an affectionate look back at life in a black Mississippi neighborhood from the mid-1940s to the dawn of the civil rights movement, based on the autobiographical novel by Clifton Taubert. See also *4 Little Girls,* Spike Lee's acclaimed 1997 documentary about the turning point in the civil rights movement—the bombing of the 16th Street Baptist Church, and *The Untold Story of Emmett Louis Till,* Keith A. Beauchamp's documentary film about one of the most horrific murders in the civil rights era (for grades 7 and up).

Audio: See Duke University's oral history project composed of the memories of those who lived in the segregated South: "Behind the Veil." Different portions of that collection can be heard (using RealAudio's free plug-in) on the Internet at American RadioWorks' "Remembering Jim Crow." The RadioWorks site also includes excellent slide shows of images taken during the period: see http:www.americanradioworks.org/features/remembering/index.html. Two years before the famed bus boycott in Montgomery, Alabama, black citizens in Baton Rouge, Louisiana, staged what's believed to be the first-ever organized protest of Jim Crow laws in the South: see http:www.npr.org/templates/story/story.php?storyId=1304304. On the fortieth anniversary (August 28, 2003) of the civil rights march on Washington, Minnesota Public Radio devoted two hours to the event, including a rebroadcast of the entire sixteen-minute "I Have a Dream" speech, which originally was supposed to be only four minutes long, and Pulitzer Prize–winning historian Roger Wilkins's powerful recollections of MLK the man, not the icon: all are at: http:news.minnesota.publicradio.org/programs/midday/listings/md20030825.shtml. *Say It Plain* is a sixty-minute anthology of African American political oratory designed for the ear and the eye, including recordings that range from Booker T. Washington and Marcus Garvey to Martin Luther King Jr. and Barack Obama. (See American RadioWorks: http:americanradioworks. publicradio.org/features/sayitplain/index.html.)

The Ruby in the Smoke (series)

BY PHILIP PULLMAN

Grades 5 and up 230 pages
Laurel Leaf (paperback), 1988

Not one to take himself too seriously despite his many awards, Pullman will produce a fairy tale parody (*I Was a Rat!*) one minute and a heart-stopping thriller like this the next. His own description of the Sally Lockhart series goes like this: "Historical thrillers, that's what these books are. Old-fashioned Victorian blood-and-thunder. Actually, I wrote each one with a genuine cliché of melodrama right at the heart of it on purpose: the priceless jewel with a curse on it, the madman with a weapon that could destroy the world, the situation of being trapped in a cellar with the water rising, the little illiterate servant girl from the slums of London who becomes a princess."

The Ruby in the Smoke contains one of the great read-aloud openings. In 1872 on a cold October afternoon in the London financial district, a young girl steps out of a hansom cab and into the second paragraph: "She was a person of sixteen or so—alone, and uncommonly pretty. She was slender and pale, and dressed in mourning, with a black bonnet under which she tucked back a straying twist of blond hair that the wind had teased loose. She had unusually dark brown eyes for one so fair. Her name was Sally Lockhart; and within fifteen minutes, she was going to kill a man."

There is absolutely no chance of your attention wandering after that. *Note:* It is Sally's *question* that will kill the man (heart attack). These books are for experienced listeners.

The Sally Lockhart quartet: *The Ruby in the Smoke; The Shadow in the North; The Tiger in the Well;* and *The Tin Princess.* Related books: *The December Rose* by Leon Garfield and *The Case of the Baker Street Irregular* by Robert Newman. More on the author online at: www.philip-pullman.com.

Rules of the Road

BY JOAN BAUER

Grades 6 and up 201 pages
Putnam/Puffin, 1998

Jenna Boller is a savvy sixteen-year-old salesgirl at a Chicago shoe store when she is spotted by the crusty matriarch of the shoe chain and given an unusual summer job; driving her from Chicago to Dallas. Considering Jenna just got her driver's license, this is no small challenge. Along the way, they visit various stores in the chain, assess the strengths and weaknesses of each, and discover that the shoe company is the object of a takeover bid by a cheapskate rival chain. In Dallas, the bid comes to a head and Jenna's courage—something she honed while coping all her life with an alcoholic father—comes to the rescue. The "rules of the road," as applied here, are the rules of life, family, and business that keep us balanced when unexpected curves appear. This is a wise, witty, and moving novel that has deservedly won awards and praise. Sequel: *Best Foot Forward.* Also by the author: *Hope Was Here.*

Sarah Bishop

BY SCOTT O'DELL
Grades 5 and up   *184 pages*
Houghton Mifflin, 1980
Based on a historic incident, this is the story of a determined young girl who flees war-torn Long Island after her father and brother are killed at the outbreak of the Revolutionary War. In the Connecticut wilderness, she takes refuge in a cave, where she begins her new life. *Sarah Bishop* makes an interesting comparative study with two other read-aloud novels dealing with children running away, *Slake's Limbo* (n) and *My Side of the Mountain* (n). Each depicts the subject of the "runaway" at a different point in history. For experienced listeners. O'Dell's stories often focus on independent, strong-willed young women. For related Revolutionary War titles, see *My Brother Sam Is Dead* (n).

Scorpions

BY WALTER DEAN MYERS
Grades 7 and up   *216 pages*
Harper, 1988
This award-winning novelist has drawn upon his childhood in Harlem to give us a revealing and poignant look at an African American family facing the daily pressures of urban poverty. While seventh-grader Jamal Hicks struggles to resist the pressures to join a neighborhood gang, he is watching his family being torn apart by the crimes of an older brother and a wayward father. Moreover, his relationship with school is disintegrating under a combination of his own irresponsibility and an antagonistic principal. Unable to resist the peer pressure, Jamal makes a tragic decision involving a handgun. Readers-aloud should be aware that some of the book's dialogue is written in black dialect.

In 1993, NPR gave a tape recorder to two boys living in Chicago public housing and allowed them to produce a documentary eventually called *Ghetto Life 101*. Several years later, the two boys again recorded life in their projects, this time after a five-year-old had been hurled to his death from a fourteenth-floor window by two other young children. If ever there was audio to add another dimension to Myers's urban novel *Scorpions*, these two NPR programs are it. They can still be heard online at: http:www.sound-portraits.org/on-air/remorse/.

Author study: *Bad Boy, a Memoir.* You can also listen via the Internet to a one-hour interview with the author (*Diane Rehm Show,* July 7, 2004) at: http:www.wamu.org/programs/dr/04/07/01.php. Related books: *Gun-stories: Life-Changing Experiences with Guns* by S. Beth Atkin; *Killing Mr. Griffin* (n); and *Twelve Shots: Outstanding Short Stories About Guns,* collected by Harry Mazer.

The Secret Garden
BY FRANCES HODGSON BURNETT
Grades 2–5   240 pages
Numerous publishers
Few books spin such a web of magic about their audiences as does this 1911 children's classic about the sulky orphan who comes to live with her cold, unfeeling uncle on the windswept English moors. Wandering the grounds of his immense manor house one day, she discovers a secret garden, locked and abandoned. This leads her to discover her uncle's invalid child hidden within the mansion, her first friendship, and her own true self. While this is definitely for experienced listeners, try to avoid the abridged versions, since too much of the book's flavor is lost in those. Also by the author: *Little Lord Fauntleroy; A Little Princess*; and *The Lost Prince.* Two recent books by Eva Ibbotson are so reminiscent of Burnett's genre, you'd almost think she'd come back from the dead: *The Star of Kazan* (n) and *Journey to the River Sea* (n). Other books: *Mandy* by Julie Edwards and *Understood Betsy* (n).

Sideways Stories from Wayside School
BY LOUIS SACHAR
Grades 2–5   124 pages
Random House, 1990
Thirty chapters about the wacky students who inhabit the thirtieth floor of Wayside School, the school that was supposed to be built one story high and thirty classes wide, until the contractor made a mistake and made it thirty stories high! If you think the building is bizarre, wait until you meet

the kids who inhabit it. Sequels: *Wayside School Is Falling Down* and *Wayside School Gets a Little Stranger.* Also by the author: *Holes* (n); *Johnny's in the Basement;* and *There's a Boy in the Girls' Bathroom.* Other humorous books: *Skinnybones* (s); *The Best Christmas Pageant Ever* (s); and *Tales of a Fourth-Grade Nothing* (n).

The Sign of the Beaver

BY ELIZABETH GEORGE SPEARE
Grades 3 and up   *135 pages*
Houghton Mifflin, 1983
This is the story of two boys—one white, the other American Indian—and their coming of age in the Maine wilderness during the Colonial period. It is also a study of the awkward relationship that develops when the starving white boy is forced to teach the reluctant Indian to read in order for both of them to survive. Related books on the relationship between white settlers and Indian neighbors: *Encounter* (p); *Return to Hawk's Hill* by Allan W. Eckert; *Sing Down the Moon* by Scott O'Dell (n); and *Weasel* (n).

Slake's Limbo

BY FELICE HOLMAN
Grades 5–8   *117 pages*
Atheneum, 1984
A fifteen-year-old takes his fears and misfortunes into the New York City subway one day, finds a hidden construction mistake in the shape of a cave near the tracks, and doesn't come out of the underground system for 121 days. The story deals simply but powerfully with the question, Can anyone be an island unto himself? It is also a story of survival, personal discovery, and the plight of today's homeless. This book makes interesting comparative study with three other books that discuss running away, hiding, and personal discovery: *Inventing Elliot* (n); *My Side of the Mountain* (n); and *Sarah Bishop* (n).

Sour Land

BY WILLIAM H. ARMSTRONG
Grades 4–8   *116 pages*
Harper, 1971
This is the little-known sequel to the Newbery-winning *Sounder,* and a better read-aloud. Here we meet the unnamed boy from *Sounder,* now grown, teaching in a small black school, maintaining his decency and dignity while the lethal shadow of racism lurks in the corner. For related books, see *Roll of Thunder, Hear My Cry* (n).

Space Race (series)

BY SYLVIA WAUGH

Grades 2–5 $\qquad$ *241 pages*

Delacorte/Dell, 2000

It's a bit sad that some truly worthy books were overlooked in the hulla-baloo over Harry Potter, and this is a case in point. In its simplest terms, it is the story of a pair of aliens from the planet Ormingat, eleven-year-old Thomas Derwent and his father. They are just completing an undercover five-year research visit to earth where they assumed the appearance and ways of earthlings and spent this idyllic time in a contemporary English village. Their next-door neighbor has informally adopted and cared for them in grandmotherly fashion. Under such circumstances, it's little won-der that Thomas is heartbroken when his father informs him that their mission is complete and it's time to return "home." His parting from his best friend, Mickey, and the neighbor are touching and believable, though neither has any idea of the family's real identity. Yet Thomas has been pre-pared for their eventual return and is resigned to its inevitability.

It is inevitable because their spaceship is timed to leave earth on exactly December 26, no sooner, no later. Exactly. If they were to miss it—well, that's never happened in 250 years of exploration. What neither father nor son anticipates is a traffic accident on their way to the ship (and a third of the way into the book). It separates the pair, landing Thomas in the hospi-tal where he fakes trauma and shock symptoms while waiting for some kind of dramatic rescue by his father. His father, meanwhile, has been ren-dered the size of an insect, and the accident's impact has flattened him atop the roof of a speeding car. Recovering from that, he must find his buried spaceship and await instructions from Ormingat as to if, how, and when he should rescue his son. The second volume, *Earthborn,* is about a twelve-year-old girl and her alien family, followed by the final volume, *Who Goes Home?*

One small cautionary note for classroom readers-aloud: On page 66, there is a pair of four-letter words ("damn" and "hell") uttered in desper-ation by the driver of the truck involved in the accident. Later in the book there are several very reverent references to God, so perhaps they balance each other out—if such things are of concern.

The Star of Kazan

BY EVA IBBOTSON

Grades 2–5 $\qquad$ *405 pages*

Dutton, 2004

If you've been yearning for the good, solid, old-fashioned storytelling that made *The Secret Garden* and *Anne of Green Gables* the favorites of devoted readers for a century, look no further than this book.

Near the turn of the last century in Austria and Germany, a young girl is being raised by two maiden Austrian housekeepers who discovered her as an abandoned baby in a church. Young Annika now lives with them in the house where they work for three finicky professors. It's an idyllic life for all, though the child does dream that someday her mother will return to claim the child she misplaced.

And then the great upheaval: the woman who had abandoned the child twelve years earlier arrives to claim her. Frau Edeltraut von Tannenberg is as aristocratic and snobby as her name implies but she is, after all, the mother Annika has dreamed of all her life. Simply put, Annika's dream has come true, and her adopted family's worst nightmare has come with it. Heartbroken at her departure, her Austrian family reassures themselves that it is best for the child. After all, in her mother's huge German estate she will be able to enjoy all the luxuries they could never afford to give her. But all is not what it appears, and the ensuing chapters are filled with disappointments, deceits, cruel relatives, sheltering servants, buried treasure, scheming lawyers, loyal friends, and perilous last-minute rescues.

One of Ibbotson's favorite tools is foreshadowing and she plants intriguing clues in chapters that usually end with a cliff-hanger. Ibbotson also offers a clear sense of the creeping infection called nationalism that would envelope Germany in the coming years and lead to two world wars.

An integral part of both the setting and the plot is the world famous Lipizzaner stallions and their home at the Spanish Riding School of Vienna. Several Web sites offer colorful views of the animals and their training: www.lipizzaner.com/Intro.asp and www.lipizzaner.at/index2.html.

To hear a BBC interview with the author, go online to: www.bbc.co.uk/schoolradio/english/meettheauthors_prog02_eva_ibbotson.shtml. Also by the author: *Journey to the River Sea* (n). Related books: all of Frances Hodgson Burnett's children's books and *Understood Betsy* (n).

Stormbreaker (series)

BY ANTHONY HOROWITZ

Grades 5–8   *234 pages*

Philomel, 2000

When fourteen-year-old Alex Rider is informed that his bachelor uncle/guardian has died in an auto accident, he's understandably distressed. But he's also perplexed by the news that he wasn't wearing his seatbelt—something he was fanatical about wearing. He's even more confused when two men show up at the funeral wearing loaded shoulder holsters under their jackets. Why guns at a bank manager's funeral? Before long his questions bring him into Britain's top-secret intelligence agency, and he may not make it out alive. As someone has noted elsewhere, if James Bond had a kid-relative, it would have been Alex Rider. This first book in a fast-paced, increasingly popular series by Horowitz has, like most thrillers, a certain amount of violence, though none of it gratuitous, and far tamer than you'd find in an Arnold Schwarzenegger film. Books like this don't produce Newbery Awards but they're very likely to produce a kid who likes to read at least as much as he likes to play video games. For an excellent five-minute BBC interview with the author (complete with video), look online at: http: news.bbc.co.uk/1/hi/programmes/breakfast/4415169.stm. Sequels: *Point Blank; Skeleton Key; Eagle Strike; Scorpia;* and *Ark Angel.* Also by the author: *Raven's Gate.* Related book: Gordon Korman's On the Run series.

Stuart Little

BY E. B. WHITE
Grades K–3   *130 pages*
Harper, 1945

Stuart is a very, very small boy (two inches) who looks exactly like a mouse. This leaves him at a decided disadvantage living in a house where everyone else is normal size, including the family cat. White's first book for children, it is filled with beautiful language and lots of adventures as Stuart struggles to find his way in the world—an important job for all children, even if they don't look like a mouse. *Stuart Little* is such a good book that even though the most influential librarian in the United States tried to block its publication, it's still around more than sixty years later. Also by the author: *Charlotte's Web* (n). Related books: *The Mouse and the Motorcycle* (n) and the Dimwood Forest tales by Avi, beginning with *Poppy* (n). For older listeners: the Redwall series by Brian Jacques (see *Martin the Warrior* [n]).

Tales from the Homeplace

BY HARRIET BURANDT AND SHELLEY DALE
Grades 3–6   *154 pages*
Dell, 1999

Family is one thing we all have in common. It can be a great resource for stories. In that tradition comes this collection of nine true episodes about a family of eight children and their parents, living on the Texas plains in the midst of the Depression. Besides family, though, you must have a story, a conflict or challenge, and this collection has that and more. These are strong people who must withstand the torments of the Texas climate and economy in hard times. The events recounted here come mainly from the stories passed down to Harriet Burandt from her mother and relatives who are the eight children in the book, and each tale is self-contained and riveting. Take, for instance, the first chapter in which Irene escorts her siblings to the creek for a swim while their parents are away for the day. She always had to be stern with them, but on this day she'll need more than strictness when she spies a mountain lion lurking in the bushes while they swim.

Tales of a Fourth-Grade Nothing

BY JUDY BLUME
Grades 3–5   *120 pages*
Dutton, 1972
A perennial favorite among schoolchildren, this novel deals with the irksome problem of a kid brother whose hilarious antics complicate the life of his fourth-grade brother, Peter. Sequels: *Otherwise Known as Sheila the Great; Superfudge* (caution: *Superfudge* deals with the question, Is there a Santa Claus?); *Fudge-a-Mania;* and *Double Fudge.* Also by the author: *Freckle Juice.*

Tangerine

BY EDWARD BLOOR
Grades 6 and up   *294 pages*
Harcourt Brace, 1997
To call this a sports novel (though it certainly is that) is to ignore its wide range of topics: prejudice, evil, repressed memories, corruption, ecology, botany, and good old academic bureaucracy. Add those topics to the friendships developed on the athletic field and you've got a remarkable first novel by Mr. Bloor, who has spent years in the classroom with adolescents— and it shows. The book does start a bit slowly for a read-aloud, so you'll need to give it thirty pages or so. By then, the pattern of seventh-grader Paul Fisher's life and family appear in bold relief: a commandeering mother, a father who lives exclusively through the high school football exploits of his oldest son, Erik, and Erik himself—a dark figure who moves through the corners of Paul's life like someone carrying a hand grenade with a loose pin. Side note: the Florida tourism office will not be recommending this book. Related book: *Inventing Elliot* (n); *Killing Mr. Griffin* (n); and *Plague Year* (n).

Thank You, Jackie Robinson

BY BARBARA COHEN
Grades 5–7   *126 pages*
Lothrop, 1988

In the late 1940s, we meet young Sam Green, a rare breed known as the True Baseball Fanatic and a Brooklyn Dodger fan. His widowed mother runs an inn, and when she hires a sixty-year-old black cook, Sam's life takes a turn for the better. The two form a fast friendship and begin to explore the joys of baseball in a way the fatherless boy has never known. A tender book that touches on friendship, race, sports, personal sacrifice, and death. Related books: *Finding Buck McHenry* (n); *In the Year of the Boar and Jackie Robinson* (n); *Teammates* by Peter Golenbock; and an excellent paperback series by Dan Gutman about a boy who time travels using his baseball cards, including *Jackie and Me.*

Thunder Cave

BY ROLAND SMITH
Grades 4–8   *250 pages*
Hyperion, 1997
For "buckle-your-seatbelts" adventure, this one ranks with the best. After the sudden death of his mother, fourteen-year-old Jacob (half Hopi Indian) makes his way to Kenya, Africa, in search of his father, a biologist studying elephant behavior in a remote area. Along the way, he masters the fine art of international politics (with Kenyan immigration officials); survives a trio of local thugs who beat him unconscious, strip him to his underwear, and steal his mountain bike; and encounters a Kenyan brush fire, a marauding lion, and a life-threatening bout of diarrhea.

Thanks to the author's background knowledge of African and exotic animals, the twists are handled quite plausibly. He also connects the wandering boy to a Masai witch doctor (college graduate with a degree in philosophy) who offers an excellent study in similarities between American Indian and Masai cultures. *Caution:* Jacob occasionally utters an expletive— nothing integral to the story, but be prepared. The book received national social studies citations. Sequels: *Jaguar* and *The Last Lobo.* Related book: *Listening for Lions* (n).

Toliver's Secret

BY ESTHER WOOD BRADY
Grades 3–5   *166 pages*
Crown, 1988
During the Revolutionary War, ten-year-old Ellen Toliver is asked by her ailing grandfather to take his place and carry a secret message through British lines. What he estimates to be a simple plan is complicated by Ellen's exceptional timidity and an unforeseen shift by the British. The book becomes a portrait of Ellen's personal growth—complete with a heart-stopping

crisis in each chapter. Related books: *The Little Ships* and *The Greatest Skating Race,* both by Louise Borden.

The True Confessions of Charlotte Doyle

BY AVI

Grades 4 and up   *215 pages*

Orchard, 1990

Winner of a Newbery Honor medal, this is the exciting tale of an obstinate thirteen-year-old girl who is the lone passenger aboard a merchant ship sailing from England to the United States in 1832. The crew is bent on mutiny, the captain is a murderer, and within weeks the girl is accused of murder, tried by captain and crew, and sentenced to hang at sea. Avi is at his finest with this "first-person" adventure, exploring history, racism, feminism, and mob psychology.

Other books by Avi: *The Barn;* the Beyond the Western Sea series; I—*The Escape from Home* and II—*Lord Kirkle's Money; Crispin: Cross of Lead; Good Dog; Nothing But the Truth* (n); *Poppy* (n); *The Secret School;* and *Wolf Rider* (n). Avi's Web site: www.avi-writer.com. Listen to a one-hour interview with Avi online at: http:news.minnesota.publicradio.org/programs/midmorning/listings/mm20040621.shtml (scroll to June 22, 2004, second hour).

Tuck Everlasting

BY NATALIE BABBITT

Grades 4–7   *124 pages*

Farrar, Straus & Giroux, 1975

A young girl stumbles upon a family that has found the "fountain of youth," and in the aftermath there is a kidnapping, a murder, and a jailbreak. This touching story suggests a sobering question: What would it be like to live forever? For experienced listeners. Also by the author: *Search for Delicious.*

The Twenty-One Balloons

BY WILLIAM PÈNE DU BOIS

Grades 4–6   *180 pages*

Viking, 1947

This long-ago Newbery winner is a literary smorgasbord; there are so many different and delicious parts one hardly knows which to mention first. The story deals with a retired teacher's attempts to sail by balloon across the Pacific in 1883, his crash landing and pseudo-imprisonment on the island of Krakatoa, and, finally, his escape. The book is crammed with nuggets of science, history, humor, invention, superior language, and marvelous artwork. For experienced listeners.

Understood Betsy

BY DOROTHY CANFIELD FISHER

Grades 2–5
Henry Holt, 1999

229 pages

Written in 1917 by one of America's most celebrated writers, this is the classic story of a timid, almost neurotic orphan child (Betsy) being raised by her overprotective city-dwelling aunts. Then a family illness requires the child be sent to live with "stiff-necked" rural relatives in Vermont and she must stand on her own two feet, do chores, and speak for herself—all of which causes a heart-warming metamorphosis. As a novel, even as a psychological or historical profile, the book is enormously successful. One of its original intentions was to promote the Montessori method of education at the beginning of the twentieth century. Related books: *Journey to the River Sea* (n); *Listening for Lions* (n); *Mandy* by Julie Edwards; *The Secret Garden* (n); and *The Star of Kazan* (n).

Weasel

BY CYNTHIA DEFELICE

Grades 2–6
Atheneum, 1990

119 pages

Set in Ohio in 1839, this realistic look at the American frontier focuses on a widower and his two children as they confront racism, violence, and the elements. Most of the challenge comes in the person of Weasel, a former government "Indian fighter" who captures both father and son. A fast-paced, first-person adventure story, it also describes the plight of the American Indian and America's own "ethnic cleansing." Also by the author: *The Apprenticeship of Lucas Whittaker.* Related books: *Buffalo Knife; Flaming Arrows; Perilous Road;* and *Winter Danger,* all by William O. Steele; and *The Sign of the Beaver* (n).

A Week in the Woods

BY ANDREW CLEMENTS

Grades 3–6
Simon & Schuster, 2002

190 pages

Once again, the author proves himself a master of the school setting. Here he gives us a fifth-grade nature trip into the woods, a wealthy know-it-all new kid in town, and a science teacher. The teacher is a decent, hard-working man but he's not perfect. And sometimes when you've been in a business for twelve years and you're the best at what you do, you're tempted to think you know it all. It's an easy trap to fall into. This teacher, who thinks he's seen all kinds of kids, thinks he's got the new kid figured out perfectly and that what the kid needs is a hard lesson or two.

The teacher may be an expert at reading kids' behavior, but he's misread this child's heart. In resolving the conflict, Clements gives us a solid dose of outdoor survival tips, as well as tips on how classmates might make the life of newcomers a lot easier. For other books by the author, see *Frindle* (s).

When the Tripods Came (Tripods series)

BY JOHN CHRISTOPHER

Grades 5 and up   *151 pages*

Dutton, 1988

An updating of H. G. Wells's *The War of the Worlds,* this is the prequel to one of modern science fiction's most popular juvenile series: The Tripods. When invaders from space take over earth and begin implanting brain-control devices among the humans, a group of rebellious teens lay the groundwork for the invaders' destruction. The series includes (in order): *The White Mountains; The City of Gold and Lead;* and *The Pool of Fire.* Related book: *City of Ember* (n).

Where the Red Fern Grows

BY WILSON RAWLS

Grades 3 and up   *212 pages*

Doubleday, 1961

A ten-year-old boy growing up in the Ozark mountains, praying and saving for a pair of hounds, finally achieves his wish. He then begins the task of turning the hounds into first-class hunting dogs. It would be difficult to find a book that speaks more definitively about perseverance, courage, family, sacrifice, work, life, and death. The long chapters are easily divided, but bring a box of tissues for the final ones. Also by the author: *Summer of the Monkeys.* The author's recitation of his life story ("Dreams Can Come True") is available on audiocassette; for details, see www.trelease-on-reading.com/rawls.html. For other dog books, see page 246.

Wolf Rider: A Tale of Terror

BY AVI

Grades 7 and up   *224 pages*

Aladdin, 2000

This is breathtaking, plausible, and compelling reading and my first recommendation for "reluctant-reader" teens. When fifteen-year-old Andy accidentally receives a random phone call from a man claiming he's killed a college coed, nobody believes him. And when everyone writes it off as a prank, Andy sets out to find the anonymous caller in a race against death and the clock. Read any version of "The Boy Who Cried Wolf" before reading aloud this book. *Caution:* There is a small number of expletives in the text. For other books about and by Avi, see *The True Confessions of Charlotte Doyle* (n). Related books: *Inventing Elliot* (n); *Killing Mr. Griffin* (n); and *Plague Year* (n).

The Wonderful Wizard of Oz
BY L. FRANK BAUM
Grades 1 and up   *260 pages*
Numerous publishers
Before your children are exposed to the movie version, treat them to the magic of this 1900 book, which many regard as the first American fairy tale as well as among our earliest science fiction. (Incidentally, the book is far less terrifying for children than the film version.) The magical story of Dorothy and her friends' harrowing journey to the Emerald City is but the first of many books about the Land of Oz. Among those sequels, one is regarded as the best—*Ozma of Oz*. Author study: Michael Patrick Hearn's *The Annotated Wizard of Oz: The Centennial Edition* (Norton, 2000) and *L. Frank Baum: Creator of Oz* by Katharine M. Rogers (St. Martin's, 2002). On the Web: www.eskimo.com/~tiktok/index.htm.

Woodsong
BY GARY PAULSEN
Grades 5 and up   *132 pages*
Simon & Schuster, 1990
Using the same tension he infuses into his novels, the author gives us a nonfiction journal about living off the land while training a dog team for the Iditarod. Powerful and breathtaking nonfiction—but not for the faint of heart or weak-stomached. Also by the author: *My Life in Dog Years*, reminiscences of his favorite dogs. For other Paulsen titles, see *Hatchet* (n); for more dog stories, see page 246.

The Year of Miss Agnes
BY KIRKPATRICK HILL
Grades 2–5   *128 pages*
Aladdin, 2002
Set in a remote and impoverished Alaskan bush village in 1948, this heartwarming story is told through the eyes of a ten-year-old Athabascan village girl (Fred), who watches as the new school teacher arrives. Everyone assumes that Miss Agnes will leave like the rest have. After all, how could she

stand the smell? They're wrong, of course. She stays and takes over not just the one-room schoolhouse but also the hearts of everyone in the village, including Fred's deaf sister who's never been to school. Out go all the old ways and in come records, pictures from all over the world, maps, and a Robin Hood read-aloud—anything to inspire learning in the bush. You'll be surprised by how Alaskan village kids can relate to Sherwood Forest. Miss Agnes demonstrates that programs don't teach, teachers do, and what an example she is! Also by the author: *Toughboy and Sister* and *Winter Camp*, a survival story.

Poetry

The Cremation of Sam McGee

BY ROBERT W. SERVICE; TED HARRISON, ILLUS.

Grades 4 and up   30 pages
Greenwillow, 1987

Once one of the most memorized poems in North America, this remains the best description of the sun's strange spell over the men who toil in the North. After seeing this edition, you will find it difficult to hear the words without picturing Harrison's artwork. Also by the author and illustrator: *The Shooting of Dan McGrew.* Two excellent collections of Service's poetry: *Best Tales of the Yukon* (Running Press) and *Collected Poems of Robert Service* (Dodd). Related title: *Once Upon a Tomb: Gravely Humorous Verses* by J. Patrick Lewis.

Danitra Brown, Class Clown

BY NIKKI GRIMES; E. B. LEWIS, ILLUS.

Grades 4–7   32 pages
HarperCollins, 2005

One of today's most acclaimed poets, Grimes uses fourteen short poems to trace the school year for two African American friends, touching the highs and lows for the pair who are as different as night and day in their outlooks. The title comes from the poem in which Zuri passes a note that is intercepted by a boy and read aloud to the class. Danitra knew this would be more embarrassment than Zuri could stand, so she immediately jumped up and acted like a clown in front of the class, offering just enough distraction to save her friend. This volume is the substance of friendship and childhood for middle graders.

Jim's Favorite Stories in Rhyming Verse
(in order of complexity)

The Neighborhood Mother Goose
  by Nina Crews
Over in the Meadow
  by Olive A. Wadsworth
Over in the Garden
  by Jennifer Ward
Chicka Chicka Boom Boom
  by Bill Martin, Jr.
The Napping House
  by Audrey Wood
The Wheels on the Bus
  by Maryann Kovalski
*This Is the House That Was Tidy
  and Neat*
  by Teri Sloat
The Foot Book
  by Dr. Seuss
Duck in a Truck
  by Jez Alborough
Sheep in a Jeep
  by Nancy Shaw
Jesse Bear, What Will You Wear?
  by Nancy White Carlstrom
The Day the Babies Crawled Away
  by Peggy Rathman
Shoe Baby
  by Joyce Dunbar

Snip Snap! What's That?
  by Mara Bergman
Madeline
  by Ludwig Bemelmans
Micawber
  by John Lithgow
Here Come the Aliens!
  by Colin McNaughton
Where's My Teddy?
  by Jez Alborough
*Timothy Cox Will Not Change
  His Socks*
  by Robert Kinerk
The Recess Queen
  by Alexis O'Neill
Kermit the Hermit
  by Bill Peet
If I Ran the Zoo
  by Dr. Seuss
The Friend
  by Sarah Stewart
Casey at the Bat
  by Ernest L. Thayer, illustrated
  by C. F. Payne
Who Swallowed Harold?
  by Susan Pearson

Honey, I Love
BY ELOISE GREENFIELD; DIANE AND LEO DILLON, ILLUS.
Grades PreS–3   *42 pages*
Harper, 1976
Sixteen short poems about the things and people children love: friends, cousins, older brothers, keepsakes, mother's clothes, music, and jump ropes.

Set against an urban background, the poems elicit both joyous and bitter-sweet feelings.

If You're Not Here, Please Raise Your Hand: Poems About School
BY KALLI DAKOS; G. BRIAN KARAS, ILLUS.

Grades 1–8   64 pages

Simon & Schuster, 1990

As a classroom teacher, Kalli Dakos has been down in the trenches with all the silliness, sadness, and happiness of elementary school. Can't you tell just from the title? Also by the author: *Don't Read This Book Whatever You Do! More Poems About School.* Related books: *I Thought I'd Take My Rat to School: Poems for September to June,* selected by Dorothy M. Kennedy; *Lunch Money and Other Poems About School* by Carol D. Shields; *Somebody Catch My Homework* and *A Thousand Cousins,* both by David L. Harrison.

I Invited a Dragon to Dinner and Other Poems to Make You Laugh Out Loud
CHRIS L. DEMAREST, ILLUS.

Grades PreS–2   32 pages

Philomel, 2002

In this zany collection of twenty-three original poems (by different authors), there is a dragonload of fun. In between the opening poem about a mouse family that overruns the house and the closing poem about a little girl's bedtime prayer, there are dining dragons, crazy mothers, a scary attic, an invisible guest, the biggest sandwich in the world, detestable vegetables, the girl who swallowed a squirrel, and the tickle that went out of control.

The New Kid on the Block
BY JACK PRELUTSKY; JAMES STEVENSON, ILLUS.

Grades K–4   160 pages

Greenwillow, 1984

One of the most prolific poets for children, Prelutsky has collected more than a hundred of his most outrageous and comical characters, attempting simply to amuse and please children—which he does, for example, with a poem about the taken-for-granted blessings of having your nose on your face instead of in your ear, and the one about Sneaky Sue who started playing hide-and-seek a month ago and still can't be found. Also by the author: *The Dragons Are Singing Tonight; It's Raining Pigs and Noodles; Nightmares: Poems to Trouble Your Sleep; A Pizza the Size of the Sun;* and *The Random House Book of Poetry for Children* (page 285) and *Read-Aloud Rhymes for the Very Young* (po).

The Random House Book of Poetry for Children

SELECTED BY JACK PRELUTSKY; ARNOLD LOBEL, ILLUS.
Grades K–5   *248 pages*
Random House, 1983
One of the best children's poetry anthologies ever, showing that poet Jack
Prelutsky recognizes the common language of children. The 572 selected
poems (from both traditional and contemporary poets) are short—but long
on laughter, imagery, and rhyme. They are grouped into fourteen categories
that include food, goblins, nonsense, home, children, animals, and seasons.

Read-Aloud Rhymes for the Very Young

COLLECTED BY JACK PRELUTSKY; MARC BROWN, ILLUS.
Grades Tod–K   *88 pages*
Knopf, 1986
Here are more than two hundred little poems (with full-color illustrations)
for little people with little attention spans, to help both to grow.

Timothy Cox Will Not Change His Socks

BY ROBERT KINERK; STEPHEN GAMMELL, ILLUS.
Grades K–2   *30 pages*
Simon & Schuster, 2005
One thing about Timothy: when he sets his mind, there's no changing it.
So when he decides not to change his socks for a month, it quickly becomes a contest of wills between Timothy and classmates, teachers, town
officials, neighbors, pets, police, and even firefighters. Told in rhyming verse
that is reminiscent of Dr. Seuss (like Horton, Timothy is faithful to his
word 100 percent), Timothy's experience also becomes a learning experience for him and the reader (don't waste your time and energy on something as trivial as socks). Related book: *Horton Hatches the Egg* by Dr. Seuss.

Where the Sidewalk Ends

BY SHEL SILVERSTEIN
Grades K–8   *166 pages*
Harper, 1974
Without question, this is the best-loved collection of poetry for children,
selling more than two million hardcover copies in twenty-five years. When
it comes to knowing children's appetites, Silverstein was pure genius. The
titles alone are enough to bring children to rapt attention: "Bandaids"; "Boa
Constrictor"; "Crocodile's Toothache"; "The Dirtiest Man in the World";
and "Recipe for a Hippopotamus Sandwich." Here are 130 poems that will

either touch childen's hearts or tickle their funny bones. Also by the author: *A Light in the Attic* and the short novel *Lafcadio, the Lion Who Shot Back* (s). Listen to a fifty-minute memorial tribute to Silverstein on NPR's *Talk of the Nation* (May 11, 1999), online at: http:discover.npr.org/features/feature. jhtml?wfId=1049873.

Anthologies

Does God Have a Big Toe?

BY MARC GELLMAN
Grades 1–7   *88 pages*
Harper, 1989
Along with being a mother lode of wisdom and inspiration, the Bible has been a rich source of literature and inspiration for those who look for the common thread of story in all life. Because the Bible lends itself to diverse interpretations, scholars often create stories of their own to explain it. In this case, Rabbi Marc Gellman has taken twenty biblical episodes and given us twenty midrashim—"new stories about old stories." Its success is largely due to Gellman's wit and the reverence he maintains throughout. Sequel: *God's Mailbox: More Stories About Stories in the Bible.* Also: *How Do You Spell God? Answers to the Really Big Questions from Around the World* by Rabbi Marc Gellman and Monsignor Thomas Hartman.

Guys Write for Guys Read

EDITED BY JON SCIESZKA; ASSORTED ILLUSTRATORS
Grades 4 and up   *227 pages*
Viking, 2005
A few years ago, popular children's author Jon Scieszka (*The True Story of the Three Little Pigs* [p]) founded a Web site (www.guysread.com) devoted to motivating boys to read more. He then solicited other male writers to write short pieces (few go more than two to three pages) about "guy stuff," stories that boys really enjoy. There are ninety-two pieces here, from the ridiculous to the sublime, from sports to music, fiction and nonfiction, excerpted from books and magazines, text and cartoons—it's all here, complete with body sounds and smells, mixed with a heavy syrup of humor. Related books: *Grossology: The Science of Really Gross Things!* by Sylvia Branzei; *The Secret Knowledge of Grown-ups* (p); and *Uncle John's Bathroom Reader for Kids Only!* (a).

Hey! Listen to This: Stories to Read Aloud

BY JIM TRELEASE

Grades K–4   *410 pages*
Penguin, 1992

Here are forty-eight read-aloud stories from the top authors of yesterday and today. Arranged in categories such as school days, food, families, folk and fairy tales, and animals, the selections include entire chapter excerpts as well as complete stories. There are also full-page biographical profiles of the authors. Also by the author: *Read All About It!* (a), an anthology for grades five and older, and *The Read-Aloud Handbook*. On the Web: www. trelease-on-reading.com/hey.html.

Never Cry "Arp!"

BY PATRICK MCMANUS

Grades 4 and up   *133 pages*
Henry Holt, 1996

Patrick McManus has long been breaking up readers of *Outdoor Life,* and this collection of essays on his wilderness and camping adventures expertly displays his funny-bone talents. You could say he's the Dave Barry of the outdoors. If you can read the first two pages of this book with a straight face, you'll hate the book. Related books: *The Secret Knowledge of Grown-ups* (p) and *Guys Write for Guys Read* (a).

On the Edge

EDITED BY LOIS DUNCAN

Grades 9 and up   *211 pages*
Simon & Schuster (paperback), 2001

In this third volume of taut psychological tales for teens (*Night Terrors* and *Trapped!*), the acclaimed novelist Lois Duncan offers a dozen original short stories from some of today's best young-adult writers, each dealing with young people teetering on the brink of something. They are ideal for reading aloud to this age group but certainly not for the timid. Certainly one objective of a collection like this is to whet students' appetites for more and this accomplishes that, provoking a genuine hunger for more writings by these authors. Duncan herself has written some of the very best in the psycho-thriller genre, including: *I Know What You Did Last Summer; Killing Mr. Griffin;* and *Ransom*.

Paul Harvey's "The Rest of the Story"

BY PAUL HARVEY JR.
Grades 6 and up   *234 pages*
Bantam, 1978
This collection of essays from broadcaster Paul Harvey's five-minute radio show, *The Rest of the Story,* is perfect for teachers and parents trying to win older students to the art of listening. Nearly all of these pieces deal with famous people, past and present. The person's name is saved for the last few lines of the tale and serves as an O. Henry–type punch line. The eighty-one stories average four minutes in length. Sequel: *More of Paul Harvey's "The Rest of the Story."*

Read All About It!

BY JIM TRELEASE
Grades 5 and up   *487 pages*
Penguin, 1993
For parents and teachers at a loss for what to read to preteens and teens, here are fifty selections—from classics to newspaper columns, fiction and nonfiction, humor and tragedy. Each story is introduced by a biographical profile of the author—like "Whatever Happened to Harper Lee?" (*To Kill a Mockingbird*). Also by the author: *Hey! Listen to This* (a), an anthology for grades K–4, and *The Read-Aloud Handbook.* On the Web: www.trelease-on-reading.com/aai.html.

Scary Stories to Tell in the Dark

COLLECTED BY ALVIN SCHWARTZ; STEPHEN GAMMELL, ILLUS.
Grades 5 and up   *112 pages*
Lippincott, 1981
Dipping into the past and the present, the author presents twenty-nine American horror stories and songs guaranteed to make your listeners cringe. The text includes suggestions for the reader-aloud on when to pause, when to scream, even when to turn off the lights. The selections run the gamut from giggles to gore and average two pages in length. In addition, a source section briefly traces each tale's origin in the United States. (Discretion is advised because of the subject matter.) Sequels: *More Scary Stories to Tell in the Dark* and *Scary Stories 3: More Tales to Chill Your Bones.*

Uncle John's Bathroom Reader for Kids Only!

BY THE BATHROOM READERS INSTITUTE

Grades 3–7   *324 pages*

Bathroom Readers Press

Crude as the title may sound, this book's contents more than make up for it. I've been a fan of this series since it started with adult editions (more than six at last count) and it's a delight to see the editors recognize the importance of *young* bathroom readers. To be honest about the title, this is an even better bedroom or kitchen table reader. Consider the variety covered in this edition: ubiquitous "body music" articles (burps and hiccups); the truth behind Aesop's fables, the Pony Express, the "dollar," yo-yos, popsicles, snowboards, Sylvester and Tweety, Bugs Bunny, and Little League; amazing kids' accomplishments; the history of bathrooms; toys that flopped; everything you ever needed to know about lightning. Got the idea? My bookstore had numerous editions, but not in the children's section; look for it in Humor/Reference. On the Web: www.bathroomreader.com.

Fairy and Folk Tales

Household Stories of the Brothers Grimm

TRANSLATED BY LUCY CRANE; WALTER CRANE, ILLUS.

Grades 2 and up   *269 pages*

Dover (paperback), 1963

This collection of fifty-three tales contains the Grimms' most popular works in a translation that is easily read aloud and includes more than one hundred illustrations. The maturity and listening experience of your audience should determine its readiness to handle the subject matter, complexity of plot, and language of these unexpurgated versions.

Individual Grimm volumes: *The Elves and the Shoemaker,* retold by Freya Littledale; *The Four Gallant Sisters,* retold by Eric A. Kimmel; *Hansel and Gretel,* retold by Rika Lesser; *Iron Hans,* illustrated by Marilee Heyer; *Rapunzel,* retold by Barbara Rogasky; *Rose Red and the Bear Prince,* retold by Dan Andreasen; *Rumpelstiltskin,* retold by Paul O. Zelinski; *Seven in One Blow,* retold by Eric A. Kimmel, *Sleeping Beauty,* retold by Trina Schart Hyman; and *Snow White & Rose Red,* illustrated by Gennady Spirin.

Jim's Favorite Fairy Tale Parodies

Beware of Boys
  by Tony Blundell
Cinder-elly
  by Frances Minters
Cindy Ellen: A Wild Western
  Cinderella
  by Susan Lowell
The Cowboy and the
  Black-eyed Pea
  by Tony Johnson
Folklore and Fairy Tale
  Funnies
  edited by A. Spiegelman and
  F. Mouly (comic book)
The Giant and the Beanstalk
  by Diane Stanley
Goldie and the Three Bears
  by Diane Stanley
Goldilocks Returns
  by Lisa Campbell Ernst
Humphrey, Albert, and the
  Flying Machine
  by Kathryn Lasky
I Was a Rat
  by Philip Pullman (novel)
Jim and the Beanstalk
  by Raymond Briggs
The Jolly Postman
  by Janet and Allan Ahlberg
Kate and the Beanstalk
  by Mary Pope Osborne
Little Red Riding Hood:

A Newfangled Prairie Tale
  by Lisa C. Ernst
The Paper Bag Princess
  by Robert Munsch
The Principal's New Clothes
  by Stephanie Calmenson
Rumpelstiltskin's Daughter
  by Diane Stanley
Scuttle's Big Wish
  by Sean and Ryan Delonas
Sleeping Ugly
  by Jane Yolen
Somebody and the Three Blairs
  by Marilyn Tolhurst
Tales from the Brothers Grimm and
  the Sisters Weird
  by Vivian Vande Velde
  (short stories)
The Three Little Rigs
  by David Gordon
The Three Little Wolves and the
  Big Bad Pig
  by Eugene Trivizas
The True Story of the Three Little
  Pigs
  by John Scieszka
The Ugly Truckling
  by David Gordon
The Wolf Who Cried Boy
  by Rob Hartman
The Wolf's Story
  by Toby Forward

Mightier Than the Sword: World Folktales for Strong Boys

COLLECTED AND TOLD BY JANE YOLEN

Grades 3–6   *100 pages*

Harcourt Brace, 2003

Folktale expert Jane Yolen offers fourteen tales from around the world, each demonstrating that male heroes can overcome adversity by using their wits instead of their swords.

The People Could Fly: American Black Folktales

BY VIRGINIA HAMILTON; LEO AND DIANE DILLON, ILLUS.

Grades 3–6   *174 pages*

Knopf, 1985

Rich with rhythm, energy, and humor, these twenty-four stories were kept alive by slave tellers and include Bruh Rabbit, Gullah, and freedom-trail adventures. Related book: *Tales of Uncle Remus,* retold by Julius Lester.

Rapunzel

ADAPTED BY PAUL O. ZELINSKY

Grades 1–4   *32 pages*

Dutton, 1997

Of all the fairy tale picture books in the marketplace, this is perhaps the most lushly illustrated and thus deserving its Caldecott Medal. Borrowing from both the Grimms and previous versions from France and Italy, Zelinsky's retelling might make it the best of all, especially when coupled with his Italian Renaissance oil illustrations of the fair damsel locked in the tower by the evil sorceress. No other illustrator has captured as many Caldecott honors as Zelinksy, including runner-up awards for *Hansel and Gretel; Rumpelstiltskin;* and *Swamp Angel.*

Red Ridin' in the Hood and Other Cuentos

BY PATRICIA SANTOS MARCANTONIO; RENATO ALACAO, ILLUS.

Grades 4 and up   *181 pages*

Farrar, Straus & Giroux, 2005

When the author was growing up as a Mexican American in Colorado, she loved the traditional fairy tales but mourned the absence of Latino culture in them. She solved that problem by writing these eleven versions as though they were set in the barrio itself. The title story, "Red Ridin' in the Hood," has a contemporary urban-Latino setting; Roja's mother has dispatched her with food for her ill *abuelita* (grandmother), along with instructions to wear the new red dress her *abuelita* made for her, to take the bus, and to avoid

Forest Avenue. Instead, the daughter saves the bus fare and travels down Forest Avenue where a brown low-rider Chevy begins to follow her. Very well written, these tales are closer to the Grimms' versions than Disney's, and the illustrations are not for the meek. My personal favorite is "Juan and the Pinto Bean Stalk," in which the irresponsible Juan, wearing baggy pants and a bandana, wants to do nothing but watch TV.

The Serpent Slayer and Other Stories of Strong Women

BY KATRIN TCHANA; TRINA SCHART HYMAN, ILLUS.

Grades 3–6   *105 pages*

Little, Brown, 2000

This handsome collection of eighteen fairy tales from around the world focuses on heroines and is handsomely illustrated by one of the most talented Caldecott winners.

Tales from the Brothers Grimm and the Sisters Weird

BY VIVIAN VANDE VELDE

Grades 6 and up   *128 pages*

Harcourt Brace, 1995

The author takes thirteen traditional fairy tales, turns them on their heads, and spins them with a grand and sometimes dark sense of humor. Thus she gives us a Hansel and Gretel who deserved to be baked to a crisp, while part of the problem for Jack (of beanstalk fame) was his hangover!

Tatterhood and Other Tales

BY ETHEL JOHNSTON PHELPS

Grades 2 and up   *174 pages*

Feminist Press, 1979

An excellent collection of fast-moving tales with witty, resourceful, and confident heroines (not heroes) from different cultures.

Notes

Introduction

1. Michael Winerip, "Off to College, Perfect Score in Hand," *New York Times,* August 20, 2003.
2. Claudia Wallis, "How to Make a Better Student," *Time,* October 19, 1998, pp. 78–96.
3. June Kronholz, "Preschoolers' Prep," *Wall Street Journal,* July 12, 2005, pp. B1, B4; also "Growing Tutoring Business in the U.S.," Part 1, *Morning Edition,* National Public Radio, June 6, 2005; also "Tutoring Industry Grows Due to No Child Left Behind Act," *Morning Edition,* National Public Radio, June 7, 2005; Mary C. Lord, "Little Scholars Big Business as More Parents Seek to Give Kids an Edge; Learning Centers Thrive," *Boston Globe,* April 10, 2005; and Susan Saulny, "A Lucrative Brand of Tutoring Grows Unchecked," *New York Times,* April 4, 2005, pp. A1, A19.
4. "Schools Drop Nap Time for Testing Preparation," Associated Press, *Atlanta Journal-Constitution,* October 3, 2003.
5. Dirk Johnson, "Many Schools Putting an End to Child's Play," *New York Times,* pp. A1, A16. The quote is from former Atlanta schools superintendent Benjamin O. Canada, who is also a former Portland, Oregon, superintendent.
6. The so-called Mozart effect is largely a myth and has nothing to do with improving IQ but rather with spatial-temporal reasoning; it was tested only on college students, and the effect wore off in ten to fifteen minutes. One of its chief researchers, Frances H. Rauscher, is amused by the mass misinterpretation of the Mozart data. See Ellen Winner and Lois Hetland, "The Arts and Academic Achievement: What the Evidence Shows," *Journal of Aesthetic Education* 20, no. 4 (1986): 6; and Mary Ann Zehr, "'Mozart Effect' Goes Only So Far, Study Says," *Education Week,* September 27, 2000. See also "Project Zero" at http://www.pzweb.harvard.edu/ and http://pzweb.harvard.edu/Research/Reap/REAPExecSum.htm.

7. "P. C. Watch," *New York Times,* Education, April 24, 2005, p. 7. After the assistant superintendent cancelled the event, community backlash forced its return, but this gives you an idea of how small a role logic plays when the government's shadow looms large. Once we could have expected such thoughts to emanate from Leningrad, but from Lincoln, Rhode Island?

8. Kate Zernike, "Ease Up, Top Universities Tell Stressed Applicants," *New York Times,* December 7, 2000, pp. A1, A29.

9. Anyone who thinks higher standards and high-stakes testing can eradicate poverty's effects on children's school scores is ignoring the best scientific research in education. In *Parsing the Achievement Gap: Baselines for Tracking Progress,* Paul E. Barton, a senior researcher at Educational Testing Service (ETS), the world's largest testing agency, examined the social factors that produced glaring differences in achievement between poor and advantaged children, gaps that are "not closed by either higher standards or a more rigorous curriculum." The seven areas are: parent participation, student mobility (household moves), lead (paint) poisoning, hunger and nutrition, reading to young children, television watching, and parent availability. Unless changes are made to these factors, test results will remain the same, no matter how high the standards, and no one has ever produced research to prove otherwise. (Paul E. Barton, *Parsing the Achievement Gap: Baselines for Tracking Progress* [Princeton, NJ: Educational Testing Service, 2003]). Researcher Gerald W. Bracey, like others, has always pointed to poverty as the main culprit in the achievement gap and impoverished children's low scores: "Poverty is not an excuse; it's a condition. Like gravity, it affects everything." Gerald W. Bracey, "The Trouble with Research, Part 2," *Phi Delta Kappan,* April 2004, pp. 635–36; see also Anahad O'Connor, "Rise in Income Improves Children's Behavior," *New York Times,* October 21, 2003, p. F5.

10. Jay Mathews, "Let's Have a 9-Hour School Day," *Washington Post,* August 16, 2005; online at http://www.washingtonpost.com/wp-dyn/content/article/2003/09/16/AR2005032304299.html.

11. Using weekdays, weekends, and summers, the KIPP charter schools extend the school day by 70 percent. See Caroline Hendrie, "KIPP Looks to Re-create School Success Stories," *Education Week,* October 30, 2002, p. 6; also Jay Mathews, "Study Finds Big Gains for KIPP Charter Schools Exceed Average," *Washington Post,* August 11, 2005.

12. Julian E. Barnes, "Unequal Education," *Newsweek,* March 29, 2004, pp. 67–75.

13. Lesley Mandel Morrow, "Home and School Correlates of Early Interest in Literature," *Journal of Educational Research,* vol. 76, March/April 1983, pp. 221–30.

14. Leonard Pitts Jr., "My First Reader Started Me Down Path to Award," *Miami Herald,* April 9, 2004; see also http://www.miami.com/mld/miamiherald/living/columnists/leonard_pitts/8390196.htm.

15. Jerry West, Kristin Denton, and Elvira Germino-Hausken, *America's Kindergartners: Findings from the Early Childhood Longitudinal Study, Kindergarten Class of 1998–99, Fall 1998,* Office of Educational Research and Improvement, NCES 2000-070 (Washington, DC: U.S. Department of Education, 2000).

16. Lawrence E. Gladieux and Watson Scott Swail, "Beyond Access: Improving the Odds of College Success," *Phi Delta Kappan,* May 2000, pp. 688–92.

17. Gerald W. Bracey, "April Foolishness: The 20th Anniversary of *A Nation at Risk,*" *Phi Delta Kappan,* April 2003, pp. 661–621; online at http://www.pdkintl.org/kappan/k0304bra.htm. See also Richard Rothstein, "America's National Crises, Both Real and Imagined," *New York Times,* October 10, 2001, p. A14.

18. Thomas L. Friedman, *The World Is Flat* (New York: Farrar, Straus & Giroux, 2005); Thomas L. Friedman, "It's a Flat World, After All," *New York Times Magazine,* April 3, 2005; also interview with Friedman, *Fresh Air,* National Public Radio, April 14, 2005; online at http://www.npr.org/templates/story/story.php?storyId=4600258.

19. Saritha Rai, "M.B.A. Students Bypassing Wall Street for a Summer in India," *New York Times,* August 10, 2005, pp. C1, C3.

20. Michael Wilson, "Butts in the Street? The Least of Their Problems," *New York Times,* August 10, 2005.

21. *Trends in Educational Equity of Girls and Women,* U.S. Department of Education (Washington, DC: National Center for Education Statistics, March 2000). See also Cornelius Riordan, "The Silent Gender Gap: Reading, Writing, and Other Problems for Boys," *Education Week,* November 17, 1999, pp. 46; Christina Hoff Sommers, "Where the Boys Are," *Education Week,* June 22, 1996, pp. 42, 52; Christina Hoff Sommers, "The War Against Boys," *Atlantic Monthly,* May 2000, pp. 59–74.

22. Peter Y. Hong, "A Growing Gender Gap Tests College Admissions," *Los Angeles Times,* November 21, 2004.

23. Alaina Sue Potrikus, "Report Shows Academic Achievement Gap Between Girls, Boys," Knight Ridder Newspapers, September 19, 2003. To review a summary of the OECD's report on the male slide, "Education at a Glance, 2003," go to: http://www.oecdwash.org/PUBS/BOOKS/RP034/rp034ed.htm.

24. She told me I could quote her; her name was Nita Epting.

25. Clyde C. Robinson, Jean M. Larsen, and Julia H. Haupt, "Picture Book Reading at Home: A Comparison of Head Start and Middle-Class Preschoolers," *Early Education and Development,* vol. 6, no. 3, July 1995, pp. 241–52.

26. Janelle M. Gray, "Reading Achievement and Autonomy as a Function of Father-to-Son Reading" (Master's thesis, California State University, Stanislaus, CA, 1991). Since the gender gap appears to be international in scope, many nations are studying the issue. England's National Literacy Trust devotes a section of its Web site to the latest research (from preschool to secondary, including U.S. material)—valuable downloadable information worth sharing in school newsletters at www.literacytrust.org.uk/Research/Fatherreviews.html.

27. Mary A. Foertsch, *Reading In and Out of School,* Educational Testing Service/Education Information Office (Washington, DC: U.S. Department of Education, May 1992).

28. Richard C. Anderson, Elfrieda H. Hiebert, Judith A. Scott, and Ian A. G. Wilkinson, *Becoming a Nation of Readers: The Report of the Commission on Reading,* U.S. Department of Education (Champaign-Urbana, IL: Center for the Study of Reading, 1985). See also Diane Ravitch and Chester Finn, *What Do Our 17-Year-Olds Know?* (New York: Harper & Row, 1987).

29. "Students Cite Pregnancies as a Reason to Drop Out," Associated Press, in *New York Times,* September 14, 1994, p. B7.

30. Jennifer Cheeseman Day and Eric C. Newburger, *The Big Payoff: Educational Attainment and Synthetic Estimates of Work-Life Earnings,* Current Population Reports, (Washington, DC, U.S. Census Bureau, 2002); online at: http://www.census.gov/prod/2002pubs/p23-210.pdf. See also Melissa Lee, "When It Comes to Salary, It's Academic," *Washington Post,* July 22, 1994, p. D1. The Census Bureau reports the following lifetime earnings:

No high school diploma: $609,000
High school diploma: $821,000
Some college: $993,000
Associate's degree: $1,062,000
Bachelor's degree: $1,421,000
Master's degree: $1,619,000
Doctorate: $2,142,000
Profession—doctor, lawyer: $3,013,000

31. The following chart appeared in the ACT's data report for the 2004 test taken by 1.2 million college applicants, and shows that as family income increases, the student's scores rise commensurately (http://www.act.org/news/data/05/pdf/data.pdf). The highest possible ACT score is 36.

Estimated Family Income	Average Score
Less than $18,000	17.9
$18,000–$24,000	18.6
$24,000–$30,000	19.3
$30,000–$36,000	19.8
$36,000–$42,000	20.3
$42,000–$50,000	20.9
$50,000–$60,000	21.3
$60,000–$80,000	21.9
$80,000–$100,000	22.5
More than $100,000	23.5

See also "Trends in Reading Scores by Parents' Highest Level of Education" in M. Perie, R. Moran, and A. D. Lutkus, *NAEP 2004 Trends in Academic Progress: Three Decades of Student Performance in Reading and Mathematics,* U.S. Department of Education, Institute of Education Sciences, National Center for Education Statistics (Washington, DC: Government Printing Office, 2005), pp. 36–38.

32. Eugene Rogot, Paul D. Sorlie, and Norman J. Johnson, "Life Expectancy by Employment Status, Income, and Education in the National Longitudinal Mortality Study," *Public Health Reports,* vol. 107, July–August 1992, pp. 457–61; see also Jack M. Guralnik et al., "Educational Status and Active Life Expectancy Among Older Blacks and Whites," *New England Journal of Medicine,*

July 8, 1993, pp. 110–16; E. Pamuk et al., *Health, United States, 1998: Socio-economic Status and Health Chartbook* (Hyattsville, MD: National Center for Health Statistics, 1998); Janny Scott, "Life at the Top in America Isn't Just Better, It's Longer: Three Heart Attacks, and What Came Next," *New York Times,* May 16, 2005, pp. A1, A14, A15; and Robert Pear, "Researchers Link Income Inequality to Higher Mortality Rates," *New York Times,* April 19, 1996, p. A12. The income-mortality rate is not just a U.S. link but international in scope. Faculty from the Harvard School of Public Health reported that as the income of nations, states, and counties became less and less equal, their mortality rate worsened. Also Michael Marmot, "Life at the Top," *New York Times,* Weekend, February 27, 2005, p. 13: "Americans with more income or education have better health than Americans with less; a Swedish Ph.D. graduate has longer life expectancy than a Swede with a Master's degree; a British civil servant at the top of the employment hierarchy has greater longevity than one not quite at the top." Among mortality findings reported by Marmot, a mortality expert, was what researchers call the "Oscar" effect. Academy Award winners live four years longer than their fellow nominees and multiple winners live six years longer. Why? "Once you win, you've got a reputation to live up to; even if you weren't so inclined, you get surrounded by an entourage that's also heavily invested in your reputation," said Dr. Donald Redelmeier, one of the researchers. "So you end up sleeping properly every night, eating well, exercising regularly every day." The higher your success in life, the greater your life expectancy. Related sources: Michael Marmot, *The Status Syndrome: How Social Standing Affects Our Health and Longevity* (New York: Times Books, 2004); D. A. Redelmeier and S. M. Singh, "The Survival of Academy Award Winning Actors and Actresses," *Annals of Internal Medicine,* 2001, 134:955–62 (PDF available at http://www.annals.org/cgi/reprint/134/10/955.pdf.)

33. Students scoring As, Bs, or Cs don't drop out. The ones who cannot read well enough to achieve those grades are the most likely to withdraw.

34. See note 31.

35. Paul E. Barton and Richard J. Coley, "Captive Students: Education and Training in America's Prisons," Educational Testing Service (Princeton, NJ: ETS Policy Information Center, 1996). More education lowers the chance of going to prison, and twenty years of research (J. Gerber) shows a positive connection to a lower recidivism rate with more education while in prison. See also: Ian Buruma, "What Teaching a College-Level Class at a Maximum-Security Correctional Facility Did for the Inmates—and for Me," *New York Times Magazine,* February 20, 2005, pp. 38–41. Despite the fact that every study of the inmate population shows the recidivism rate is dramatically lower for those who exit prison with a diploma than for those without one, America has done everything it can to keep the recidivism rate high. You'd almost think the legislators' best friends were all in the prisons-for-profit business. Between 1995 and 2005, the number of prisons offering college degree programs dropped from 350 to approximately one dozen. Also Tamar Lewin, "Inmate Education Is Found to Lower Risk of New Arrest," *New York Times,* November 16, 2001, p. A18.

36. These figures vary in the literature. See Barton and Coley, "Captive Students" and the National Institute for Literacy (NIFL) Correctional Education Facts, online at http://www.nifl.gov/nifl/facts/correctional.html.

37. Edward B. Fiske, "Can Money Spent on Schools Save Money That Would Be Spent on Prisons?" *New York Times,* September 27, 1989, p. B10; also National Institute for Literacy, *Correctional Education Facts,* online at nifl.gov/nifl/facts/correctional.html.

38. Harold L. Hodgkinson, *The Same Client: The Demographics of Education and Service Delivery Systems* (Washington, DC: Institute of Educational Leadership/Center for Demographic Policy, 1989), p. 16.

Chapter 1: Why Read Aloud?

1. M. Perie, R. Moran, and A. D. Lutkus, *NAEP 2004 Trends in Academic Progress: Three Decades of Student Performance in Reading and Mathematics* (NCES 2005-464). U.S. Department of Education, Institute of Education Sciences, National Center for Education Statistics. (Washington, DC: Government Printing Office, 2005).

2. Tom Bradshaw, Bonnie Nichols, Kelly Hill, and Mark Bauerlein, *Reading At Risk: A Survey of Literary Reading in America,* Research Division Report No. 46 (Washington, DC: National Endowment for the Arts, June 2004); online at http://www.nea.gov/pub/ReadingAtRisk.pdf.

3. "National Household Education Survey" (NHES), National Center for Education Statistics (Washington, DC: Government Printing Office, 1999).

4. Perie et al., *NAEP 2004 Trends in Academic Progress.*

5. Richard C. Anderson, Elfrieda H. Hiebert, Judith A. Scott, and Ian A.G. Wilkinson, *Becoming a Nation of Readers: The Report of the Commission on Reading,* U.S. Department of Education (Champaign-Urbana, IL: Center for the Study of Reading, 1985), p. 23.

6. Ibid., p. 51.

7. Keith E. Stanovich, "Matthew Effects in Reading: Some Consequences of Individual Differences in the Acquisition of Literacy," *Reading Research Quarterly,* Fall 1986, pp. 360–407; Richard Anderson, Linda Fielding, and Paul Wilson, "Growth in Reading and How Children Spend Their Time Outside of School," *Reading Research Quarterly,* Summer 1988, pp. 285–303.

8. *Literacy: Profiles of America's Young Adults,* National Assessment of Educational Progress (Princeton, NJ: Educational Testing Service, 1987).

9. "Getting Students Ready for College: What Student Engagement Data Can Tell Us," The High School Survey of Student Engagement (Bloomington: Indiana University, 2005); online at http://www.iub.edu/~nsse/hssse/pdf/college_prep_hssse05.pdf.

10. Gordon Rattray Taylor, *The Natural History of the Brain* (New York: E. P. Dutton, 1979), pp. 59–60.

11. Stanovich, "Matthew Effects in Reading"; Anderson, Fielding, and Wilson, "Growth in Reading and How Children Spend Their Time Outside of School"; Richard L. Allington, "Oral Reading," in *Handbook of Reading Research,* P. David Pearson, ed. (New York: Longman, 1984), pp. 829–64. Also Warwick B. Elley and Francis Mangubhai, "The Impact of Reading on

Second Language Learning," *Reading Research Quarterly,* Fall 1983, pp. 53–67; Irwin Kirsch, John de Jong, Dominique LaFontaine, Joy McQueen, Juliette Mendelovits, and Christian Monseur, *Reading for Change: Performance and Engagement Across Countries, Results from Pisa 2000,* Organisation for Economic Co-operation and Development (OECD); online at http://213.253.134.29/OECD/pdfs/browseit/9602071e.pdf; Foertsch, *Reading In and Out of School.*

12. Warwick B. Elley, *How in the World Do Students Read?* (Hamburg: International Association for the Evaluation of Educational Achievement, 1992). Available from the International Reading Association, Newark, DE.

13. Lizette Alvarez, "Suutarila Journal: Educators Flocking to Finland, Land of Literate Children," *New York Times,* April 9, 2004. Also Sean Coughlan, "Education Key to Economic Survival: Finland Has Often Been Hailed as One of the Most Successful Education Systems in Europe," BBC News, November 23, 2004; online at: http://news.bbc.co.uk/1/hi/education/4031805.stm.

14. Elley, *How in the World?*

15. Ina V. S. Mullis, Michael O. Martin, Eugene J. Gonzalez, and Ann M. Kennedy, *PIRLS 2001 International Report: IEA's Study of Reading Literacy Achievement in Primary School in 35 Countries* (Chestnut Hill, MA: International Association for the Evaluation of Educational/International Study Center, Boston College, 2003), p. 95.

16. Report of the National Reading Panel: *Teaching Children to Read: An Evidence-Based Assessment of the Scientific Research Literature on Reading and Its Implications for Reading Instruction—Reports of the Subgroups* (Washington, DC: National Institute of Child Health and Human Development, NIH, Publication 00-4754, 2000); online at www.nationalreadingpanel.org, or www.nichd.nih.gov/publications/nrp/report.pdf.

17. Joanne Yatvin, "Babes in the Woods: The Wanderings of the National Reading Panel," *Phi Delta Kappan,* January 2002, pp. 364–369. Also, Joanne Yatvin, "I Told You So! The Misinterpretation and Misuse of the National Reading Panel Report," *Education Week,* April 30, 2003, pp. 44, 56. Yatvin was far from alone in her misgivings about the panel's findings. Dr. Richard Allington, a leading reading researcher for thirty-five years, compiled an entire book on the erroneous assumptions of the panel: *Big Brother and the National Reading Curriculum: How Ideology Trumped Evidence* (Portsmouth, NH: Heinemann, 2002). In addition, Dr. Elaine M. Garan found so many inconsistencies in the panel's report that she was able to build a small handbook on how to circumvent many of the questionable federal mandates, using the NRP's own words and recommendations: *Resisting Reading Mandates* (Portsmouth, NH: Heinemann, 2002), as well as a second volume on the politics behind government imposed reading reforms: *In Defense of Our Children: When Politics, Profit, and Education Collide* (Portsmouth, NH: Heinemann, 2004). Also Dr. Stephen Krashen, "The NRP Report on Fluency: More Smoke and Mirrors—A Critique of the National Reading Panel Report on Fluency," *Phi Delta Kappan,* vol. 83, no. 2 (October 2001), pp. 119–123.

18. Kristen Denton and Jerry West, *Children's Reading and Mathematics Achievement in Kindergarten and First Grade* (Washington, DC: U.S. Department of

Education, NCES, 2002), pp. 16, 20; PDF file available at http://nces.ed.
gov/pubs2002/2002125.pdf.

19. There are several versions of the NRP report, all available at http://www.
nationalreadingpanel.org/Publications/publications.htm. The full report is
called *Teaching Children to Read: An Evidence-Based Assessment of the Scientific
Research Literature on Reading and Its Implications for Reading Instruction—
Reports of the Subgroups* (449 pages). It was accompanied by a 32-page summary report (with the same title as the larger report but without the words
"Reports of the Subgroups"). Since nobody expected local, state, or federal
offices to read 449 pages, the summary, coupled with some slick 60-page,
full-color booklets with titles such as *Put Reading First: The Research Building
Blocks for Teaching Children to Read,* were distributed to legislators, school
districts, and child-care centers throughout the United States. The summary and booklets, produced in conjunction with a public relations company (Widmeyer-Baker) that has been a major client of McGraw-Hill/
Open Court, ended up contradicting, warping, or misinterpreting much of
the larger report and repositioning it to agree with the curriculum in certain highly scripted commercial reading series. For example, Elaine Garan
noted in her 2004 book *In Defense of Our Children: When Politics, Profit, and
Education Collide* that the NRP *summary* said, "Across all grade levels, sys-
tematic phonics instruction improved the ability of good readers to spell."
The *full report,* on the other hand, said: "The effect size for spelling [for children in second through sixth grades] was not statistically different from
zero. . . . [Phonics was] not more effective than other forms of instruction
in producing growth in spelling." See also Steven L. Strauss, "Challenging
the NICHD Reading Research Agenda," *Phi Delta Kappan,* February 2003,
pp. 438–42; Elaine M. Garan, *Resisting Reading Mandates,* pp. 8, 23, 41,
70–72. The "unscientific" accusations didn't stop with the National Reading Panel. There was so much evidence of conflict of interest between
education publishers and people either working for Reading First or con-
tracted to them that the inspector general of the Department of Education
opened a full-scale investigation in late summer 2005 of the charges that
many of the consultants for Reading First were consulting for private publishing houses on their reading programs and then evaluating programs for
the Department of Education. See Kathleen Kennedy Manzo, "States
Pressed to Refashion Reading First Grant Designs; Documents Suggest
Federal Interference," *Education Week,* September 7, 2005; online at http://
www.edweek.org/ew/articles/2005/09/07/02read.h25.html; also Kathleen Kennedy Manzo, "Publishers Question Fairness of 'Reading First' Process," *Education Week,* September 7, 2005; online at www.edweek.org/ew/
articles/2005/09/07/02readside.h25.html/ew/articles/2005/09/07/02read.h25.
html; "Special Report: Reading First Under Fire, IG Targets Conflicts of
Interest, Limits on Local Control," and "When Research Goes to Market,
Is It a Good Thing for Education?" both by Andrew Brownstein and Travis
Hick, Thompson Title I Online, August, 2005, at www.titleionline.com/
libraries/titleionline/news_desk/tio050826.html; and www.titleionline.com/
libraries/titleionline/news_desk/tio050825.html.

20. Denton and West, *Children's Reading and Mathematics Achievement.*

21. Adriana G. Bus, Marinus H. van IJzendoorn, and Anthony D. Pellegrini, "Joint Book Reading Makes Success in Learning to Read: A Meta-Analysis on Intergenerational Transmission of Literacy," *Review of Educational Research,* vol. 65, no. 1, Spring 1995, pp. 1–21.

22. Warwick B. Elley, "Vocabulary Acquisition from Listening to Stories," *Reading Research Quarterly,* vol. 24, Spring 1989, pp. 174–187.

23. Mullis, Martin, Gonzalez, and Kennedy, *PIRLS 2001 International Report.*

24. For more on monastic table reading, see Eric Hollas, OSB, "Food for Thought: Monastic Table Reading," *Abbey Banner,* Spring 2003, pp. 10–11.

25. "Reign of the Reader," *Reading Today,* International Reading Association, December 2001/January 2002, p. 30; Gary R. Mormino and George E. Pozzetta, *The Immigrant World of Ybor City: Italians and Their Latin Neighbors in Tampa, 1885–1985* (Gainesville, FL: Florida Sand Dollar Books, University Press of Florida, 1998); also Edward Rothstein, "Connections: What It Takes to Bring Tears to an Unsentimental Reader's Eyes," *New York Times,* June 15, 2002, p. A19; "Reading 2: Ybor City's Cigar Workers," ParkNet, National Park Service, http://www.cr.nps.gov/nr/twhp/wwwlps/lessons/51ybor/51facts2.htm.

26. Elton G. Stetson and Richard P. Williams, "Learning from Social Studies Textbooks: Why Some Students Succeed and Others Fail," *Journal of Reading,* September 1992, pp. 22–30.

27. Jerry West, Kristin Denton, and Elvira Germino-Hausken, *America's Kindergartners: Findings from the Early Childhood Longitudinal Study, Kindergarten Class of 1998–99, Fall 1998,* Office of Educational Research and Improvement, NCES 2000-070 (Washington, DC: U.S. Department of Education, 2000).

28. Courtney B. Cazden, *Child Language and Education* (New York: Holt, Rinehart and Winston, 1972).

29. Psychologist Burton L. White, interviewed in "Training Parents Helps Toddlers," *New York Times,* October 2, 1985, p. C1.

30. George A. Miller and Patricia M. Gildea, "How Children Learn Words," *Scientific American,* September 1987, pp. 94–99.

31. Betty Hart and Todd Risley, *Meaningful Differences in the Everyday Experience of Young American Children* (Baltimore, MD: Brookes Publishing, 1996). For a downloadable six-page condensation of the book: Betty Hart and Todd R. Risley, "The Early Catastophe: The 30 Million Word Gap by Age 3," *American Educator* (American Federation of Teachers), Spring 2003; online at http://www.aft.org/pubs-reports/american_educator/spring2003/index.html. This can be freely disseminated to parents, according to the AFT Web site. See also Paul Chance, "Speaking of Differences," *Phi Delta Kappan,* March 1997, pp. 506–7.

32. George Farkas and Kurt Beron, "Family Linguistic Culture and Social Reproduction: Verbal Skill from Parent to Child in the Preschool and School Years," paper delivered March 31, 2001, to annual meetings of the Population Association of America, Washington, DC; online at http://www.pop.psu.edu/~gfarkas/paa301.pdf. Also Karen S. Peterson, "Moms' Poor Vocabulary Hurts Kids' Future," *USA Today,* April 12, 2001, p. D8.

33. Here's what is printed at the bottom of the article: "Articles may be reproduced for noncommercial personal or educational use only; additional permission is required for any other reprinting of the documents." That entire spring issue is an easy-to-understand treasure of research on children's language and reading comprehension—free for downloading at http://www. aft.org/pubs-reports/american_educator/spring2003/index.html.

34. Donald P. Hayes and Margaret G. Ahrens, "Vocabulary Simplification for Children: A Special Case for 'Motherese,'" *Journal of Child Language,* vol. 15, 1988, pp. 395–410.

35. Ibid.

36. Caroline Hendrie, "Chicago Data Show Mixed Summer Gain," *Education Week,* September 10, 1999, pp. 1, 14. See also Diane Ravitch, "Summer School Isn't a Solution," *New York Times,* March 3, 2000, A25.

37. Olga Emery and Mihaly Csikszentmihalyi, "The Socialization Effects of Cultural Role Models in Ontogenetic Development and Upward Mobility," *Child Psychiatry and Development and Human Development,* Fall 1981, pp. 3–18.

38. Bruno Bettelheim, *The Uses of Enchantment: The Meaning and Importance of Fairy Tales* (New York: Knopf, 1976), pp. 3–6.

39. Kirsch, de Jong, LaFontaine, McQueen, Mendelovits, and Monseur, *Reading for Change: Performance and Engagement Across Countries,* pp. 106–110; online at http://213.253.134.29/OECD/pdfs/browseit/9602071e.pdf.

40. *Time,* February 1, 1988, pp. 52–58; also Mark D. O'Donnell, "Boston's Lewenberg Middle School Delivers Success," *Phi Delta Kappan,* March 1997, pp. 508–12. The *Kappan* article describes how O'Neill didn't affect just the language arts curriculum. He also spearheaded a physical rebirth in the school and a remarkable six-week physical education program built around Project Adventure, an intense climbing regimen. There is also a detailed description of O'Neill's adventures with an often inept school department and an obstructionist custodial union, and the resulting triumph of the school. For his work at Lewenberg, O'Neill was named one of the inaugural recipients of the Heroes in Education award, presented by *Reader's Digest* to educators with original and effective methods.

41. Howard W. French, "Tokyo Dropouts' Vocation: Painting the Town," *New York Times,* March 12, 2000, pp. A1, A18: "In the place of the nose-to-the-grindstone ethic of long study hours and single-minded focus on exams and careers that helped build postwar Japan, the motto of the current 15- to 18-year-olds seems to be that girls and boys just want to have fun." Since 1997, Japan has seen its school dropout rate increase by 20 percent. See also Norimitsu Onishi, "An Aging Island Embraces Japan's Young Dropouts," *New York Times,* June 6, 2004, p. A3; Miki Tanikawa, "Free to Be," *New York Times,* Education, January 12, 2003, pp. 36, 38.

42. David Snowden, *Aging with Grace: What the Nun Study Teaches Us About Leading Longer, Healthier, and More Meaningful Lives* (New York: Bantam, 2001), pp. 117–18; Kathryn P. Riley, David A. Snowden, Mark F. Desrosiers, and William R. Markesbery, "Early Life Linguistic Ability, Late Life Cognitive Function, and Neuropathology: Findings from the Nun Study," *Neurobiology of Aging,* vol. 26, no. 3, 2005, pp. 341–47; also Pam Belluck, "Nuns Offer Clues to Alzheimer's and Aging," *New York Times,* May 7, 2001.

Chapter 2: When to Begin (and End) Read-Aloud

1. These remarks were made during a half-hour interview (September 3, 1979) with Dr. Brazelton conducted by John Merrow for *Options in Education*, a co-production of National Public Radio and the Institute for Educational Leadership of the George Washington University.
2. Anthony J. DeCasper and Melanie J. Spence, "Prenatal Maternal Speech Influences Newborns' Perception of Speech Sounds," *Infant Behavior and Development*, 1986, vol. 9, no. 2, pp. 133–50.
3. Marjory Roberts, "Class Before Birth," *Psychology Today*, May 1987, p. 41; Sharon Begley and John Carey, "The Wisdom of Babies," *Newsweek*, January 12, 1981, pp. 71–72.
4. Dorothy Butler, *Cushla and Her Books* (Boston: The Horn Book, 1980).
5. Lizette Alvarez, "Educators Flocking to Finland, Land of Literate Children," *New York Times*, April 9, 2004. See also Sean Coughlan, "Education Key to Economic Survival," BBC News, November 23, 2004; online at http://news.bbc.co.uk/1/hi/education/4031805.stm; Gerald W. Bracey, "American Students Near the Top in Reading," *Phi Delta Kappan*, February 1993, pp. 496–97. You'll find everything you need to know about the Finnish reading philosophy in the following: Leonard B. Finkelstein, "Finland's Lessons: Learning Thrives in a Land Where It Is Respected," Commentary, *Education Week*, October 18, 1995, p. 31; Viking Brunell and Pirjo Linnakylä, "Swedish Speakers' Literacy in the Finnish Society," *Journal of Reading*, February 1994, pp. 368–75; Pirjo Linnakylä, "Subtitles Prompt Finnish Children to Read," *Reading Today* (Newark, DE: International Reading Association, October/November 1993), p. 31.
6. Warwick B. Elley, *How in the World Do Students Read?* (Hamburg: International Association for the Evaluation of Educational Achievement, July 1992). Available from the International Reading Association, Newark, DE, $16/$12.
7. David Elkind, *The Hurried Child: Growing Up Too Fast Too Soon*, 3rd ed. (Cambridge, MA: Perseus/DaCapo, 2001).
8. Dolores Durkin, *Children Who Read Early* (New York: Teachers College, 1966) and Margaret M. Clark, *Young Fluent Readers* (London: Heinemann, 1976). See also Anne D. Forester, "What Teachers Can Learn from 'Natural Readers,'" *Reading Teacher*, November 1977, pp. 160–66.
9. Ina V. S. Mullis, Michael O. Martin, Eugene J. Gonzalez, and Ann M. Kennedy, "PIRLS 2001 International Report: IEA's Study of Reading Literacy Achievement in Primary School in 35 Countries," International Association for the Evaluation of Educational Achievement (IEA) (Chestnut Hill, MA: International Study Center, Boston College, 2003); online at http://pirls.bc.edu/isc/publications.html.
10. Ina V. S. Mullis, John A. Dossey, Jay R. Campbell, Claudia A. Gentile, Christine Sullivan, and Andrew Latham, *NAEP 1992 Trends in Academic Progress*, Office of Educational Research and Improvement (Washington, DC: U.S. Department of Education, June 1994). See also Paul E. Barton and Richard J. Coley, *America's Smallest School* (Princeton, NJ: Educational Testing Service, Policy Information Center, 1992), pp. 12–19.

11. Ibid., pp. 105–24.

12. Andrew Biemiller, "Oral Comprehension Sets the Ceiling on Reading Comprehension," *American Educator,* Spring 2003; online at www.aft.org/pubs-reports/american_educator/spring2003/biemiller.html.

13. Nell K. Duke, "For the Rich It's Richer: Print Experiences and Environments Offered to Children in Very Low- and Very High-Socioeconomic Status First-Grade Classrooms," *American Educational Research Journal,* vol. 37, no. 2, Summer 2000, pp. 441–78.

14. Jerome Kagan, "The Child: His Struggle for Identity," *Saturday Review,* December 1968, p. 82. See also Steven R. Tulkin and Jerome Kagan, "Mother-Child Interaction in the First Year of Life," *Child Development,* March 1972, pp. 31–41.

15. Further examples of "concept-attention span" can be found in Kagan, "The Child: His Struggle for Identity," p. 82.

16. Donald Roberts, Ph.D., et al., *Kids & Media @ The New Millennium* (Menlo Park, CA: The Henry J. Kaiser Family Foundation, November 1999); online at www.kff.org/content/1999/1535/ChartPack.pdf. See also Victoria J. Rideout, Elizabeth A. Vandewater, and Ellen A. Wartella, *Zero to Six: Electronic Media in the Lives of Infants, Toddlers, and Preschoolers* (Menlo Park, CA: The Henry J. Kaiser Family Foundation, 2003); online at http://www.kff.org. Thirty-five percent of all families with young children now eat their meals with the television on "always" or "most of the time."

17. Lesley Mandel Morrow, "Home and School Correlates of Early Interest in Literature," *Journal of Educational Research,* vol. 76, March/April 1983, pp. 221–30. See page xvi here for charts on this study.

18. Richard C. Anderson, Elfrieda H. Hiebert, Judith A. Scott, and Ian A. G. Wilkinson, *Becoming a Nation of Readers: The Report of the Commission on Reading,* U.S. Department of Education (Champaign-Urbana, IL: Center for the Study of Reading, 1985), p. 51.

19. G. Robert Carlsen and Anne Sherrill, *Voices of Readers: How We Come to Love Books,* National Council of Teachers of English (Urbana, IL: NCTE, 1988).

20. A sample *Cosby* script page can be found at http://www.trelease-on-reading.com/cosby_script.html.

21. In the interest of fairness, four different factors were taken into account by reading specialist Kathy Nozzolillo in determining the Harris-Jacobson reading level for the script: semantic difficulty, syntactic difficulty, vocabulary, and sentence length.

22. Andrew Biemiller, "Oral Comprehension Sets the Ceiling on Reading Comprehension," *American Educator,* Spring 2003; online at www. aft.org/pubs-reports/american_educator/spring2003/biemiller.html. See also Thomas G. Devine, "Listening: What Do We Know After Fifty Years of Research and Theorizing?" *Journal of Reading,* January 1978, pp. 296–304.

23. The original dust jacket copy for *The Cat in the Hat* included the words "Many children . . . will discover for the first time that they don't need to be read to any more," as noted in Judith and Neil Morgan's *Dr. Seuss and Mr. Geisel* (New York: Random House, 1995), p. 155.

24. Constance L. Hays, "David Ogilvy, 88, Father of Soft Sell in Advertising, Dies," *New York Times,* July 22, 1999.

25. Miriam Martinez and William H. Teale, "Reading in a Kindergarten Classroom Library," *Reading Teacher,* February 1988, pp. 568–72; Barbara Martin Palmer, Rose Marie Codling, and Linda B. Gambrell, "In Their Own Words: What Elementary Students Have to Say About Motivation to Read," *Reading Teacher,* October 1994, pp. 176–78.

26. Robert McCrum, William Cran, and Robert MacNeil, *The Story of English* (New York: Viking, 1986), pp. 19, 20, 32.

27. John Ritter, "Why English Is Language of Aviation," *USA Today,* January 18, 1996, p. 2A.

28. Andrew Adam Newman, "Actors You've Never Heard of Are Becoming the Ones Heard Most," *New York Times,* January 15, 2005, p. 13B.

29. Carl B. Smith and Gary M. Ingersoll, "Written Vocabulary of Elementary School Pupils," ERIC document ED323564, pp. 3–4.

30. John Holt treated this concept at length in "How Teachers Make Children Hate Reading," *Redbook,* November 1967.

31. Stephen Krashen, *The Power of Reading,* 2nd ed. (Portsmouth, NH: Libraries Unlimited and Heinemann, 2004); also William Powers, John Cook, and Russell Meyer, "The Effect of Compulsory Writing on Writing Apprehension," *Research in the Teaching of English,* 13, 1979, pp. 225–30; and Harry Gradman and Edith Hanania, "Language Learning Background Factors and ESL Proficiency," *Modern Language Journal,* 75, 1991, pp. 39–51.

32. Arthur N. Applebee, Judith A. Langer, Ina V. S. Mullis, Andrew S. Latham, and Claudia A. Gentile, *NAEP 1992 Writing Report Card,* Educational Testing Service (Washington, DC: U.S. Department of Education, 1994).

33. Jacques Barzun, *Begin Here* (Chicago: University of Chicago Press, 1991), pp. 114–16. Barzun is one of the grand old men of American letters (author of thirty books, including a National Book Award finalist for *From Dawn to Decadence: 500 Years of Western Cultural Life* at age ninety-two) and former dean of the graduate faculty and provost of Columbia University. His advice should never be taken lightly.

34. Sam Dillon, "What Corporate America Cannot Build: A Sentence," *New York Times,* December 7, 2004, p. A23.

35. Eric R. Kandel, James H. Schwartz, and Thomas M. Jessell, eds., *Principles of Neural Science,* third ed., Center for Neurobiology and Behavior, College of Physicians and Surgeons of Columbia University and the Howard Hughes Medical Institute (Norwalk, CT: Appleton & Lange, 1991): "The visual system is the most complex of all the sensory systems. The auditory nerve contains about 30,000 fibers, but the optic nerve (visual) contains one million, more than all the dorsal root fibers entering the entire spinal cord!"

36. John Katzman, Andy Lutz, and Erik Olson, "Would Shakespeare Get into Swarthmore?" *Atlantic Monthly,* March, 2004. See also "Hemingway, Shakespeare Might Flunk SAT Essay Test," *Weekend Edition,* National Public Radio, February 21, 2004; online at http://www.npr.org/templates/story/story.php?storyId=1690907.

37. The poster corporation for this concept was Enron. See Bethany Mclean and Peter Elkind, *The Smartest Guys in the Room* (New York: Portfolio/Penguin, 2003).

Chapter 3: The Stages of Read-Aloud

1. The speech can be heard at Minnesota Public Radio's *Midday Show* for September 9, 2004; online at http://server-us.imrworldwide.com/cgi-bin/b?cg=news-clickthru&ci=us-mpr&tu=http://news.mpr.org/play/audio.php?media=/midday/2004/09/22_midday2.
2. Peter W. Jusczyk and Elizabeth A. Hohne, "Infants' Memory for Spoken Words," *Science,* September 26, 1997, pp. 1984–85.
3. Anthony J. DeCasper and Melanie J. Spence, "Prenatal Maternal Speech Influences Newborns' Perception of Speech Sounds," *Infant Behavior and Development,* 1986, vol. 9, no. 2, pp. 133–50. See also Gina Kolata, "Rhyme's Reason: Linking Thinking to Train the Brain?" *New York Times,* February 19, 1995, p. E3.
4. "The Experience of Touch: Research Points to a Critical Role," *New York Times,* Science Times, February 2, 1988, p. 17.
5. Linda Lamme and Athol Packer, "Bookreading Behaviors of Infants," *Reading Teacher,* February 1986, pp. 504–9; Michael Resnick et al., "Mothers Reading to Infants: A New Observational Tool," *Reading Teacher,* May 1987, pp. 888–94.
6. A. Ninio and J. S. Bruner, "The Achievement and Antecedents of Labeling," *Journal of Child Language,* vol. 5, 1978, pp. 1–15.
7. A. Ninio, "Picture Book Reading in Mother-Infant Dyads Belonging to Two Subgroups in Israel," *Child Development,* vol. 51, 1980, pp. 587–90.
8. Warwick B. Elley, "Vocabulary Acquisition from Listening to Stories," *Reading Research Quarterly,* vol. 24, Spring 1989, pp. 174–87.
9. Keith E. Stanovich, "Matthew Effects in Reading: Some Consequences of Individual Differences in the Acquisition of Literacy," *Reading Research Quarterly,* Fall 1986, pp. 360–407.
10. David Yaden, "Understanding Stories Through Repeated Read-Alouds: How Many Times Does It Take?" *Reading Teacher,* February 1988, pp. 556–60.
11. David B. Yaden Jr., Laura B. Smolkin, and Alice Conlon, "Preschoolers' Questions About Pictures, Print Conventions, and Story Text During Reading Aloud at Home," *Reading Research Quarterly,* Spring 1989, pp. 188–214.
12. Joannis K. Flatley and Adele D. Rutland, "Using Wordless Picture Books to Teach Linguistically/Culturally Different Students," *Reading Teacher,* December 1986, pp. 276–81; Donna Read and Henrietta M. Smith, "Teaching Visual Literacy Through Wordless Picture Books," *Reading Teacher,* May 1982, pp. 928–52; J. Stewig, *Children and Literature* (Chicago: Rand McNally, 1980), pp. 131–58.
13. Jane Gross, "Seeing Rise in Child Abuse, Hospitals Step in to Try to Stop the Battering," *New York Times,* April 5, 1994, p. A18.
14. Ibid.
15. Ann Jones, "Crimes Against Women," *USA Today,* March 10, 1994, p. 9A.
16. Carol Jago, "An Interview with Alfie Kohn," *California English,* Winter 1995.
17. Mary A. Foertsch, *Reading In and Out of School,* National Center for Statistics/U.S. Department of Education (Princeton, NJ: Educational Testing Service, 1992), pp. 10–11.

18. Richard Anderson, Linda Fielding, and Paul Wilson, "Growth in Reading and How Children Spend Their Time Outside of School," *Reading Research Quarterly,* Summer 1988, pp. 285–303.

19. Patricia Greenfield and Jessica Beagles-Roos, "Radio vs. Television: Their Cognitive Impact on Children of Different Socioeconomic and Ethnic Groups," *Journal of Communications,* Spring 1988, pp. 71–92.

20. Robertson Davies, *One Half of Robertson Davies* (New York: Viking, 1977), p. 1.

21. Nancy Pearl, *Book Lust: Recommended Reading for Every Mood, Moment, and Reason* (Seattle, WA: Sasquatch Books, 2003); and Nancy Pearl, *More Book Lust: Recommended Reading for Every Mood, Moment, and Reason* (Seattle, WA: Sasquatch Books, 2005).

22. Dr. Marie Carbo today is a nationally recognized figure in reading circles, heading the National Learning Styles Institute. For more information, see http://www.nrsi.com/.

23. Marie Carbo, "Teaching Reading with Talking Books," *Reading Teacher,* December 1978, pp. 267–73.

24. Personal e-mail correspondence.

25. Personal e-mail correspondence.

Chapter 5: Sustained Silent Reading: Reading Aloud's National Partner

1. Report of the National Reading Panel: *Teaching Children to Read: An Evidence-Based Assessment of the Scientific Research Literature on Reading and Its Implications for Reading Instruction—the Summary Report* (Washington, DC: National Institute of Child Health and Human Development, NIH, Publication 00-4754, 2000), p. 13. Available online at http://www.nichd.nih.gov/publications/nrp/smallbook.pdf.

2. The NRP's own scientific standards have come under severe attack since the report was issued, the most notable being Steven L. Strauss, "Challenging the NICHD Reading Research Agenda," *Phi Delta Kappan,* vol. 84, no. 6, February 2003, pp. 438–42; also Joanne Yatvin, "Babes in the Woods: The Wanderings of the National Reading Panel," *Phi Delta Kappan,* January 2002, pp. 364–69; and James Cunningham, "The National Reading Panel Report," review, *Reading Research Quarterly,* July/August/September 2001, pp. 326–35.

3. Stephen Krashen, "More Smoke and Mirrors: A Critique of the National Reading Panel Report on Fluency," *Phi Delta Kappan,* October 2001, pp. 119–23; also Stephen Krashen, "Is In-School Free Reading Good for Children? Why the National Reading Panel Report Is (Still) Wrong," *Phi Delta Kappan,* February 2005, pp. 444–47; James Cunningham, "The National Reading Panel Report"; and Elaine M. Garan, *Resisting Mandates: How to Triumph with the Truth* (Portsmouth, NH: Heinemann, 2002) pp. 22–24.

4. Keith E. Stanovich, "Matthew Effects in Reading: Some Consequences of Individual Differences in the Acquisition of Literacy," *Reading Research*

Quarterly, Fall 1986, pp. 360–407; also Richard L. Allington, "Oral Reading," in *Handbook of Reading Research,* P. David Pearson, ed. (New York: Longman, 1984), pp. 829–64; Warwick B. Elley and Francis Mangubhai, "The Impact of Reading on Second Language Learning," *Reading Research Quarterly,* Fall 1983, pp. 53–67; and Mary A. Foertsch, *Reading In and Out of School,* National Center for Statistics/U.S. Department of Education (Princeton, NJ: Educational Testing Service, 1992).

5. Irwin Kirsch, John de Jong, Dominique LaFontaine, Joy McQueen, Juliette Mendelovits, and Christian Monseur, *Reading for Change: Performance and Engagement Across Countries—Results from Pisa 2000,* Organisation for Economic Co-Operation and Development (OECD); online at http://213.253. 134.29/OECD/pdfs/browseit/9602071e.pdf.

6. Warwick B. Elley, *How in the World Do Students Read?* (Hamburg: International Association for the Evaluation of Educational Achievement, July 1992).

7. P. L. Donahue, K. E. Voelkl, J. R. Campbell, and J. Mazzeo, *NAEP 1998 Reading Report Card for the Nation and States.* (Washington, DC: U.S. Department of Education, Office of Educational Research and Improvement, National Center for Education Statistics, 1999); also Ina V. S. Mullis et al., *NAEP 1992 Trends in Academic Progress,* ETS / Office of Educational Research and Improvement (Washington, DC: U.S. Department of Education, June 1994). Also found in *America's Smallest School: The Family,* Educational Testing Service, at www.ets.org/research.

8. Robert A. McCracken, "Instituting Sustained Silent Reading," *Journal of Reading,* May 1971, pp. 521–24, 582–83.

9. Stephen Krashen, *The Power of Reading,* second ed. (Portsmouth, NH: Libraries Unlimited and Heinemann, 2004).

10. S. Jay Samuels, "Decoding and Automaticity: Helping Poor Readers Become Automatic at Word Recognition," *Reading Teacher,* April 1988, pp. 756–60; also Richard Anderson, Linda Fielding, and Paul Wilson, "Growth in Reading and How Children Spend Their Time Outside of School," *Reading Research Quarterly,* Summer 1988, pp. 285–303.

11. Richard C. Anderson, Elfrieda H. Hiebert, Judith A. Scott, and Ian A. G. Wilkinson, *Becoming a Nation of Readers: The Report of the Commission on Reading* (Champaign-Urbana, IL: Center for the Study of Reading, 1985), p. 119.

12. Mark Sadoski, "An Attitude Survey for Sustained Silent Reading Programs," *Journal of Reading,* May 1980, pp. 721–26.

13. Richard Allington is the author of *Big Brother and the National Reading Curriculum: How Ideology Trumped Evidence* (Heinemann) and *What Really Matters for Struggling Readers* (Longman).

14. Richard Allington, "If They Don't Read Much, How They Gonna Get Good," *Journal of Reading,* October 1977, pp. 57–61.

15. Anderson et al., "Growth in Reading," p. 152.

16. Edward Fry and Elizabeth Sakiey, "Common Words Not Taught in Basal Reading Series," *Reading Teacher,* January 1986, pp. 395–98.

17. Robert A. McCracken and Marlene J. McCracken, "Modeling Is the Key to Sustained Silent Reading," *Reading Teacher,* January 1978, pp. 406–8. See

also Linda B. Gambrell, "Getting Started with Sustained Silent Reading and Keeping It Going," *Reading Teacher,* December 1978, pp. 328–31.

18. Alan Neuharth, "Why Newspapers Are More Popular in Asia," *USA Today,* Op-ed, June 3, 2005, p. 15A; also Alan Neuharth, "Why Are Newswpapers So Popular in Japan?" *USA Today,* Op-ed, November 26, 2004, p. 13A.

19. Jason Singer, "Lonesome Highways: In Japan, Big Tolls Drive Cars Away," *Wall Street Journal,* September 15, 2003, pp. A1, A15.

20. Howard W. French, "The Rising Sun Sets on Japanese Publishing," *New York Times Book Review,* December 10, 2000, p. 51.

21. Barbara Heyns, *Summer Learning and the Effects of Schooling* (New York: Academic Press, 1978). See also Doris R. Entwistle and Karl L. Alexander, "Summer Setback: Race, Poverty, School Composition, and Mathematical Achievement in the First Two Years of School," *American Sociological Review,* 57, 1992, pp. 72–84; Barbara Heynes, "Schooling and Cognitive Development: Is There a Season for Learning?" *Child Development,* vol. 58, 1987, pp. 1151–60; Larry J. Mikulecky, "Stopping Summer Learning Loss Among At-Risk Youth," *Journal of Reading,* April 1990, pp. 516–21; Harris Cooper, Barbara Nye, Kelly Charlton, James Lindsay, and Scott Greathouse, "The Effects of Summer Vacation on Achievement Test Scores: A Narrative and Meta-Analytic Review," *Review of Educational Research,* vol. 66, no. 3, Fall 1996, pp. 227–68; Richard L. Allington and Anne McGill-Franzen, "The Impact of Summer Setback on the Reading Achievement Gap," *Phi Delta Kappan,* September 2003, pp. 68–75.

22. Jimmy Kim, "Summer Reading and the Ethnic Achievement Gap," *Journal of Education for Students Placed at Risk (JESPAR),* vol. 9, no. 2, 2004, pp. 169–88; see also Debra Viadero, "Reading Books Is Found to Ward Off 'Summer Slump,'" *Education Week,* May 5, 2004.

23. Paul E. Barton, *Parsing the Achievement Gap* at http://www.ets.org/research/pic/parsing.pdf.

24. Greg Toppo, "Poor, Minority Kids Face Long Odds in Education," *USA Today,* November 24, 2003, p. 7D.

25. Jay R. Campbell, Catherine M. Hombo, and John Mazzeo, *NAEP 1999 Trends in Academic Progress: Three Decades of Student Performance,* U.S. Department of Education (Washington, DC: National Center for Education Statistics, 2000); online at http://nces.ed.gov/nationsreportcard. For international comparison, see Irwin Kirsch et al., *Reading for Change: Performance and Engagement Across Countries, Results from Pisa 2000.*

26. Stephen Krashen, "Does Accelerated Reader Work?" *Journal of Children's Literature* (2003) vol. 29 (2): 9, pp. 16–30, online at http://www.sdkrashen.com/articles/does_accelerated_reader_work/index.html.

27. Linda M. Pavonetti, Kathryn M. Brimmer, and James F. Cipielewski, "Accelerated Reader: What Are the Lasting Effects on the Reading Habits of Middle School Students Exposed to Accelerated Reader in Elementary Grades?" *Journal of Adolescent and Adult Literacy,* vol. 46, no. 4, December 2002 / January 2003. See also Jean M. Stevenson and Jenny Webb Camarata, "Imposters in Whole Language Clothing: Undressing the Accelerated Reader Program," *Talking Points,* Whole Language Umbrella/National Council of

Teachers of English, vol. 11, no. 2, April/May 2000, pp. 8–11. I don't agree with everything in this article, but there are some points that are very valid.

28. John T. Guthrie, "Contexts for Engagement and Motivation in Reading" at http://www.readingonline.org/articles/handbook/guthrie/, and in M. L. Kamil, P. B. Mosenthal, P. D. Pearson, and R. Barr eds., *Handbook of Reading Research: Volume III* (New York: Erlbaum, 2000), pp. 403–22. See also M. Csikszentmihalyi, "Literacy and Intrinsic Motivation," *Daedalus*, 1990, vol. 119, pp. 115–40, and M. Csikszentmihalyi, "Literacy and Intrinsic Motivation," in S. R. Graubard, ed., *Literacy* (New York: Noonday, 1991) pp. 115–40.

29. Kirsch et al., *Reading for Change.*

30. "The Man with Two Brains," *New York Times,* Education, October 9, 1989, p. 6E.

31. Dave Anderson, "Erskine Recalls Lessons Learned from Jackie Robinson and His Own Son," *New York Times,* Sports, February 14, 2005; also Carl Erskine, *What I Learned from Jackie Robinson* (New York: McGraw-Hill, 2005).

32. Stephen D. Krashen and Kyung-Sook Cho, "Acquisition of Vocabulary from the Sweet Valley Kids Series: Adult ESL Acquisition," *Journal of Reading,* May 1994, pp. 662–67; similar results were accomplished in the Sponce English Language Program at the University of Southern California, using Harlequin romances. See also Rebecca Constantino, "Pleasure Reading Helps, Even If Readers Don't Believe It," *Journal of Reading,* March 1994, pp. 504–5.

33. G. Robert Carlson and Anne Sherrill, *Voices of Readers: How We Come to Love Books* (Urbana, IL: National Council of Teachers of English, 1998); Krashen, *The Power of Reading,* pp. 91–110.

34. Viking Brunell and Pirjo Linnakylä, "Swedish Speakers' Literacy in the Finnish Society," *Journal of Reading,* February 1994, pp. 368–75.

35. Leslie Campbell and Kathleen Hayes, "Desmond Tutu," interview from *The Other Side's Faces of Faith,* pp. 23–26. For a free copy of this booklet, write to 300 Apsley St., Philadelphia, PA 19144.

36. Arthur Schlesinger Jr., "Advice from a Reader-Aloud-to-Children," *New York Times Book Review,* November 25, 1979.

37. Sid T. Womack and B. J. Chandler, "Encouraging Reading for Professional Development," *Journal of Reading,* February 1992, pp. 390–94.

38. Stanley I. Mour, "Do Teachers Read?" *The Reading Teacher,* January 1977, pp. 397–401. This study was somewhat skewed in favor of teachers because the subjects were more motivated professionally as graduate students. If anything, the results would be worse with teachers not as professionally involved. Included in the numbers were 202 females and 22 males, 6 counselors, 6 principals, 5 supervisors; most of the teachers (145) were elementary level. See also Kathleen Stumpf Jongsma, "Just Say Know!" *Reading Teacher,* March 1992, pp. 546–48.

39. Tom Bradshaw and Bonnie Nichols, Kelly Hill, and Mark Bauerlein, *Reading at Risk: A Survey of Literary Reading in America,* National Endowment for the Arts (Washington, DC: NEA, Research Division, Report no. 46, 2004), online at http://www.nea.gov/pub/ReadingAtRisk.pdf; Nicholas Zill and Marianne Winglee, *Who Reads Literature?* (Cabin John, MD: Seven Locks Press, 1990).

40. Cheryl B. Littman and Susan S. Stodolsky, "The Professional Reading of High School Academic Teachers," *Journal of Educational Research,* vol. 92, no. 2, November 1998, p. 75.

41. I borrowed the "date" analogy from the novelist Kurt Vonnegut Jr., who, when asked if you could actually teach a person how to write, replied indignantly that such teaching is the job of an editor—the person who teaches the writer how to behave on "a blind date with a total stranger"—the "reader." See Kurt Vonnegut Jr., "Despite Tough Guys, Life Is Not the Only School for Real Novelists," *New York Times,* May 24, 1999, pp. B1, B2.

42. Margaret G. McKeown, Isabel L. Beck, Richard C. Omanson, and Martha T. Pople, "Some Effects of the Nature and Frequency of Vocabulary Instruction on the Knowledge and Use of Words," *Reading Research Quarterly,* vol. 20, no. 5, 1985, 522–35; see also Steven A. Stahl, "How Words Are Learned Incrementally over Multiple Exposures," *American Educator,* Spring 2003, pp. 18–19.

Chapter 7: The Print Climate in the Home, School, and Library

1. President Ronald Reagan and New York governor Mario Cuomo, 1984; the Cuomo speech is listed as one of the "Top 100 American Speeches" in the Online Speech Bank, available at http://www.americanrhetoric.com/speeches/cuomo1984dnc.htm.

2. Lesley Mandel Morrow, "Home and School Correlates of Early Interest in Literature," *Journal of Educational Research,* vol. 76, March/April 1983, pp. 221–30.

3. Susan B. Neuman and Donna Celano, "Access to Print in Low-Income and Middle-Income Communities: An Ecological Study of Four Neighborhoods," *Reading Research Quarterly,* vol. 36, no. 1, January/February/March 2001, pp. 8–26; and Susan B. Neuman, Conna C. Celano, Albert N. Greco, and Pamela Shue, *Access for All: Closing the Book Gap for Children in Early Education* (Newark, DE: International Reading Association, 2001).

4. Nell K. Duke, "For the Rich It's Richer: Print Experiences and Environments Offers to Children in Very Low- and Very High-Socioeconomic Status First-Grade," *American Educational Research Journal,* vol. 37, no. 2, Summer 2000, pp. 441–78.

5. Stephen S. Krashen, *The Power of Reading* (Portsmouth, NH: Heinemann and Libraries Unlimited, 2004).

6. Jeff McQuillan, *The Literary Crisis: False Claims, Real Solutions* (Portsmouth, NH: Heinemann, 1998).

7. Richard Allington, Sherry Guice, Kim Baker, Nancy Michaelson, and Shouming Li, "Access to Books: Variations in Schools and Classrooms," *Language and Literacy Spectrum,* Spring 1995, pp. 23–25. Also Richard L. Allington and Sherry Guice, "Something to Read: Putting Books in Their Desks, Backpacks, and Bedrooms," in Phillip Dreyer, ed., *Vision and Realities in Literacy: Sixtieth Yearbook of the Claremont Reading Conference* (Claremont, CA: Claremont Reading Conference, 1996), p. 5.

8. Keith Curry Lance, Marcia J. Rodney, and Christine Hamilton-Pennell, *How School Librarians Help Kids Achieve Standards: The Second Colorado Study,* Colorado State Library, Colorado Department of Education; Keith Curry Lance, Lynda Welborn, and Christine Hamilton-Pennell, *The Impact of School Media Centers on Academic Achievement,* Colorado Department of Education. Copies may be ordered through Libraries Unlimited, P.O. Box 6633, Englewood, CO 80155 (tel: 800-237-6124). See also Christine Hamilton-Pennell, Keith Curry Lance, Marcia J. Rodney, and Eugene Hainer, "Dick and Jane Go to the Head of the Class," *School Library Journal,* April 2000, pp. 44–47.

9. Jay R. Campbell, Catherine M. Hombo, and John Mazzeo, *NAEP 1999 Trends in Academic Progress: Three Decades of Student Performance,* U.S. Department of Education (Washington, DC: National Center for Education Statistics, 2000); online at http://nces.ed.gov/nationsreportcard.

10. Ina V. S. Mullis, Michael O. Martin, Eugene J. Gonzalez, and Ann M. Kennedy, "PIRLS 2001 International Report: IEA's Study of Reading Literacy Achievement in Primary School in 35 Countries," International Association for the Evaluation of Educational Achievement (IEA) (Chestnut Hill, MA: International Study Center, Boston College, 2003); online at http://pirls.bc.edu/isc/publications.html.

11. Warwick B. Elley, *How in the World Do Students Read?* (Hamburg: International Association for the Evaluation of Educational Achievement, July 1992). Available from the International Reading Association, Newark, DE, $16/$12 (U.S.).

12. The studies can be found online at http://www.ala.org/aaslTemplate. cfm?Section=studentachieve.

13. James C. Baughman, "School Libraries and MCAS Scores," paper presented at library symposium, Graduate School of Library and Information Science, Simmons College, Boston, MA, October 26, 2000; online at http://web. simmons.edu/~baughman/mcas-school-libraries/.

14. C. Contantino and Stephen Krashen, "Differences in Print Environment for Children in Beverly Hills, Compton, and Watts," *Emergency Librarian,* vol. 24, no. 4, (1997), pp. 8–9. See also Stephen Krashen, "Bridging Inequity with Books," *Educational Leadership,* January 1998, pp. 19–22.

15. Many of Krashen's findings and recommendations can be found in the document *Every Person a Reader: An Alternative to the California Task Force Report on Reading* by Stephen D. Krashen, from Language Education Associates, online at http://www.languagebooks.com/books/every_person_a_reader.html.

16. Kathleen Kennedy Manzo, "California Continues Phaseout of Whole Language Era," *Education Week,* July 9, 1997, p. 15.

17. Duke Helfand and Doug Smith, "Elementary Schools Post Lower Scores," *Los Angeles Times,* August 17, 2004, p. B1; Duke Helfand and Jean Merl, "Pace of School Gains Slows Down: Statewide, Fewer Than Half Meet Their Goals, a Sharp Decline from Last Year," *Los Angeles Times,* October 29, 2004, p. B1; and Duke Helfand, "Study Offers Grim Look at Schools," *Los Angeles Times,* January 4, 2005, p. B1, B8.

18. According to Michael Gorman, president of American Library Association, August 16, 2005.

19. James Ricci, "A Saving Grace in the Face of Our School Library Scandal," *Los Angeles Times Magazine,* November 12, 2000.

20. Nell K. Duke, "For the Rich It's Richer: Print Experiences and Environments Offers to Children in Very Low- and Very High-Socioeconomic Status First-Grade Classrooms," pp. 441–78.

21. Julian E. Barnes, "Unequal Education," *Newsweek,* March 29, 2004, pp. 67–75; also Greg Toppo, "Teacher of the Year: Let Teachers Teach," *USA Today,* April 19, 2005, p. 5D. In 2004, during Black History Month, *New York Times* education columnist Michael Winerip visited Williams Elementary School in Mount Vernon, New York. The school serves 90 percent poverty-level children with 10 percent from homeless shelters. As for the school library, most books had copyrights from the fifties and sixties, when the school served a white population. This made most of the nonfiction collection impossibly out of date and offered a dearth of relevant current fiction for children. Harry Potter? None. Gary Paulsen? One. Langston Hughes? None. The shelves weren't bare, though; there were books on television (copyright 1955) and the telephone (1967). See Michael Winerip, "At Poor Schools, Time Stops on the Library Shelves," *New York Times,* March 10, 2004, p. A21.

22. Robin Keefe, BookEnds, 6520 Platt Avenue, No. #331, West Hills, CA 91307; online at www.bookends.org.

23. Brigid Hubberman, Family Reading Partnership, 54 Gunderman Road, Ithaca, NY 14850; online at www.familyreading.org.

24. David Mazor, Reader to Reader, Inc., 24 Mt. View Circle, Amherst, MA 01002; online at www.readertoreader.org. To hear a three-minute interview with Mazor from *Marketplace,* American Public Radio, September 7, 2005, go online to http://www.publicradio.org/tools/media/player/start/ 00:00:04:56.0/end/00:00:08:17.0/marketplace/morning_report/2005/09/ 07_mktmorn0850.ram.

25. Doreen Carvajal, "Reading the Bottom Line," *New York Times Magazine,* April 6, 1997, pp. 76–77.

26. Dean E. Murphy, "Moving Beyond 'Shh' (and Books) at Libraries," *New York Times,* March 7, 2001, pp. 1A, 20A.

27. Patricia Cohen, "Spaces for Social Study: Architects Are Rethinking Libraries as Places to See and Be Seen," *New York Times,* Education Life, August 1, 2004.

28. Jack Hitt, "The Theory of Supermarkets," *New York Times Magazine,* March 10, 1996, pp. 56–61, 94, 98.

29. Robin Fields, and Melinda Fulmer, "Markets' Shelf Fees Put Squeeze on Small Firms," *Los Angeles Times,* January 29, 2000, pp. 1A, 26A.

30. Jann Sorrell Fractor et al., "Let's Not Miss Opportunities to Promote Voluntary Reading: Classroom Libraries in the Elementary School," *Reading Teacher,* March 1993, pp. 476–84.

31. Mary B. W. Tabor, "In Bookstore Chains, Display Space Is for Sale," *New York Times,* January 15, 1996, pp. A1, D8.

32. Mike Oliver is now principal at James Zaharis Elementary School, 9410 E. McKellips Road, Mesa, AZ 85207.

33. Pamela Harper, "After a Long Search, He Finds a Real Treasure," *Santa Barbara News Press,* December 7, 1988, p. B5.

Chapter 8: Lessons from Oprah, Harry, and the Internet

1. Iris C. Rotberg, ed., *Balancing Change and Tradition in Global Education Reform* (Lanham, MD: Rowman & Littlefield Education, 2004). Rotberg's book on education reform in sixteen countries showed that few other countries use testing in the lower grades and almost none hold teachers accountable for student grades. She wrote in *Education Week,* "[It is] ironic because a major impetus for the testing movement was our perception that other countries were outperforming the United States in international test-score comparisons. Yet, in our attempt to be more like the countries we most admire, we have adopted practices that few of these countries use." Iris C. Rotberg, "The Bigger Picture: U.S. Education in a Global Context," *Education Week,* Commentary, February 9, 2005.

2. D. T. Max, "The Oprah Effect," *New York Times Magazine,* December 26, 1999, pp. 36–41.

3. Laurel Graeber, "New Book Clubs: Mothers, Daughters and Discussion," *New York Times,* April 24, 1997, p. B4.

4. See also Terry A. Jewell and Donna Pratt, "Literature Discussions in the Primary Grades," *Reading Teacher,* May 1999, pp. 842–50.

5. *Caddie Woodlawn* by Carol Ryrie Brink, *Bridge to Terabithia* by Katherine Paterson, *Roll of Thunder, Hear My Cry* by Mildred Taylor, *Maniac Magee* by Jerry Spinelli, and *Holes* by Louis Sachar, to name a few. If you've ever had misgivings about the Newbery Awards (who hasn't?), you might take strength from E. J. Graff's skeptical essay for Salon.com titled "A Gold Star for Tedium." You can read it at http://dir.salon.com/books/feature/2001/01/25/newbery/index.html.

6. Fox Butterfield, "Crime in Schools Fell Sharply Over Decade, Survey Shows," *New York Times,* November 20, 2004.

7. Online at http://www.teenpregnancy.org/america/.

8. Associated Press, "Smoking and Drug Use by Teenagers Drop Again," *New York Times,* December 22, 2004.

9. Online at http://www.catholicinsider.com/scripts/index.php.

10. Online at http://www.ala.org/ala/oif/challengessupport/dealing/Default1208.htm.

11. William Sloane Coffin, *Credo* (Louisville, KY: Westminster John Knox Press, 2004).

12. Catherine Sheldrick Ross, "If They Read Nancy Drew, So What? Series Book Readers Talk Back," *Library and Information Science Research* (LISR), vol. 17, 1995, pp. 201–36. This research won the American Library Association's research award in 1995. A shortened version appeared in *School Library Media Quarterly,* Spring 1996, pp. 165–71.

13. Harvey Graff, *The Literacy Myth* (San Diego, CA: Academic, 1979), p. 39. Quoting an editorial from the *Christian Guardian,* July 31, 1850.

14. Roger Kimball, "Closing Time? Jacques Barzun on Western Culture," *New Criterion,* June 2000; online at http://www.newcriterion.com/archive/18/jun00/barzun.htm.

15. "For It Was Indeed He," *Fortune Magazine,* April 1934; also found in Sheila Egoff, G. T. Stubbs, and L. F. Ashley, eds., *Only Connect* (New York: Oxford University Press, 1969), pp. 41–61.

16. Sheldrick Ross, "If They Read Nancy Drew, So What?"

17. Barbara A. Bruschi and Richard J. Coley, "How Teachers Compare: The Prose, Document, and Quantitative Skills of America's Teachers," ETS Policy Information Center (Princeton, NJ: Educational Testing Service, March 1999). Available on the Web at www.ets.org/research/pic/compare.html.

18. G. Robert Carlsen and Anne Sherrill, *Voices of Readers: How We Come to Love Books* (Urbana, IL: National Council of Teachers of English, 1988).

19. Joel Achenbach, "Search for Tomorrow," *Washington Post,* February 15, 2004, p. D1.

20. Nate Stulman, "The Great Campus Goof-Off Machine," *New York Times,* Op-ed, May 15, 1999.

21. Paul Attewell, Belkis Suazo-Garcia, and Juan Battle, "Computers and Young Children: Social Benefit or Social Problem?" *Social Forces,* September 2003.

22. "Computers and Student Learning: Bivariate and Multivariate Evidence on the Availability and Use of Computers at Home and at School," Thomas Fuchs and Ludger Woessmann, researchers at the University of Munich, CESifo Working Paper No. 1321, November 2004; online at http://www.cesifo.de/~DocCIDL/cesifo1_wp1321.pdf

23. Elizabeth Weise, "One Click Starts the Avalanche," *USA Today,* August 8, 2000, p. 3D.

24. J. Markwell and D. W. Brooks, "Broken Links: The Ephemeral Nature of Educational WWW Hyperlinks," *Journal of Science Education and Technology,* vol. 11, 2002, pp. 105–108; also J. Markwell and D. W. Brooks, "Link Rot Limits the Usefulness of Web-based Educational Materials in Biochemistry and Molecular Biology," *Biochemistry and Molecular Biology Education,* vol. 31, 2003, pp. 69–72; online at http://www-class.unl.edu/biochem/url/broken_links.html; also Andrew Trotter, "Too Often, Educators' Online Links Lead to Nowhere," *Education Week,* December 4, 2002, pp. 1, 15.

25. Walter C. Clemens Jr., "Without Books on Paper, So Much Is Lost," *New York Times,* letter to the editor, May 17, 2005. The writer is a professor at Boston University.

26. Your best bet might be to just "Google" the name because sites like this keep changing addresses online. As of 2006, the address was http://www.ala.org/gwstemplate.cfm?section=greatwebsites&template=/cfapps/gws/default.cfm. (I must confess to being honored as one of ALA's "great sites.")

27. Online at http://www.sldirectory.com/virtual.html.

28. Jeffrey Selingo, "When a Search Engine Isn't Enough, Call a Librarian," *New York Times,* February, 5, 2004, p. 7.

29. Mark F. Goldberg, "Joltin' Joe and the Pursuit of Excellence," *Phi Delta Kappan,* January 1997, pp. 395–97.

30. Ian Austen, "The Case of the Flickering Pixels," *New York Times,* February 3, 2000, pp. D1, D9.

31. Catherine Greenman, "Printed Page Beats PC Screen for Reading, Study Finds," *New York Times,* August 10, 2000, p. E11.

32. Quoted in Robert Darnton, "The New Age of the Book," *New York Review of Books,* March 18, 1999, p. 5.

33. June Kronholz, "PowerPoint Goes to School," *Wall Street Journal,* November 12, 2002, pp. B1, B6.

34. Kevin Stevens, "Incoming: Two Sides of PowerPoint," *New York Times,* letter to the technology section, June 7, 2001, p. E6.

35. Clifford Stoll, *Silicon Snake Oil* (New York: Doubleday, 1995).

36. Irwin Kirsch, John de Jong, Dominique LaFontaine, Joy McQueen, Juliette Mendelovits, and Christian Monseur, "Reading for Change: Performance and Engagement Across Countries, Results from Pisa 2000," Organisation for Economic Co-Operation and Development (OECD); online at http://213.253.134.29/OECD/pdfs/browseit/9602071e.pdf.

37. Herb Katz and Laura Sokal, "Masculine Literacy: One Size Does Not Fit All," *Reading Manitoba,* vol. 24, no. 1, 2003, pp. 4–8. This was a research grant funded by the Social Sciences and Humanities Research Council of Canada and the University of Winnipeg.

38. Stephen Krashen, *The Power of Reading,* second ed. (Portsmouth, NH: Libraries Unlimited and Heinemann, 2004).

39. G. Robert Carlson and Anne Sherrill, *Voices of Readers: How We Come to Love Books* (Urbana, IL: National Council of Teachers of English, 1998); also Krashen, *The Power of Reading,* pp. 91–110.

40. Johnson quoted in *Forty Thousand Sublime and Beautiful Thoughts,* compiled by Charles Noel Douglas, first published in 1890 and enlarged in 1904.

Chapter 9: TV, Audio, and Technology: Hurting or Helping Literacy?

1. Dimitri A. Christakis, MD, MPH; Frederick J. Zimmerman, PhD; David L. DiGiuseppe, MS; and Carolyn A. McCarty, PhD, "Early Television Exposure and Subsequent Attentional Problems in Children," *Pediatrics,* vol. 113, no. 4, April 2004, pp. 708–713; online at www.aap.org/advocacy/releases/tvapril.pdf. See also the National Public Radio *Morning Edition* report "Study Links TV, Attention Disorders in Kids," April 5, 2004. The four-minute story and interview with one of the researchers can be heard online for free at www.npr.org/rundowns/segment.php?wfld=1812501.

2. Victoria J. Rideout, Elizabeth A. Vandewater, and Ellen A. Wartella, *Zero to Six: Electronic Media in the Lives of Infants, Toddlers, and Preschoolers* (Menlo Park, CA: Henry J. Kaiser Family Foundation, 2003); online at http://www.kff.org.

3. Linda Carroll, "The Problem with Some 'Smart Toys': (Hint) Use Your Imagination," *New York Times,* October 26, 2004, pp. F5, F12. See also Tamar Lewin, "See Baby Touch Screen. But Does Baby Get IT?" *New York Times,* December 15, 2005, p. 1.

4. Dina L. G. Borzekowski and Thomas N. Robinson, "The Remote, the House, and the No. 2 Pencil," *Archives of Pediatrics & Adolescent Medicine* 159, 2005, pp. 607–13.

5. Donald F. Roberts, PhD; Ulla G. Foehr, MA; and Victoria Rideout, MA, *Generation M: Media in the Lives of 8–18-Year-Olds* (Menlo Park, CA: Henry J. Kaiser Family Foundation, 2005); online at http://www.kff.org.

6. Ibid.

7. Judith Owens et al., "Television-Viewing Habits and Sleep Disturbance in School Children," *Pediatrics,* September 8, 1999, p. 552.

8. Pam Belluck, "Reason Is Sought for Lag by Blacks in School Effort," *New York Times,* July 4, 1999, pp. A1, A12. See also Debra Viadero, "Even in Well-Off Suburbs, Minority Achievement Lags," *Education Week,* March 15, 2000; Debra Viadero and Robert C. Johnston, "Lifting Minority Achievement: Complex Answers," *Education Week,* April 5, 2005; Debra Viadero, "Lags in Minority Achievement Defy Traditional Explanations," *Education Week,* March 22, 2000; and Abigail Thernstrom and Stephan Thernstrom, *No Excuses: Closing the Racial Gap in Learning* (New York: Simon & Schuster, 2004).

9. Donald Roberts, Ulla G. Foehr, Victoria Rideout, and Mollyann Brodie, PhD, *Kids & Media @ The New Millennium* (Menlo Park, CA: Henry J. Kaiser Family Foundation, 1999).

10. Derrick Z. Jackson, "Too Much TV Takes a Heavy Toll on Blacks," *Atlanta Journal-Constitution,* October 22, 2002, p. A17.

11. Patricia A. Williams, Edward H. Haertel, Geneva D. Haertel, and Herbert J. Walberg, "The Impact of Leisure-Time Television on School Learning: A Research Synthesis," *American Educational Research Journal,* vol. 19, no. 1, Spring 1982, pp. 19–50.

12. Online at www.aap.org/healthtopics/mediause.cfm.

13. Jed Gaines, executive director, Read Aloud America, Inc., 1937 Keeaumoku Street, Honolulu, HI 96822, or info@readaloudamerica.org.

14. A parent-attendance formula devised by Joan Moorman, a principal in Covina, California, has been equally impressive through the years. It was published in *Principal* magazine and can be read at my Web site: www.trelease-on-reading.com/whatsnu_moorman.html.

15. I have no connection whatsoever with this company or product. I paid in full for my copy of the Time-Scout Monitor; it was not a product review copy. For more information, see www.time-scout.com.

16. Arthur M. Schlesinger Jr., *A Life in the Twentieth Century* (Boston, MA: Houghton Mifflin, 2000).

17. Irwin Kirsch, John de Jong, Dominique LaFontaine, Joy McQueen, Juliette Mendelovits, and Christian Monseur, *Reading for Change: Performance and Engagement Across Countries, Results from Pisa 2000,* Organisation for Economic Co-Operation and Development (OECD); online at http://213.253. 134.29/OECD/pdfs/browseit/960207le.pdl; also "OECD Pisa 2003 Results: Young Finns Still at the OECD Top," Ministry of Education Finland, 2003; online at http://www.minedu.fi/minedu/education/pisa/results2003.html.

18. Lizette Alvarez, "Educators Flocking to Finland, Land of Literate Children," *New York Times,* International, April 9, 2004; see also Sean Coughlan, "Education Key to Economic Survival," BBC News, November 23, 2004; online at http://news.bbc.co.uk/go/pr/fr/-/1/hi/education/4031805.stm; and Pirjo Linnakylä, "Subtitles Prompt Finnish Children to Read," *Reading Today* (IRA bimonthly), October/November 1993, p. 31.

19. Warwick B. Elley, *How in the World Do Students Read?* (Hamburg: International Association for the Evaluation of Educational Achievement, July 1992).

20. Susan B. Neuman and Patricia Koskinen, "Captioned Television as 'Comprehensible Input': Effects of Incidental Word Learning from Context for

Language Minority Students," *Reading Research Quarterly,* vol. 27, 1992, pp. 95–106; P. S. Koskinen, R. S. Wilson, L. Gambrell, L. and C. J. Jensema, *ERS Spectrum: Journal of School Research and Information* vol.4, no. 2, 1986, pp. 9–13; Patricia S. Koskinen, Robert M. Wilson, Linda B. Gambrell, and Susan B. Neuman, "Captioned Video and Vocabulary Learning: An Innovative Practice in Literacy Instruction," *Reading Teacher,* September 1993, pp. 36–43; Robert J. Rickelman, William A. Henk, and Kent Layton, "Closed-Captioned Television: A Viable Technology for the Reading Teacher," *Reading Teacher,* April 1996, pp. 598–99.

21. Helen Aron, "Bookworms Become Tapeworms: A Profile of Listeners to Books on Audiocassette," *Journal of Reading,* November 1992, pp. 208–12.

22. I prefer using this URL in my searches (if it still works by the time you read this): http://search.npr.org/search97cgi/s97_cgi?ResultTemplate=allow_re_sort.hts&newQuery=1.

23. Peter Johnson, "NPR, On a Roll with Listeners," *USA Today,* March 20, 2002, p. 3D.

Bibliography

Adams, Marilyn Jager. *Beginning to Read: Thinking and Learning About Print— A Summary.* Champaign-Urbana, IL: University of Illinois, Center for the Study of Reading, 1990.

Allington, Richard. *Big Brother and the National Reading Curriculum: How Ideology Trumped Evidence.* Portsmouth, NH: Heinemann, 2002.

Anderson, Richard C., Elfrieda H. Hiebert, Judith A. Scott, and Ian A. G. Wilkinson. *Becoming a Nation of Readers: The Report of the Commission on Reading.* Champaign-Urbana, IL: University of Illinois, Center for the Study of Reading, 1985.

Applebee, Arthur N., Judith A. Langer, Ina V. S. Mullis, Andrew S. Latham, and Claudia A. Gentile. *NAEP 1992 Writing Report Card.* Educational Testing Service. Washington, DC: U.S. Department of Education, 1994.

Bae, Yupin, Susan Choy, Claire Geddes, Jennifer Sable, and Thomas Snyder. *Trends in Educational Equity of Girls and Women.* Washington, DC: U.S. Government Printing Office, 2000.

Barton, Paul E. *Parsing the Achievement Gap: Baselines for Tracking Progress.* Princeton, NJ: Educational Testing Service, 2003.

Barton, Paul E., and Richard J. Coley. *America's Smallest School: The Family.* Princeton, NJ: Educational Testing Service, 1992.

———. *Captive Students: Education and Training in America's Prisons.* Princeton, NJ: Educational Testing Service Policy Information Center, 1996.

Barzun, Jacques. *Begin Here.* Chicago, IL: University of Chicago Press, 1991.

Beatty, Alexandra S., Clyde M. Reese, Hilary R. Persky, and Peggy Carr. *NAEP 1994 U.S. History Report Card.* Washington, DC: U.S. Department of Education, Office of Educational Research and Improvement, 1994.

Berliner, David C., and Bruce J. Biddle. *The Manufactured Crisis.* Reading, MA: Addison-Wesley, 1996.

Bettelheim, Bruno. *The Uses of Enchantment: The Meaning and Importance of Fairy Tales.* New York: Knopf, 1976.

Bradshaw, Tom, Bonnie Nichols, Kelly Hill, and Mark Bauerlein. *Reading At Risk: A Survey of Literary Reading in America.* National Endowment for the Arts. Washington, DC: NEA, Research Division, Report No. 46, 2004.

Bruer, John T. *The Myth of the First Three Years.* New York: The Free Press/ Simon & Schuster, 1999.

Bruner, Jerome S., Allison Jolly, and Kathy Sylva, eds. *Play—Its Role in Development and Evolution.* New York: Penguin, 1976.

Bruschi, Barbara A., and Richard J. Coley. *How Teachers Compare: The Prose, Document, and Quantitative Skills of America's Teachers.* Princeton, NJ: Educational Testing Service ETS Policy Information Center, March 1999.

Butler, Dorothy. *Cushla and Her Books.* Boston: The Horn Book, 1980.

Campbell, Jay R., Catherine M. Hombo, and John Mazzeo. *NAEP 1999 Trends in Academic Progress: Three Decades of Student Performance.* U.S. Department of Education. Washington, DC: National Center for Education Statistics, 2000. Also available at http://nces.ed.gov/nationsreportcard.

Carlsen, G. Robert, and Anne Sherrill. *Voices of Readers: How We Come to Love Books.* Urbana, IL: National Council of Teachers of English, 1988.

Carson, Ben. *Gifted Hands: The Ben Carson Story.* Grand Rapids, MI: Zondervan, 1990.

Cazden, Courtney B. *Child Language and Education.* New York: Holt, Rinehart and Winston, 1972.

Clark, Margaret M. *Young Fluent Readers.* London: Heinemann, 1976.

Coffin, William Sloane. *Credo.* Louisville, KY: Westminster John Knox Press, 2004.

Coley, Richard J. *An Uneven Start: Indicators in Inequality in School Readiness.* Princeton, NJ: Policy Information Center, ETS, 2002.

Csikszentmihalyi, M., K. Rathnude, and S. Whalen. *Talented Teenagers: The Roots of Success and Failure.* New York: Cambridge University Press, 1993.

Davies, Robertson. *One Half of Robertson Davies.* New York: Viking, 1977.

Denton, Kristen, and Jerry West. *Children's Reading and Mathematics Achievement in Kindergarten and First Grade.* Washington, DC: U.S. Department of Education, NCES, 2002. Online at http://nces.ed.gov/pubs2002/2002125.pdf.

Donahue, Patricia L., Kristin E. Voelki, Jay R. Campbell, and John Mazzeo. *NAEP 1998 Reading Report Card for the Nation and the States.* Washington, DC: U.S. Department of Education, NCES, 1999. Online at http://nces.ed.gov/.

Durkin, Dolores. *Children Who Read Early.* New York: Teachers College, 1966.

Egoff, Sheila, G. T. Stubbs, and L. F. Ashley. *Only Connect.* New York: Oxford University Press, 1969.

Elkind, David. *The Hurried Child: Growing Up Too Fast Too Soon.* 3rd ed. Cambridge, MA: Perseus/DaCapo, 2001.

Elley, Warwick B. *How in the World Do Students Read?* Hamburg: International Association for the Evaluation of Educational Achievement, 1992.

Emery, Kathy, and Susan Ohanian. *Why Is Corporate America Bashing Our Public Schools?* Portsmouth, NH: Heinemann, 2004.

Ferguson, Ronald F. *What Doesn't Meet the Eye: Understanding and Addressing Racial Disparities in High-Achieving Suburban Schools.* Northern Central Regional Educational Laboratory, 2002. Online at http://www.nerel.org/gap/ferg.

Foertsch, Mary A. *Reading In and Out of School.* Educational Testing Service/ Education Information Office. Washington, DC: U.S. Department of Education, May 1992.

Friedman, Thomas L. *The World Is Flat.* New York: Farrar, Straus & Giroux, 2005.

Garan, Elaine M. *In Defense of Our Children: When Politics, Profit, and Education Collide.* Portsmouth, NH: Heinemann, 2004.

———. *Resisting Mandates.* Portsmouth, NH: Heinemann, 2002.

Goleman, Daniel. *Emotional Intelligence: Why It Can Matter More Than IQ.* New York: Bantam, 1995.

Goodman, Kenneth, Patrick Shannon, Yvonne Freeman, and S. Murphy. *Report Card on Basal Readers.* New York: Richard Owen, 1988.

Gopnik, Alison, Andrew N. Meltzoff, and Patricia K. Kuhl. *The Scientist in the Crib.* New York: Morrow, 1999.

Graff, Harvey. *The Literacy Myth.* San Diego, CA: Academic, 1979.

Graubard, S. R., ed. *Literacy.* New York: Noonday, 1991.

Hart, Betty, and Todd Risley. *Meaningful Differences in the Everyday Experience of Young American Children.* Baltimore, MD: Brookes Publishing, 1996.

Heyns, Barbara. *Summer Learning and the Effects of Schooling.* New York: Academic Press, 1978.

Hodgkinson, Harold L. *The Same Client: The Demographics of Education and Service Delivery Systems.* Washington, DC: Institute of Educational Leadership, 1989.

Kamil, M. L., P. B. Mosenthal, P. David Pearson, and R. Barr, eds. *Handbook of Reading Research.* Vol. III. New York: Erlbaum, 2000.

Kandel, Eric R., James H. Schwartz, and Thomas M. Jessell, eds. *Principles of Neural Science.* 3rd ed. Center for Neurobiology and Behavior, College of Physicians and Surgeons of Columbia University and the Howard Hughes Medical Institute. Norwalk, CT: Appleton & Lange, 1991.

Kirsch, Irwin, John de Jong, Dominique LaFontaine, Joy McQueen, Juliette Mendelovits, and Christian Monseur. *Reading for Change: Performance and Engagement Across Countries—Results from Pisa 2000.* Organisation for Economic Co-operation and Development (OECD). Online at http:// 213.253.134.29/OECD/pdfs/browseit/9602071e.pdf

Kohn, Alfie. *Punished by Rewards: The Trouble with Gold Stars, Incentive Plans, A's, Praise, and Other Bribes.* Boston: Houghton Mifflin, 1993.

Krashen, Stephen. *The Power of Reading.* 2nd ed. Portsmouth, NH: Libraries Unlimited and Heinemann, 2004.

———. *Writing: Research: Theory and Applications.* Torrance, CA: Laredo Publishing Company, 1984.

Kubey, Robert, and Mihaly Csikszentmihalyi. *Television and the Quality of Life.* Hillsdale, NJ: Erlbaum, 1990.

Lance, Keith Curry, Lynda Welborn, and Christine Hamilton-Pennell. *The Impact of School Media Centers on Academic Achievement.* Englewood, CO: Libraries Unlimited, 1993.

Lance, Keith Curry, Marcia J. Rodney, and Christine Hamilton-Pennell. *How School Librarians Help Kids Achieve Standards: The Second Colorado Study.* Denver, CO: Colorado State Library, 2000.

Lee, E., and David T. Burkam. *Inequality at the Starting Gate: Social Background Differences in Achievement as Children Begin School.* Washington, DC: Economic Policy Institute, 2002.

Manguel, Alberto. *A History of Reading.* New York: Viking, 1996.

Maraniss, David. *When Pride Still Mattered: A Life of Vince Lombardi.* New York: Simon & Schuster, 1999.

Marmot, Michael. *The Status Syndrome : How Social Standing Affects Our Health and Longevity.* New York: Times Books, 2004.

McCrum, Robert, William Cran, and Robert MacNeil. *The Story of English.* New York: Viking, 1986.

McLean, Bethany, and Peter Elkind. *The Smartest Guys in the Room.* New York: Portfolio/Penguin, 2003.

McQuillan, Jeff. *The Literary Crisis: False Claims, Real Solutions.* Portsmouth, NH: Heinemann, 1998.

Morgan, Judith, and Neil Morgan. *Dr. Seuss and Mr. Geisel.* New York: Random House, 1995.

Mormino, Gary R., and George E. Pozzetta, *The Immigrant World of Ybor City: Italians and Their Latin Neighbors in Tampa, 1885–1985.* Gainesville, FL: Florida Sand Dollar Books/University Press of Florida, 1998.

Mullis, Ina V. S., J. R. Campbell, and A. E. Farstrup. *NAEP 1992 Reading Report Card for the Nation and States.* Washington, DC: National Center for Education Statistics, U.S. Government Printing Office, 1993.

Mullis, Ina, John A. Dossey, Jay R. Campbell, Claudia A. Gentile, Christine O'Sullivan, and Andrew Latham. *NAEP 1992 Trends in Academic Progress.* Washington, DC: Office of Educational Research and Improvement, U.S. Department of Education, 1994.

Mullis, Ina, Michael O. Martin, Eugene J. Gonzalez, and Ann M. Kennedy. *PIRLS 2001 International Report: IEA's Study of Reading Literacy Achievement in Primary School in 35 Countries.* Chestnut Hill, MA: International Association for the Evaluation of Educational/International Study Center, Boston College, 2003.

NAEP 2004 Trends in Academic Progress: Three Decades of Student Performance in Reading and Mathematics. U.S. Department of Education, Institute of Education Sciences, National Center for Education Statistics, National Assessment of Educational Progress, selected years, 1980–2004.

National Assessment of Educational Progress. *Literacy: Profiles of America's Young Adults.* Princeton, NJ: Educational Testing Service, 1987.

Neuman, Susan B., Conna C. Celano, Albert N. Greco, and Pamela Shue. *Access for All: Closing the Book Gap for Children in Early Education.* Newark, DE: International Reading Association, 2001.

Nielsen Media Research. *2000 Report on Television: The First 50 Years.* New York: Nielsen Media Research, 2000.

Niles, J. A., and L. A. Harris. *New Inquiries in Reading Research and Instruction.* Rochester, NY: National Reading Conference, 1982.

Ogbu, John U. *Black American Students in an Affluent Suburb: A Study of Academic Disengagement.* Mahwah, NJ: Lawrence Erlbaum Associates, 2003.

Ohanian, Susan. *One Size Fits Few: The Folly of Educational Standards.* Portsmouth, NH: Heinemann, 1999.

Pamuk, E., D. Makuc, K. Heck, C. Reuben, and K. Lockner. *Health, United States, 1998: Socioeconomic Status and Health Chartbook.* Washington, DC: U.S. Government Printing Office, 1998.

Pearl, Nancy. *Book Lust: Recommended Reading for Every Mood, Moment, and Reason.* Seattle, WA: Sasquatch Books, 2003.

————. *More Book Lust.* Seattle, WA: Sasquatch Books, 2005.

Pearson, P. David, ed. *Handbook of Reading Research.* New York: Longman, 1984.

Perie, M., R. Moran, and A. D. Lutkus. *NAEP 2004 Trends in Academic Progress: Three Decades of Student Performance in Reading and Mathematics.* U.S. Department of Education, Institute of Education Sciences, National Center for Education Statistics. Washington, DC: Government Printing Office, 2005.

Pratt, Rebecca et al. *The Condition of Education 2000.* Washington, DC: U.S. Department of Education, NCES, 2000. Online at http://nces.ed.gov/pubsearch/index/asp.

Ravitch, Diane, and Chester Finn. *What Do Our 17-Year-Olds Know?* New York: Harper & Row, 1987.

Report of the National Reading Panel: Teaching Children to Read—An Evidence-Based Assessment of the Scientific Research Literature on Reading and Its Implications for Reading Instruction; Reports of the Subgroups. Washington, D.C.: National Institute of Child Health and Human Development, NIH, Publication 00-4754, 2000. Online at www.nationalreadingpanel.org, or www.nichd.nih.gov/publications/nrp/report.pdf.

Rideout, Victoria J., Elizabeth A. Vandewater, and Ellen A. Wartella. *Zero to Six: Electronic Media in the Lives of Infants, Toddlers, and Preschoolers.* Menlo Park, CA: The Henry J. Kaiser Family Foundation, 2003. Online at http://www.kff.org.

Roberts, Donald F., Ulla G. Foehr, Victoria Rideout, and Mollyann Brodie. *Kids & Media @ The New Millennium.* Menlo Park, CA: The Henry J. Kaiser Family Foundation, 1999. Online at www.kff.org/content/1999/1535/ ChartPack.pdf.

Roberts, Donald F., Ulla G. Foehr, and Victoria Rideout. *Generation M: Media in the Lives of 8–18-Year-Olds.* Menlo Park, CA: The Henry J. Kaiser Family Foundation, 2005. Online at http://www.kff.org.

Rotberg, Iris C., ed. *Balancing Change and Tradition in Global Education Reform.* Lanham, MD: Rowman & Littlefield Education, 2004.

Rumbaut, Ruben G., and Wayne A. Cornleiu. *California's Immigrant Children: Theory, Research, and Implications for Education Policy.* San Diego, CA: Center for U.S.-Mexican Studies, University of California, 1996.

Schlesinger Jr., Arthur M. *A Life in the Twentieth Century.* Boston, MA: Houghton Mifflin, 2000.

Snow, Catherine E., M. Susan Burns, and Peg Griffin, eds. *Preventing Reading Difficulties in Young Children.* Washington, DC: National Academy Press, 1998.

Snowden, David. *Aging with Grace: What the Nun Study Teaches Us About Leading Longer, Healthier, and More Meaningful Lives.* New York: Bantam, 2001.

Starting Points: The Report of the Carnegie Task Force on Meeting the Needs of Young Children. New York: Carnegie Corporation, 1994.

Stoll, Clifford. *Silicon Snake Oil.* New York: Doubleday, 1995.

Taylor, Gordon Rattray. *The Natural History of the Brain.* New York: E. P. Dutton, 1979.

Thernstrom, Abigail, and Stephan Thernstrom. *No Excuses: Closing the Racial Gap in Learning.* New York: Simon & Schuster, 2004.

Trends in Educational Equity of Girls and Women. U.S. Department of Education. Washington, DC: National Center for Education Statistics, March 2000.

The 2000 Kids Count Data Book. Baltimore, MD: Annie E. Casey Foundation, 2000. Online at www.aecf.org/kidscount/kc2000/.

Underhill, Paco. *Why We Buy: The Science of Shopping.* New York: Simon & Schuster, 1999.

Vernez, Georges, Richard Krop, and C. Peter Ryde. *Closing the Education Gap: Benefits and Costs.* Santa Monica, CA: Rand Corporation, 1999.

West, Jerry, Kristin Denton, and Elvira Germino-Hausken. *America's Kindergartners: Findings from the Early Childhood Longitudinal Study, Kindergarten Class of 1998–99, Fall 1998.* Washington, DC: U.S. Department of Education, NCES, 2000.

Zill, Nicholas, and Marianne Winglee. *Who Reads Literature?* Cabin John, MD: Seven Locks Press, 1990.

Subject Index
for the Text

*Page numbers in **bold** indicate section devoted to a subject.*
For books listed in the Treasury, see the Author-Illustrator Index, pp. 335–40.

Author-Illustrator Index
for the Treasury

*Italics are for illustrator only; ★ after page number gives location
of a group of books by an author or illustrator.*

Grateful acknowledgment is made for permission to use the following copyrighted works:

Page 60—Illustration from *All About Alfie* by Shirley Hughes. Copyright © 1997 by Shirley Hughes. Used by permission of HarperCollins Publishers.

PHOTOGRAPH CREDITS
Unless otherwise indicated, photographs are by Jim Trelease.
Page 11—Cigar makers, used by permission of Tampa-Hillsborough County Public Library System.
106—Bill and Gabe McMahan, used by permission.
124—Brandon Keefe, used by permission.
125—Brigid Hubberman, used by permission.
133—Peralta Trail Elementary rain gutters, used by permission.
159—Dr. Ben Carson, used by permission of Johns Hopkins Children's Center.

CHARTS
Page xvi—Based on "Home and School Correlates of Early Interest in Literature," *Journal of Educational Research,* April 1983.
xviii—Based on findings by Center for Disease Control, www.cdc.gov/tobacco/research_data?economics/consumpt.htm.
9—Based on Richard J. Coley, *An Uneven Start: Indicators of Inequality in School Readiness* (Princeton, N.J.: Policy Information Center, ETS, 2002).
83—Based on Stephen Krashen, *The Power of Reading,* 2nd ed. (Portsmouth, N.H.: Heinemann, 2004).
85—Based on *Long-Term Trend Reading Assessment,* U.S. Department of Education, NAEP, 2004.
88—Based on findings by Center for Summer Learning, Johns Hopkins University.
95—Based on the report *Reading for Change: Performance and Engagement Across Countries, Results from Pisa 2000,* Organisation for Economic Co-Operation and Development (OECD).
161—Based on the study "The Remote, the House, and the No. 2 Pencil," *Archives of Pediatrics & Adolescent Medicine,* July 2005 (vol. 159).
163—Based on the study "Association of Television Viewing During Childhood with Poor Educational Achievement," *Archives of Pediatrics & Adolescent Medicine,* July 2005 (vol. 159).

Available from Jim Trelease:

The Read-Aloud Handbook: Sixth Edition
For more than two decades, millions of parents and educators have turned to Jim Trelease's beloved classic to help countless children become avid readers through awakening their imaginations and improving their language skills. Now this new edition of *The Read-Aloud Handbook* imparts the benefits, rewards, and importance of reading aloud to children of a new generation. Supported by delightful anecdotes as well as the latest research, *The Read-Aloud Handbook* offers proven techniques and strategies—and the reasoning behind them—for helping children discover the pleasures of reading and setting them on the road to becoming lifelong readers.

ISBN 0-14-303739-0

Hey! Listen to This
Stories to Read Aloud
This delightful anthology brings together forty-eight read-aloud stories—from folktales like "Uncle Remus" to favorite classics like *Charlotte's Web*—that parents and teachers can share with children ages five to nine.

ISBN 0-14-014653-9

Read All About It!
Great Read-Aloud Stories, Poems, and Newspaper Pieces for Preteens and Teens
This wonderfully diverse treasure of fifty read-aloud pieces will turn young people on to the many pleasures of reading, sparking their interest with selections ranging from an autobiographical sketch by Maya Angelou to "Casey at the Bat" to a moving story about two Holocaust survivors.

ISBN 0-14-014655-5